Human Security

About the Peace and Security in the 21st Century Series

Until recently, security was defined mostly in geopolitical terms with the assumption that it could be achieved only through at least the threat of military force. Today, however, people from as different backgrounds as planners in the Pentagon and veteran peace activists think in terms of human or global security, where no one is secure unless everyone is secure in all areas of their lives. This means that it is impossible nowadays to separate issues of war and peace, the environment, sustainability, identity, global health, and the like.

The books in this series aim to make sense of this changing world of peace and security by investigating security issues and peace efforts that involve cooperation at several levels. By looking at how security and peace interrelate at various stages of conflict, the series explores new ideas for a fast-changing world and seeks to redefine and rethink what peace and security mean in the first decades of the new century.

Multidisciplinary in approach and authorship, the books cover a variety of topics, focusing on the overarching theme that students, scholars, practitioners, and policymakers have to find new models and theories to account for, diagnose, and respond to the difficulties of a more complex world. Authors are established scholars and practitioners in their fields of expertise.

In addition, it is hoped that the series will contribute to bringing together authors and readers in concrete, applied projects, and thus help create, under the sponsorship of Alliance for Peacebuilding (AfP), a community of practice.

The series is sponsored by the Alliance for Peacebuilding, http://www.allianceforpeacebuilding.org, and edited by Charles Hauss, government liaison.

Human Security

Theory and Action

David Andersen-Rodgers
California State University, Sacramento

Kerry F. Crawford
James Madison University

ROWMAN & LITTLEFIELD
Lanham • Boulder • New York • London

Executive Editor: Dhara Snowden
Associate Editor: Rebecca Anastasi
Senior Marketing Manager: Amy Whitaker

Credits and acknowledgments for material borrowed from other sources, and reproduced with permission, appear on the appropriate page within the text.

Published by Rowman & Littlefield
A wholly owned subsidiary of The Rowman & Littlefield Publishing Group, Inc.
4501 Forbes Boulevard, Suite 200, Lanham, Maryland 20706
www.rowman.com

Unit A, Whitacre Mews, 26–34 Stannary Street, London SE11 4AB, United Kingdom

British Library Cataloguing in Publication Information Available

Library of Congress Cataloging-in-Publication Data Available
ISBN 9781442273764 (cloth : alk. paper)
ISBN 9781442273771 (pbk. : alk. paper)
ISBN 9781442273788 (electronic)

♾™ The paper used in this publication meets the minimum requirements of American National Standard for Information Sciences—Permanence of Paper for Printed Library Materials, ANSI/NISO Z39.48–1992.

Printed in the United States of America

Contents

Tables, Boxes, and Figures

TABLES

BOXES

FIGURES

Abbreviations

African Union (AU)
Amnesty International (AI)
Armed Forces Revolutionary Council (AFRC)
Association of Southeast Asian Nations (ASEAN)
C40 Cities Climate Leadership Group (C40)
Carbon dioxide (CO_2)
Centers for Disease Control and Prevention (CDC)
Chlorofluorocarbons (CFCs)
Civil Defense Forces (CDF)
Civilians in Conflict (CIVIC)
Convention on the Elimination of All Forms of Discrimination against
    Women (CEDAW)
Gulf Cooperation Council (GCC)
Defense of Marriage Act (DOMA)
Demobilization, disarmament, and reintegration (DDR)
Democratic Republic of the Congo (DRC)
"Don't Ask, Don't Tell" policy (DADT)
European Union (EU)
Famine Early Warning Systems Network (FEWS NET)
Female genital mutilation (FGM)
Food and Agriculture Organization (FAO)
Force Intervention Brigade (FIB)
GLBTQ Legal Advocates & Defenders (GLAD)
Global Gender Gap Index (GGGI)
Gender Inequality Index (GII)
Group of 7 (G7)
Group of 20 (G20)

Human Development Index (HDI)
Human Rights Watch (HRW)
Human Security Unit (HSU)
Hydrochlorofluorocarbons (HCFCs)
Hydrofluorocarbons (HFCs)
Inter-Agency Working Group on Human Security (IAWGHS)
Interagency Standing Committee (ISAC)
Intergovernmental organizations (IGOs)
Intergovernmental Panel on Climate Change (IPCC)
Internally displaced persons (IDPs)
International Commission on Intervention and State Sovereignty (ICISS)
International Committee of the Red Cross (ICRC)
International Covenant on Civil and Political Rights (ICCPR)
International Covenant on Economic, Social and Cultural Rights (ICESCR)
International Criminal Court (ICC)
International Fund for Agricultural Development (IFAD)
International nongovernmental organizations (INGOs)
International relations (IR)
International Rescue Committee (IRC)
Lesbian, Gay, Bisexual, Transgender, and Queer/Questioning (LGBTQ)
Mano River Women's Peace Network (MARWOPNET)
Médecins Sans Frontières (also Doctors without Borders) (MSF)
Millennium Development Goals (MDGs)
National Congress for the Defense of the People (CNDP)
National Patriotic Front of Liberia (NPLF)
Nationally determined contributions (NDCs)
Nongovernmental organizations (NGOs)
North Atlantic Treaty Organization (NATO)
Office for the Coordination of Humanitarian Affairs (OCHA)
Open Working Group (OWG)
Organization of American States (OAS)
Organisation for Economic Co-operation and Development (OECD)
Peace Accord Matrix (PAM)
Peace Research Institute Oslo (PRIO)
Peacebuilding Commission (PBC)
Popular Revolutionary Movement (MPR)
Protection of Civilians (POC)
Responsibility to Protect (R2P)
Revolutionary Armed Forces of Colombia (FARC)
Revolutionary United Front (RUF)
Security sector reform (SSR)
Supplemental Nutrition Assistance Program (SNAP)

Sustainable Development Goals (SDGs)
Transnational advocacy networks (TANs)
Truth and reconciliation commissions (TRCs)
United Nations (UN)
United Nations Action against Sexual Violence in Conflict (UN Action)
United Nations Children's Fund (UNICEF)
United Nations Commission on the Status of Women (CSW)
United Nations Department of Peacekeeping Operations (UNDPKO)
United Nations Development Programme (UNDP)
United Nations Economic and Social Council (ECOSOC)
United Nations Emergency Force I (UNEF I)
United Nations Framework Convention on Climate Change (UNFCCC)
United Nations High Commissioner for Refugees (UNHCR)
United Nations Humanitarian Stabilization Mission in Haiti (MINUSTAH)
United Nations Office on Drugs and Crime (UNODC)
United Nations Organization Mission in the Democratic Republic of the
    Congo (MONUC)
United Nations Organization Stabilization Mission in the Democratic Repub-
    lic of the Congo (MONUSCO)
United Nations Mission for Ebola Emergency Response (UNMEER)
United Nations Mission in Sierra Leone (UNAMSIL)
United Nations Mission in South Sudan (UNMISS)
United Nations Multidimensional Integrated Stabilization Mission in the
    Central African Republic (MINUSCA)
United Nations Multidimensional Integrated Stabilization Mission in Mali
    (MINUSMA)
United Nations Transition Assistance Group (UNTAG)
United Nations Trust Fund for Human Security (UNTFHS)
United States Department of Agriculture (USDA)
Universal Declaration of Human Rights (UDHR)
Uppsala Conflict Data Program (UCDP)
Women, Peace, and Security (WPS)
World Food Program (WFP)
World Health Organization (WHO)

Acknowledgments

We gratefully acknowledge support from the International Studies Association James N. Rosenau Postdoctoral Fellowship program, the Mr. and Mrs. F. Claiborne Johnston Jr. Endowment Junior Faculty Grant Program of James Madison University, and the Sacramento State Research and Creative Activity Faculty Awards Program.

The manuscript benefited from the guidance of numerous colleagues and anonymous reviewers. We wish to thank Jessica Adolino, Marie-Claire Antoine, Chris Blake, Chip Hauss, Patrick James, James Rae, and the staff at Rowman & Littlefield, especially Rebecca Anastasi, Mary Malley, and Dhara Snowden.

Our students, who helped us to realize the need for a book like this one, also deserve our thanks. They both inspired and challenged us, and we are heartened by the growing interest in human security among university students.

Last, but never least, we wish to thank our families for their support and patience.

Section I

INTRODUCTION TO HUMAN SECURITY

Chapter 1

Human Security—A New Security?

Learning Objectives

This chapter will enable readers to:

1. Recall and discuss essential characteristics of human security.
2. Identify differences between national, global, and human security.
3. Identify the various actors tasked with the provision of national, global, and human security.
4. Identify and describe the concept of a human security norm and its implications.

WHAT IS SECURITY?

What is security? In its most basic form, security is protection from harm. The field of security studies, traditionally housed within the broader discipline of international relations, has mostly been concerned with two forms of security: national and global. **National security** focuses on the protection of the individual state from external harm and internal challengers or instability, whereas **global security** focuses on the protection of the stability of the system of states (see table 1.1). How states and groups or systems of states have sought to maintain their security has, at times, led to severe harm to the human populations that live within them. We can look to the internment of Japanese-Americans in the United States during World War II for one example of how a national response to an external threat can lead to hardship and insecurity for individuals and communities within the state. After the attack on Pearl Harbor in December 1941, more than 100,000 individuals of Japanese

Table 1.1.   Security Approaches and Purposes

Security Approach	Purpose of Security Provision
National Security	To protect the state from external threats and internal instability
Global Security	To protect the stability of the system of states
Human Security	To protect individuals and their communities from threats to their well-being and physical security

heritage—a majority of whom were U.S. citizens—living near the Pacific coast were forcibly relocated to camps in interior states out of fear that they might pose a national security risk if their allegiance was to Japan. It was not until 1988 that the U.S. government formally apologized and compensated interned families through the Civil Liberties Act. "Security" does not always have the same implications for individuals, states, and the globe, and there are different approaches to achieving security, as well as diverging understandings of who ought to provide security and for whom security ought to be provided. Building on both theoretical concepts and historical examples, this book explores a third approach to security that seeks to ensure the protection of individuals and communities from harm: human security.

RESPONSIBILITY FOR SECURITY

The overarching theme of this book is the question of responsibility for the provision of security. We examine the shift in responsibility for security from states alone to the combination of states and exogenous (outside) actors; such actors may include humanitarian agencies, nongovernmental organizations (NGOs), foreign states, transnational social movements, and international organizations. The responsibility for **security provision** is distinct from the doctrine of Responsibility to Protect, which we take up in chapter 5. We use the term "security provision" to convey the general practice of preventing or mitigating harm, or providing assistance and resources in response to situations of insecurity at the individual, state, or international levels. As chapter 3 discusses, many types of actors are capable of engaging in security provision in the national, global, and human security approaches.

Traditional understandings of security focus on the state as the primary guarantor of protection and stability. A **state** is a centralized political entity that holds territory, has a stable population, and is recognized as legitimate by its population and the other states in the world; China, the United States, Brazil, Tanzania, Portugal, and Australia are examples of states. These understandings stem from the notion of the **social contract**, or the agreement between individuals and a government that the latter will provide for the common security in exchange for the allegiance of its people. This system of states as providers for their people has been unquestioned for centuries. When we discuss state or national security, we focus on the security and stability of the political entity of the state and its territorial integrity; a state that is secure is able to defend its borders, protect its population from outside threats, manage internal challenges and instability, and continue its political and economic functions. A state that is secure, according to traditional understandings, fulfills its social contract with its population by providing for the safety and stability of the land and people.

Modern security problems, however, may be **globalized** and beyond the ability of any one state to address. The interconnected world in which we live allows people from all over the globe to exchange goods, services, and ideas; it also allows security threats to cross borders quickly and easily. Challenges to public health—epidemics, drug-resistant illnesses, rising costs of medications—do not respect territorial borders. Similarly, environmental threats—rising global temperatures, sea level rise, drought, strong hurricanes, or typhoons—have the potential to have an impact on all states. Many of the threats affecting human security, including the daily lives of individuals, also threaten national security, yet these are problems that states must work together to address.

In addition to global threats, people and communities may face insecurity as a result of their own state's policies or national insecurity. Sometimes the state does not provide security but, instead, directly undermines the security of its own people. The 1994 Rwandan genocide is one such example: the political party in charge of the government actively called for the extermination of Tutsis and moderate Hutus; members of the Rwandan army, National Police, and government-supported militias killed between 500,000 and 1,000,000 Rwandan civilians. Genocide is one extreme among a number of challenges that a national government may pose to human security. Other challenges include unequal access to rights and services for people on the basis of sex or race, economic policies that exacerbate poverty, and poor health services. Some threats to human security are not intentional but result from a state's lack of capacity or ability to provide the services, rights, and stability that are essential to protect individuals from harm. For instance, a state with a large amount of territory (land) but a limited ability to enforce laws or maintain security throughout that territory may find itself unable to prevent or control the rise of militias or non-state armed groups that seek to gain territory or resources. Violence against civilians caused by such non-state armed groups is not a direct result of intentional harm by the state but, instead, is related to the state's lack of capacity to provide for the security of the population.

Yet when a state is unable to protect human security, whether from globalized or internal threats, does responsibility shift to other actors? Can outside organizations or other states provide the security a state is unable or unwilling to provide? **Collective security organizations**, like the North Atlantic Treaty

Organization (NATO) or the United Nations (UN), are one type of exogenous or outside actor tasked with the provision of security. These organizations, made up of nation-states, seek to cooperate to protect all of their members from harm. **Humanitarian organizations**, such as Médecins Sans Frontières or Doctors without Borders (MSF) or the International Committee of the Red Cross (ICRC), are organizations that seek to protect individuals from harm, regardless of political affiliation, ethnic or racial identity, or any other characteristic. These non-state actors are unaffiliated with state governments and provide aid in response to natural disasters, war and armed conflict, and public health crises. States may also seek to provide assistance to other states or people or groups within those other states. A state may engage in **humanitarian intervention**, or the use of force within another state to protect people from harm, when another government's policies and instability cause destruction and insecurity. States may also offer **humanitarian assistance**, provision of aid and support without the use of force, in response to natural disasters, famine, or public health crises in another state. In today's world, outside organizations and states have the potential to become involved in security issues and problems far from their geographical bases.

The world has changed dramatically since the first political communities banded together to protect each other from outside threats. States and their people face threats of a global nature, states harm their own people, and increasingly influential and capable non-state actors or collective security organizations offer another option for the protection of communities and populations. Traditional notions of security—those that focus on the state as the primary guarantor of security for its people—are unable to account fully for the shifting responsibility for security provision and the new types of protectors and protection that we can see in the world today. These traditional notions are not, however, obsolete. In the midst of rising nationalist and populist sentiments within some wealthy Western states, threats posed by transnational terrorism, efforts to foster collaborative responses to problems like climate change and global hunger, and other complex problems in our interconnected and globalized world, security studies and policymaking require nuanced, careful analysis of competing and complementary security approaches and perspectives on security provision. Therefore, we aim to foster such careful thinking through an examination of human security in armed conflict and durable human security.

HUMAN SECURITY: AN EMERGING GLOBAL NORM

The United Nations Development Programme's (UNDP) 1994 Human Development Report issued the first comprehensive and direct definition of human security. The report observed that the concept of security had for too long focused entirely on conflicts between states and the threats to their borders, while individual people have always understood security to mean stability in their daily lives and the safety of their surroundings. Within the context of this conceptual divide between what makes the state secure and the types of security that individual human beings wish for themselves and their communities, the Human Development Report identified **human security** as a twofold concept: first, "safety from the constant threats of hunger, disease, crime and repression"; and second, "protection from sudden and hurtful disruptions in the pattern of our daily lives—whether in our homes, in our jobs, in our communities, or in our environment" (United Nations Development Programme 1994, 3). Human security, then, exists when individuals and communities are safe from both chronic, long-term threats to their well-being and from more sudden threats to their physical safety. Human security, in its broadest sense, is not just about protection from *physical* harm but about stability, well-being, freedom, and the capacity of individuals to thrive. Individuals need protection from war and weapons but also protection from adversity through the promotion of equity and basic human rights. Because of its dual focus on imminent and chronic threats to safety and well-being, those who seek to ensure human security for all people address not only wars and national security crises but also societal norms and institutions, as well as global factors, that contribute to day-to-day insecurity and systematic harm for people and their communities. Put simply, if people feel that their basic needs are met today and will continue to be met for the foreseeable future, such that they are empowered to live full lives, we would say that those people have human security.

UNDP's 1994 Human Development Report outlines four fundamental characteristics of human security that make the concept easier to understand and apply.

1. Human security is a universal concern; it affects all people in all areas of the world.
2. Its components are interdependent; if one population is suffering from chronic hunger, war, or air pollution, the effects of that insecurity extend globally in some way, whether directly or indirectly.
3. Human security is more easily established through prevention than intervention; for example, it is easier and cheaper to prevent malaria transmission through the use of mosquito-repelling bed nets than to treat a malaria patient with medications or to respond to a large outbreak of malaria.
4. Human security is people-centered; it focuses on the daily lives of individuals and their communities, their overall well-being, and their potential to live a free and healthy life (United Nations Development Programme 1994, 22–23).

Human security is concerned with the protection of *individuals* from harm. But what constitutes harm? During violent conflict it is not just those doing the fighting who are at risk of death or injury. Modern warfare increasingly targets noncombatant populations. Ethnic cleansing and genocide, such as the Islamic State's targeting of Iraq's Yezidi population beginning in 2014 or Serb forces' targeting of Bosnian Muslims in the mid-1990s, are the starkest examples. Sexual violence in armed conflict, the recruitment of child soldiers, and the use of indiscriminate weapons such as landmines are all profound threats to human security in armed conflict. Terrorism, the deliberate targeting of civilians by non-state actors, also violates principles of human security. Additionally, individual security can be threatened by more than just guns, bombs, and direct physical attack. Environmental degradation, insufficient access to food, or lack of appropriate health infrastructures, both in and outside of armed conflict, pose real challenges to human security, as well as national and global security by extension. When we discuss protection, the responsibility for providing protection and fostering human security, and the justification for protection, we refer to the broad sense of protection as the absence of physical threats, the provision of basic needs, and the foundation for empowerment.

Where the responsibility to protect and empower individuals lies and the methods by which those goals are implemented are highly contested. Thus, the study of human security encompasses a range of problematic issues that require an examination of both the governance of human populations and the underlying politics that inform that governance. In the two decades since it was first articulated, human security has become a core function of the policies of some states as well as intergovernmental and nongovernmental organizations. The foreign policy initiatives of Canada and Japan, in particular, illustrate how states may take different approaches to promoting human security. Canada has focused on the "freedom from fear" elements of human security, prioritizing protection from imminent physical harm. Japanese foreign policy has emphasized the "freedom from want" aspects of human security, focusing on development and protection of an adequate standard of living (Commission on Human Security 2003, iv, Hanlon and Christie 2016, 4–9). Both approaches are rooted in the 1994 Human Development Report, with deeper roots in the Universal Declaration of Human Rights and U.S. president Franklin Delano Roosevelt's "Four Freedoms" speech (given on January 6, 1941), and they form the backbone of the concept of human security. (See chapters 2, 3, and 8 for additional discussion.)

A wide acceptance of the relevance and importance of freedom from fear and freedom from want creates a human security norm. A **norm,** generally speaking, is a commonly accepted belief or idea that provides standards for behavior. A **human security norm** is a consensus, among a significant group of states and international organizations, that individuals and communities are entitled to protection from harm and that outside actors (including foreign states or organizations) may assist in providing this protection as necessary. To say that a human security norm exists is to say that the lives of individuals and communities matter within global political discussions.

It is not enough, however, to simply claim that human populations should be protected from harm. This, in and of itself, is not generally a contested point. How that protection occurs, what constitutes protection (simply safeguarding against direct physical threats, defending human rights and dignity, or some combination thereof), and the extent of responsibility allotted to various actors, however, are. For example, many conflicts result in the large-scale displacement of human populations. When such displacement occurs, governments, nongovernmental organizations, and international organizations all must consider whether and how to respond. The refugee flows resulting from the civil war in Syria, for example, led to a wide range of responses from states into which the refugees moved, ranging from attempts to close borders (as Hungary did) to relative openness (as Germany demonstrated). How, then, do these decisions get made? Why are some human security issues addressed while others seem to be routinely ignored?

Understanding Security Approaches

We can begin to answer these questions by thinking about how individuals, states, and the global system of states justify protection toward themselves and others. Protection for oneself in its most basic form can be understood in terms of **self-interest**. In most circumstances, an individual, state, or even the global system as a whole will see the perpetuation of its own survival as its primary goal. Yet, individuals, states, and the global system also pursue policies aimed at protecting others even without the existence of a norm promoting human security. The state has an incentive to protect individuals living within its borders, as the stability that protection provides should contribute to its long-term survival. Nevertheless, protection by the state is not absolute and under certain circumstances the state may consider some individuals expendable. The state also has an incentive to protect the global system, particularly if it considers the current status quo beneficial. This logic extends to the global system's interests in preserving the state (see table 1.2).

If we work through each cell—or box—within table 1.2, we can see how self-interest will guide individuals, states, and the global system to offer forms of protection to themselves and the level both immediately above or

Table 1.2.   Justifications for Security Provision without a Human Security Norm

		Who Provides Security?		
		Individual	*State*	*System*
For Whom Is Security Provided?	**Individual**	Self-interest	Preservation of the state, but individual may be expendable	Only if protection of individual can be linked to maintenance of the system
	State	If status quo favors individual	Self-interest	Preservation of the system, but an individual state may be expendable
	System	Only if protection of the system is linked to security of the individual	If status quo favors the state	Self-interest

below them, even without a consensus around the importance of human security and the protection of the individual. Individuals, for example, can protect the state through such acts as military service, paying taxes, and pledging fidelity when they perceive the state to be beneficial to them. While a state may be able to coerce such behavior in the short term, taking measures to create a cohesive national identity can, in the long term, be a more effective strategy. The state, then, is motivated to provide protection to individuals in such a way that garners that loyalty. Of course, without an embedded human security norm the state also may be motivated to eliminate those individuals who don't adhere to its form of national identity.

What is perhaps less obvious is why the global system would concern itself with protecting the individual. Under assumptions of self-interest, a global system whose primary interest is in self-preservation should not be overly concerned with the protection of individuals if the integrity of the states that make up that system is not in jeopardy. However, as will be discussed in chapter 2, a vast majority of the work being conducted by the institutional structure initially designed to preserve the global system is focused on what could be labeled human security issues.

The United Nations High Commissioner for Refugees (UNHCR) is one example of an international agency that works to establish human security for specific populations, individuals who have been displaced by armed conflict or humanitarian crises. UNHCR is tasked with directly assisting refugees and displaced populations and coordinating other organizations and agencies that seek to provide assistance and resolve issues that contribute to displacement. UNHCR is not a state entity but, instead, an international agency within the United Nations system. Efforts toward human rights promotion, peacekeeping, protections for displaced populations, poverty reduction, and sustainable development goals epitomize the type of human security work being pursued by global and regional organizations.

What effects does the development of a human security norm have on the relationships between the system, the state, and the individual? For one, we should expect to see a stronger linkage between the global and the individual. Instead of a self-interested system with a purpose of maintaining the global status quo alone, we will see the international system organize itself to protect the security of individuals as well. It will do so by creating organizations and rules that reflect its growing acceptance of human security as a priority. Individuals, on the other hand, will see the value of engaging global actors when advocating for their security. **Transnational advocacy networks**—individuals and organizations who are connected through their pursuit of a common goal—emerge and engage with international institutions and states to create change. The international coalition that came together in the 1990s and successfully banned antipersonnel landmines through the Ottawa Treaty is one example of a transnational advocacy network of organizations and individuals working to improve human security by reducing the use of indiscriminate weapons. The closure of the gap between the global and the individual puts pressure on the state to adopt policies that also reflect the prioritization of human security.

Thus, we should expect to see three changes in behavior as a human security norm becomes more clearly articulated and accepted by individuals, their states, and the broader global system. The process should follow what is understood as the norm development cycle (Finnemore and Sikkink 1998). First, individuals will adopt and promote the discourse of human security more broadly when advocating for their rights. They will emphasize the importance of their well-being and the protection of their fundamental rights, perhaps even directly challenging the prioritization of state security concerns. Second, states will enact domestic policies that reflect human security discourse and, at least in principle, support global organizing around human security norms. Even if states do not abandon their concern for political stability, they will begin to speak about the rights and protection of individuals and communities at home and abroad. Third, international organizations will work to create a global bureaucracy that promotes human security norms. Organizations, such as the United Nations, will begin to discuss the security and rights of individuals and groups, especially in times of crisis and threats against human rights; beyond discussion, these organizations may themselves take action—such as ordering economic sanctions or deploying a peacekeeping operation—or call on states to take action in response to human security threats. These changes reflect a shifting understanding of responsibility for the provision of security.

Table 1.3 illustrates the ways in which the justifications for protection shift when a human security norm guides individual-, state-, and system-level behavior and beliefs. It should be clear that today's global system does not reflect one in which a human security norm has been universally accepted by individuals, states, organizations, or the broader global system. Nor do we claim that the presence of said norm is the sole factor informing when and how security is provided. States continue to be driven by their national interests and are reluctant to intervene in other states when mass atrocities are committed. The armed conflicts and humanitarian crises in Rwanda, Darfur, and Syria all provide painful examples of the states' reluctance to

Table 1.3. Justifications for Security Provision Incorporating a Human Security Norm

		Who Provides Security?		
		Individual	*State*	*System*
	Individual	Self-interest	Preservation of the state, but individual may be expendable *or* Protection of the individual because it is the right thing to do *or* Protection of the individual because it is politically costly to harm the individual	Protection of the individual because it is the right thing to do *or* Protection of the individual because it is politically costly to permit harm to the individual
For Whom Is Security Provided?	**State**	If status quo favors individual	Self-interest *or* Protection of the state in the interest of protecting the population	Protection of the state in the interest of protecting population
	System	If status quo favors individual	If status quo favors state *or* Protection of the system in the interest of protecting the state population *or* Protection of the system in the interest of protecting the global population	Self-interest *or* Protection of the system in the interest of protecting the population

protect against humanitarian crises. Even for those individuals, states, and organizations that deliberately try to incorporate a human security norm, justifications for providing security will still reflect a range of motivations— the presence of and compliance with a norm will not necessarily snuff out self-interest. For example, states may commit their armed forces through unilateral (single-state) or multilateral (cooperation of multiple states) action in a humanitarian crisis, but each state's motivation may be different and will range from a purely humanitarian goal to save as many lives as possible to a more strategic approach related to resources, national interests, or political alliances tied up in the conflict. For this reason, table 1.3 still includes the self-interested justifications for security provision seen in table 1.2; even if human security matters to some or many international actors, there will still be reasons for individuals, states, and the international system to act on the basis of self-interest and we will still see occasions on which human security is not a priority. Individuals, states, and even the system still wish to survive, but in a world full of individuals, states, and organizations guided by a human security norm the ways in which these actors seek to promote their survival and protect others will look different from a world without a human security norm. Further, individuals, states, and organizations may comply with a norm not because they believe in its appropriateness and value but because *others* do and to violate a norm held by others in the global system would be politi- cally—and sometimes economically—costly. There are also strategic reasons for states and global security actors to pursue a human security approach. Providing for basic needs, eliminating scarcity and discrimination or oppres- sion, protecting communities from violence, and helping individuals realize opportunities are not exclusively a normative endeavor; success in these areas can be key to ensuring the state's political and economic stability, stabilizing a region after armed conflict, or countering transnational threats like terrorism and violent extremism.

In sum, a world motivated by a human security norm is one in which individuals, states, and the system may work to prioritize the security of indi- viduals, but the norm is not accepted by all international actors and is not the only factor motivating these policies. In such a world of mixed motivation, it can be difficult to determine when a norm is compelling behavior or when a behavior, that would be pursued regardless, is using the language of the norm to give that action justification. One reason why it will remain difficult to clearly observe the norm's impact is that, although human security, state security, and global security can be at odds, there are significant points of overlap and complementarity among them. In other words, the three security approaches we discuss are often synchronous. We will explore these points, as well as the ways in which human, state, and global security are at odds, throughout the book.

BOX 1.1. "THINK ABOUT IT . . ."—HOW DO WE KNOW "SECURITY" WHEN WE SEE IT?

1. What does "security" look like in our daily lives?

Consider the people, objects, or routines that make you feel safe and secure in your daily life. Working through these questions will give you a sense of what security means to you, personally:

a. What comes to mind when you picture the word "security" in your own daily life?
b. Who or what (institutions, individuals, objects) provides for your security?
c. Who or what has the potential to threaten your security?

2. What does "security" look like from your national government's perspective?

Now, imagine that you are in charge of national security, the safety and protection of your homeland. Working through these questions will help you envision what national security is:

a. What comes to mind when you picture a secure state?
b. Who or what provides for the security of the state?
c. Who or what has the potential to threaten the state's security?

3. What does "security" look like from a global perspective?

Picture a world that is safe and secure for all people in all states and nations. Working through these questions will prompt you to think about what global security looks like:

a. What comes to mind when you picture a secure world?
b. Who or what should provide for global security?
c. Who or what has the potential to threaten global security?

PLAN OF THE BOOK

Building on the concepts presented in this chapter the first section proceeds by examining the historical foundations of human security. Chapter 2 explores how the idea of human security evolved. Why did human security as we understand it today emerge in the 1990s? The focus in this chapter is on the three aspects that created a global political environment conducive to the emergence of human security: the changing nature of war, the expanded role of the United Nations, and greater recognition of human rights within the international community. The chapter discusses the shifting justification for and conduct of war, the discussion of human development in the UN, and the origin of contemporary human rights discourse after World War II and the reinvigoration of human rights protection in the 1990s. The chapter concludes by discussing what is meant by the term "human security approach" and introducing the differences between protection in war (human security in armed conflict) and durable human security (long-term or "peacetime" human security).

Chapter 3 discusses the implementation of human security concepts by introducing the range of actors involved in the provision of human security and competing perspectives on security provision. This chapter serves as a reference point for proceeding chapters and offers an overview of the human security landscape. A vignette exploring the evolution of the Millennium Development Goals and Sustainable Development Goals introduces these important initiatives in the context of the discussion of the expanded range of relevant actors in human security provision.

Chapter 4 expands on the foundational concepts of human rights and freedoms presented in chapter 2 and traces the roots of modern human rights. Human security depends in large part on the recognition and protection of human rights, and this chapter discusses the connection between the development of international human rights discourse and the pursuit of human security. The concept of "new" human rights is introduced, with a particular focus on LGBTQ rights and opposition to female genital mutilation, to demonstrate that what constitutes a right is subject to change over time.

Armed Conflict and Human Security

The book's second section discusses human security in armed conflict and war. Human security related to armed conflict involves protecting individuals from direct physical harm or the threat thereof. Armed conflict triggers some of the most urgent physical, social, political, and psychological threats to short- and long-term well-being.

Chapter 5 draws on arguments about responsibility from the first chapter to discuss how human security–based justifications for intervention have been used since the ending of the Cold War. It highlights how acute conflict creates high levels of human security threats. This chapter will include a section on Just War Theory and the emergence of Responsibility to Protect (R2P). This chapter will also highlight some of the key concerns that an overreliance on militarized interventions creates regarding questions of human security and the role of outside intervenors and local actors. As the first international intervention authorized with an explicit R2P mandate, the NATO-led intervention in Libya in 2011 is the vignette presented in this chapter.

Chapter 6 examines how human security issues are (or are not) addressed during peace processes with a focus on the various actors that participate in these processes. It discusses comprehensive peace accords and the evidence that suggests that accords that include a broader range of human security–focused issues have greater chances for durable success. This chapter will explore women's involvement in peace negotiations in Liberia to demonstrate the effectiveness of inclusive peace processes.

Chapter 7 looks at human security through the frame of peacebuilding, or rebuilding society after intrastate or interstate armed conflict. Peacebuilding encompasses the scope of efforts to transition a society from war to peace, including rule-of-law provisions, infrastructure, social services, combatant demobilization, economy, and politics. Using UN peacekeeping efforts as a central illustration of how the international community cooperates in peacebuilding efforts in vastly different contexts, the chapter explores both short- and long-term initiatives. Additionally, the chapter examines the ways that transitional justice mechanisms, including post-conflict tribunals, truth and reconciliation commissions, and special courts, contribute to human security. The exploration of transitional justice mechanisms ties into the broader concepts of retributive and restorative justice, which the authors introduce and relate back to the human security approach. The chapter examines the Democratic Republic of the Congo to highlight the difficulties peacebuilding and transitional justice actors have for carrying out their mandates.

Durable Human Security

In addition to considering the impact of armed conflict on human security and the ways in which security needs change in war, we also discuss what we call **durable human security**. Durable human security includes the dimensions of security that are not necessarily related to armed conflict—though they may certainly exist in wartime—but threaten the daily lives and livelihoods of individuals and communities through dysfunctional norms or institutions that create the conditions for harm. Durable human security incorporates the concepts of freedom from want and freedom from fear, as both are essential for the realization of long-term, sustainable human security. When states are unable to provide the ingredients for durable human security—such as effective public health institutions, adequate food supply, protection from widespread poverty and inequality, environmental protection and stability, gender equality, and human rights—both individuals and the state will face insecurity and instability. It is important to consider these issues of durable human security when looking at the broad picture of what security means and how individuals and communities can live without fear, so the book's third section provides a view of durable security from multiple perspectives. Chapter 8 bridges sections II and III with a discussion of the transition from the concept of human security in armed conflict to the notion of durable or "peacetime" human security.

Chapter 9 looks at the impact of public health crises on human, national, and global security. Public health crises present acute threats to the individual and community but also trigger a broader effect on state stability and economic growth if the threat is widespread. Illustrating the key differences between chronic and sudden individual health problems and health *security* threats, the chapter revisits the notion of a threshold for human security concerns and discusses the threat posed by and responses to the Ebola outbreak in West Africa in 2014. Using the cholera outbreak in Haiti in 2011 as an example, the chapter also addresses the perversity of human security actions that create health security threats.

Chapter 10 provides an overview of the ways in which gender equality, or a lack thereof, can impact both human and national security. Through an introduction of the Gender Inequality Index (GII) and the Global Gender Gap Index (GGGI), the chapter illustrates the multifaceted nature of gender equality and the impact of gender discrimination on many dimensions of social, political, and economic life. The chapter identifies the links between gender inequality and decreased human security and state and global instability. The vignettes in this chapter examine the progress of and obstacles facing gender equality efforts developed from within and outside of the state in Afghanistan and Sweden.

Chapter 11 examines climate change and the role of environmental instability in shaping human, national, and global security. The chapter introduces the scientific evidence for climate change and general predictions of its effects before turning to international efforts and failures to address the widespread challenge. The chapter's vignette focuses on the latest global climate summit, COP21, through the perspective of the Marshall Islands to bring awareness to the acute climate-related threats facing island nations in particular.

Chapter 12 discusses the roots and effects of hunger, malnutrition and undernutrition, and dysfunctional distribution of resources. The discussion revisits the impacts of climate change introduced in chapter 11 to underscore the widespread and chronic nature of food insecurity and the need for international cooperation to address its causes and effects. The vignettes in chapter 12 offer a glimpse into the problem of food security in both fragile and wealthy states by exploring food insecurity in the United States and famine in South Sudan.

Applying Human Security

The fourth and final section of the book applies the concepts presented in previous sections to security policy and practice. Chapter 13 returns to the three views of security to synthesize the concepts and challenges presented in the preceding chapters. The discussion presents the requirements for effective and durable human security and aims to promote critical thinking and analysis by highlighting the advantages of and challenges to utilizing the human security approach to respond to twenty-first-century security threats. The chapter also highlights the example of transnational terrorism and the potential contributions a human security response could make. The discussion is designed to prime the reader to consider the promise and pitfalls of human security before turning to the thought exercise in the final chapter.

Chapter 14 may form the basis of classroom simulations or simply serve as a thought exercise for readers outside of the classroom. It presents ways to integrate a human security framework in global policymaking, offering readers a sense of the practical application of the book's central concepts. Rather than presenting a traditional vignette, as in the preceding chapters, the final chapter sets up an exercise based on the terrorism example presented in chapter 13, guiding the reader through an exploration of alternative approaches (based on the different approaches to security) to the problem of transnational and domestic terrorism perpetrated by non-state actors. The chapter will offer readers the opportunity to explore a complex issue with multiple possibilities for action, illustrating the challenges security practitioners, policymakers, and academics face when confronting a range of human and traditional security issues.

Discussion Questions

1. What is human security?
2. What is national security?
3. Do efforts to promote national security threaten or undermine efforts to provide human security?
4. How might efforts to improve national security enhance the security of individuals?
5. In what ways might efforts to provide human security threaten or undermine efforts to promote national security?
6. How might efforts to provide human security increase national security?
7. Are there any agencies, organizations, or institutions that provide for national security *and* human security?
8. What is a human security norm and how does it impact the behavior of (a) individuals, (b) states, and (c) the global system?
9. How does today's globalized world impact national security?

10. What are other examples of humanitarian organizations that you have encountered in the news?

11. What are the key differences between durable human security and human security in armed conflict? What are the similarities?

FURTHER READING AND WEB RESOURCES

Commission on Human Security. *Human Security Now.* New York: United Nations, 2003. Available: http://www.un.org/humansecurity/content/human-security-now

FDR and the Four Freedoms Speech, FDR Presidential Library and Museum web page: https://fdrlibrary.org/four-freedoms

International Committee of the Red Cross web page: https://www.icrc.org/en/homepage

Médecins Sans Frontières web page: http://www.msf.org/

United Nations Development Programme. *Human Development Report 1994.* New York: Oxford University Press, 1994. Available: http://hdr.undp.org/sites/default/files/reports/255/hdr_1994_en_complete_nostats.pdf

For Deeper Discussion

Shahrbanou Tadjbakhsh and Anuradha M. Chenoy. *Human Security: Concepts and Implications.* New York: Routledge, 2007.

REFERENCES

Commission on Human Security. *Human Security Now.* New York: United Nations, 2003.

Finnemore, Martha, and Kathryn Sikkink. "International Norm Dynamics and Political Change." *International Organization* 52, no. 4 (1998): 887–917.

Hanlon, Robert J., and Kenneth Christie. *Freedom from Fear, Freedom from Want: An Introduction to Human Security.* North York, Ontario: University of Toronto Press, 2016.

United Nations Development Programme. *Human Development Report.* New York: Oxford University Press, 1994.

Chapter 2

Historical Foundations of Human Security

Learning Objectives

This chapter will enable readers to:

1. Identify the three central characteristics of the political context for the emergence of human security.
2. Identify the foundational principles for human security, including human rights and human development.
3. Compare and contrast human security in war and durable human security.
4. Identify and discuss the motivations and characteristics of a human security approach.

THE POLITICAL CONTEXT FOR A NEW SECURITY

The fall of the Berlin Wall in November 1989 and the subsequent ending of the Cold War brought hope for a more peaceful world, free of superpower rivalry. That hope, however, was soon muted by the breakup of Yugoslavia, Iraq's invasion of Kuwait, and civil wars in Rwanda, Liberia, Somalia, the Democratic Republic of Congo, and elsewhere. While the number of **intrastate wars**, wars being fought within states rather than between states, had been rising for years, images of the starving and maimed being shown on people's television sets around the world, coupled with increased activism by civil society groups, put more pressure on governments and international organizations to develop policies that emphasized the physical and legal protection of humans. With the rapidly changing nature of the international system as a backdrop, earnest discussion of human security within the UN and among state policymakers began during the early 1990s. Three key inter-national political developments provided a supportive environment for the emergence of human security: a shift in the character of war, an expanded role for the UN after the end of the Cold War, and an increased recognition of human rights. This chapter explores each of these developments in turn before turning to a discussion of the human security approach.

The Changing Character of War

The romanticized notion of war being fought between trained soldiers on a battlefield removed from civilian populations has never been one that matched the historic reality. Ancient texts belie such myths of war; Thucydides' *History of the Peloponnesian War*, for example, talks of Athenians killing all Melian men of military age and enslaving their women and children prior to colonizing their territory. In the twentieth century the introduction of strategic bombing, nuclear weapons, and the rise of identity-based conflicts delineated even further the distinction between military and civilian targets. Thus, when discussing the changing nature of war, it should not be understood simply as a metric. While we can measure whether wars are becoming more or less frequent or more or less violent, there have also been changes in how we think about war as either a justified or unjustified human activity. This section examines both these changes in the context of three major historical events: the ending of the Cold War and its aftermath, the terrorist attacks on September 11, 2001, and the Arab Spring.

The first major event was the ending of the Cold War itself. Global politics for years had been deeply embedded within a framework of superpower rival-ries and ideational differences. During the Cold War most states were aligned in some capacity with either the United States or the Soviet Union. In fact, the influence of the superpower rivalry on global politics was so dominant that the group of states that chose not to align themselves with one side or the other were known as the Non-Aligned Movement. The ending of the Cold War, therefore, caused a major jolt to the international system as states had to adapt their foreign policies away from their former superpower patrons. This had different impacts on different regions. In Latin America the elimina-tion of ideological rivalries helped bring an end to civil wars in El Salvador and Guatemala (although Colombia's civil war continued on for more than twenty-five years). It also helped usher in a wave of democratization to many formerly authoritarian regimes as the United States intervened less frequently in domestic affairs in the region once it became less fearful that leftist parties would align with the Soviet Union.

Many states in Africa and the former Soviet states, on the other hand, saw a number of civil wars either begin or intensify. Several states with weakened authoritarian leaders saw a subsequent rise in ethnopolitical conflict as competing identity groups challenged their rule and battled for greater control of the state. Thus, in the aftermath of the Cold War there was a substantial shift from ideational conflicts to identity-based conflicts. One consequence of this shift was that in many of these conflicts parties were not divided by what they believed (i.e., communism versus capitalism) but by their ethnic or religious identity. This shift led to the deliberate targeting of civilians based on their ethnic or religious identity, as was seen in Rwanda, the former Yugoslavia, and Darfur.

While the ending of the Cold War certainly reduced the risk of a nuclear Armageddon it is not readily obvious whether it became a more or less violent world. One way to determine this is by measuring the intensity of conflict for any given period by calculating the total number of **battle deaths**. Battle deaths are deaths that occur due to combat in two-sided conflict with at least one of those sides being a state. During the Cold War, for example, three conflicts saw over one million battle deaths: the Vietnam War (2,097,705), the Korean War (1,254,811), and the Chinese Civil War (1,200,000). In addition, the Iran–Iraq War (1980–1988) had 644,500 battle deaths and the Afghan Civil War (1978–2002) had 562,995 battle deaths (Lacina and Gleditsch 2005, 154). In contrast, no conflict since the end of the Cold War has reached these totals of people killed in conflict (although Syria may come close). Battle deaths, however, are distinct from **one-sided violence**, which is violence perpetrated against noncombatants without fear of reciprocation. The 1994 Rwandan genocide, for instance, is considered one-sided violence, as are executions or the firing on of nonviolent protesters (Lacina and Gleditsch 2005). In addition, many deaths during wartime are caused by **indirect violence**, or the harm caused to civilians due to the indirect consequences of war such as decreased access to food, clean water, or health care.

The Democratic Republic of the Congo (DRC) provides a stark example of the difference between two-sided conflict and indirect violence. According to the Peace Research Institute Oslo's (PRIO) Battle Deaths dataset, the best estimate of the number of battle deaths in the DRC between 1996 and 2008 was 151,618. However, a mortality study conducted by the International Rescue Committee (IRC) on the effects of the civil war estimated that the conflict and its aftermath were responsible for an excess of 5.4 million deaths to the general population. Some of these deaths were due to one-sided violence by armed actors, while many others were due to the decreased access to food, clean water, and health care services that are indirect consequences of war.[1] Needless to say, only examining one aspect of war obscures how it deeply affects a broader swath of the population.

In addition, the conflicts of the 1990s saw greater activism on a global scale that brought attention to the suffering of people during warfare. The

International Campaign to Ban Landmines, discussed further in the final section of this chapter, drew focus on how an indiscriminate weapon, the landmine, could cause suffering to the greater population long after a peace accord was signed. This activism, and others like it, helped transform the discourse around war and bring renewed attention to its devastating consequences to civilian populations. It should be made clear that the deliberate targeting of civilians, as well as the indirect violence suffered by civilians during wartime, has always been historic realities of armed conflict. Thus, the shift toward a greater focus on human security issues following the Cold War should not diminish our recognition of the violations to human security that occurred prior. What the end of the Cold War did do was remove the political constraints that had prevented those activists, organizations, and governments from bringing greater attention to human security concerns. That said, there were a number of trends in the conduct of war—such as ethnic cleansing, use of rape as a weapon of war, and forced displacement—that lent greater urgency to a new human security discourse.

The terrorist attacks directed against the United States by al Qaeda operatives on September 11, 2001, represented a second type of human security problem. **Terrorism** is the use of violence by non-state actors toward non-military targets and noncombatant populations; the ultimate goal is to send a message to the state in which the terrorist organization is based, the population of that state, or to foreign states and populations. While terrorism as a form of violence and political communication was not new, the magnitude of the attacks, as well as the emphasis by al Qaeda on targeting the U.S. symbolic centers of power, was new. The aftermath of the attacks on September 11, 2001, presented a number of challenges for the human security agenda. One, which began to emerge within the context of ethnopolitical conflict but took on new significance with the rise of transnational terrorism, was the accountability of non-state actors to instruments of international law and the question of who has the authority to respond to non-state actors residing within the territory of another sovereign state.

Did September 11 and the U.S.-led response represent a setback to the human security agenda? In many ways the response to September 11 mirrored a traditional state-centric security response. The United States and its NATO coalition first overthrew the Afghan government, which at the time was led by the Taliban, rather than targeting al Qaeda directly. The battle of Tora Bora (al Qaeda's suspected hideout) did not occur until after the Taliban government was deposed—two months after the initial invasion. The overthrow of the Taliban regime and the insertion of a pro-Western government in its place then gave NATO the authority to operate freely throughout Afghanistan. The intervention in Afghanistan (and the subsequent intervention in Iraq) led to many core human security questions, including

the responsibilities of intervening states to protect vulner
the role of the United Nations in authorizing military inter
human security goals can be properly met through the for
hegemonic power, and how international bodies and legal
be applied to non-state actors. These questions will be fu
chapters 13 and 14.

Finally, the Arab Spring, which began in Tunisia in December 2010 when a college-educated Tunisian street vendor, Mohamed Bouazizi, set himself on fire to protest the widespread joblessness and lack of opportunities faced by many young people, led to a series of social protests throughout the Arab world. These protests, which took place in Tunisia, Egypt, Syria, Libya, Yemen, Bahrain, and other Arab states, called on governments to reform themselves toward greater openness and political participation. States responded in multiple ways to the protest. Some led to moderate reforms. In Egypt the authoritarian leader, Hosni Mubarak, was overthrown. In Libya a UN-authorized international coalition helped lead to the overthrow of Muammar Gaddafi. However, in both these cases the ousting of the authoritarian leader did not lead to improved human security. In fact, one could make a strong argument that in the aftermath of these protests human security has weakened. The most glaring example is the Arab Spring protests in Syria, which led to what has become one of the most violent and destructive post–Cold War conflicts and the greatest refugee crisis since World War II. The violence, instability, and lack of effective rule of law have contributed to the rise of violent non-state actors such as the so-called Islamic State and interventions by multiple states, including the United States and Russia. The Arab Spring protests and the subsequent violent conflicts that arose from them raise a number of questions about our current understanding of human security, particularly as it relates to the responsibility that a state has to protect its own citizens and the responsibilities of others when the state fails to do so.

What these changes demonstrate is that we should not equate state security with individual security, as one does not guarantee the other. At times, efforts by states to improve their own security have had devastating consequences for their own citizens; however, the void that is left when the state weakens or disappears also has dramatic consequences for human security.

The UN's New Role

The emergence of human security–related efforts is linked not only to the apparent need for a different view of security, as made clear by the horrific intrastate wars and transnational advocacy efforts to monitor human rights abuses and violence against civilians in the 1990s, but also to the recognition of the potential for a more significant role for a global institution founded to establish global peace and security. The end of the Cold War and the UN's role in authorizing the U.S.-led response to Iraq's invasion of Kuwait in 1990 brought hope in many quarters that the UN could play a more direct part in resolving conflict. In his report to the Security Council in June 1992, UN secretary-general Boutros Boutros-Ghali mapped out a new, more influential role for a post–Cold War UN. The report, *An Agenda for Peace*, highlighted the need and opportunities to make UN efforts toward preventive diplomacy, peacekeeping, and mediation more efficient and effective. Each of these related efforts is focused on preventing and resolving armed conflict through peaceful means, and each envisions more active involvement on the part of the UN. In the context of the UN's role in the maintenance of international peace and security, the secretary-general cited the responsibility of all elements of the organization and its members to work toward achieving human security (Secretary-General 1992). The reference to this new approach to security makes sense, given the report's focus on maintaining peace in a world that had very recently been dominated by a decades-long conflict between two superpower states whose principal focus was ensuring the survival of their political influence. In short, the human security norm began to take shape as the once-taken-for-granted centrality of superpower states and their influence started to wane.

However, the expanded vision presented in *An Agenda for Peace* was quickly challenged by conflicts in Somalia, the former Yugoslavia, and Rwanda. Each of these conflicts saw human deprivation on such a large scale that they overwhelmed the UN's capacities to act effectively. Indecisiveness on how to respond, Member States' unwillingness to commit resources, regional and global politics, and rivalries all plagued the UN response to these conflicts. These early failures should not overshadow the successes that a more active United Nations has had. For instance, when UN peacekeeping forces are present in the tenuous post-conflict period the situation is more likely to remain peaceful. UNHCR has helped many post-conflict states successfully manage their displaced populations and assisted refugees in the early stages of the resettlement process. UN system-wide efforts to improve the representation of women within peacekeeping forces, state governments, and UN agencies have led to modest, but meaningful, advances in more equitable and gender-sensitive policy and post-conflict reconstruction efforts.

While *An Agenda for Peace* focused on what are typically seen as traditional security concerns—the prevention, resolution, and management of violent conflict—the Human Development Report focused on an alternative understanding of development. As we noted in chapter 1, the 1994 Human Development Report offered the first comprehensive definition of human security as safety from both chronic threats and sudden interruptions to the daily lives of individuals. **Human development** is an approach to international development that seeks to improve the well-being and capabilities of individuals and communities, rather than focusing solely on the wealth and growth of the economy in which those individuals live. Whereas traditional economic development approaches aim to expand the economy, a human development approach aims to enrich people's lives by focusing state resources toward improving health, access to education, job skills development, and other goals that secure the well-being of individuals. Given the opportunity to live a longer and healthier life, pursue a quality education, and obtain the skills necessary to engage in rewarding employment, an individual will contribute substantially to his or her home state's economic, political, and social stability. The ripple effects of a life full of rewarding opportunities and overall well-being extend throughout the individual's family—especially to children—and social network. In theory, successful human development will lead to a more stable economy and economic growth by empowering individuals, helping them to improve their skills and abilities, and giving them a wider array of choices and opportunities to improve their livelihoods. One way to measure human development is through the **Human Development Index (HDI)**, created by economist Mahbub ul Haq in 1990 and used in UNDP's Human Development Reports. HDI is a measure of growth that attempts to account for human capabilities and opportunities and, therefore, takes into account indicators that measure a population's health and life expectancy, access to education, and standard of living. Human development offers a more holistic view of economic growth and development and provides a basis for the freedom from want aspect of human security.

Increased Recognition of Human Rights

A third factor contributing to the introduction and promotion of a human security norm unfolded in tandem with the UN's increased role in global affairs: nongovernmental organizations (NGOs), transnational advocacy networks (TANs), and other non-state actors increased their advocacy on behalf of human rights and the victims and survivors of human rights violations. **Human rights** are the rights to which all human beings—regardless of their nationality, sex, ethnicity, race, religion, language, state or territory of residence, or any other factor or status—are entitled simply by virtue of being human. Such rights are universal (meaning all humans everywhere are entitled to them) and inalienable (meaning no one can deprive another person of their rights except through the due process of law). Examples of human rights include liberty, life, equality before the law, access to education, and freedom to practice a religion. Human rights are, by their very nature, focused on the individual; protection of human rights requires protection of individuals and their freedoms. Increased prioritization and monitoring of human rights by NGOs and TANs called attention to the many threats confronting individuals and communities, whether those threats were posed by the government, non-state actors like armed groups and militias, or more globalized challenges like environmental instability.

Although activism on behalf of human rights became more common in the 1990s, the concept of human rights has a much longer history. The **Universal Declaration of Human Rights (UDHR)**, adopted by the UN General Assembly on December 10, 1948, documented much of what we understand about human rights today and listed specific human rights. (See chapter 4 for a full discussion of human rights and box 4.1 for the list of rights enumerated in the UDHR.) Early discussion of human rights, articulated by ancient Greek and Roman philosophers and legal systems, medieval religious texts and doctrine, and political philosophers and popular revolutions of the eighteenth century, preceded the UDHR by centuries. The UDHR became a landmark text, however, because it was the first international statement of human rights and the first to apply to all people everywhere. Drafted and adopted after World War II, the UDHR was a response to the atrocities and violations of individual security and rights that occurred in all states affected by the war. The international agreement formed a basis for the understanding and protection of fundamental freedoms and human rights. Just as human rights issues were far from the top of the list of global priorities during earlier times of colonial expansion, economic depression, and world wars, the potential outbreak of war among superpower states stifled much discussion of human rights after the UDHR's adoption in 1948.

In spite of its historical importance, the UDHR does not have the legally binding force of a treaty in its own right, but the UN General Assembly adopted two succeeding agreements in 1966 to complete the **International Bill of Human Rights**. Intense debate over the scope and form of the International Bill of Human Rights demonstrates the impact of national security and ideological concerns on human rights issues. The **International Covenant on Economic, Social and Cultural Rights (ICESCR)** and the **International Covenant on Civil and Political Rights (ICCPR)** (both entered into force in 1976) have the legally binding force of treaties; states that signed the covenants are obligated to uphold the rules and procedures agreed upon in the documents. Negotiated and adopted at the height of the Cold War, the ICESCR and ICCPR display the global political divisions of the time, with the former championed by the Soviet Union and the latter favored by the United States. While human rights are universal and inalienable in theory, states are aware of their unique abilities to protect certain rights more than others, and of their inability or unwillingness to guarantee some rights. The Soviet Union based its political ideology on providing for the economic and social stability of its people, so rights to education, employment, and leisure time fit naturally with the state's goals and vision. The United States, on the other hand, advocated freedoms of religion, speech, and assembly, freedoms that resemble those in the U.S. Constitution. Many states, of course, signed on to and ratified both Covenants, but that there are two Covenants when the original intention was to create and implement *one* legally binding agreement on human rights demonstrates the power of state interests in regulating human rights. Yet, as the UN gained more influence in the 1990s and intrastate wars featured grave human rights abuses, NGOs and TANs pushed states and international organizations to recognize and protect the human rights of individuals and communities. At the close of the twentieth century, states were not the only significant players in international politics; instead, states often felt real pressure from NGOs and TANs, and at the UN. Although the UDHR and the two Covenants—the ICESCR and the ICCPR—were adopted decades prior, the collective efforts of NGOs and TANs in the 1990s to monitor the human rights abuses in intrastate wars; to secure the rights of women, children, and minority groups; and to question the central focus on the security and well-being of the state-led to renewed international recognition of human rights.

The international campaign to recognize and protect women's rights as human rights is one example of a human rights cause that met with great success in the mid-1990s, thanks to the persistence of NGOs and individual advocates. Efforts and advocacy during the UN Decade for Women (1975–1985) produced the Convention on the Elimination of All Forms of Discrimination against Women (CEDAW), a legally binding international agreement, adopted in 1979, that outlines efforts to protect women from gender-based discrimination such as unequal pay and lack of property rights. The UN formed the Commission on the Status of Women, which then organized UN World Conferences on Women in Mexico (1975), Copenhagen (1980), Nairobi (1985), and Beijing (1995). The international movement to secure women's rights strengthened through these conferences because NGOs and advocates had a common forum to share ideas and strategies, solicit the support of state governments, and publicly shame governments or groups that violated women's human rights. The Beijing Platform for Action, adopted in 1995, recognized the need for urgent action in response to various forms of gender-based inequality related to poverty, education, health, violence, war, the economy, political participation, and the environment, among other concerns (United Nations 1995). The realization that violence against women occurred on a massive scale in the bloody intrastate wars in the former Yugoslavia and Rwanda gave the movement further momentum and solidified international legal recognition of sexual violence as a human rights violation and a war crime. Legal and political acknowledgment and protection of women's rights as human rights came about through the increased influence of the UN, NGOs, and advocacy networks in a time of international political upheaval surrounding the breakup of a world superpower (the Soviet Union) and horrific intrastate wars that broadcast images of atrocities onto television screens across the world. Discussion of human security was thus a natural complement to the expanding recognition of human rights.

BOX 2.1. "THINK ABOUT IT . . ."—WHAT MOTIVATES INTERNATIONAL ACTORS TO CHOOSE HUMAN SECURITY?

Different international actors (states, international organizations, NGOs, and individuals) may have different motivations for advocating or opposing a human security norm, or calling for a human security or traditional state security approach to a specific problem. Consider each of the situations listed here. Research each situation to identify the goals of the listed action.

Consider the context for the development of human security discussed in this chapter, as well as the motivations for action introduced in chapter 1—self-interest, protection of the individual, protection of states, and protection of the global system—and any other factors that you think may explain each situation. Given the global political context and the identity of each intervening state or organization, does each situation appear to be motivated by a human security approach, a state security approach, a global security approach, or some combination of these approaches? Does each situation uphold or challenge the human security norm?

1. Deployment of UN peacekeepers in Bosnia and Herzegovina from 1995 to 2002
2. U.S.-led intervention in Iraq beginning in 2003
3. NATO-led, UN-authorized intervention in Libya in 2011
4. Multistate intervention in Syria beginning in 2014

HUMAN SECURITY: A NEW APPROACH TO SECURITY

When international actors—including states, international organizations (IOs), NGOs, TANs, other non-state actors, and individuals—adopt a **human security approach**, they seek to ensure the protection of individuals and communities from harm and create a stable and equitable society that allows them to thrive. This approach complements and conflicts with the two other security approaches introduced in chapter 1, state or national security and global security. We contend, and seek to demonstrate through our exploration of the range of human security concerns presented in this book, that the human security approach is a necessary tool or lens for twenty-first-century policymakers, security providers, and researchers. We do not argue that state security or global security is irrelevant in the modern era; however, on the contrary, the often synchronous nature of the three approaches suggests that each offers important insights into security threats, effective solutions, and responsibility for security provision.

A human security approach places the individual at the center of the political, humanitarian, development, military, or human rights effort. This reorientation of security practice is not easy, but it is conceivable. The transnational effort to ban antipersonnel landmines (introduced in chapter 1), led by the International Campaign to Ban Landmines, demanded that states focus on the security of individuals even at the expense of cost-effective defensive security tactics. Antipersonnel landmines can serve as a relatively cheap method to slow or stop an adversary's advance by making terrain too dangerous to cross. However, landmines do not have mechanisms that allow them to distinguish between combatants and civilians, and they can lie dormant for an indeterminate amount of time, which has caused injury and death among civilian populations during and long after active armed conflict. By condemning the use of a traditional weapon for the indiscriminate harm it posed during and after war, advocates made clear that they prioritized human security over military strategy and they asked states and the UN to do the same. The risk to noncombatants far outweighed the utility of landmines. The fact that a majority of states in the international system signed and ratified the resulting Ottawa Treaty demonstrates that states can be persuaded to place the security of individuals and communities ahead of traditional security interests, given sufficient advocacy and awareness of the human costs at stake.

Some states have worked to promote human security goals through support for various forms of humanitarian assistance and peacebuilding activities in war-torn states. Some middle-power states, such as Japan, Norway, and Canada, have explicitly integrated human security goals into their foreign policy agendas, as mentioned in chapter 1. For Japan, these efforts have largely focused on freedom from want issues, pursuing human development goals through economic assistance. Canada, on the other hand, has focused its efforts on freedom from fear issues with a specific emphasis on public safety, protection of civilians, conflict prevention, governance and accountability, and peace support operations. Development agencies of various states often provide grants for governments and nongovernmental organizations to incorporate human security approaches into their activities. Conversely, other branches within the same government pursuing a different set of goals can sometimes contradict these efforts. Policy confusion caused by the co-implementation of competing approaches can undermine a state's ability to achieve any of its goals, so coordination is essential.

The prioritization of human security by any given state will largely be contingent on who is elected. Both Japan and Canada's human security agendas faltered with the election of governments more circumspect of human security goals—although the 2015 election of Prime Minister Justin Trudeau appears to once again place human security on Canada's foreign policy agenda. The election of Donald Trump in the United States led to a quick reversal of the U.S. policies that had fit within a human security framework. Thus, it would be unlikely that in a system in which states were the sole actor that the human security approach would be engaged in any meaningful way in the long term without being subordinated to various interpretations of a state's national or global security goals. It is for this reason that realists and much of the security studies literature tend to dismiss human security approaches. These critics argue that any human security approach implemented by a state would only be pursued in order to advance a more important national security interest.

Still, adopting a human security approach does not necessarily mean that international actors will abandon self-interest and a traditional security approach altogether; states and other international actors may adopt a human security approach to resolve one situation while maintaining a traditional national security approach in other efforts. One example is the U.S. humanitarian relief effort in response to the 2004 Indian Ocean earthquake and tsunami: the U.S. government pledged $35 million in aid and sent additional direct naval humanitarian assistance to the affected states in 2004 (Weisman 2004); at the same time, the United States was embroiled in national debates over immigration, post-9/11 security concerns, and its military operations in Iraq and Afghanistan, each of which involved a strong focus on the preservation of national (traditional) security. The United States did not give up its national security interests to pursue a human security approach in response to the earthquake and tsunami, but by the same token human security efforts were not completely eclipsed during a time of intense national focus on traditional security concerns.

Human Security in Armed Conflict and Durable Human Security

A human security approach can apply to situations involving armed conflict as well as longer-term "peacetime" concerns. We discuss these two branches of human security as human security in armed conflict and durable human security, in keeping with the Human Development Report's definition of human security as protection from both sudden and chronic threats. In January 2001 the UN established the Commission on Human Security and in May 2003 the Commission's co-chairs, Sadako Ogata and Amartya Sen, released a report—*Human Security Now*—outlining a definition for human security and steps the international community should take to achieve freedom from want and freedom from fear for all people (Commission on Human Security 2003, iv). *Human Security Now* defines human security as the protection of "the vital core of all human lives in ways that enhance human freedoms and human fulfillment" (Commission on Human Security 2003, 4). The focus of a human security approach, as laid out in *Human Security Now*, is the protection of freedoms, protection from severe and chronic threats, and empowerment through support for individual strengths and goals. The report does not, however, provide a specific list of protections and capabilities that constitute human security. Paragraph 143 of United Nations General Assembly Resolution 60/1 (otherwise known as the 2005 World Summit Outcome document) articulates a similarly broad view of human security, as follows:

> We stress the right of people to live in freedom and dignity, free from poverty and despair. We recognize that all individuals, in particular vulnerable people, are entitled to freedom from fear and freedom from want, with an equal opportunity to enjoy all their rights and fully develop their human potential. To this end, we commit ourselves to discussing and defining the notion of human security in the General Assembly. (United Nations General Assembly 2005)

We adopt this broad view of human security and seek to refine it through discussion of responsibility for security provision and the connection between insecurity and harmful norms or flawed or failed institutions.

What one person in one society considers to be vital or important will not be the same as what someone else in another context might consider essential to achieve human security. A human security approach is best when it is dynamic, adapting to the political, social, economic, environmental, and other constraints and opportunities in a particular situation. Although this makes universally applicable policies and programs difficult—or nearly impossible—using a true human security approach, all efforts that seek to protect and empower the individual share a common fundamental characteristic: placement of the individual's safety, dignity, and opportunities at the center of any effort.

Armed conflict requires a different set of protections and considerations for individuals than peacetime, given the immediate physical and existential risks associated with active hostilities. Human insecurity in armed conflict results from the breakdown of positive norms and functional institutions, eroding or eliminating the protections and rights that individuals and their communities may have enjoyed in peacetime (or worsening the situation of groups that were already insecure or marginalized prior to conflict). A human security approach to conflict-related threats may involve the following general protections, as well as others that are unique to the context of the conflict: provision of medical care to all parties and the protection of medical staff; protection, basic necessities, and shelter for individuals and groups displaced by the fighting; international or regional assistance with the protection of civilians from hostilities (humanitarian intervention); international or regional assistance with mediation and peace negotiations; reconstruction of infrastructure and services after the conflict; transitional justice processes and mechanisms to restore order and peace and to prevent the outbreak of violence in the future. Put more simply, a human security approach to armed conflict seeks to treat the wounded and dying, protect innocent bystanders from physical harm, and help move from conflict to peaceful normalcy and good governance as efficiently and effectively as possible. The chapters that follow in section II address each of these protections and processes in turn.

Durable human security deals with longer-term, or chronic, threats and seeks to establish stable societies that treat all individuals and groups with equal respect for their rights and freedoms. A durable human security approach, like human security in armed conflict, prioritizes the individual and group while working toward the ultimate goal of creating stability in states, regions, and the global system. A lack of durable human security is the result of harmful societal norms—including systematic discrimination and inequality—and institutions that lack the capacity or mandate to protect all individuals. When norms and institutions prioritize some individuals and communities and place others at a disadvantage, durable human security is threatened. Still, it is important to remember that for an issue to rise to the level of a human *security* concern, the problem should be systematic or widespread, arising from some flaw in overall governance. Threats to durable human security may include poverty and income inequality; health crises (crucially, but not limited to, the outbreak of contagious diseases); gender, racial, ethnic, or social inequality and discrimination against people on the basis of their sex, gender, sexual orientation, race, ethnicity, nationality, religion, or other facets of their identity; climate change; and food insecurity (including famine, malnutrition, and undernutrition). Although threats to durable human security may not kill an individual immediately—as an attack in a war zone might—in the long run they can devastate individuals, families, society, the state, and the global system. Durable human security seeks to make life better for everyone, with the ultimate effect of making states more stable and peaceful. Section III discusses the major threats to durable human security and efforts to mitigate them; specifically, chapter 8 examines the connections between human security in armed conflict and durable human security. These security threats are not simply normative or moral concerns; they can have a long-term effect on states' domestic stability and foreign policy successes. A shrewd policymaker will see the strategic value in bolstering human security.

A New Approach and Its Challenges

New norms and approaches to solving the world's problems are shaped by the global political context of the time; human security is no exception. The concept of human security was introduced during a time of global upheaval: the changing character of war from interstate to predominantly intrastate conflicts, the expanded role and increased legitimacy of the UN, and greater global consideration of human rights laid the foundation for a new approach to security. Although the emergence of a human security norm and the application of a human security approach in practice does not signal states' abandonment of their self-interests, states, the UN, organizations, and advocacy networks have made efforts to place individuals at the center of policies, aid programs, and armed interventions.

This new approach to security is not a cure-all for the world's problems, of course, and human security is the subject of much debate. A reasonable critique of human security as a concept is that, in attempting to account for a wide range of security threats, it becomes unwieldy; if a concept includes everything, it means nothing (Paris 2001). Furthermore, and quite troubling from a practical policymaking and humanitarian perspective, if the concept of human security expands beyond the context of armed conflict, and what we call durable human security threats are met with traditional security policy solutions—primarily military responses—then the discussion of human security could risk inviting more armed interventions to counteract civil and human rights problems (Grayson 2003, Liotta 2002, MacFarlane and Khong 2006). Ultimately, this could leave people at greater risk for harm. On the other hand, traditional security-focused entities, like state armed forces and foreign policy agencies, are already beginning to incorporate ideas central to human security into their strategies and operations (Reveron and Mahoney-Norris 2011). Adding to the discussion, some scholars urge that recognition of the importance of freedom from want—or durable human security—is essential to ensuring overall human security and perhaps even addressing the root causes of conflict (Hanlon and Christie 2016).

The debate over human security, and especially over the kinds of threats and challenges that should be included as human security threats, is still unfolding. We take the broad view of human security, including both insecurity in armed conflict and threats to well-being in times of relative peace. By examining the ways in which various issues and threats can become human security issues and how they in turn affect national and global security, we aim to foster critical thinking about the notion of security from each of the three approaches, as well as improved understanding of the utility of the concept of human security.

Discussion Questions

1. Would the human security norm have emerged without the increase in intrastate wars?

2. What are the advantages and disadvantages of an expanded role for the UN?
3. How does a human development approach differ from a traditional development approach?
4. How do your human rights shape your daily life?
5. Which human rights does your state appear to respect most? Which human rights does your state seem to ignore?
6. Think of a foreign state with which you are familiar. Which human rights does this state appear to respect most? Which human rights does this state seem to ignore?
7. What are the most pressing threats to durable human security in your community?
8. The concept of human security, as we understand it today, took shape in the 1990s and early 2000s, as discussed throughout this chapter. Given what you now know about human security and the context in which the human security norm emerged, consider each of the following time periods and identify the barriers to human security in each context:
   a. The interwar period, 1918–1939
   b. The Cold War, 1947–1991

NOTE

1. A subsequent study by the Human Security Report challenged the methodology of the IRC findings and instead pegs the number of excess deaths in the DRC as between 863,000 and 2.4 million people. While substantially lower, the number still dwarfs the number of battle deaths (Human Security Report Project 2011).

FURTHER READING AND WEB RESOURCES

Commission on Human Security. *Human Security Now*. New York: United Nations, 2003. http://www.un.org/humansecurity/content/human-security-now

United Nations. *Beijing Platform for Action*. 1995. http://www.un.org/womenwatch/daw/beijing/platform/

United Nations. *The Universal Declaration of Human Rights*. 1948. http://www.un.org/en/universal-declaration-human-rights/

United Nations Department of Peacekeeping Operations web page. http://www.un.org/en/peacekeeping/

United Nations Development Programme, Human Development Index web page. http://hdr.undp.org/en/content/human-development-index-hdi

United Nations Development Programme, Human Development Reports web page. http://hdr.undp.org/en/humandev

United Nations General Assembly. "An Agenda for Peace: Preventive Diplomacy and Related Matters." 1992. http://www.un.org/documents/ga/res/47/a47r120.htm

United Nations Office of the High Commissioner for Human Rights web page. http://www.ohchr.org/EN/Issues/Pages/WhatareHumanRights.aspx

For Deeper Discussion

Human Security Report Project. *Human Security Report 2009/2010: The Causes of Peace and the Shrinking Costs of War*. Simon Fraser University, Oxford: Oxford University Press, 2011.

Peace Research Institute Oslo (PRIO), Battle Deaths Data. https://www.prio.org/Data/Armed-Conflict/Battle-Deaths/

REFERENCES

Commission on Human Security. *Human Security Now*. New York: United Nations, 2003.

Grayson, Kyle. "Securitization and the Boomerang Debate: A Rejoinder to Liotta and Smith-Windsor." *Security Dialogue* 34, no. 3 (2003): 337–43.

Hanlon, Robert J., and Kenneth Christie. *Freedom from Fear, Freedom from Want: An Introduction to Human Security*. North York, Ontario: University of Toronto Press, 2016.

Human Security Report Project. *Human Security Report 2009/2010: The Causes of Peace and the Shrinking Costs of War*. Simon Fraser University, Oxford: Oxford University Press, 2011.

Lacina, Bethany, and Nils Petter Gleditsch. "Monitoring Trends in Global Combat: A New Dataset of Battle Deaths." *European Journal of Population* 21 (2005): 145–66.

Liotta, P.H. "Boomerang Effect: The Convergence of National and Human Security." *Security Dialogue* 33, no. 4 (2002): 473–88.

MacFarlane, S. Neil, and Yuen Foong Khong. *Human Security and the UN: A Critical History*. Bloomington: Indiana University Press, 2006.

Paris, Roland. "Human Security: Paradigm Shift or Hot Air?" *International Security* 26, no. 2 (2001): 87–102.

Reveron, Derek S., and Kathleen A. Mahoney-Norris. *Human Security in a Borderless World*. Boulder, CO: Westview Press, 2011.

Secretary-General, United Nations. *An Agenda for Peace: Preventive Diplomacy, Peacemaking and Peace-Keeping*. A/47/277-S/24111, 1992.

United Nations. "Beijing Declaration and Platform for Action." *Fourth World Conference on Women*. September 15, 1995. http://www.un.org/womenwatch/daw/beijing/platform/ (accessed December 3, 2015).

United Nations General Assembly. "2005 World Summit Outcome." *A/Res/60/1*. New York, October 24, 2005.

Weisman, Steven R. "Irate over 'Stingy' Remark, U.S. Adds $20 Million to Disaster Aid." *New York Times*, December 29, 2004. http://www.nytimes.com/2004/12/29/world/worldspecial4/irate-over-stingy-remark-us-adds-20-million-to-disaster-aid.html (accessed November 24, 2015).

Chapter 3

Human Security Actors

Learning Objectives

This chapter will enable readers to:

1. Identify types and examples of actors who contribute to the provision of human security.
2. Identify types and examples of actors who degrade human security.
3. Recognize and discuss the Millennium Development Goals (MDGs), Sustainable Development Goals (SDGs), and their role in fostering human security.
4. Recognize and discuss different perspectives on security.

Up to this point we have discussed the political and historical context in which human security developed as a norm. The articulation of any norm, however, does not have much significance until it is reflected in practice. Thus, human security needs to be understood in the context of those actors with the capabilities to implement the human security approach. This chapter, therefore, offers readers an overview of the types of actors that provide or degrade human security. Furthermore, this chapter explores the implementation of the human security approach by key actors, the obstacles and threats to human security posed by certain types of actors, and perspectives on the responsibility for security provision. The chapter is not intended to provide an exhaustive catalogue of every human security provider or detractor; it aims, instead, to help the reader think critically about human security provision. It is intended to serve as a guide for the chapters that follow.

The first section, "Security Providers," examines the types of actors that contribute to human security. In comparison with national and global security, the range of actors and mechanisms involved in the provision of human security is wider and more diverse. The diversity of actors and mechanisms through which human security can be established makes this approach to security less concrete and more complex than the other two security approaches. The wide range of actors and mechanisms, however, serves to bring previously silenced voices into the discussion of individual needs and wants if discussions surrounding new initiatives and policies are sufficiently inclusive.

The chapter's second section, "Challenges to Security and Stability," explores the types of actors that degrade human security, whether as a direct strategy or an unintended consequence of their actions. The range of actors contributing to insecurity contains many similarities when we look at the different approaches to security, but, as with a consideration of human security providers, the range of actors that may pose human security threats expands beyond those that would normally be considered threats to state or global security and stability.

The vignette in this chapter explores the Millennium Development Goals (MDGs) and the Sustainable Development Goals (SDGs) to provide an illustration of how actors at the local, state, and global levels can coordinate their efforts to address a broad range of human security threats.

Human security is neither completely independent of nor seamlessly integrated into national or global security. To achieve human security, states must be secure and the international system should be stable. We contend that this statement is also true in reverse: that state and global security benefit from the realization of human security, that stability at the individual level flows up to the national and international levels. The question of how best to provide human security, however, is a difficult one. There are competing perspectives on security, the responsibility for providing it, and who should benefit from security provision. In the fourth section of the chapter, "Perspectives on Security," we explore some of the perceptions of security that lead to conflicts and congruence among the three approaches to security discussed in the book before turning to concluding thoughts.

SECURITY PROVIDERS

As chapters 1 and 2 introduced, the focus or purpose of security provision differs across the national, global, and human security approaches. The three approaches to security, then, involve different actors tasked with responsibility for security provision and prioritize different beneficiaries of security efforts. This section briefly discusses the types of actors that provide for national and global security before introducing the broad range of actors involved in human security provision. (See table 3.1 for a list of types of security providers.)

National Security Providers

Providers of state or national security are united in their shared goal of keeping the state safe from external threats and internal instability. Since the purpose of national security is to ensure that the state is safe from external threats and internal challenges to the government's stability, efforts to keep the state secure focus squarely on maintaining the state's borders and ability to govern its territory. This prioritization means that the state will pursue policies aimed at keeping its external and internal challengers in check. Thus, national security is protected primarily through the state's armed forces, as well as security-focused agencies. In addition, international agreements and alliances can bolster a state's influence and capabilities. The state's armed forces serve the dual function of deterring or responding to external threats—threats of harm from other states or non-state actors—and maintaining internal order if the state's stability is threatened by violent challengers from within the state, such as insurgents or revolutionary movements. Intelligence and law enforcement agencies can detect and respond to potential threats from within and outside the state. Border protection agencies serve the function of maintaining control of the flow of people and goods at the state's territorial borders. Beyond military and police security providers, a state's foreign service agencies and diplomatic corps help to manage the state's position in the world, maintain its alliances, protect its interests, and project its values. During crises, a state's diplomatic corps often works to reach an optimal outcome without having to resort to military force. Similarly, collective security agreements, alliances, and multilateral organizations help states band together with allies and other states with similar goals to strengthen their capacity to respond to external threats—perhaps from an adversary with superior military capability—and provide reassurance of assistance if a conflict or crisis should arise.

A secure state can have positive implications for individuals and communities. A strong military, for example, can ensure that a state is not invaded, which provides the benefit of protection from the effects of armed conflict for everyone living within the state's borders. Without an explicit focus on human security, however, the human security benefits of state security provision are by-products or externalities, not the direct objectives, of national security providers. Furthermore, the human and national security approaches can be in conflict, especially in times of crisis when the state responds to perceived or actual threats by restricting human and civil rights or targeting specific communities within the domestic population or foreign populations. In states where human rights are routinely disregarded and where the population has little recourse to address grievances with the state, human security in its broad sense is difficult, if not impossible, to achieve. As chapters 2 and 4 discuss, human rights are central to human security and any attempt by the state to secure itself through human rights restrictions—even temporary restrictive measures—places the national security approach at odds with the human security approach.

Global Security Providers

The global security approach is a logical extension of the national or state security approach, but its emphasis is on the stability of the state-based international system. In a world characterized by interdependent states and complex, borderless threats like transnational terrorism, cyberattacks, and climate change, it is difficult for states to consider their security interests and threats in isolation from the wider world. Global security exists when there is international order, when crises and armed conflicts are isolated and do not threaten overall peace and stability, and when the balance of power among states is relatively stable. Many of the security providers that contribute to state security also contribute to global security because the existence of stable states ensures the overall stability of the international system. Stable states are states that have achieved national or state security and are not threatened by major crises like widespread famine, insurgency or armed conflict, epidemic disease, or economic collapse. Along with state stability, global security is well protected when the strong states in the system are generally in favor of the status quo. If strong states perceive that their state security and interests are well served by the **international order**—the political, economic, and normative arrangements in the international system—and have no pressing interest in changing the structure of global politics, then they will work to maintain international order and stability—or they will simply abstain from not threatening it. If, however, at least one strong state views the international order as unjust or if a state or group of states pursues aggressive or expansionist policies to gain more power, then global security will decrease.

Security providers within the global security approach, then, are the states and organizations or arrangements that promote and protect stability in the international system; without stability, there cannot be true global security. In addition to stable states, the types of actors that provide global security include regional blocs, **intergovernmental organizations** (IGOs), international law and agreements, multilateral collective security arrangements, and multilateral military and peacekeeping mechanisms. **Regional blocs** or groupings—including the European Union (EU), Association of Southeast Asian Nations (ASEAN), the African Union (AU), the Cooperation Council for the Arab States of the Gulf (or the Gulf Cooperation Council, GCC) and the Organization of American States (OAS)—are formal institutions that reduce barriers to economic and political cooperation. These arrangements promote regional stability, and in turn global stability, by facilitating discussions, transparency, interdependence, and the development of shared norms among states. IGOs similarly provide member states with forums for discussion and resource sharing, avenues for communication and transparency about goals and planned policies or military actions, and mechanisms for socialization and development of new norms. IGOs may be global in nature (as in the case of the United Nations and its agencies) or membership may be limited to states with similar political, economic, or military interests and identities (as with the Organisation for Economic Co-operation and Development [OECD], the Group of 7 [G7], or the Group of 20 [G20]).

Multilateral collective security agreements or organizations function as both coordination and socialization forums—not unlike IGOs or regional blocs—and as a means of deterring external attacks on member states. Collective security agreements, like NATO, are based on member states' commitment to defend one another, to respond to any attack on any member state as an attack on all member states; by pledging to share military resources, the weaker states gain protection from the stronger members and the stronger members expand their influence and capacity. Assuming the deterrent effect of collective security works as intended and member states themselves comply with international norms and laws prohibiting aggression, these arrangements promote global stability by decreasing the likelihood of armed conflict. Multilateral military and peacekeeping operations seek to protect global security by responding to situations that threaten to upset regional or international stability or violate accepted international norms. Multilateral military and peacekeeping mechanisms involve the collaboration of many states with a shared goal of restoring peace in a conflict-affected region with the larger goal of maintaining international stability. These operations are usually authorized by, and work under the supervision of, the UN, although some involve coordination between the UN and NATO. (See chapters 5, 6, and 7 for in-depth discussion of humanitarian intervention, peacekeeping, and peacebuilding.)

Finally, international law, treaties, and agreements foster global security by placing limitations on what states can and cannot do without fear of repercussion from other states or IGOs. International law includes prohibitions on aggression or expansion (states cannot legally start wars without just cause, for revenge, or to acquire more territory or resources), certain types of weapons (antipersonnel landmines and chemical weapons are considered unacceptable), and human rights violations, among other things. These accepted rules promote global stability by providing states with reasonable expectations about other states' behavior and incentives for complying with the international community's expectations.

Overall, global security and stability require a careful balance of diplomacy, resource sharing, transparency, and cooperation. In the post–World War II international order, much of this work has been done through the UN and Member States' interactions in UN forums. The key to global security and the focus of security providers is to protect the international system from the kinds of shocks that result from widespread crises and armed conflict.

Human Security Providers

The question of who provides human security is at the heart of this book.

As table 3.1 demonstrates, the same actors that provide state and global security are also the ones most often called on to provide human security—and they often do. When the actors discussed in the previous two sections either reorient their strategies and operations to account for human security threats and needs, or when human security is supported as a result of the provision of state or global security, then we can consider these actors to be human security providers, as well.

It is important to revisit the importance of the state in the provision of human security once again, as the stable state, at least within the construct of the current international system, is *the* actor without which human security cannot be achieved. As noted previously and in the previous chapters, one of the state's primary functions is to protect against external threats and internal instability. In the state security approach, the purpose of this function is to maintain the state's ability to govern its territory and to survive as a political entity. This continued stability and protection from external harm creates a situation that can be conducive to human security, provided the state does not infringe upon human rights and the security of individuals and communities in its pursuit of national security. In providing for the common defense and establishing and maintaining institutions and norms that make the state secure *and* recognize the rights, freedoms, and needs of individual people, the state forms the foundation for human security.

UN General Assembly Resolution 66/290 (2012) makes the role of the state explicit by noting, "Human security does not replace State security," and "Governments retain the primary role and responsibility for ensuring the survival, livelihood and dignity of their citizens" (United Nations General Assembly 2012, 2). When it provides not only the common defense of the population from threats and instability, but also establishes social safety nets to protect against threats to durable human security and maintains institutions and norms that foster equal opportunities and fulfillment of human and civil rights, the state is the most important provider of human security. It can also be the most formidable threat to human security, as we discuss later in this chapter.

Table 3.1. Security Approaches, Goals, and Providers

Security Approach	Purpose of Security Provision	Main Security Providers
National Security	To protect the state from external threats and internal instability	State armed forces State intelligence agencies Local- and state-level law enforcement agencies State border protection agencies Foreign service and diplomatic corps Multilateral collective security agreements and alliances
Global Security	To protect the stability of the system of states	Stable states Strong states in favor of the status quo Intergovernmental organizations (IGOs) Regional blocs and organizations International law, treaties, and agreements *Multilateral collective security agreements* Multilateral military and peacekeeping mechanisms
Human Security	To protect individuals and their communities from threats to their well-being and physical security	*Stable states* *State armed forces* *State intelligence agencies* *Local- and state-level law enforcement agencies* *State border protection agencies* *Foreign service and diplomatic corps* *Multilateral collective security agreements* *Multilateral military and peacekeeping mechanisms* *Strong states in favor of the status quo* *Intergovernmental organizations (IGOs)* *Regional blocs and organizations* *International law, treaties, and agreements* Nongovernmental organizations (NGOs)—international NGOs and local NGOs Social movements and advocacy networks Civil society Local community organizations Individuals

Alongside—or in the absence of—the state as security provider, several other types of actors contribute to human security. A stable international order, but one which also includes millions of people who suffer from extreme food insecurity, poverty, and marginalization, may be acceptable from a national or global security perspective but would not be characterized by human security for all. When the national and global security providers discussed previously ignore these conditions, others step in. In the remainder of this section we turn to these other human security providers, those whose work does not always immediately register in considerations of state and global security.

Chapters 1 and 2 explored the UN's role at the epicenter of the development of human security as a concept. Through the 1994 Human Development Report and continued discussions of the importance of recognizing the roles and needs of individuals and specific groups in peace, security, and development, the UN became a key incubator of the concept of human security (Mac-Farlane and Khong 2006). IGOs like the UN provide states with a framework for coordination and communication that promotes global stability and, for many states, national security; its role in the conceptual development of human security and implementation of programs that promote human security make the UN a key human security provider, as well. This is particularly notable when we look at the many agencies and units within the UN system that are tasked with human security–related missions.

The UN Trust Fund for Human Security (UNTFHS) finances UN programs that address human security issues in armed conflict and relative peacetime; in supporting initiatives to rebuild conflict-affected regions, reduce extreme poverty, and provide assistance after natural disasters strike (to name only three of the many efforts), UNTFHS takes a broad view of human security and one that is consistent with the UN's focus on both freedom from fear and freedom from want. The Human Security Unit (HSU), which manages the UNTFHS, was established in May 2004 and works with regional IGOs, non-governmental organizations, academics, and civil society to develop tools and programs that implement human security. The HSU, crucially, takes General Assembly and Security Council resolutions and translates them into programs around the world.

Outside of the HSU but within the UN system, agencies such as UNDP, the Office for the Coordination of Humanitarian Affairs (OCHA), Office of the UN High Commissioner for Refugees (UNHCR), the World Food Program (WFP), the Food and Agriculture Organization (FAO), UN Action against Sexual Violence in Conflict (UN Action), UN Women, UN Department of Peacekeeping Operations (UNDPKO), and the World Health Organization (WHO) are several of the agencies and units within the UN system that undertake work relevant to the human security approach. Each of these offices and agencies is focused on a specific set of issues related to the UN's more general mission of maintaining international peace and security. For example, as chapter 6 will discuss in greater depth, several recent UN peace-keeping operations have been assigned specific civilian protection mandates, placing UNDPKO in a position to consider human security in conflict zones. The WHO, discussed in chapter 9, helps states coordinate their responses to communicable disease outbreaks and other threats to individual health and well-being, positioning WHO's work within the human security approach. Separately, each agency or unit possesses a wealth of information on its set of issues and maintains networks of contacts within and outside of the UN system. When entities with a connection to human security combine their capabilities in cross-cutting efforts, they have the potential to implement comprehensive programs and provide effective tools to respond to the complex security issues that arise today.

To coordinate the human security efforts of diverse UN entities and outside experts, the HSU supports the Inter-Agency Working Group on Human Security (IAWGHS), which began meeting in October 2014. The IAWGHS helped the HSU develop a Framework for Cooperation to ensure system-wide application of the human security approach. The Framework for Cooperation document, released in September 2015, ties the human security approach to the central mission of the UN, envisions a more comprehensive approach to human security, and lays out a shared understanding of human security based on General Assembly Resolution 66/290 (United Nations Human Security Unit 2015). The Framework for Cooperation notes that "the human security approach can contribute to and strengthen the work of the United Nations system," underscoring the complementary nature of the three approaches to security and the importance of human security for the realization of broader global political objectives (United Nations Human Security Unit 2015, 5).

Nongovernmental organizations (NGOs) are another group of important human security actors. NGOs are organizations that focus on a particular issue or set of issues and operate independently of states and IGOs. These organizations usually function on a not-for-profit basis and depend on support from donors, which may include individuals, corporations, other organizations, states (often through funds designated for foreign aid or domestic social programs), and IGOs. The International Committee of the Red Cross (ICRC) is a prominent NGO with a long history of providing humanitarian assistance in armed conflicts and natural disasters and maintaining political neutrality. Médecins Sans Frontières (MSF), too, sends medical personnel to conflict zones, humanitarian crises, and regions affected by natural disaster to provide medical care but is also known for its activist stance and history of speaking out against injustice. For example, in May 2017 the head of MSF-Italy criticized G7 leaders for framing the displacement crisis as a national security issue rather than a humanitarian one (Médecins Sans Frontières 2017). In 2015, MSF also condemned Ukrainian separatists in Lugansk who refused MSF permission to access the region. They have also been extremely vocal in condemning those who have targeted and bombed medical facilities. Human Rights Watch (HRW) and Amnesty International (AI) monitor human rights violations and spread global awareness of systematic abuses and grave insecurity to generate political, economic, and social pressure for change. Some NGOs focus on particular groups of people, like Save the Children (focused on children's well-being and security) or Promundo (focused on improving gender justice and equality through engagement with men and boys). NGOs often work in tandem with other NGOs, IGOs, states, international financial institutions, corporations, and civil society to achieve common goals and reach larger populations.

Local participation in human security initiatives is especially important, given in-country NGOs' and local civil society groups' familiarity with the security needs, cultural considerations, political situation, and other factors relevant to human security provision. When we think about human security provision, the work should not necessarily flow from the top (international level) down, as it is easy to envision when we consider the central role of the UN in human security discussions. Instead, the human security approach should involve collaboration between security providers at all levels, engaging the insights and preferences of the individuals whose security is at stake. Research on peacebuilding has demonstrated that local populations are skeptical of outside actors' efforts to impose values or institutions on society, especially when local communities' concerns are not taken into account. This type of security initiative without collaboration can lead to flawed or failed programs and sustained insecurity (Autesserre 2014). Human security efforts function most efficiently and effectively when local stakeholders have a voice in decision-making and program implementation; individuals and communities must perceive efforts as legitimate for human security initiatives to work, and local groups know what will resonate and work best in their communities.

When different types of human security providers, ranging from the local to international levels, work together with a focus on a specific issue and a shared goal, they form a transnational advocacy network (see chapter 1). TANs may include actors at all levels of the international system, including locally and internationally focused NGOs, IGOs, sympathetic states, businesses and other donors, and influential individuals (e.g., celebrities, former heads of state, Nobel laureates, or currently serving policymakers), and civil society groups (e.g., campus organizations, professional associations, or clubs). Networks amplify the concerns of local NGOs or civil society groups working to change situations of insecurity or stop human rights violations; by connecting local actors with international resources, visibility, and the political leverage of IGOs and states, TANs place pressure on the state or other actor responsible for creating the problem or threat (Keck and Sikkink 1998). By connecting multiple human security providers around a single issue or set of connected issues, TANs enable organizations, states, and other entities to share expertise and resources, ideally providing a more comprehensive and effective response to a human security problem.

Advocacy networks have formed around a multitude of issues, including (but not limited to) environmental protection and sustainability, the proliferation of weapons and limitations on certain types of weapons, women's rights, the rights of children in war, indigenous rights, and global hunger. Not all issues or cases will generate a response from a relevant transnational advocacy network. NGOs must be mindful of their limited resources, ability to assist in a given situation or crisis, and donors' preferences (Carpenter 2007). When the most reputable and influential NGOs consider an issue or particular case deserving of attention, other NGOs and human security providers in the TAN will follow suit; these NGOs are considered the "gate-keepers" of transnational advocacy (Carpenter 2010, 2011). IGOs are constrained by their member states' politics and preferences and the global political environment, although IGOs likewise tend to develop their own bureaucracies and practices and can place constraints on their member states (Barnett and Finnemore 2004). The UN's limited ability to respond to human rights violations during the Cold War is a prime example of the limitations imposed on IGOs by powerful member states and the structure of the international system. Another factor that determines the global response to a particular problem is public attention (or lack thereof): public outcry can be fickle, limited to certain areas of the world, and short-lived. Public attention can shape states' willingness to address an issue, donors' interest in an issue, and NGOs' capacity (especially in terms of funding) to respond to an issue. Public recognition of a problem is also shaped by the actions of states, NGOs, and IGOs and the extent to which those actors consider an issue to be a problem, leading to a virtuous circle or vicious cycle of recognition or nonrecognition. TANs gain momentum when global public opinion supports action, and public recognition is similarly bolstered by the actions of TANs.

Human security exists when individuals and communities are safe from threats to their physical security and long-term well-being. In evaluating the need for collaboration among human security actors, the HSU's Framework for Cooperation notes that "there is growing acknowledgement that most of today's development or humanitarian challenges are the confluence of multiple factors that are interconnected and mutually reinforcing, and as such require greater integration of activities across the United Nations system" (United Nations Human Security Unit 2015, 3–4). We can apply this call for action and integration to the broader range of human security providers, both within and outside of the UN system. The human security approach has the potential to make security practice more inclusive, to spread out the burden of security provision across multiple types of actors, and to bring new ideas and experiences to the table for more effective and comprehensive policymaking in response to complex twenty-first-century threats.

This type of security provision requires effective governance at the level of the state, effective state institutions and social norms conducive to the realization of freedom from fear and freedom from want. While the focus of human security is the individual—and, by extension, the community—the primary onus to provide this security remains with the state. Where the state is unable or unwilling to fulfill this responsibility, the wide range of human security actors discussed here can fill in gaps in capacity or persuade the state to change. Human security cannot exist where human rights are routinely violated, where the state is fragile or failing, where systematic discrimination and inequality (of any form) are tolerated or promoted by the state's institutions and norms, where opportunities for self-sufficiency and well-being are few or limited to particular social groups, or where the threat of violence is pervasive. It requires all relevant actors to operate as if a human security norm exists and matters, factoring in the effects of policy decisions and security provision on individuals and communities. The key challenge—or opportunity—is to promote communication and collaboration among human security providers and to expand the discussion of security needs and provision to all relevant stakeholders.

CHALLENGES TO SECURITY AND STABILITY

Just as there is significant overlap among the actors that provide state, global, and human security, there are types of actors that challenge security at multiple levels. In this section we will consider sources of insecurity to highlight the differences and similarities between security concerns within each of the approaches.

Threats to State and Global Security

State security is, again, concerned with the survival of the political entity of the state and protection of the government and its territory from external threats and internal instability. The types of threats that are central to the state security approach, then, arise from foreign actors and domestic challengers. Rival state armed forces and weapons capabilities present the most traditional threat to state security, especially if those rival states have expansionist objectives (these are particularly concerning for states in the same region) or engage in aggressive behavior. Since the end of World War II the threat and proliferation of nuclear weapons has constituted a pressing concern for both nuclear- and non-nuclear-armed states. There is a long-standing debate in policymaking and academic circles about the effect of nuclear proliferation; this discussion centers on whether having more nuclear-armed states would increase global stability and state security by decreasing the threat of war or whether the spread of nuclear weapons decreases global stability and state security by increasing the risk of miscalculation, accidental deployment, or weapons falling into the hands of terrorist actors (Sagan and Waltz 2002).

States also worry about threats from non-state actors. Since the terrorist attacks of September 11, 2001, in the United States; March 11, 2004, in Spain; and July 7, 2005, in the United Kingdom, transnational terrorist organizations have become a central concern of many Western states and the threat posed by these actors has shaped these states' foreign policy priorities. The use of terrorism by non-state actors with grievances against states predated these attacks, but the nature and scale of violence have shifted in recent years toward highly visible attacks with the intention of producing large numbers of civilian casualties. Transnational terrorist networks and domestic insurgents, militias, and paramilitary groups can erode the state's security and ability to govern portions of its territory, depending on the nature, severity, and frequency of attacks. If non-state challengers to the state's authority have sway with the domestic population or large numbers of foreign nationals, the state's legitimacy and ability to govern can be further weakened. Transnational and domestic criminal networks, including groups trafficking in drugs, weapons, or people, can have a similarly destabilizing effect, and there is often overlap between illicit activities and the financing of terrorist groups and other armed actors. Improved communications technology allows groups to recruit through social media, encrypt messages to avoid detection from intelligence and law enforcement agencies, and reorganize and strategize after strategic setbacks, making non-state actors more influential and difficult for the state to thwart than in the past.

Nevertheless, the range of threats beyond the adversarial state is not limited to people, groups, and the weapons they use. States face a range of global phenomena that threaten to destabilize the state, harm the population, or strain resources. These phenomena include, but are not limited to, climate change, depletion of vital natural resources, pandemic disease, large migration flows, global financial crises and economic instability, and cybersecurity threats. As states grapple with challenges to their security in the twenty-first century, they are compelled to consider novel approaches and collaboration with other states and non-state security providers, but it can be difficult for policymakers to stray from the traditional security approach and tactics when decision-making practices are rooted in them. (For a discussion of international practices, see Adler and Pouliot 2011.)

The same actors and phenomena that challenge state security may also threaten global security and stability. As we discussed in the previous section on security providers, there is a clear link between stable states and a stable international system; similarly, there is a strong link between threats to state stability and threats to global stability and security. It stands to reason, then, that expansionist states and their weapons, transnational terrorist groups and criminal networks with sufficient capabilities to upset the normal functions of ordinary strong states, and global phenomena that destabilize states and regions can all challenge the order and stability of the international system.

As states craft their responses to national security threats, some perceive a need to turn inward, to take a more isolationist stance in response to an increasingly interconnected world and the challenges that come with it. Another potential challenge to global security and stability that may conflict with the state security approach is the nascent trend among donor states toward economic and foreign policy nationalism and a withdrawal from formal and informal arrangements that facilitate cooperation. Two events in 2016—the June 23 "Brexit" vote in which a slim majority of voters in the United Kingdom elected to leave the European Union and the November 8 election of Donald Trump as president of the United States on an "America First" platform—signaled the potential for a reversal of the trend toward global collaboration and integration in favor of more nationally focused or unilateral policy initiatives. We introduce this here as a potential challenge, but not an absolute one, given the novelty of these developments and the danger in generalizing too readily based on still-unfolding policy developments within a handful of states. It is important to note, however, that the ever-present possibility of any number of states refocusing their foreign policy efforts away from global security and human security issues at any point could have the effect of upsetting the system if the effects are significant enough, just as an expansionist state's campaign to annex territory can upset the global balance of power and international order. Global security and stability depend on balance, communication, and maintenance of peaceful relations, which make this approach to security particularly vulnerable to abrupt changes.

Threats to Human Security

Many of the key providers of state and global security also function as human security providers. By that same token, the actors and phenomena that degrade state and global security also threaten human security; human security is jeopardized by global instability, and it cannot exist when the state is fragile, failing, embroiled in armed conflict, or otherwise seriously threatened. The actors and phenomena that challenge state and global security affect human security differently or more immediately, although the overall effect of decreased state or global security is similar in the long run. For example, non-state armed groups may extract resources from communities, exploit or abuse civilians in armed conflict, or target individuals in terrorist attacks. These actors ultimately seek to destabilize the state, but they do so through direct harm to individuals and communities. Like the people and groups that constitute threats, the phenomena that challenge state and global security can also affect human security first; this point is clearest when considering pandemic disease (the effects of which devastate individuals, families, and communities before jeopardizing the security of the state or international community), climate change (see chapters 11 and 12 for discussions of famine and climate refugees, respectively), and financial crises (in which individuals stand to lose their jobs, homes, and self-sufficiency). Precisely because human security may be affected before state and global security are challenged, the human security approach accounts for a wider range of threats to security. This approach requires practitioners, policymakers, and researchers to widen their perspectives on what constitutes a security threat, but the linkages between human, state, and global security—as explored in the chapters in sections II and III—justify the conceptual complexity.

It is important to note here that some of the key providers of state and global security may also have the effect of degrading human security. Even though human, state, and global security can be synchronous much of the time, there are clear points of conflict between the approaches. We can look at cases of ethnic cleansing and genocide—in Germany and occupied territories before and during World War II, in Bosnia and Kosovo in the 1990s, in Rwanda in 1994, and in Sudan and South Sudan in the 2000s—to see how a state can quickly turn its means of protection (military, law enforcement, intelligence agencies, and even communications infrastructure) against segments of its population. Genocidal campaigns begin with the language of threats, in which a group is cast as the enemy, an other, and a threat to the state or to other groups within the state. These examples are, of course, cases of extreme human insecurity.

We can also look at more common threats to human security that exist within the context of relatively secure states and a stable international system. Food insecurity is one such example; episodic or chronic food insecurity can affect individuals and communities within wealthy, developed states as well as in fragile states. Food insecurity can result from policy failures that create the conditions for famine, from strategic starvation in which belligerents withhold food supplies from a population, or from insufficient social safety nets (see chapter 12 for a full discussion of food security). If the state's institutions and social norms are insufficient to protect individuals from—or directly create threats to—their physical safety and well-being, then human and state security are in conflict. Similarly, if the state lacks the capacity to provide for the physical safety and well-being of its population (including access to vital services, fulfillment of human rights, and enjoyment of equal opportunities), this insufficient capacity creates human security threats.

The actors and phenomena that threaten human, state, and global security share a common theme: they degrade governance, destabilize institutions, and challenge norms. To achieve human security, it is necessary (but, as discussed previously, insufficient) to maintain state and global security. There is a great deal of overlap between the approaches, and accounting for the common threats to each type of security helps to determine the most effective policies and approaches to achieving overall security. Understanding the points of conflict and confluence helps practitioners, policymakers, and researchers craft more effective security initiatives. This conclusion leads to another question: what do efforts to improve human security and overcome threats look like in practice? The next section examines the global effort to achieve human development and reduce poverty and associated threats. The Millennium Development Goals and Sustainable Development Goals are two related global initiatives that have brought states, IGOs, NGOs, and communities together to create the conditions for improved well-being.

EXPLORING GLOBAL COLLABORATION AND EVOLVING GOALS: THE MDGS AND SDGS

The shifts in global politics discussed in chapter 2—the changing nature of war, the UN's expanded role in international affairs, and increased recognition of human rights after the end of the Cold War—and awareness of the unevenness of global development created a context that was conducive to the pursuit of global governance related to development, human rights, and protection of marginalized or underrepresented individuals and communities. One such governance effort involved long-term development goals with a focus on human rights and needs. In 2000, the **Millennium Development Goals (MDGs)**—eight global human development goals with a target date of 2015—focused UN Member States' and international organizations' efforts on fostering development through attention to hunger, health, gender inequality, education, and other durable human security issues. Table 3.2 enumerates the eight MDGs, which gained the support of 191 UN Member States and 22 international organizations (United Nations n.d.).

The MDGs arose from broader considerations of the UN's role in the twenty-first century and how UN agencies and Member States might go about fulfilling the UN's central mission of maintaining peace and security in the world. The Report of the Panel on United Nations Peace Operations—otherwise known as the Brahimi Report (United Nations General Assembly

Table 3.2. The MDGs and SDGs, Side by Side

Millennium Development Goals (MDGs): 2000–2015	Sustainable Development Goals (SDGs): 2015–2030
MDG 1: Eradicate extreme poverty and hunger MDG 2: Achieve universal primary education MDG 3: Promote gender equality and empower women MDG 4: Reduce child mortality MDG 5: Improve maternal health MDG 6: Combat HIV/AIDS, malaria, and other diseases MDG 7: Ensure environmental sustainability MDG 8: Global partnership for development	SDG 1: End poverty in all its forms everywhere SDG 2: End hunger, achieve food security and improved nutrition and promote sustainable agriculture SDG 3: Ensure healthy lives and promote well-being for all at all ages SDG 4: Ensure inclusive and equitable quality education and promote lifelong learning opportunities for all SDG 5: Achieve gender equality and empower all women and girls SDG 6: Ensure availability and sustainable management of water and sanitation for all SDG 7: Ensure access to affordable, reliable, sustainable and modern energy for all SDG 8: Promote sustained, inclusive and sustainable economic growth, full and productive employment and decent work for all SDG 9: Build resilient infrastructure, promote inclusive and sustainable industrialization and foster innovation SDG 10: Reduce inequality within and among countries SDG 11: Make cities and human settlements inclusive, safe, resilient and sustainable SDG 12: Ensure sustainable consumption and production patterns SDG 13: Take urgent action to combat climate change and its impacts SDG 14: Conserve and sustainably use the oceans, seas and marine resources for sustainable development SDG 15: Protect, restore and promote sustainable use of terrestrial ecosystems, sustainably manage forests, combat desertification, and halt and reverse land degradation and halt biodiversity loss SDG 16: Promote peaceful and inclusive societies for sustainable development, provide access to justice for all and build effective, accountable and inclusive institutions at all levels SDG 17: Strengthen the means of implementation and revitalize the Global Partnership for Sustainable Development

Source: UN Millennium Project (http://www.unmillenniumproject.org/goals/)

Source: Sustainable Development Knowledge Platform (https://sustainabledevelopment.un.org/sdgs)

2000a)—disclosed the shortcomings of and challenges facing UN-led peace operations, exemplified most painfully by the UN's failure to respond to genocide in Rwanda and the massacre of civilians in Srebrenica in the 1990s, and suggested improvements. The Brahimi Report called for stronger commitments from Member States and UN-level institutional changes to support effective conflict prevention and peacebuilding, improved efforts to build up and reform local police organizations, inclusion of human rights specialists in peacebuilding, enhanced financial support and rapid deployment capabilities, and clear, feasible mandates for peace operations. The high-level review of UN peace operations focused on the freedom from fear aspect of human security and how the UN and Member States might improve their efforts to protect individuals and communities from imminent threats to their physical security after the shocking failures to do so in Rwanda and Bosnia.

At the same time, UN agencies and Member States were also exploring improvements in global economic development with the objective of improving the well-being of the world's poor; from September 6 to 8, 2000, most of the world's leaders gathered at UN Headquarters in New York at the Millennium Summit to consider this task. The Millennium Declaration (United Nations General Assembly 2000b) resulted from the summit and called for the world's states to observe international human rights law and international humanitarian law and foster sustainable development. The Millennium Declaration contains eight chapters focused on key issue areas that formed the basis for what would become the MDGs: values and principles; peace, security, and disarmament; development and poverty eradication; protecting our common environment; human rights, democracy, and good governance; protecting the vulnerable; meeting the special needs of Africa; and strengthening the United Nations (United Nations General Assembly 2000b).

Drawing from this broader institutional context, the MDGs laid out quantifiable goals with clear targets and an explicit timeframe for their achievement. The structure and content of the MDGs reflect the perspectives of the individuals who drafted the goals, the interests of donor states and organizations, and the global political context of the year 2000. The MDGs were drafted by a small group of experts in the basement of UN Headquarters through a process that was casual enough that MDG 7—ensuring environmental sustainability—was accidentally left out until the head of the UN Development Programme at the time, Lord Mark Malloch-Brown, walked past the head of the UN environmental program and was suddenly struck by the omission (Tran 2012). In 2012 Malloch-Brown recalled, while reflecting on the comparison between the MDG drafting process and the process that would later lead to the SDGs, that the small team had to consider the interests and priorities of various global constituencies and that the final list of MDGs reflected the human rights approach of the UNDP's Human Development

Report, the market-oriented development approach of the World Bank, and target-focused approach of donors from the OECD (Tran 2012). The MDGs had to please multiple donor states and organizations, as well as the full UN membership, requiring the drafters to use language and establish goals and targets that would appease competing views on what constitutes development and how far the enforcement of certain rights should go (MDG 3 on gender equality, for example, met some opposition from more conservative states). In seeking universal acceptance of the goals from Member States, drafters of both the MDGs and the SDGs had to leave democracy and accountable government institutions out of the lists of goals.

The MDGs were written and accepted in 2000, in a time of post–Cold War relative optimism before the global political context shifted abruptly just one year later as Western donor states—led by the United States—began to focus their foreign policy efforts on combating transnational terrorism. Laudable achievements reached through the MDGs include a 40 percent drop in HIV/AIDS infections since 2000, more than 50 percent decreases in the number of children out of school and in child mortality (measured against 1990 levels), and more than one billion fewer people living in extreme poverty (measured against 1990 levels) (United Nations Development Programme n.d.). Still, the realization of the MDGs by 2015 was uneven, with some goals meeting more success than others and some states achieving greater gains than others, and critics note that the metrics used to assess progress are of questionable reliability (Jurkovich 2016, MDG Gap Task Force 2015, Sandbu 2015). The MDGs took on a broad range of durable human security concerns but were drafted by a small group of people with little input from those most affected by the problems the MDGs sought to address. The path to the SDGs, in contrast, speaks to the evolution of global efforts to improve human security by expanding access to the negotiating table and working to ensure that global governance efforts recognize the diverse contexts and needs of the world's population.

The **Sustainable Development Goals (SDGs)**—also known as the Global Goals—developed from the framework of the MDGs and analysis of the progress still to be made when the MDGs expired in 2015. There are still hungry people in the world. Children are still out of school. Efforts to improve the sustainability of natural resources and energy sources have fallen short. The SDGs consist of seventeen goals (with 169 targets across all of the goals) that pick up where the MDGs left off and run through an end date of 2030 (United Nations General Assembly 2015). The more inclusive drafting process for the SDGs began shortly before the Rio+20 Conference in June 2012, twenty years after the initial United Nations Conference on Environment and Development in Rio de Janeiro in 1992 (see chapter 11 for the connection between the Rio Earth Summit and the broader effort to address climate change). The outcome document of the Rio+20 Conference, *The Future We*

Want, established central themes to be addressed by the SDGs and called for a coordinated process leading to goals that are aspirational, easily communicated, and feasible, taking varying state and local capacities and resources into consideration. Unlike in the process leading to the MDGs, sustainability was central to the creation of the SDGs from the start, as noted in *The Future We Want*: states renewed their "commitment to sustainable development and to ensuring the promotion of an economically, socially and environmentally sustainable future for our planet and for present and future generations" (United Nations General Assembly 2012).

The Rio+20 Conference outcome document called for an Open Working Group (OWG) to draft the goals and their targets. This thirty-seat group was established by the UN General Assembly in January 2013 and included more than thirty states, as groups of states shared seats (United Nations General Assembly 2013). In July 2012, just before the formation of the OWG, UN secretary-general Ban Ki-moon established a High-Level Panel of Eminent Persons on the Post 2015 Development Agenda to consider the UN's development role moving forward from the MDGs. The Panel was tasked with holding inclusive discussions that integrated insights for the post-2015 agenda from civil society groups, individuals in the private sector, UN personnel, and academics, in addition to the state representatives on the panel (High-Level Panel on the Post-2015 Development Agenda n.d.). The Panel's final recommendations resulted from the discussion with academics, regional organizations, more than 500 civil society groups, and 250 heads of corporations. These recommendations centered on continuing the work started by the MDGs, especially with a core focus on ending extreme poverty, but called for more emphasis on the devastating (and development-inhibiting) role played by armed conflict and violence and the potential for climate change to hamper the UN's development agenda if left unaddressed (High-Level Panel of Eminent Persons on the Post-2015 Development Agenda 2013).

The SDGs, newly accepted and largely untested at the time of writing, provide a framework for collaboration among a wide array of actors involved in global human security efforts. The more inclusive drafting process for the SDGs led to a greater number of goals with more nuanced targets. It is important to note, as well, that the SDGs are all interdependent, and success or failure in one will help or hinder the others. For example, SDG 4 calls for "inclusive and equitable quality education," SDG 8 seeks to "promote sustained, inclusive and sustainable economic growth," and SDG 10 aims to "reduce inequality within and among countries" (United Nations n.d.). Each of these three goals shares an explicit focus on reducing inequality and barriers to opportunity, and efforts to reach one of the goals will advance progress toward the others: education itself is a powerful equalizer; inclusive economic growth and reduced social inequality improve access to quality education; and improved equality within the state and more broadly within the international community increases both sustainable development and access to quality education. The creation, implementation, and limitations of the MDGs and SDGs speak to the need for global collaboration to achieve human security. While the MDGs and SDGs are cast in the language of development, the conditions created by the achievement of the goals would advance the protection of individuals from threats to their physical security and well-being in both the immediate and long terms.

The MDGs and SDGs originated at the international level, largely from within the UN architecture, and require a cosmopolitan view of security provision and governance that emphasizes the shared burden all of people, communities, states, and organizations to band together to solve the world's problems. Nevertheless, fostering local- and state-level involvement or buy-in with global development goals can help skeptical constituencies see the merit in such efforts. To the extent that the SDGs appeal to, involve, and improve the capacity of local communities and states struggling in our inter-connected world, the case can be made that the goals and targets strengthen local and national security and serve related interests. We now turn to the question of these different perspectives on security provision.

BOX 3.1. "THINK ABOUT IT . . ."—GLOBAL–LOCAL PARTNERSHIPS AND PERSPECTIVES ON SECURITY

In 2016 the office of the UN High Commissioner for Refugees observed that every minute in 2015 an average of 24 people had to flee their homes. By the end of 2015, there were 65.3 million internally displaced persons or refugees. The UNHCR's tally of displaced persons had never surpassed sixty million before the most recent refugee crisis (Edwards 2016). Estimates of displacement caused by World War II are around sixty million, just below the level of the current refugee crisis (Zampano, Moloney, and Juan 2015). (See chapter 5 for additional discussion of internally displaced persons and refugees.) Record displacement calls for vastly increased security provision and humanitarian assistance.

A look at just one arrival point in Europe, the island of Lesvos in Greece, shows the wide range of actors—from individuals through UN agencies—involved in providing assistance to refugees. In a span of only three months in 2015, UNHCR had set up 226 Refu-gee Housing Units and distributed 77,000 non-food items (between September and November 2015) through a presence of dozens of UN staff members (United Nations High Commissioner for Refu-gees 2015). Prominent NGOs like Médecins Sans Frontières and the

International Rescue Committee provided medical, psychological, and other humanitarian assistance to refugees arriving on the island from war-torn states.

One January 2016 report in *The Guardian* newspaper questioned whether or not there were too many NGOs operating in Lesvos, with a count of eighty-one organizations at the time. Residents and public officials in Lesvos expressed both appreciation for the outpouring of help and concern about the lack of coordination between some organizations and local government (Nianias 2016).

Individuals, too, have stepped in to provide assistance on the island by offering translation services, meals, shelter, boats, and other supplies (Gaglias 2016). A diverse set of security providers with different skills, resources, and perspectives has the potential to improve the response to any humanitarian crisis, especially a large-scale crisis like record forced displacement; still, careful coordination and clear communication among these actors are keys to improving outcomes for the vulnerable populations in question—here, refugees.

By August 2016, the number of refugees arriving in Greece decreased with a politically controversial deal between the European Union and Turkey. The agreement forced refugees arriving in Greece to be returned to Turkey in exchange for the resettlement in Europe of Syrians who had sought asylum in Turkey. The one-for-one deal left refugees in a state of uncertainty amid the new restrictions and diminished global attention to the plight of refugees on Lesvos, other Greek islands, and along the European migration routes.

Tourism in Lesvos also decreased in the wake of the refugee crisis, causing concern about the local economy and threatening the livelihoods of Greek nationals, thus creating another dimension of insecurity (Alderman 2016).

Explore the following resources for information on the refugee crisis:

BBC News, "Migrant Crisis: Migration to Europe Explained in Seven Charts," March 4, 2016: http://www.bbc.com/news/world-europe-34131911
UNHCR, "Figures at a Glance": http://www.unhcr.org/en-us/figures-at-a-glance.html
UNHCR, "Global Forced Displacement Hits Record High," June 20, 2016: http://www.unhcr.org/en-us/news/latest/2016/6/5763b65a4/global-forced-displacement-hits-record-high.html
Nick Squires, "A Year on from EU-Turkey Deal, Refugees and Migrants in Limbo Commit Suicide and Suffer from Trauma," *The Telegraph*,

March 14, 2017: http://www.telegraph.co.uk/news/2017/03/14/year-eu-turkey-deal-refugees-migrants-limbo-commit-suicide-suffer/

Emily Tamkin, "Did Turkey Just Kill the Refugee Deal with Europe?" *Foreign Policy*, March 17, 2017: http://foreignpolicy.com/2017/03/14/did-turkey-just-kill-the-refugee-deal-with-europe/

Kondylia Gogou, "The EU-Turkey Deal: Europe's Year of Shame," Amnesty International, March 20, 2017: https://www.amnesty.org/en/latest/news/2017/03/the-eu-turkey-deal-europes-year-of-shame/

Explore the following resources for information about European and global public opinion of refugees:

Pew Research Center, "European Opinions of the Refugee Crisis in 5 Charts," September 16, 2016: http://www.pewresearch.org/fact-tank/2016/09/16/european-opinions-of-the-refugee-crisis-in-5-charts/

Amnesty International, "Refugees Welcome Index Shows Government Refugee Policies out of Touch with Public Opinion," May 19, 2016: https://www.amnesty.org/en/latest/news/2016/05/refugees-welcome-index-shows-government-refugee-policies-out-of-touch/

Pew Research Center, "Immigration Attitudes" page: http://www.pewresearch.org/topics/immigration-attitudes/

After reviewing the aforementioned resources, consider the following questions:

1. What are the advantages of the involvement of a diverse set of security providers in a situation like the arrival of hundreds of thousands of refugees on Lesvos? What are the disadvantages of the diversity of security providers?
2. Are there ways in which individuals, NGOs, local governments, national governments, and intergovernmental organizations (like the UN) can better coordinate to ensure more comprehensive security provision for refugees? How might efforts improve?
3. How do differing national public opinions of refugees affect the viability of a local, national, or global effort to provide human security?
4. According to the nationalist security perspective, which actor(s) would be responsible for providing security to refugees? How would the nationalist security perspective view the effect on the local economy in Lesvos?

PERSPECTIVES ON SECURITY

For the diverse array of security providers to work together to achieve common goals, like the MDGs and SDGs, there must be some degree of mutual trust and shared norms and an absence of global disruptions or instability. Assumptions about what constitutes security, who or what provides it or ought to provide it, and who or what threatens it are inherent in any approach to security. When we consider security provision, especially human security provision, we must take into account the ways in which individuals seek to maintain or improve their own security. To date, this is missing from much of the research on and discussion of human security.

International Relations (IR) literature in the realist paradigm characterizes states as self-interested actors. We know that individuals are similarly preoccupied with their safety and well-being. If the individual is at the center of security in the human security approach, then it is a useful exercise to consider the competing perspectives through which individuals assess their security and how best to achieve it. The concept of "security" to an individual generally involves a combination of economic, physical, and cultural aspects, and each person makes conscious or subconscious decisions every day in pursuit of their security. Pursuing one's own security does not necessarily guarantee an interest in pursuing or providing security for others; in fact, it can be easy to view security gains for others as security threats to oneself. Just as realist IR posits that states pursuing their self-interest will inevitably end up in situations of insecurity and less-than-ideal outcomes in a world made up of similarly self-interested states, individuals may also perceive security to be a win-lose (or zero-sum, in the language of realist IR) situation in which security for oneself must come at the expense of security for others.

The human security approach developed out of recognition of human rights as universal and human development as essential. As the concept of human security developed, so too did the expectation that the state and international community (especially the United Nations) would promote and protect human rights and pursue human development. Yet it is not clear that recognition of universal human rights and the importance of human development or the expectation that states and international organizations will provide these are accepted without question. Individual security perspectives come about through a confluence of experience, norms, interests, and beliefs, all of which vary across communities, even within the same state or region. In short, individuals may not see human security conceived as a global, top-down endeavor as the best way to guarantee their own security, and the conflict between individual perspectives on security and approaches to security can lead to flawed policy initiatives (see Autesserre 2014 for research on the effects of this incompatibility).

We can group individual security perspectives into three broad categories: nationalist, nativist, and cosmopolitan (see table 3.3). The **nationalist perspective on security** tracks closely with the traditional or state security and global security approaches. According to this perspective, the individual believes security is best provided by the state for the citizens of the state. The state is the primary provider of security and the individual expects to receive protection from the state, as established by the notion of the social contract (discussed in chapter 1). With the state as the central security provider, the provision of foreign aid and assistance through unilateral or multilateral efforts is not guaranteed in this perspective; foreign aid and assistance are also not out of the question, especially if one state's security situation benefits from helping another state's population.

The **nativist perspective on security** places the primary security provider closer to home. Security, according to this perspective, is best provided by a group or groups below the level of the state, including sectarian, ethnic, religious, racial, or other identity groups. Because the state is not seen as the primary guarantor of security in this perspective, individuals may come to rely on, support, or participate in non-state armed groups such as militias, insurgent factions, or terrorist organizations in response to situations of real or perceived insecurity. The nativist perspective may arise when the state is incapable of or unwilling to provide protection for all segments of the population, meaning the state has failed in its responsibility to provide security. It may also be present when the state *is* able and willing to provide security for its population, but when segments of the population instead associate effective security provision with their own identity group rather than with the broader state. The nativist perspective is similarly suspect of global policy efforts to provide security.

The third perspective, the **cosmopolitan perspective on security**, holds that security is best provided through global cooperation and acceptance of norms and governance institutions. The cosmopolitan perspective leads individuals to see their security as closely aligned with the security of others around the world, regardless of differences in identity, nationality, and lived experiences. Individuals who see the world from a cosmopolitan viewpoint see global institutions and agreements as necessary components of overall security but emphasize the importance of local and state participation in

Table 3.3. Security Perspectives and Their Implications

Security Perspective	Implications
Nativist	Security is best provided by one's own local kinship group.
Nationalist	Security is best provided by the state for the citizens of that state.
Cosmopolitan	Security is best provided by groups agreeing on sets of norms that govern behavior between them.

shared efforts. The cosmopolitan perspective envisions security policies and initiatives as functioning best when they are created through inclusive processes that incorporate diverse insights and experiences. Civil society organizations are most likely to adhere to this perspective, which tracks most closely (but not completely) with the human security approach: because much of the human security discourse has taken a top-down approach, and because the cosmopolitan perspective values the contributions of local actors, the match is not entirely seamless.

The three different perspectives on security and security provision have the potential to affect human security policy implementation. This effect exists on both sides of security provision: the population in need of assistance will have a perspective on the most logical or capable security provider, and the population or constituents of the state, IGO, or other entity tasked with security provision will also have a perspective on the appropriateness of that role. To examine how perspectives come into play in global human security provision, we can take the example of the nativist perspective on assistance. If a nativist perspective exists within the key constituencies in a donor state, then there will be pressure on that state to limit the resources directed to communities that are perceived as different, foreign, or incompatible with the identity of the potential donor or security provider. An example of this can be seen in the response to the Syrian refugee crisis among segments of the population within the United States and in some European states. Some constituencies within these states, states which have a history of resettling refugees, have pushed back against the notion that their communities have an obligation to provide for and take in refugees who practice a different religion, come from a different culture, and speak a different language (see the resources in box 3.1 for links to public opinion on the refugee crisis). Similarly, a nativist perspective within a population in need of assistance would lead to acceptance of assistance from states or groups with a shared identity, but less so from those perceived as different, foreign, or incompatible with the needs and identity of the local population. One example is that of efforts by NGOs, UN entities, or foreign states to promote gender equality and women's rights in culturally conservative states; such efforts may meet with resistance if those efforts are perceived by constituencies within the local population as an attempt to impose Western values (see chapter 10 for further discussion). If individuals' unique perspectives on security are not taken into account when states, IGOs, NGOs, and other security providers determine their response to a given situation of insecurity, there is an underlying risk of failure, or at least inefficiency.

We revisit these three perspectives throughout the book to discuss potential obstacles to the human security approach. Human security is not doomed to failure in the light of these competing views on security provision, but practitioners, policymakers, and researchers would do well to be mindful of these perspectives and invite dialogue and frame human security initiatives in a way that engages and reconciles rather than ignores and exacerbates the potential obstacles arising from competing perspectives.

Concluding Thoughts

Human security is neither completely independent of nor seamlessly integrated into the state and global security approaches. As we explored in this chapter, many of the actors that create security or insecurity in one approach also have an impact on the others. For this reason, we maintain the assumption throughout the book that the three approaches to security are synchronous in some cases and conflictual in others. To achieve human security, the world needs secure states with functional institutions and social norms that promote the core values central to human security (namely, human rights), while also promoting inclusive dialogue to account for and navigate competing security perspectives. To achieve human security, the world also needs a relatively stable international system in which far-reaching threats are absent and states are in concert with one another.

There is not a perfect formula for the achievement of human security, and we do not seek to propose one in this book. Likewise, there is a multitude of security providers and threats that we could address in this chapter and throughout the book, but no single volume can account for all the world's heroes or problems. We hope instead that the discussions in this book will help readers to think about the enduring questions of who or what provides and threatens security in every sense of the word and apply the concepts presented here to the myriad security challenges facing the world today.

Discussion Questions

1. Think about a human security issue that you have heard or read about before (e.g., refugee resettlement, famine, civilian protection in armed conflict, or systematic racial discrimination). Who are the main contributors to this problem? Who are the central actors working to solve this problem and create human security? Do the different actors work together or is the effort disjointed?
2. How might improved human security within your state affect your state's national security?
3. The SDGs are significantly more complex and comprehensive than the MDGs, largely as a result of the more inclusive drafting process that led to the SDGs. How might the longer list of goals and targets affect global progress toward achievement of the goals?

4. What are the potential effects of political polarization on human, national, and global security? What efforts, if any, might be undertaken to foster collaboration?

FURTHER READING AND WEB RESOURCES

High-Level Panel on the Post-2015 Development Agenda: http://www.post2015hlp. org

Open Working Group on Sustainable Development Goals: https://sustainabledevelop-ment.un.org/owg.html

Progress towards the Sustainable Development Goals, Report of the Sec-retary-General, E/2016/75*: http://www.un.org/ga/search/view_doc. asp?symbol=E/2016/75&Lang=E

United Nations High Commissioner for Refugees (UNHCR). *Global Trends: Forced Displacement in 2015*, June 20, 2016. https://s3.amazonaws.com/ unhcrsharedmedia/2016/2016-06-20-global-trends/2016-06-14-Global-Trends-2015.pdf (accessed June 22, 2017)

United Nations Human Security Unit. *Strategic Plan 2014–2017*. 2014. http://www. un.org/humansecurity/sites/www.un.org.humansecurity/files/hsu%20documents/ HSU%20Strategic%20Plan%202014-2017%20Web%20Version.pdf (accessed June 28, 2017)

United Nations Trust Fund for Human Security: http://www.un.org/humansecurity/ about-human-security/human-security-all

For Deeper Discussion

Amanda Murdie. *Help or Harm: The Human Security Effects of International NGOs*. Stanford, CA: Stanford University Press, 2014.

Andrew H. Kydd and Barbara F. Walter. "The Strategies of Terrorism." *International Security* 31, no. 1 (2006): 49–80.

Fiona Robinson. *The Ethics of Care: A Feminist Approach to Human Security*. Phila-delphia, PA: Temple University Press, 2011.

Michael Barnett and Martha Finnemore. *Rules for the World: International Organiza-tions in Global Politics*. Ithaca, NY: Cornell University Press, 2004.

REFERENCES

Adler, Emanuel, and Vincent Pouliot. "International practices." *International Theory* 3, no. 1 (2011): 1–36.

Alderman, Liz. "Greek Villagers Rescued Migrants. Now They Are the Ones Suffer-ing." *New York Times*, August 17, 2016.

Autesserre, Séverine. *Peaceland: Conflict Resolution and the Everyday Politics of International Intervention*. Cambridge: Cambridge University Press, 2014.

Barnett, Michael, and Martha Finnemore. *Rules for the World: International Organizations in Global Politics*. Ithaca, NY: Cornell University Press, 2004.

Carpenter, R. Charli. "Governing the Global Agenda: Gate-keeping and Issue Adoption in Transnational Advocacy Networks." In *Who Governs the Globe?*, by Deborah Avant, Martha Finnemore, and Susan Sell. Cambridge: Cambridge University Press, 2010.

Carpenter, R. Charli. "Setting the Advocacy Agenda: Theorizing Issue Emergence and Nonemergence in Transnational Advocacy Networks." *International Studies Quarterly* 51, no. 1 (2007): 99–120.

Carpenter, R. Charli. "Vetting the Advocacy Agenda: Networks, Centrality and the Paradox of Weapons Norms." *International Organization* 65, no. 1 (2011): 69–102.

Commission on Human Security. *Human Security Now*. New York: United Nations, 2003.

Edwards, Adrian. *Global Forced Displacement Hits Record High*. June 20, 2016. http://www.unhcr.org/en-us/news/latest/2016/6/5763b65a4/global-forced-displacement-hits-record-high.html (accessed June 23, 2017).

Gaglias, Alexis. "The Hidden Heroes of Greece's Refugee Crisis." *The Huffington Post*, June 2, 2016.

Hanlon, Robert J., and Kenneth Christie. *Freedom from Fear, Freedom from Want: An Introduction to Human Security*. North York, Ontario: University of Toronto Press, 2016.

High-Level Panel of Eminent Persons on the Post-2015 Development Agenda. *A New Global Partnership: Eradicate Poverty and Transform Economies through Sustainable Development*. New York: United Nations, 2013.

High-Level Panel on the Post-2015 Development Agenda. *About*. http://www.post2015hlp.org/about/ (accessed June 21, 2017).

Jurkovich, Michelle. "Venezuela Has Solved Its Hunger Problem? Don't Believe the U.N.'s Numbers." *The Monkey Cage–The Washington Post*, September 21, 2016.

Keck, Margaret E., and Kathryn Sikkink. *Activists beyond Borders*. Ithaca, NY: Cornell University Press, 1998.

MacFarlane, S. Neil, and Yuen Foong Khong. *Human Security and the UN: A Critical History*. Bloomington: Indiana University Press, 2006.

MDG Gap Task Force. *Millennium Development Goal 8: Taking Stock of the Global Partnership for Development*. New York: United Nations, 2015.

Médecins Sans Frontières. *G7 Fails to Provide Humane Response to Global Displacement Crisis*. May 27, 2017. http://www.doctorswithoutborders.org/article/g7-fails-provide-humane-response-global-displacement-crisis (accessed July 14, 2017).

Nianias, Helen. "Refugees in Lesbos: Are There Too Many NGOs on the Island?" *The Guardian*, January 5, 2016.

Sagan, Scott D., and Kenneth N. Waltz. *The Spread of Nuclear Weapons: A Debate Renewed*. 2nd edition. New York: W.W. Norton, 2002.

Sandbu, Martin. "Critics Question Success of UN's Millennium Development Goals." *Financial Times*, September 15, 2015.

Tran, Mark. "Mark Malloch-Brown: Developing the MDGs Was a Bit Like Nuclear Fusion." *The Guardian*, November 16, 2012.

United Nations Development Programme. *Background on the Goals*. http://www.undp.org/content/undp/en/home/sustainable-development-goals/background.html (accessed June 21, 2017).

United Nations Development Programme. *Human Development Report*. New York: Oxford University Press, 1994.

United Nations General Assembly. "Follow-Up to Paragraph 143 on Human Security of the 2005 World Summit Outcome." *A/Res/66/290*. New York, October 25, 2012.

United Nations General Assembly. "Open Working Group of the General Assembly on Sustainable Development Goals." *A/67/L.48/Rev.1*. New York, January 15, 2013.

United Nations General Assembly. "Report of the Panel on United Nations Peace Operations." *A/55/305-S/2000/809*. New York, August 21, 2000a.

United Nations General Assembly. "The Future We Want." *A/Res/66/288*. New York, September 11, 2012.

United Nations General Assembly. "Transforming Our World: The 2030 Agenda for Sustainable Development." *A/Res/70/1*. New York, October 21, 2015.

United Nations General Assembly. "United Nations Millennium Declaration." *A/55/L.2*. New York, September 8, 2000b.

United Nations High Commissioner for Refugees. "Lesvos Island-Greece Factsheet." *UNHCR*. November 12, 2015. http://www.unhcr.org/en-us/protection/operations/5645ddbc6/greece-factsheet-lesvos-island.html (accessed June 23, 2017).

United Nations Human Security Unit. *Framework for Cooperation for the System-Wide Application of Human Security*. New York, September 2015.

United Nations. *Sustainable Development Goals*. https://sustainabledevelopment.un.org/sdgs (accessed July 5, 2017).

United Nations. *We Can End Poverty: Millennium Development Goals and beyond 2015*. http://www.un.org/millenniumgoals/ (accessed June 21, 2017).

Zampano, Giada, Liam Moloney, and Jovi Juan. "Migrant Crisis: A History of Displacement." *The Wall Street Journal*, September 22, 2015.

Chapter 4

Human Rights and Human Security

Learning Objectives

This chapter will enable readers to:

1. Identify the historical and philosophical origins of human rights.
2. Examine the role of human rights in establishing human security.
3. Identify and discuss the role of states and non-state actors in securing human rights.
4. Apply the concept of universal rights to the case studies of advocacy on behalf of LGBT rights and advocacy against female genital mutilation.

Human rights are universal, fundamental, and inalienable; this means they are the most basic rights, which apply to all people without regard to any aspect of their identity, and they cannot be withheld or taken away except through the due process of law. Discussion of human rights, or more generally of the protections and freedoms to which people are entitled, predates the discussion of human security by thousands of years, but the continued violation of the rights of individuals and communities around the world led NGOs, TANs, and the UN to redouble their efforts to secure such rights at the close of the twentieth century. The dual emphases on the sanctity of the individual and the relationship between the individual and the state at the heart of human rights scholarship, advocacy, and policy discussions create a strong link between human rights and human security.

By providing, protecting, and respecting human rights, states and the international community lay the groundwork for the individual's ability to thrive. From the strategic perspective of the state, securing human rights ensures peace and stability within the domestic population—contentedness does not lead to unrest—and enhances or maintains the state's reputation within the international community through compliance with human rights law and norms. From the global perspective, observance of human rights indicates compliance with the norms of the international community, which is desirable not only from a normative perspective but also from a global security perspective since stable states are less likely to engage in armed conflict. In chapter 2 we discussed the role of increased recognition of human rights in the development and promotion of a human security norm. In this chapter we explore the concept of human rights more fully and discuss the connection between human rights fulfillment and the establishment of human security.

THE ROOTS OF HUMAN RIGHTS

The understanding of a common humanity that connects all people on a fundamental level and the recognition of a moral or religious authority higher than that of the political order have supported the notion of human rights for centuries. Human rights are protected under national and international law, although the reality is that these rights are protected to varying degrees depending on the state or the international community's willingness or ability to step in and enforce human rights laws. At times it is the state itself that violates the human rights of some portion or all of its population. An extreme example of this is the genocide perpetrated by Adolf Hitler and the Nazi forces in Germany and other European states from 1933 to 1945: the Nazi regime and its armed forces deprived millions of individuals of their employment, freedom of movement, access to education, freedom to marry, freedom to have and raise children, and, ultimately, the right to life. Indeed, the profound humanitarian tragedies of the Holocaust and in World War II more broadly inspired much of the content of the Universal Declaration of Human Rights (UDHR, introduced in chapter 2) three years after the war's end. Human rights, then, form the conceptual roots of human security: human rights are articulated, recognized, and enforced to protect the individual.

Long before anyone spoke directly of the term "human security," individuals were believed to be entitled to basic rights and freedoms, first among them the right to life. The concept of human rights existed even before the international community documented a consensus around such rights in the UDHR. At the most basic level we can understand human rights to be those rights and freedoms that one might reasonably expect to be entitled to in daily life. Historically, concepts related to human rights evolved from religious and philosophical understandings of a morality or authority beyond the person or people with power in a society. This sense of a universal set of principles is at the center of what ancient Greek philosophers called natural law. **Natural**

law refers to a foundational (or basic), unchanging morality that serves as a guide to human behavior at all times in all places. As an example, a common or natural sense of right and wrong would prohibit most people from taking the life of another person except in extreme circumstances; this common inhibition is suggestive of natural law. Stoic philosophers also referred to **natural rights**, or privileges to which all rational human beings are entitled (Cranston 1962, 4). Human rights articulated in the twentieth century are rooted in the principles of natural law and natural rights.

Eastern and Western religious and secular traditions have typically shared a consensus of the rights to which human beings are entitled; these generally include life, justice, and dignity. Interestingly, in addition to the core belief that human life is sacred and to be protected, core texts and philosophers observe the importance of order and the state. For example, the Christian gospels permit obedience to earthly kings (or states), noting that Christians may participate in war if the state deems a war necessary, even though the gospels send a more broadly pacifist message and the Ten Commandments of Judeo-Christian faith forbid killing.

Natural Rights

From the foundation of natural law seventeenth-century philosophers derived the concept of natural rights, which closely resemble human rights. Prominent thinkers in the Age of Reason and Age of Enlightenment invoked natural law to challenge the notion of the **divine right of kings**, which held that rulers were not subject to human authority but to divine—or absolute—authority. This notion prohibited the people from challenging a ruler's legitimacy or right to govern. Natural law, with its emphasis on *human* morality and basic individual rights, provided a foundation from which philosophers could articulate a set of rights common to all people, which cannot be disregarded or abridged by rulers. Natural rights are closely tied to what would later be called human rights and refer to those rights and freedoms to which all individuals are entitled by virtue of being human. John Locke, Jean-Jacques Rousseau, Thomas Hobbes, Immanuel Kant, and Thomas Paine, among other philosophers, envisioned a world in which individuals are free and equal, the state is limited in its scope and reach, and the state and its citizens are tied together willingly through the social contract (discussed in chapter 1). The consensual nature of the agreement between citizen and state lays the foundation for the expectation that the state will respect and protect certain individual rights. One of the most basic natural rights is liberty: individuals are free to do as they wish in pursuit of their own fulfillment. Natural rights give individuals their freedom, agency, and independence; natural law is the set of common principles that place limitations on individuals, but these principles are presumably innate rather than decreed by a government or ruler. Although they are often *also* written into law, natural rights and natural law should guide human behavior even in the absence of such legal constraints. To return to the example of natural law, despite being entitled to liberty by virtue of being human (natural rights), that liberty ends where another human's right to live is concerned because an innate sense of right and wrong prohibits murder (natural law).

Locke, writing at the time of the English Revolution of 1688, contested that individuals have the natural rights of life, liberty, and property (Cranston 1962, 1–3). At the time, this was a revolutionary idea. On December 16, 1689, the Parliament of England passed the Bill of Rights, which placed limits on the monarchy's powers and established the rights and authority of Parliament and of individuals. The individual rights described in the Bill of Rights included the right of Protestants to bear arms in self-defense, the right of individuals to be free from cruel and unusual punishment, the right to a public jury trial, and protection from excessive fines or bail (Cranston 1983, 1). By emphasizing the individual's rights and needs and constraining (at least to some extent) the monarchy, the Bill of Rights reflected the concepts of natural rights and natural law. Of course, not all philosophers and certainly not all political actors were supportive of the idea of natural rights. Jeremy Bentham, David Hume, and Edmund Burke were three prominent thinkers who opposed the notion that natural rights are somehow innate, or that they exist outside of human-authored law. Bentham saw "natural rights" and the declarations arising from them as governments' attempts to resist real change by making lofty rhetorical statements; individual rights should instead come through the creation of laws (Cranston 1983, 4). Hume and Burke, who rarely agreed with Bentham on philosophical matters, were similarly wary of "natural rights" because they saw the potential for such rhetoric to be used to justify uprisings and revolutions in pursuit of what were considered unrealistic goals, like equality for all people (Cranston 1983, 4). They were right about the inspiration for political revolutions: both the American and French Revolutions were justified on the basis of individual rights and freedoms—at least for some people.

The American Declaration of Independence, adopted on July 4, 1776, contended that all people (at the time just men were explicitly named and enslaved men were not included) are born equal and are entitled to the natural rights (granted by their Creator) of "life, liberty, and the pursuit of happiness" (Declaration of Independence 1776). The U.S. Constitution (ratified in 1788), and especially the Bill of Rights (introduced in 1789), further specified the rights of individuals relative to the state, including the rights of freedom of speech, assembly, and religion, the right to keep and bear arms, freedom from arbitrary search and seizure, and the right to a speedy and public jury trial, among other rights. The French Declaration of the Rights of Man and Citizen, passed in the National Constituent Assembly in August 1789, echoed the rights enumerated by the Americans, stating that individuals (again, men at the time) are born free and have equal rights and that the state's purpose is to provide, protect, and observe the natural rights of liberty, property, security, and resistance to oppression. Because individuals had lived for so long under monarchical rulers who failed to grant, protect, or observe individual rights, there was immense popular support for revolution within the United States of America and France (Cranston 1983, 2). The three documents—the Declaration of Independence, the Constitution, and the Declaration of the Rights of Man and Citizen—reflected philosophical discussions of natural rights *and* strengthened the foundation for discussion of human rights.

The many roots of human rights underscore the notion that some form of universal humanity binds us all together, that each person is entitled to certain rights and protections simply on the basis of being human.

HUMAN RIGHTS AND THE PROTECTION OF A COMMON HUMANITY

At the root of discussions of human rights is the interest in protecting that common humanity by protecting the security, freedom, and well-being of individuals. Some rights require governments to take action or actively provide something (these are often called "positive rights," as discussed in this chapter), while others require the government to refrain from taking an action that would harm or constrain an individual (these are called "negative rights," as discussed in this chapter). All human rights are linked by the common premise that the individual matters, so much so that when the human rights of one person are violated, the common thread of humanity frays. This section looks at international efforts to preserve the sanctity of the individual.

So many terrible things happened on such a large scale in the first half of the twentieth century that the newly formed UN General Assembly adopted the first common declaration of human rights, the UDHR. The UDHR was adopted on December 10, 1948, and, even though it is not a legally binding document (meaning states are not obligated by law to comply with it as they would be if it were a convention or treaty), it still represents the cornerstone of global discussions of human rights since it was the first and most comprehensive international document enumerating human rights. (See box 4.1.) From the late 1800s through the mid-1900s, the focus of international conventions and agreements was on protecting humanity in warfare (expressed in international humanitarian law). Although the UDHR gives us a list of rights that should certainly apply during the extreme duress of warfare, the rights within the declaration are intended to be preserved and protected every day all over the world. All Member States of the UN are expected (but, again, not legally obligated) to comply with the UDHR; they are encouraged to provide and protect the listed rights. The UDHR underpins all **international human rights law** after World War II, and it was intended to be a statement of the most basic or minimal list of human rights.

The UDHR was never intended to be the final word on human rights; in fact, its principles have been carried over into conventions and treaties that *are* legally binding. In 1966 the UN General Assembly adopted two legally binding covenants on human rights—the International Covenant on Civil and Political Rights (ICCPR) and the International Covenant on Economic, Social and Cultural Rights (ICESCR)—both introduced in chapter 2. The ICCPR enshrines the rights that most closely resemble those articulated by the American Declaration of Independence, the U.S. Constitution, and the French Declaration of the Rights of Man and Citizen. The ICESCR focuses on rights that require states to take action to provide social and economic protections. Drafted, negotiated, and adopted during the Cold War, when tensions between the United States and the Soviet Union were high, the ICCPR and ICESCR reflect the interests and priorities of the states that championed each one; interests and priorities diverged sufficiently to make a single covenant politically untenable. Together the UDHR, ICCPR, and ICESCR comprise the International Bill of Human Rights. This framework is one that places the responsibility for providing, protecting, and preserving human rights in the hands of states. By signing and ratifying the ICCPR and ICESCR, states agree to respect human rights and provide or abstain from violating such rights. States, then, are at the center of discussions of human rights and human security.

With the end of the Cold War and the increased presence and strength of NGOs, non-state actors have the ability to monitor and report on progress toward human rights fulfillment as well as human rights violations. The UN and its agencies, including the General Assembly, Human Rights Council, and the High Commissioner for Human Rights, also have varying capabilities to comment on and take action in response to human rights violations. When these organizations and agencies comment on human rights violations, they tend to focus on the state, or at least on the state's inability to protect rights when a non-state actor is violating them (as in the case of a state that lacks the capacity to stop abuse by non-state armed groups within its borders, or a state that lacks the legal framework and investigative capabilities to address oppression of or violence against particular groups of people). While states are not the only entities responsible for monitoring and contributing to the preservation of human rights, states are at the center of discussions of human rights, precisely because of the assumption that the primary responsibility of the state is to protect the security and rights of its people.

BOX 4.1. HUMAN RIGHTS IN THE UNIVERSAL DECLARATION OF HUMAN RIGHTS

This text paraphrases the Articles of the UDHR, 1948. The full text is available through the United Nations UDHR web page: http://www. un.org/en/universal-declaration-human-rights/.

1. All human beings are born free and equal in dignity and rights.
2. All human beings are entitled to the rights and freedoms in the UDHR and no right or freedom may be denied on the basis of individual identity or place of residence.
3. All human beings have the right to life, liberty, and security of their person.
4. No human being may be enslaved.
5. No human being may be tortured or subjected to cruel or inhuman punishment.
6. All human beings have the right to recognition as a person before the law.
7. All human beings should be free from discrimination and are entitled to equal protection under the law.
8. All human beings have a right to legal recourse if their rights are violated.
9. No human being may be arbitrarily arrested, detained, or exiled.
10. All human beings are entitled to a fair, public, and impartial trial if criminal charges are brought against them.
11. All human beings charged with a crime have the right to be presumed innocent until proven guilty according to the law; no human being may be charged with committing a crime if no crime was committed.
12. All human beings are entitled to their privacy and protection from interference in their privacy, family, home, correspondence, and reputation.
13. All human beings have the right to freedom of movement and residence within their state; all human beings have the right to leave any state and to return to their home state.
14. All human beings have the right to seek asylum in other states.
15. All human beings have the right to a nationality and no human being may be denied the right to change nationalities.
16. All human beings have the freedom to marry and form a family without discrimination; no human being may be forced into marriage; marriage is entitled to protection by the state.

17. All human beings have the right to own property; no human being may be arbitrarily deprived of their property.
18. All human beings have the right to freedom of thought, conscience, and religion.
19. All human beings have the right to freedom of opinion and expression.
20. All human beings have the right to freedom of peaceful assembly and association; no human being may be forced to join an association.
21. All human beings have the right to participate in their home state's government; all human beings have the right to equal access to public services in their home state; and the will of the people should be the basis of the government's authority.
22. All human beings have the right to social security and the realization of their economic, social, and cultural rights.
23. All human beings have the right to work, to choose their employment, and to enjoy fair working conditions; all human beings have the right to equal pay for equal work; all human beings who work have the right to compensation and—if necessary—social protection; all human beings have the right to join unions.
24. All human beings have the right to rest and leisure time.
25. All human beings have the right to a standard of living that ensures health and well-being for themselves and their family; motherhood and childhood are entitled to special protections and all children are entitled to the same protection.
26. All human beings have the right to an education; education should promote respect for human rights, tolerance, understanding, and global friendship; and all parents have the right to choose the kind of education their children receive.
27. All human beings have the right to participate in the cultural life of their community; all human beings have the right to protection of their intellectual property.
28. All human beings are entitled to a global order that protects the rights in the UDHR.
29. All human beings have duties to the community that supports their rights; all human beings are subject to limitations of their rights only with regard to respect for the rights of others; no rights or freedoms may be exercised in ways contrary to the principles and purpose of the United Nations.
30. None of the rights in the UDHR may be interpreted as implying the right of any state, group, or person to do anything intended to destroy the rights and freedoms set forth by the UDHR.

Conceptualizations of Human Rights

We can view human rights through three different, but related, distinctions. First, we can understand human rights in terms of civil and political rights or economic, social, and cultural rights. Or we might also look at certain rights as belonging to one of several generations of human rights. Finally, a third distinction is that between positive and negative rights. We can even discuss human rights in some combination of these three distinctions.

Civil and political rights are most easily understood as the human rights that allow individuals to participate fully in society—including and especially in political processes—without fear of discrimination or harm. Civil and political rights were conceived to protect individuals from state repression, discrimination, and overreach and rights such as freedom of assembly, speech, and religion, as well as security of person and property, bring to mind the natural rights advocated by the philosophers and political revolutions in the seventeenth and eighteenth centuries. Much of what we discuss today as civil and political rights is built on the foundation of natural rights; indeed, these rights are visible in the U.S. Declaration of Independence, the U.S. Bill of Rights, and the French Declaration of the Rights of Man and Citizen. The UDHR, of course, also establishes these rights as universal human rights. **Economic, social, and cultural rights** are likewise laid out in the UDHR. These rights take the concept of human rights one step further, establishing that the state and its agencies must provide certain services and resources as needed to enable individuals to thrive. Such rights include the right to food, housing, and education.

Karel Vasak, during his tenure as the secretary-general of the International Institute of Human Rights, discussed human rights in generational categories. **First-generation rights** are chiefly civil and political rights, the earliest human rights discussed by philosophers and political actors. These rights establish the basis for a more participatory and less discriminatory society in which individuals do not need to fear state-perpetrated interference or harm. **Second-generation rights** apply the notion of human rights to the vision of a more egalitarian society in which individuals' basic needs (food, shelter, education, and employment) are met. Both first- and second-generation rights are in the UDHR, and the UDHR itself does not distinguish between them, but the ICCPR and ICESCR are divided along these lines, with the former containing first-generation rights and the latter focusing on second-generation rights. The term **third-generation rights** is broader than the first two categories and encompasses a wider range of rights specific to groups of people, identities, and even the environment. Although human rights are universal in theory, in reality certain groups are routinely denied their human rights (or even their full humanity) and third-generation rights seek to remedy this. Two examples of international agreements establishing third-generation rights, or peoples' rights, are the Declaration on the Rights of Indigenous Peoples (adopted by the UN General Assembly in 2007) and the Convention on the Rights of the Child (which was adopted by the UN General Assembly in 1989 and entered into force in 1990). Third-generation rights include the right to cultural heritage, minority rights, children's rights, women's rights, and environmental rights, among others. Not all human rights agreements, statements, or documents are legally binding: the Declaration on the Rights of Indigenous Peoples is a General Assembly resolution and, as such, is nonbinding; the Convention on the Rights of the Child is a treaty and is therefore binding on states that have signed and ratified it.

The term **positive rights**, also used by Vasak, indicates that the provision of a certain right requires someone (usually the government, but possibly also an agency, institution, or fellow human) to *do something* or take action to provide that right if necessary. Examples of positive human rights include the rights to food, education, shelter, and health care, all of which are generally considered economic, social, and cultural rights. Each of the aforementioned rights requires someone to provide food, public schools, adequate shelter, and health services if an individual cannot access those resources on their own. Civil and political rights can also be positive rights; one such example is the right to legal representation for those who must stand trial but cannot afford a lawyer or counselor. **Negative rights**, on the other hand, require someone to abstain from a specific action; the enjoyment of such rights requires the government, other entities or institutions, or people not to affect an individual's choices, freedoms, or beliefs, or actions. Most often such rights are civil and political rights, including freedom of speech and religion (no one should stop an individual from speaking their mind or practicing—or not practicing—a religion), security of person and property (no one should take an action that harms a person or their home or possessions), right to life, and freedom from torture. Negative rights loosely correspond with first-generation rights, while positive rights are more closely aligned with second- and third-generation rights.

There is some disagreement over the usefulness of these distinctions between human rights, especially regarding the three generations of rights and the categorization of rights as positive or negative. One such critique, made by Maurice Cranston, is that since second- and third-generation rights usually require resources that may not always be available, these cannot be true human rights (Cranston 1967). Still, employing alternative conceptualizations helps us to envision how the discussion of human rights has evolved over centuries and how the prioritization of certain human rights will vary by state, community, and individual identity.

**BOX 4.2. "THINK ABOUT IT . . ."—HOW WELL
DO YOU KNOW YOUR HUMAN RIGHTS?**

If you had to list your human rights, before reading this chapter and the UDHR, could you have done it? Which rights would you have included in your list?

If you could have listed only a few of your human rights, why do you think this is the case?

Where and when did you first learn about your human rights?

What are the potential consequences of *not* knowing your human rights?

What can be done to improve global awareness of human rights?

Which human rights does the government of your state (country) seem to respect most?

Are there any human rights that are not adequately protected in your state? If so, has there been any advocacy or policy effort to change this?

NEW HUMAN RIGHTS AND CHANGING DIALOGUES

What counts as a human right is subject to change over time as norms, beliefs, identities, and laws evolve. Just as the notion of human security was introduced and has gained greater acceptance because of the historical and political context of the 1990s and 2000s, "new" human rights can be introduced and adopted given a hospitable political, social, and/or cultural climate. We can look at changes in human rights through two different lenses: claims to human rights made by a group of people who share a particular identity; and new recognition of a particular act as a violation of human rights. To explore both of these types of changes in human rights, we briefly look at the push for Lesbian, Gay, Bisexual, Transgender, and Queer/Questioning (LGBTQ) rights in the United States and the transnational campaign against female genital mutilation (FGM).

LGBTQ Rights Movement

For much of the twentieth century in the United States, if you did not conform to the established norms of gender and sexuality you could be barred from working for the government, serving in the military, or even gathering at bars. Homosexuality was considered a mental illness, a perversion, and—in the eyes of the government in 1950—a security risk (United States Senate 1950); from January 1, 1947, to August 1, 1950, 1,700 applications for federal jobs were rejected on the basis of homosexuality or "other sex perversion" (Davidson 2012). Employees were subject to intrusive investigations into their private lives. The "Don't Ask, Don't Tell" (DADT) policy on LGBTQ military personnel, in effect from February 1994 until its repeal in September 2011, prohibited discrimination and harassment of LGBTQ personnel or applicants, as well as investigations into the sexuality of personnel or applicants; in this respect it loosened prior federal restrictions on employment. Yet DADT also barred openly LGBTQ persons from serving in the military, citing a negative effect on morale and unit cohesion. In 2016, five years after the repeal of DADT, the U.S. military continued to grapple with the integration of transgender service members. Rights violations were not (and are not) limited to employment discrimination but extended to the right to marry and the right to be secure in one's person.

The federal Defense of Marriage Act (DOMA) of 1996 defined marriage as a union between a man and a woman and allowed states to refuse to recognize same-sex marriages granted in other states; this effectively blocked same-sex couples from federal employee benefits, Social Security benefits, bankruptcy benefits, tax returns, immigration processes, and adoption of children. In 2013, in *United States v. Windsor*, the Supreme Court ruled that DOMA violated the Due Process Clause of the Fifth Amendment, declaring it unconstitutional. Still, same-sex marriage was prohibited in many states until the Supreme Court's decision in *Obergefell v. Hodges* on June 26, 2015, established that marriage is a fundamental right to which same-sex couples are entitled under the Fifth and Fourteenth Amendments.

The 1998 murder of Matthew Shepard, a gay student at the University of Wyoming, and the resulting film and play, *The Laramie Project*, brought to light the lack of hate crime laws and legal protections for LGBTQ individuals across the United States. On October 28, 2009, the Matthew Shepard and James Byrd, Jr. Hate Crimes Prevention Act became law and through it the federal hate crime protections expanded to cover violence motivated by an individual's gender, sexuality, or perceived gender or sexuality.

Behind each legal advance was a persistent advocacy effort to secure LGBTQ civil and human rights. Organizations and advocacy efforts such as the Human Rights Campaign, the It Gets Better Project, PFLAG, and GLBTQ Legal Advocates & Defenders (GLAD) continue to work for a more inclusive society in the United States through legal advances, public discourse and education, and social support. Certainly, legal advances do not end all discrimination and violence against LGBTQ persons, as the mass shooting at the Pulse nightclub in Orlando, Florida, on June 26, 2016, and the Gloucester County, Virginia, School Board's 2016–2017 legal battle over a transgender student's access to restrooms suggest. Defining and protecting the rights of a specific group of people can be contentious, especially when perceptions about the group's shared identity polarize the population.

Similar movements working to secure LGBTQ civil and human rights are happening throughout the world. These efforts face many of the same cultural and legal obstacles that activists in the United States have faced. These movements have had more success in the Americas and Western Europe. Other parts of the world, including much of Africa, Eastern Europe, the Middle East, and Asia, have been more reluctant to recognize and expand LGBTQ rights. The LGBTQ rights movement demonstrates that the emergence of a new human rights norm does not guarantee universal acceptance or legal protection of the right; rather, broad recognition of new rights takes time and considerable effort by advocates.

The Campaign against Female Genital Mutilation

Global advocacy to eliminate the practice of FGM, based on the notion that it is a violation of girls' and women's human rights, offers a similar lesson about the challenges facing new human rights. FGM—also referred to as female genital cutting or female circumcision—involves the removal of all or a portion of external female genitalia for non-medical reasons. The procedure is usually ritualized and performed as a rite of passage by a traditional circumciser, though medical professionals in some areas will perform the procedure based on the belief that such conditions minimize the procedure's harm. The extent of the circumcision ranges from the excision of part of the clitoris to full removal of the clitoris (clitorectomy), to clitorectomy and removal of the inner labia, to the most severe form—clitorectomy, removal of the labia, and the sewing together of the outer labia to create a seal (infibulation). FGM does not provide any health benefits but creates both short- and long-term physical and emotional harm for the individual who has undergone the procedure and poses risks in childbirth that affect both mother and infant.

The fact that most females who are circumcised experience the procedure as minors has led the World Health Organization and the United Nations Children's Fund (UNICEF) (among other NGOs and international organizations) to condemn strongly the practice as a form of gender-based discrimination, a violation of the rights of the child, and a violation of the human rights of health, security, physical integrity, and life (as the procedure can lead to death), as well as freedom from torture (World Health Organization 2016). Each year an estimated three million girls in thirty states undergo FGM, and the practice is most common in states in the Horn of Africa, the Middle East, and Asia (UNICEF 2016). Still, as UNICEF indicates, FGM is a globalized concern, and women and girls in South America, Europe, Australia, and North America are also affected (UNICEF 2016).

The practice of female circumcision persists because of traditional, social, and cultural beliefs about female sexuality (the effects of the procedure decrease or eliminate female sexual desire) and the importance of virginity for marriage prospects. Advocacy against FGM has been successful when it has occurred through the framing of the procedure as contrary to religious beliefs, which avoids the language of human rights or women's rights that can often be seen as an imposition of Western values. For example, Suzanne Mubarak, former first lady of Egypt, influenced the discussion of FGM as *haram* (prohibited by Islam) and mobilized public resources to campaign against the practice (Hudson et al. 2012, 138). Other advocacy efforts, such as those by grassroots organizations in Kenya, have sought to highlight alternative coming-of-age practices for girls that empower rather than subjugate, thereby keeping important elements of ritual and tradition but reducing the occurrence of FGM and gender-based discrimination more broadly (Hudson et al. 2012, 189).

Which Rights?

Both the movement for LGBTQ rights and the campaign to end FGM highlight the tensions inherent in "new" human rights advocacy. Asserting the rights of a particular group or contending that a tradition, practice, or action is a human rights violation demands normative change—it disrupts long-held ideas. These two cases highlight the persistent questions of whose rights matter most and how the world ought to decide (or whether the broader global community should have any say at all). Because many human rights initiatives face daunting challenges before they are accepted as global norms, it can be difficult to sort out the competing perspectives. Scholars and public decision-makers sometimes point to the concept of **cultural relativism** when discussing differing views on human rights; cultural relativism holds that an individual's morals, values, and beliefs are rooted in their culture. This concept presents a counterpoint to the argument that human rights are universal, as it creates gray areas in which one can argue that in some contexts championing the rights of women, religious minorities, or the LGBTQ community challenges tradition, identity, and culture in a particular region. From the point of view of human security, it is clear that what matters most is the ability of the individual to be safe from threats and free from obstacles to empowerment. In theory, this aligns the human security approach with the notion of universal human rights. In practice, the best way to establish the individual's security and foster empowerment will vary by individual, community, state, or region, and so policy prescriptions and initiatives are best created with attention to the specific cultural, political, economic, and social context in mind.

HUMAN RIGHTS AND HUMAN SECURITY

The prominence of human rights in much of political philosophy and international political discourse emphasizes the importance of the individual. At the heart of human security are the individual human and the communities formed by individuals who share some facet of their identity. The chapters in sections I and II discuss the concept and emergence of human security as well as the interplay between human security and armed conflict. During conflict human rights are severely strained. Human rights advocates have not only worked to define more clearly what rights people have during warfare but also how violations of those rights are punished. These efforts have focused both on the responsibility of the state to protect the rights of its citizens, as well as the responsibility of the international community to stop mass human rights violations. The chapters in section III explore the concept of "durable" human security. Durable human security, as we introduced in chapters 1 and 2, relates to long-term or chronic security issues stemming from the norms and institutions within a society. When durable human security exists, individuals and groups enjoy their human rights and freedoms, they thrive in their societies, and their states are politically and economically stable. Individuals whose human rights are protected and guaranteed can work together toward long-term peace and stability because they do not live in fear that their personal security, ability to adhere to their beliefs, stability of their employment or access to education, or freedom from discrimination will suddenly be denied.

The international legal framework that protects human rights (the International Bill of Human Rights and other treaties, conventions, and declarations) establishes a foundation for durable human security and lays the groundwork for the protection of individuals from chronic harms and the provision of the basic needs that allow individuals to thrive. Which international actors are responsible for establishing durable human security? The international framework for human rights establishes the state as central to the preservation of human rights—and ultimately of human security. Recall that international treaties and conventions are binding legal agreements *between states*. States, then, take on the responsibility of ensuring that their citizens enjoy their rights and freedoms.

Of course, states do not comply fully with their international legal obligations and agreements at all times. When a state fails to provide for the human rights and human security of its population, non-state actors like NGOs, civil society networks, and international organizations like the UN act as monitors and report on the state's actions. Non-state actors play an important role in ensuring that the human rights and human security needs of individuals and groups are met. By publicly agreeing to respect human rights, states make themselves accountable and invite this form of scrutiny both from other states and from non-state actors. When states fail to meet their obligations to their people, it is not always due to malicious intentions. Sometimes states do not have the capacity to enforce domestic or international law (including the provision of human rights) within their own territory. With the rise of NGOs, actors other than the state government can become service providers, monitors and defenders of human rights, and advocates in partnership with or opposition to states. Threats to human security can be globalized threats, threats that cannot be contained within a state's borders and that are unlikely to be solved by a single-state or non-state actor. It is to these threats and the responses to them that we now turn.

Discussion Questions

1. For what reasons might states sign on to human rights treaties?
2. What common themes are visible across early human rights documents (U.S. and French declarations), the UDHR, and more recent agreements or advocacy campaigns?
3. Is a violation of human rights in one part of the world truly a threat to human rights everywhere?
4. How useful is the distinction between generations of rights? What about the distinction between civil/political and economic/social/cultural rights? Are the dual concepts of positive and negative rights helpful? Why or why not?
5. Should cultural or social differences determine the extent to which human rights may be enforced?

FURTHER READING AND WEB RESOURCES

Bill of Rights. United States National Archives. 1789. http://www.archives.gov/exhibits/charters/bill_of_rights_transcript.html

Declaration of Independence. United States National Archives. 1776. http://www.archives.gov/exhibits/charters/declaration_transcript.html

Declaration of the Rights of Man and Citizen. The Avalon Project, Yale Law School. 1789. http://avalon.law.yale.edu/18th_century/rightsof.asp

English Bill of Rights. The Avalon Project, Yale Law School. 1689. http://avalon.law.yale.edu/17th_century/england.asp

Human Rights Campaign website. http://www.hrc.org/

International Committee of the Red Cross. *Geneva Conventions and Commentaries*.
https://www.icrc.org/en/war-and-law/treaties-customary-law/geneva-conventions
Micheline R. Ishay. *The Human Rights Reader*. 2nd edition. New York: Routledge,
2007.
PBS "American Experience" Timeline, Milestones in the American Gay Rights Movement. http://www.pbs.org/wgbh/americanexperience/features/timeline/stonewall/
United Nations. *The Universal Declaration of Human Rights*. 1948. http://www.
un.org/en/universal-declaration-human-rights/

For Deeper Discussion

Clifford Bob, ed. *The International Struggle for New Human Rights*. Philadelphia:
University of Pennsylvania Press, 2009.
John Locke. *Two Treatises of Government*. London: Everyman, 2000.
Thomas Cushman, ed. *Handbook of Human Rights*. New York: Routledge, 2012.
Thomas Risse, Stephen C. Ropp, and Kathryn Sikkink, eds. *The Power of Human
Rights: International Norms and Domestic Change*. New York: Cambridge Uni-
versity Press, 1999.

REFERENCES

Cranston, Maurice. "Are There Any Human Rights?" *Daedalus* 112, no. 4 (1983):
1–17.
Cranston, Maurice. "Human Rights: Real and Supposed." In *Political Theory and the
Rights of Man*, by D. D. Raphael, 43–51. Bloomington: Indiana University Press,
1967.
Cranston, Maurice. *What Are Human Rights?* New York: Basic Books, 1962.
Davidson, Joe. "Uncle Sam Didn't Welcome Gay Employees." *The Washington Post*,
March 2, 2012.
"Declaration of Independence." *United States National Archives*. 1776. http://www.
archives.gov/exhibits/charters/declaration_transcript.html (accessed July 3, 2017).
Hudson, Valerie M., Bonnie Ballif-Spanvill, Mary Caprioli, and Chad F. Emmett.
Sex & World Peace. New York: Columbia University Press, 2012.
UNICEF. *Female Genital Mutilation/Cutting: A Global Concern*. New York: UNI-
CEF, 2016.
United Nations. "Beijing Declaration and Platform for Action." *Fourth World Con-
ference on Women*. September 15, 1995. http://www.un.org/womenwatch/daw/
beijing/platform/ (accessed December 3, 2015).
United States Senate. *Employment of Homosexuals and Other Sex Perverts in Gov-
ernment*. Interim Report, Washington, DC: United States Government Printing
Office, 1950.
World Health Organization. "Media Centre." *Female Genital Mutilation*. February 2016. http://www.who.int/mediacentre/factsheets/fs241/en/ (accessed June 30,
2016).

Section II

ARMED CONFLICT AND HUMAN SECURITY

Chapter 5

From Non-Intervention to the Responsibility to Protect

Learning Objectives

This chapter will enable readers to:

1. Understand the relationship between sovereignty and the principle of non-intervention.
2. Describe the scope and type of conflict in the international system today.
3. Examine the ways that international humanitarian law has evolved to better account for civilian protection.
4. Understand the norms leading to the Responsibility to Protect (R2P), criticisms of R2P, and how it has been applied.

SOVEREIGNTY AND THE PRINCIPLE OF NON-INTERVENTION

The human security approach both challenges and complements the national and global approaches to security. Each of the three approaches, however, must contend with a core construct of the international system: the **sovereignty** of states. Sovereignty, in its simplest form, is the idea that a state has legal jurisdiction over its territory and that other states are not to interfere in each other's internal affairs. This includes, in its strictest form, the right of the state to create laws and to determine how those laws are enforced, including the parameters by which force can be used against its citizens. It is presumed that those governing structures would be built upon the values of that state. Within a system of sovereign states the norm of **sovereign equality** entails that all states are legally equal to each other. The strict interpretation of sovereignty implies a **principle of non-intervention** by states or other out-side actors into the domestic affairs of other states, up to and including using force to stop a state from violating the human rights of its citizens. As we will see in this chapter, however, this strict interpretation of sovereignty neither matches reality nor conforms to modern legal understandings of the term. This chapter begins by exploring the concept of sovereignty and its implications for the three security approaches. We then turn to the evolving norms of protection and the development of the Responsibility to Protect (R2P) doctrine. The chapter's vignette introduces the multilateral intervention in Libya, the first explicit R2P mission, before offering concluding thoughts.

The modern-day origins of sovereignty evolved from principles articulated in the Treaty of Westphalia of 1648, which ended the Thirty Years' War. In this original articulation, sovereignty was based on the notion that monarchs were equals and had the right to rule over their subjects as they pleased, particularly in terms of determining the religion to be practiced within the state. Of course, the idea that a single individual has absolute authority over his or her subjects has been challenged by calls for **self-determination** and government that adheres to the consent of the governed. Self-determination means that the citizens of a territory have the right to choose for themselves what type of political system they are to live under and that the government is tasked with the protection of their rights. As we discussed in chapter 4, the American and French Revolutions and the political systems that arose from them were direct challenges to monarchal rule driven by the principle of self-determination. Later, the dismantling of the European imperial international order after World War II was also driven by the principle of self-determination. Today, the principle of sovereignty is the underlying legal mechanism that governs the international political system. How security is provided, and to whom, must be considered under this framework.

The state, however, is a highly contested space. Multiple factions within a state can make competing claims over who ultimately has the right to exercise control of the state. These challenges are rooted in debates on national identity and who constitutes a "true" citizen. States, therefore, face ongoing internal challenges to their domestic political institutions. To illustrate this, think about your own community. Would you say there is universal agreement on how the state should function and who should rule? Who controls the state and the types of institutions the state supports has implications for every person living in it. How are these disagreements resolved? In a state with strong institutions and democratic forms of government those challenges would ideally happen through the formation of political parties that compete through electoral politics—although it should be noted that democracies can also experience large amounts of social protest by groups who feel that their voices are not adequately represented within the current governing structure.

In more authoritarian systems of government, challenges come through riskier forms of engagement, as citizens in these types of states typically have fewer political rights and the state, when challenged, faces fewer limitations on the use of oppressive security tactics. The socioeconomic makeup of the state can also have implications for political contestation. Scholarship has shown that states with large economic and political disparities between ethnopolitical groups are more likely to experience political violence. For example, Yugoslavia, prior to descending into civil war in the early 1990s, had large economic and political disparities between the various ethnic groups (Cederman, Weidmann, and Gleditsch 2011).

How a state is contested from within has potential implications for other states' national security and for global security. A state, for example, may fear having an ally overthrown by a challenger because it would consequently lose a strategic partner or even create a new enemy that could pose a threat to its national security, as happened with the United States and Iran following the latter's 1979 Islamic Revolution. Global security, on the other hand, relies on like-minded states that accept and work within the basic parameters of that system. Therefore, reactionary states that reject that system, such as North Korea, could threaten the stability of the global system. One or two such challengers would likely be managed through containment (as we have seen with various sanctions placed on North Korea), but an increasing number of such states could disrupt the entire global security structure. (Recall the discussion of state and global security threats in chapter 3.) Because the domestic politics of states can pose threats to other states' national security and global security, there will always be the temptation for other states to interfere in the internal politics of others.

The ongoing contestation of the state has consequences for human security. An ethnically divided state, for example, could spell disaster for a minority group that does not have adequate security or legal protections. A state that does not adequately provide for the basic needs of its citizens creates the conditions in which human security is most likely to be threatened. A strict interpretation of sovereignty, however, leaves a dismal outlook for how such threats to human security could and should be addressed. Under strict interpretations of sovereignty, people that found their personal security threatened by the actions (or lack of action) of the state they live in would only be able to rely on their own or domestic sources for recourse. In many cases, this would mean that there are few options available, except, perhaps, to flee or take up arms.

The historical record shows quite clearly that despite an international system of sovereign states that is constructed on the principle of non-intervention, states have found numerous justifications to engage in intervention, whether those justifications are on national, global, or human security grounds. Therefore, a key question in international politics involves when intervention by an outside power into the affairs of another state is justified (if ever). It is under these parameters that the complex challenges to the principle of non-intervention emerge. This raises an important question: Can a state, under the guise of sovereignty, rightfully carry out actions against its citizenry that, if carried out by a foreign or occupying power, would be considered violations of international humanitarian law? If the answer is "no," then what instruments are available to prevent those actions from happening and punishing those responsible once they do happen? The other side of this question is what rights or obligations do others have to intervene in a state when that state is unable or unwilling to protect its citizens from widespread harm to a civilian population, whether harm is in the form of war, natural disaster, or famine.

Why Non-Intervention?

While sovereignty implies a principle of non-intervention, intervention by states into the affairs of others has been a permanent feature of international affairs. As already discussed, states have a key interest in how other states behave. Thus, a state's foreign policy is largely focused on how to influence other states to align their behavior more closely with the state's own interests— or at least to reduce the harm that other states' interests might cause for the state. While much of this will be pursued through diplomatic persuasion, intervention occurs when a state uses more forceful efforts to compel changes in other states' behavior. Intervention can take on many forms, with military intervention being the strongest and most visible approach; however, intervention can include economic and diplomatic tools as well.

Because the international system is **anarchic**, meaning there is no overarching authority capable of punishing rule violators, states are seen as on their own when it comes to guaranteeing their security. Such a **self-help system** means that war, if not common, is expected, as each state sees military force and other aggressive tactics as legitimate means for pursuing one's interests and compelling others to change their behavior. This world order, coupled with technological advances in weaponry, led to disastrous results in the first half of the twentieth century. The catalysts for both World War I and World War II were rooted in attempts by predatory states to expand their borders and increase their global power. Global institution building following both world wars (the League of Nations following World War I and the United Nations following World War II) were built around a desire to resolve the instability seen to be the result of a purely self-help system. Both the League of Nations and the United Nations were attempts to create a **collective security system**, in which predatory behavior by one state would elicit a collective response by all international actors (Wilkenfeld 2015). The weakness of the League of Nations was laid bare by the onset of World War II. The creation of the United Nations following World War II, therefore, tried to address those weaknesses, while also creating the mechanisms to better respond to the human suffering that occurred during that war, including the Holocaust, the deliberate targeting of civilian populations, and refugees. This happened in three ways: (1) reaffirming the principle of sovereignty, but couching it within the principle of self-determination; (2) defining the rules regarding the conduct of war between states; and (3) articulating a set of universal human rights for all peoples regardless of national origin (as discussed in chapter 4).

The principle of non-intervention is embedded within the United Nations Charter. According to Article 51 of the UN Charter, a state may take military action on its own accord only in self-defense. In other instances, the UN Security Council is tasked with overseeing matters that pose threats to international peace and security. Resolutions by the UN Security Council must pass with a majority of voting members and without a veto from any of the **permanent five members** (China, France, Russia, United Kingdom, and United States—also known as the P5). One of the pressing questions facing the UN Security Council has been: What constitutes a threat to international peace and security? Should internal conflicts fall into this category—thus becoming a legitimate concern of the Security Council? The answer over time has become a clear yes, but this position evolved slowly. Part of this evolution has been due to the rapidly changing transformation of the international system.

After World War II the world saw a steady dismantling of the European colonial system. When the UN Charter was signed in 1945 there were only forty-nine sovereign states in the world, with large portions of Africa and Asia under colonial rule by European powers. Today, there are 195 states that are officially recognized as independent and sovereign. The transition from a global system once dominated by colonialism to one of independent sovereign states opened the possibility for wide-scale conflict if newly independent states looked to shape their borders to include traditionally held territory and kinsfolk. To try to avoid this outcome, the UN system recognized newly independent states based on the boundaries that had been drawn by the former colonial powers, not adhering to any ethnic or religious divisions that might exist within those borders. This greatly reduced the amount of potential interstate conflict, but it increased the number of intrastate conflicts as different ethnic, religious, and ideological groups competed, often violently, for control of the newly formed state. The Cold War rivalry between the United States and the Soviet Union often exacerbated these conflicts, as each side sought to support and arm those groups that aligned with their political ideologies. After the Cold War, these ideological rivalries subsided, only to be replaced with ethnic or religious fissures.

The rise of identity-based conflicts led to acute violence against civilian populations that has led to a global rethinking of our conceptions of sovereignty. It is important, however, to keep in mind that this rethinking was done within the post–World War II non-intervention framework. Therefore, the means by which these changes have taken place are constrained by these institutional realities, which will be discussed further in chapter 6.

Human Insecurity in Acute Conflict

Human security is most immediately threatened during **acute conflict**. While conflict is a constant feature of interpersonal and intergroup interaction, acute conflict is conflict that has a substantial probability of violence (Sharp 1998). It is difficult to capture within a text the experience of living through war. All civilians face greater risks of violence being directed toward them during conflict. However, different people's experiences differ from conflict to conflict and even within the same armed conflict. A rural farmer, for instance, will likely face fundamentally different threats to his or her security than a poor urban dweller. During conflict, women, men, and children all experience a variety of threats (see chapter 10 on gender equality). Boys and men, for instance, are more likely to be pressed into military service or to be killed by enemy forces (Carpenter 2003). Women and girls are frequently targeted for indentured servitude or sexual violence and exploitation. There are also structural changes during wartime that threaten people's security. War destroys economies, health care systems, and agriculture, and poisons water supplies. These conditions can greatly affect the mortality rates of people living in conflict-affected areas, as they are not able to access the basic necessities for sustaining life. The loss of life due to these indirect factors is sometimes referred to as **structural violence**. In fact, the immediate and long-term damage to a state or locality's infrastructure and services are often a greater cause of human mortality than direct violence.

The type of conflict also matters in how human insecurity is affected. For example, a revolutionary group that is trying to impose their ideology onto the state might try to limit civilian casualties, as that could undermine its support among the greater population, which the group will need to rule effectively. At the same time, however, those civilians may see certain human rights severely restricted by the revolutionary ideology. Identity-driven conflicts, on the other hand, are motivated by exclusionary ideas and, therefore, are more likely to involve forced displacement, ethnic cleansing, or genocide, as groups try to recreate the state around their own ethnic or religious identity.

Have threats to human security due to armed conflict gotten worse? This is a difficult question to answer. Steven Pinker (2011) observes that violence between humans in general has significantly decreased over the past century. When we look at the number of ongoing armed conflicts since the end of the Cold War there is ample evidence that, overall, things have improved. According to the Armed Conflict Dataset, from 1991 to the mid-2000s there was a steady decline in the total number of intrastate conflicts being fought. In addition, between 2000 and 2010, the number of battle deaths per year hovered around all-time lows. Still, in other respects human security has deteriorated. Events in Syria since 2011 have demonstrated that a single conflict can have rapid devastating effects for the civilians experiencing that conflict and have broader ramifications well beyond its borders. The brutality of the conflict in Syria contributed to the highest total number of battle deaths since the end of the Cold War (Pettersson and Wallensteen 2015). In addition, this single armed conflict has led to the displacement of over eleven million people, with nearly five million refugees and more than six million internally displaced persons according to UNHCR—contributing to the highest global number of displaced persons since World War II (United Nations High Commissioner for Refugees 2016). This raises the question of whether the downward trends in violence are easily reversible under the right conditions and whether we have transitioned into an era in which the norms and structures that sustained that previous peace have eroded.

Gathering statistics on harm to civilians during conflict is difficult. Access to combat zones is often limited and armed actors rarely collect data on how their own actions harm the civilian population (although they will certainly highlight how their opponents' actions do). International organizations like the UNHCR, for example, track the number of global refugees and NGOs such as the Internal Displacement Monitoring Center gather data on the number of internally displaced persons. NGOs also play an important role in providing information on civilian casualties in conflict. Humanitarian agencies, such as Médecins Sans Frontières or the International Committee of the Red Cross (see chapter 3), often see firsthand the ways in which combatants target civilians. Other NGOs have worked to develop methods for systematically collecting data on civilian harm. The Center for Civilians in Conflict (CIVIC), for example, has found that during conflict civilians are often left to their own, often ad hoc, survival strategies. These efforts have greatly helped researchers, and policymakers have a more informed understanding of the effects of conflict on civilian populations.

Another question is whether wars have changed to such a degree that human security is being threatened in a way that is unique in comparison to previous eras. Mary Kaldor (2007) defines wars following the end of the Cold War as "new wars," that is, wars that are fought "in the context of the disintegration of states" rather than state-building exercises, which she characterizes as "old wars." According to Kaldor, "old wars" were fought in accordance with certain rules codified under the Geneva and Hague Conventions. These rules governed conduct regarding civilian casualties and prisoners of war. These rules, however, were primarily concerned with the conduct of how states engage in military action against other states. It is not always clear whether those rules should legally apply to the conduct of violent non-state actors and state responses against those actors. This legal ambiguity has contributed to the free reign that those fighting these wars have had with respect to their treatment of civilian populations.

One way that we can think about whether civilians might be particularly vulnerable to insecurity during conflict is to examine the institutional and cultural structures underlying the conflict. In many cases the violence experienced by civilians during intrastate conflict is due to weak cultural and institutional protections for specific groups. The dehumanization of a specific ethnic group and a state governing structure that organizes and directs violence toward that group would be both a cultural and an institutional breakdown and creates an acute human security problem. In other cases, a state's constitutional and legal system is structured to protect a group from discrimination and the use of violence against the group, but armed, nativist non-state actors do so anyway. These cases constitute a human security problem generated by "bad apples" at the sub-state-level and weak institutions at the state level. Understanding the roots of insecurity toward civilians helps structure our conversations on best methods for protecting them when acute conflict situations arise.

EVOLVING NORMS OF PROTECTION

The argument that civilians should be protected during warfare is not new, but how they should be protected and who is responsible for that protection remain difficult dilemmas. This section examines how norms of civilian protection have evolved over time. One important consideration is that the changing nature of both the international system and warfare has implications for how we think about these questions.

Limiting the Brutality of War: Just War Theory and International Humanitarian Law

Just War Theory, rooted in the teachings of Saint Augustine, Saint Thomas Aquinas, and later theologians, provides a framework for when, how, and for what reasons governments may engage in warfare (it is helpful to note here that the modern state system was not yet in existence when Augustine and Aquinas wrote about war). **Just wars**—wars fought with good intentions for one's own state or on behalf of others—are permissible according to Judeo-Christian texts and philosophy. The Quran similarly condones war for a just cause, chiefly in defense of Islam, and places restrictions on combat that call for the protection of women, children, and the elderly. Islamic philosophers also believed that leaders had divine authority, albeit with limited power, and tasked individuals with obedience to the state as long as the state did not demand disobedience to God. In each tradition there is an apparent tension between the sanctity of life and the necessity of state-imposed order, a trade-off that persists when wars and human rights violations occur today. Just War Theory acknowledges that violence is an inevitable aspect of the human condition, and does not seek to ban war but to "harness" it so that it may be used to achieve good ends (Hoffmann 1981, 47). At its core, Just War Theory recognizes that while war should be avoided when possible, there are circumstances in which war is an appropriate means to restore justice. Wars may be appropriate when they adhere to the constraints outlined in the three pillars of Just War Theory: *jus ad bellum*, *jus in bello*, and (the newest pillar) *jus post bellum*. The first limits the causes for which war is justifiable (e.g., in self-defense or in defense of civilians persecuted by their government). The second outlines expectations for moral behavior in warfare (e.g., injured or surrendering combatants and civilians do not pose a threat and are entitled to special protections). The third pillar has taken shape in recent years and places the responsibility for reconstruction and reestablishment of a just order after the end of armed conflict on the parties to the conflict, especially the victor.

The principles of Just War Theory have endured long after Augustine's time, embodied in the treaties and conventions that comprise **international humanitarian law**, the rules of warfare developed in the nineteenth and twentieth centuries. International humanitarian law places limitations on the use of force by states and the conduct of combatants acting on behalf of states. The will to compose and comply with laws of war arose in response to recognition of the horrors individuals experienced in armed conflict. The **Geneva Conventions** resulted from a series of meetings between states between 1864 and 1949; these international treaties outlined rights and protections related to combatants, prisoners of war, and civilians caught up in armed conflict. The International Committee of the Red Cross—which was cofounded in 1863 by Henri Dunant, who became an international humanitarian relief advocate after witnessing the mass casualties and lack of medical treatment at the Battle of Solferino in 1859—played a central role in establishing a legal framework for humanitarian assistance and protection of human life in wartime through the Geneva Conventions. The **First Geneva Convention** (1864) pertains to the welfare of wounded combatants and establishes a right to medical care and protection for International Committee of the Red Cross members working in war zones. The **Second Geneva Convention** (1906) applies to sailors in armed forces, expanding the protections of the First Geneva Convention to war at sea. The **Third Geneva Convention** (1929) establishes protections for prisoners of war. The **Fourth Geneva Convention** (1949) outlines the rights of and protections for civilians in armed conflict. The Geneva Conventions were not the only attempts to regulate the conduct of warring parties. The **Hague Convention of 1899** was a multilateral treaty that proposed a framework for conflict prevention through mediation, protocols for declarations of war, and rules for humane treatment of prisoners. Shortly thereafter, the **Hague Convention of 1907** outlawed the use of poison gas and aerial bombing (from balloons, since airplanes had yet to appear on the battlefield). The ill-fated third Hague Convention, scheduled for 1914, never occurred because of the outbreak of World War I.

International treaties and agreements seeking to keep warfare within certain moral boundaries enshrine the concepts of Just War Theory and hold states accountable for their actions. While the deliberate targeting of another state's civilians or injured combatants in war is clearly understood as a violation of international law, it is less clear whether the same legal principles applied if the action was carried out by a state against its own citizens or by non-state combatants in insurgencies, civil wars, or actions against multilateral interventions. The changing scope and nature of warfare in the twenty-first century calls into question the extent to which agreements devised by and for states apply to today's armed conflicts and the non-state parties to those conflicts.

HUMANITARIAN INTERVENTION AND THE RESPONSIBILITY TO PROTECT

Post–Cold War conflicts, driven by ethnic, tribal, or religious divisions, brought about a new discussion of how to protect individuals, particularly noncombatants, during conflict. Starvation and the disintegration of the state in Somalia, ethnic cleansing during the breakup of Yugoslavia, and the genocide in Rwanda, among other atrocities, forced the international community to consider the question of what, if anything, should be done in response to such crises. Much of the existing international legal framework dealing with **civilian protection** was focused not on intrastate conflicts, but on cases in which a state was in a conflict with another state. Thus, there has been a greater focus in international humanitarian law on protecting civilians from outside parties or occupying powers and less concern with how civilians are treated by their own state. However, with conflicts now more likely to happen within states, a growing network of global activists, both within governments and the NGO community, began to draw attention to the security threats people faced in conflict. These activists put pressure on their governments, the United Nations, and various regional organizations to develop better response mechanisms to these humanitarian crises. Consequently, the international community began to work toward creating a stronger set of mechanisms to respond to these crises, particularly when they led to mass atrocities. This has led to efforts to create a more precise legal framework, embedded within multilateral institutions, about when the use of force to intervene in the affairs of other states can be justified (Finnemore 2004). These efforts led to a more activist UN, particularly within the Office of the Secretary-General and at the Security Council, which saw the instability and human suffering caused by these conflicts as threats to international peace and security.

How civilian protection concerns translate into policy, however, has followed a disjointed and controversial path. While there is little vocal opposition to the idea that noncombatants should not be deliberately targeted during intrastate warfare, how to prevent that from occurring is not always clear. An early example of this is seen in efforts to protect **internally displaced persons (IDPs)**, people who are displaced from their homes due to conflict or natural disasters, but do not cross an international border. **Refugees**, people who are displaced from their homes and do cross an international border, are granted legal rights under the 1951 Convention relating to the Status of Refugees. This disparity between the legal protections offered to the two groups that face similar circumstances led a global group of activists and officials within the United Nations to work to create a set of guiding principles based on existing international law for states to follow with respect to their internally displaced populations. Francis Deng, who was appointed to be the UN first Special Rapporteur on the Human Rights of Internally Displaced Persons, coined the term **sovereignty as responsibility**, meaning that having the status of sovereignty means that a state has certain obligations to protect the human rights of its citizens. In the case of IDPs, this meant that a state was obligated to prevent displacement from occurring in the first place, to protect the rights of the displaced when displacement did occur, and then to find an acceptable durable solution to their displacement (Cohen 2012).

All of this, however, is complicated by the fact that states are often the actors responsible for atrocities against their own civilian populations. This, coupled with norms of non-intervention, prevented any type of serious international response. United Nations peacekeeping was originally conceived as a mechanism by which the international community could serve as neutral observers between armed actors only after a cease-fire or peace accord had been agreed upon. The peacekeeping forces, therefore, would be in the country with the state's consent and could be asked to leave at any time. Consequently, the principle of non-intervention meant that the international community would be required to stand by while mass atrocities were knowingly taking place. It is under these circumstances that justifications for **humanitarian intervention** have been made. Humanitarian interventions are military interventions, ideally under the auspices of a UN Security Council Resolution, with the intended purpose of relieving the ongoing human suffering of people living in conflict zones or areas affected by natural disasters. The term "intervention" implies that the effort happens without the consent of one or more parties to the conflict or violence, thus presenting a challenge to the sovereign norms that have governed the international system. Prior to the post–Cold War period, humanitarian interventions were essentially nonexistent, largely due to the structural limitations imposed by the Security Council veto and the presence of both the United States and the Soviet Union on the Council. While there are cases in which an intervention did relieve human suffering—such as Vietnam's intervention in Cambodia in 1979, which effectively stopped the ongoing genocide—the primary purpose of these interventions was to advance the intervening state's foreign policy goals and the relief of human suffering was more or less an unintended consequence.

After the Cold War ended, the question of whether and how to conduct humanitarian interventions became a central debate in the field of international relations. As discussed previously, the idea of using force for just cause, particularly to aid civilian populations, was not new and had been part of moralistic thinking for centuries. However, the legalization of humanitarian intervention would challenge the idea of sovereign equality, which is at the foundation of the UN Charter. The end of the Cold War rivalry between the United States and the Soviet Union, however, gave hope in some quarters that the global community could play a greater role in stopping atrocities. Soon after, international actions justified on humanitarian grounds became more common. Western powers, in particular, became much more willing to frame interventions in the language of humanitarianism. While Operation Desert Storm in 1991 was not justified on humanitarian grounds, but rather to respond to Iraq's invasion of Kuwait, the establishment of a no-fly zone in northern and southern Iraq to protect Kurd and Shiite populations once the war ended was justified on such grounds. Later, the 1999 NATO intervention in Kosovo was justified entirely on humanitarian grounds, although without Security Council approval.

BOX 5.1. "THINK ABOUT IT . . ."—RESPONSIBILITY TO PROTECT (R2P) VERSUS PROTECTION OF CIVILIANS (POC)

This chapter examines the emergence of Responsibility to Protect (R2P) as a norm aimed at protecting civilians against the most egregious war crimes and human rights violations. The following chapters use a different term: Protection of Civilians (POC). What is the fundamental difference between the two? Both concepts emerged in international discourse at relatively the same time as a response to mass atrocities committed during the mid-1990s. The Security Council first passed a resolution on POC in 1999 (Resolution 1265), and the Report of the International Commission on Intervention and State Sovereignty on the Responsibility to Protect was drafted at the end of September 2001. Both are rooted in the same goal: to protect civilians from harm from violent conflict.

Not without controversy, R2P was unanimously agreed to at the 2005 World Summit. According to the 2005 World Summit Outcome Document, R2P represents an agreement between states that they will be "prepared to take collective action" when a state "manifestly fail[s] to protect its citizens from genocide, war crimes, ethnic cleansing and crimes against humanity" (United Nations General Assembly 2005). According to R2P that action must be authorized by the UN Security Council and force is to be used only as a last resort. As the vignette in this chapter highlights, how to apply R2P in practice is riddled with challenges and controversy.

POC, on the other hand, grew from the increasing pressure on UN peacekeeping missions to be better prepared to protect civilians. POC is deeply grounded within international humanitarian law. That said, there are varied interpretations of what exactly POC means—from the protection norms found in the Geneva Conventions to the narrower goal of physically protecting civilians from harm during an ongoing peacekeeping operation. Thus, while R2P has, by many accounts, fallen out of favor, POC language is now a key component of international discourse. Protecting civilians has now become an operational requirement for peacekeeping (see chapter 7). In 2017 there were ten missions that had explicit mandates to protect civilians. Nevertheless, protection mandates often have confusing language and can suffer from promising more than what it can reasonably deliver, leaving UN peacekeepers confused on how far any given mandate extends. In some cases, peacekeepers themselves have been the perpetrators through sexual exploitation and abuse of the very populations they are supposed to be protecting.

Consider the following questions:

1. Who has the responsibility to protect civilians during conflict?
2. Should the same principles that inform the collective security system of the United Nations be extended to apply to the protection of human populations in other states?
3. What do you think about the increased use of civilian protection mandates in peacekeeping operations? What are the practical implications for peacekeeping operations which have such a mandate?
4. Does the failure to implement civilian protection mandates damage UN credibility or limit its ability to broker or maintain peace?

The use of humanitarian arguments to justify military interventions continues to increase, even in cases in which the humanitarian aims were dubious at best. Despite its deliberate targeting of civilian populations throughout the conflict, Saudi Arabia justified its intervention in Yemen on the basis of its "responsibility" to "protect the people Yemen" (Royal Embassy of Saudi Arabia Information Office 2015). This is one of the key criticisms of humanitarian interventions: it is unclear what actions by a state against its citizens should justify an intervention. Therefore, critics have argued, much of the need for intervention that one saw (or didn't see) was a reflection of powerful states' national interests rather than a just and systematic response to relieving human suffering. States from former colonies have expressed concerns about the concept of humanitarian intervention, which was typically accompanied by military force and the imposition of Western institutional structures, as a veiled form of neocolonialism. Proponents of creating a robust civilian protection regime have recognized these criticisms and sought to create a clearer and more just set of criteria for responding to mass atrocities. The primary effort through which this has happened has been the development of the **Responsibility to Protect** doctrine.

When Serbian forces began to conduct a campaign of ethnic cleansing in Kosovo in 1998, the hope for an international armed response with the backing of a UN Security Council Resolution was dashed when Russia and China made it clear that they would veto any such resolution. When NATO intervened anyway, the intervention violated Article 2(4) of the UN Charter, which prohibits the use of force without Security Council authorization. This led UN secretary-general Kofi Annan to begin a process to address more clearly the issues related to humanitarian interventions. In his 1999 opening address to the General Assembly, Annan argued that the international community had to find a balanced solution between the principle of non-intervention and a state's obligation to protect the rights of its citizens. He further argued that the UN had a role in helping states fulfill their obligations to their citizens and that any principle of intervention needed to be "fairly and consistently applied." Thus, starting in 1999 the United Nations began to systematically formalize a set of strategies to protect civilians in armed conflict (United Nations Security Council 1999).

Canada took up Annan's challenge and in 2000 established the International Commission on Intervention and State Sovereignty (ICISS). In December of 2001, it released its report, *Responsibility to Protect*. The core argument of the ICISS report is that states are obligated to protect their citizens from what are known as the four crimes: genocide, war crimes, ethnic cleansing, and crimes against humanity (see table 5.1). When the state is either unwilling or unable to do so, that responsibility becomes the obligation of the international community (Bellamy 2011). R2P is constructed around three pillars. Pillar one is the responsibility that the state has to protect its own citizens from genocide, war crimes, ethnic cleansing, and crimes against humanity. According to the secretary-general's report on implementing R2P, states can work toward fulfilling these obligations by becoming parties to the already existing human rights treaties that obligate signatories

Table 5.1.   The Four Crimes: Genocide, War Crimes, Ethnic Cleansing, and Crimes against Humanity

Crime	Definition
Genocide	Acts meant to destroy, in whole or in part, a national, ethnic, racial, or religious group (Rome Statute of the International Criminal Court 1998, Article 6)
War Crimes	The "serious violations of the laws and customs applicable in international armed conflict" (Rome Statute of the International Criminal Court 1998, Article 8)
Ethnic Cleansing	"The planned deliberate removal from a specific territory, persons of a particular ethnic group, by force or intimidation, in order to render the area ethnically homogenous" (United Nations Security Council 1994, 33)
Crimes against Humanity	Acts such as murder, extermination, enslavement, deportation or forcible transfer of population, torture, rape, enforced disappearance or persons, apartheid, or similar inhumane acts committed in a widespread or systematic attack against a civilian population (Rome Statute of the International Criminal Court 1998, Article 7)

to protect the rights of their citizens. In addition, states should integrate the principles of human rights and international humanitarian law into their domestic legal system. This commitment to protecting their citizens' rights would, presumably, lessen the chance that internal conflict in a state would escalate to the point that any of the four crimes would be committed. Pillar two is the responsibility of the international community to assist states in fulfilling their responsibility to protect. Much of the activity under pillar two falls under norm promotion. Under this pillar the international community would encourage states to fulfill their pillar one commitments and to provide technical assistance when requested. Pillar three is the responsibility of the international community to take action, with Security Council authorization, when a state refuses or is unable to fulfill its responsibility to protect its citizens from one or more of the four crimes. Thus, while R2P challenges a strict norm of non-intervention, it also limits what states can consider a justifiable reason to intervene.

According to Gareth Evans, the co-chair of ICISS, R2P was innovative in four ways (Evans 2015). First was the reframing of the debate from the right to intervene to the responsibilities that each state has to protect its own citizens and citizens in other states from mass atrocity crimes. Second, R2P expanded the range of actors beyond those that had the military capabilities to project force abroad. By focusing on the responsibility for each state to protect its own citizens (pillar one) and then moving to how outside states can assist others in reaching that obligation (pillar two), it made R2P an ongoing commitment based primarily on prevention activities. Third, R2P broadened the range of responses beyond military intervention. According to R2P, military intervention is seen as a means of last resort and pillar three activities include any number of coercive activities, such as sanctions or international criminal prosecutions, that do not include the use of force. Fourth, R2P sought to clarify when pillar three uses of force would be justified. This included Security Council authorization as well as the creation of a set of benchmarks that needed to be met in order for force to be legitimate. These benchmarks included seriousness of the harm being threatened; the motivation of the proposed military action; whether there were peaceful alternatives; the proportionality of the response; and whether more good than harm would result from the intervention.

The merits of R2P were debated at the 2005 World Summit and again in 2009 at the United Nations General Assembly. These debates demonstrated that there was an agreement between almost all states on a number of key points, including that prevention was a key component of R2P; that R2P was not a new legal principle but grounded in already established international law; that it could only be invoked to prevent or stop one of the four crimes; and that there was a need for political will in order for R2P to be successfully implemented (Hehir 2012, 52–53). While there were (and still are) critics of the doctrine, particularly around the use of pillar three, R2P was unanimously adopted at the 2005 World Summit.

Despite its unanimous adoption, R2P remains controversial for both critics and supporters. For those who saw R2P as a welcome tool for the prevention of mass atrocities, they fear that there are a number of weaknesses that could prevent its effective implementation. For one, the structural conditions under which force must be justified (i.e., through the authorization of the UN Security Council) remains in place, meaning that international action remains coupled to great power politics and the national interests of Security Council members. The secretary-general's report pleaded with Security Council members not to use their veto when a clear case of one of the four crimes being committed existed. As seen in the response to Syria's civil war, such moral restraint is difficult when one or more Security Council members see vital national interests at stake. This problem is coupled with the fact that there is no single agency within the UN system with the mandate to determine authoritatively and independently whether and when one of the four crimes is being committed. Furthermore, the UN's lack of a rapid reaction force specifically trained in responding to the four crimes means that forces must be put together on an ad hoc basis. This means that the mission is limited to the contributing states' capabilities, willingness to commit specific types of personnel (i.e., air power versus ground troops), and response time. Such problems run the risk of delegitimizing the principle of R2P when the international community is unable to respond or responds poorly. This problem is coupled by the fact that it has never been decidedly resolved whether unilateral action by a state would be permissible if the UN Security Council fails to act.

Critics suggest that R2P operates as an extension of past colonial structures and power dynamics in which the Global North continues to impose its institutions and values onto the Global South. Intervenors, it is argued, are rarely satisfied with simply preventing or stopping atrocities from occurring. If a state is willing to commit one of the four crimes once, what is to stop it from doing so again unless that government is replaced? This question helps intervenors justify much more involved interventions in which efforts are made to force the targeted states to adopt democratic and neoliberal forms of governance. Thus, one cannot decouple R2P from prior power dynamics associated with colonial rule (Mallavarapu 2015). It is important to note that this line of criticism is not making the argument that states should be able to commit any of the four crimes but that the historical power structures that R2P is embedded in perpetuate unequal power relationships between states and, thus, lack universal legitimacy.

In addition, there are criticisms about R2P's continued reliance on the use of military force, even as a last resort. There are numerous risks associated with the use of force, including the risk of accidentally targeting the civilians one is tasked with protecting. This risk is exacerbated when the intervening force relies on air power or its ground troops are not adequately trained to distinguish between those they are protecting and those they are protecting against. There is also the possibility that armed intervention and the toppling of the target state's government will lead to a power vacuum, which creates the problem of other violent groups forming in order to capture the new state, further endangering the lives of civilians. The question of timing is also important. Can force be used only when one of the four crimes has already been committed or can it be used preemptively if it is determined that one of the crimes is imminent? If force is used preemptively to prevent an atrocity, but the state later falls into chaos, then it will be difficult to determine whether the decision to intervene was a sound one. While the framers of R2P provide guidelines, based on the logic of Just War Theory, on how to make these determinations, in practice the decision to use force and the outcomes of that decision are never straightforward.

Most importantly, advocates for human security at the United Nations have worked to decouple the idea of human security from R2P. Recall that General Assembly Resolution 66/290 (2012), introduced in chapter 3, states that "human security is distinct from the responsibility to protect and its implementation" and "does not entail the threat or the use of force or coercive measures." Instead, as the resolution states, "Governments retain the primary role and responsibility for ensuring the survival, livelihood and dignity of their citizens." It can be easy to conflate the concepts of human security and R2P in our consideration of security, but it is essential to keep the distinction between overall human security and the specific doctrine of R2P in mind. R2P is one avenue through which security providers have sought to ensure protection of civilians, but it does not constitute the whole of human security.

How has R2P worked in practice? The UN Human Rights Council has been particularly eager to invoke R2P in their resolutions. Between 2008 and 2016 the Human Rights Council promoted R2P principles in twenty resolutions, particularly in response to the conflict in Syria (Global Centre for the Responsibility to Protect 2016). According to Secretary-General Ban Ki-moon, in his 2009 report on R2P, because of R2P "the world is less likely to look the other way than in the last century" (United Nations General Assembly 2009). R2P was implicitly invoked after the 2008 Kenyan presidential elections in which opposition leader Raila Odinga claimed that President Mwai Kibaki had stolen the election. The subsequent violence resulted in the death of 800 people and displaced 260,000 people. While Secretary-General Kofi Annan did not use the language of R2P when negotiating with Kenyan leadership to end the crisis, the fact that R2P was now a tool that could be invoked by the Security Council loomed over the negotiation. In addition, multiple governments were calling on Kenya to stop the bloodshed and threatened sanctions if it was unwilling to do so. Similar implicit invocations of R2P happened in Cote d'Ivoire and Guinea. Each of these cases did not invoke a pillar three–level Security Council resolution. The case of Libya, however, did, and the remainder of this chapter will examine R2P in relation to that crisis.

LIBYA AND THE RESPONSIBILITY TO PROTECT

The UN-backed intervention in Libya in 2011 marked the first case in which the doctrine of R2P was explicitly invoked within a UN Security resolution to justify a military intervention. Libya, like other states in North Africa and the Middle East during the Arab Spring, was experiencing uprisings against its long-time authoritarian leader, Colonel Muammar Gaddafi. Gaddafi responded to the uprisings with violence against the civilian population. In March 2011 Gaddafi's forces surrounded the opposition outpost city of Benghazi and, many thought, looked poised to carry out a massacre—an act that, if committed, would clearly constitute a crime against humanity. Many, including Deputy Permanent Representative to the United Nations Ibrahim O. Dabbashi, called on the international community to do something to stop the violence. The Security Council passed two resolutions, both with the purpose of protecting Libya's civilian population. The first, Resolution 1970, passed unanimously and called for financial sanctions, an arms embargo, and a referral to the International Criminal Court (United Nations Security Council 2011). The second, Resolution 1973, passed on March 17, 2011 (but with abstentions from China, Russia, Brazil, Germany, and India), authorized Member States to "take all necessary measures . . . to protect civilians and civilian populated areas in Libya" (United Nations Security Council 2011).

Following Security Council Resolution 1973, a coalition of NATO forces led by France, the United Kingdom, and the United States conducted an air assault on Gaddafi's forces and centers of power, quickly weakening his grip on power. Rebels, who had looked on the verge of defeat, were able to regroup and retake territory; however, as the campaign progressed there was worry, particularly from Secretary-General Ban Ki-moon, that the nature of the intervention with its heavy reliance on air support prevented adequate monitoring of civilian protection and wasn't stopping Gaddafi from targeting civilians. The fighting continued for several months, with NATO forces regularly backing rebel advances. In August 2011, rebel forces overthrew Gaddafi's regime.

The case was initially heralded by some as a successful application of the R2P doctrine: Libya deliberately targeted civilians in its response to anti-regime protesters and then appeared poised to carry out an indiscriminate attack on a populated urban area. The Arab Spring protests in Libya began as nonviolent protests but, after the initial crackdown by Gaddafi's forces, morphed into an armed rebellion by some parts of the opposition. Does the presence of an armed challenger change how a state may use its armed forces? Security Council Resolution 1973 was unclear on what was ultimately required to protect civilians and whether that extended to providing military support for an ongoing armed rebellion. Prior to the adoption of the resolution U.S. President Barack Obama had stated that, in order to resolve the crisis, Gaddafi must step down, so it was clearly no surprise when the NATO mission pursued that goal. But what does this mean for similar interventions? It is not hard to make the logical step that in order to protect civilians in the long run, governments that have committed or shown willingness to commit one of the four crimes in the past should ultimately be replaced. This opens the door to increased justifications under the guise of R2P for the use of force not just to protect a vulnerable civilian population but also to overthrow norm-violating governments.

Another issue related to the question of sovereignty is the role that international actors have in the post-conflict state? Following the overthrow of Gaddafi, the transitional government in Libya did not want the presence of a large UN mission. Because such missions can operate only with the consent of the recognized government, it meant that post-conflict Libya had to rely largely on its limited resources and weak state institutions to restore order—a task that proved difficult. Libya's opposition forces were not united and Libya, with its deep tribal divisions, quickly deteriorated into ongoing contestation for control of the state.

In the aftermath of the Libyan intervention R2P has been heavily criticized and some have argued that its influence has waned, particularly in relation to pillar three consensus (Hehir 2016). However, there is evidence that normative principles of R2P have continued to be a central component of international debate and have become increasingly institutionalized at the UN (Doyle 2016) and the influence of R2P continues to be seen in global efforts to protect human populations, such as the Arms Trade Treaty (Henderson 2017). Additionally, we continue to see increased calls for the protection of civilians without explicit reference to R2P. In fact, according to one study, R2P language has actually increased since the Libyan intervention (Gifkins 2016).

CONCLUSION

This chapter introduces a number of key concerns related to the question of intervention as a possible response to human security concerns. Violent conflict represents the most immediate threat to human security. Nevertheless, as the Libya case demonstrates, military responses, while they may be able to prevent immediate atrocities, do not necessarily lead to long-term, durable structural changes that improve human security over time. In addition, the use of military force always comes with the risk of escalating the violence and creating additional human security threats. It is also clear that military intervention for entirely humanitarian reasons is rarely disconnected from competing national security goals. The world does not possess a neutral force that can intervene disconnected from the broader national security concerns of other states, and it would be naïve to think that human security justifications would be sufficient enough to trump a state's national security goals. Responsibility to Protect was meant to address that, but it, too, is limited in how it can be applied. Even when faced with a moral responsibility to respond, policy options that have no chance of success should be avoided. The challenge for the human security approach, then, is to discover solutions to human security threats that are realistic within a global framework that continues to privilege sovereignty over normative concerns.

Discussion Questions

1. Do the principles of *jus ad bellum*, *jus in bello*, and *jus post bellum* offer important guidelines and limitations in twenty-first-century armed conflict? Why or why not?
2. What are the obstacles to effective human security provision arising from the principle of non-intervention? What benefits or threats to national or state security arise from the principle of non-intervention? What is the effect of observance of the non-intervention principle on global security?
3. What are the political and structural limitations facing action within each of the R2P pillars?
4. Consider a current humanitarian crisis or armed conflict. Does any aspect of that crisis or conflict fit within the notion of the four crimes?

FURTHER READING AND WEB RESOURCES

International Committee of the Red Cross, "Geneva Conventions and Commentaries": https://www.icrc.org/en/war-and-law/treaties-customary-law/geneva-conventions
"Report of the Secretary-General on the Protection of Civilians in Armed Conflict," *S/2007/643*: civiliansinconflict.org
Uppsala Conflict Data Program, Armed Conflict Dataset: http://ucdp.uu.se/#/
Yale Law School, The Avalon Project, "The Laws of War": http://avalon.law.yale.edu/subject_menus/lawwar.asp

For Deeper Discussion

Aidan Hehir. *The Responsibility to Protect: Rhetoric, Reality and the Future of Humanitarian Intervention*. Hampshire, UK: Palgrave Macmillan, 2012.

Alex J. Bellamy. *Global Politics and the Responsibility to Protect: From Words to Deeds*. London: Routledge, 2011.

Martha Finnemore. *The Purpose of Intervention: Changing Beliefs about the Use of Force*. Ithaca, NY: Cornell University Press, 2003.

Michael Walzer. *Just and Unjust Wars: A Moral Argument with Historical Illustrations*. New York: Basic Books, 1977.

Ramesh Thakur and William Maley. *Theorising the Responsibility to Protect*. Cambridge: Cambridge University Press, 2015.

REFERENCES

Bellamy, Alex J. *Global Politics and the Responsibility to Protect: From Words to Deeds*. London: Routledge, 2011.

Carpenter, Charli. "'Women and Children First': Gender, Norms, and Humanitarian Evacuation in the Balkans 1991–1995." *International Organization* 57, no. 4 (2003): 661–94.

Cederman, Lars-Erik, Nils B. Weidmann, and Kristian Skrede Gleditsch. "Horizontal Inequalities and Ethnonationalist Civil War: A Global Comparison." *American Political Science Review* 105, no. 3 (2011): 478–95.

Cohen, Roberta. "From Sovereignty to R2P." In *The Routledge Handbook of the Responsibility to Protect*, by W. Andy Knight and Frazer Egerton, 7–21. New York: Routledge, 2012.

Doyle, Michael W. "The Politics of Global Humanitarianism: The Responsibility to Protect before and after Libya." *International Politics* 53, no. 1 (2016): 14–31.

Evans, Gareth. "The Evolution of the Responsibility to Protect: From Concept and Principle to Actionable Norm." In *Theorising the Responsibility to Protect*, by Ramesh Thakur and William Maley, 16–37. Cambridge: Cambridge University Press, 2015.

Finnemore, Martha. *The Purpose of Intervention: Changing Beliefs about the Use of Force*. Ithaca, NY: Cornell University Press, 2004.

Gifkins, Jess. "R2P in the UN Security Council: Darfur, Libya and Beyond." *Cooperation and Conflict* 51, no. 2 (2016): 148–65.

Global Centre for the Responsibility to Protect. "R2P References in United Nations Human Rights Council Resolutions." October 3, 2016. http://www.globalr2p.org/resources/977 (accessed February 24, 2017).

Hehir, Aidan. "Assessing the influence of the Responsibility to Protect on the UN Security Council during Arab Spring." *Cooperation and Conflict* 51, no. 2 (2016): 166–83.

Hehir, Aidan. *The Responsibility to Protect: Rhetoric, Reality and the Future of Humanitarian Intervention*. New York: Palgrave Macmillan, 2012.

Henderson, Stacey. "The Arms Trade Treaty: Responsibility to Protect in Action?" *Global Responsibility to Protect* 9, no. 2 (2017): 147–72.

Hoffmann, Stanley. *Duties beyond Borders: On the Limits and Possibilities of Ethical International Politics.* Syracuse, NY: Syracuse University Press, 1981.

Kaldor, Mary. *Human Security: Reflections on Globalization and Intervention.* Cambridge: Polity, 2007.

Mallavarapu, Siddharth. "Colonialism and the Responsibility to Protect." In *Theorising the Responsibility to Protect,* by Ramesh Thakur and William Maley, 305–22. Cambridge: Cambridge University Press, 2015.

Pettersson, Thérése, and Peter Wallensteen. "Armed Conflicts, 1946–2014." *Journal of Peace Research* 52, no. 4 (2015): 536–50.

Pinker, Steven. *The Better Angels of Our Nature: Why Violence Has Declined.* New York: Penguin Books, 2011.

Rome Statute of the International Criminal Court. *A/CONF.183/9.* Rome, July 17, 1998.

Royal Embassy of Saudi Arabia Information Office. "Statement by Saudi Ambassador Al-Jubeir on Military Operations in Yemen." PR Newswire. March 25, 2015. http://www.prnewswire.com/news-releases/statement-by-saudi-ambassador-al-jubeir-on-military-operations-in-yemen-300056316.html (accessed July 1, 2017).

Sharp, Gene. "Nonviolent Action in Acute Interethnic Conflicts." In *The Handbook of Interethnic Coexistence,* by Eugene Weiner, 371–81. New York: Continuum Publishing, 1998.

United Nations General Assembly. "2005 World Summit Outcome." *A/RES/60/1.* New York, October 24, 2005.

United Nations General Assembly. "Implementing the Responsibility to Protect: Report of the Secretary General." *A/63/677.* New York, January 12, 2009.

United Nations High Commissioner for Refugees. *With 1 Human in Every 113 Affected, Forced Displacement Hits Record High.* June 20, 2016. http://www.unhcr.org/afr/news/press/2016/6/5763ace54/1-human-113-affected-forced-displacement-hits-record-high.html (accessed July 4, 2017).

United Nations Security Council. "Letter Dated 24 May 1994 from the Secretary-General to the President of the Security Council." *S/1994/674.* New York, May 27, 1994.

United Nations Security Council. "Report of the Secretary-General to the Security Council on the Protection of Civilians in Armed Conflict." *S/1999/957.* New York, September 8, 1999.

United Nations Security Council. "Resolution 1970 (2011)." *S/RES/1970.* New York, February 26, 2011.

United Nations Security Council. "Resolution 1973 (2011)." *S/RES/1973.* New York, March 17, 2011.

Wilkenfeld, Jonathan. *Myth and Reality in International Politics: Meeting Global Challenges through Collective Action.* New York: Routledge, 2015.

Chapter 6

Human Security in Peace Processes

Learning Objectives

This chapter will enable readers to:

1. Understand the complex process by which conflicts turn into peaceful settlements.
2. Consider how a human security lens during peace processes differs from a global security or national security lens.
3. Delineate between the multiple actors that are engaged in peace processes and think critically about their competing interests.
4. Understand changing norms regarding inclusivity during peace processes.

Violent conflict poses the most immediate threat to human security. As discussed in previous chapters, the effects of violent conflict extend well beyond the individuals that are directly engaged in the fighting and can have devastating long-term consequences. Beyond the threat to one's life and personal security, these long-term effects range from displacement from one's home, post-traumatic stress disorder, and other physical and mental health consequences. Conflict can shatter economies and livelihoods for generations. This chapter focuses on how various groups address human security issues during the peace processes meant to resolve an ongoing conflict. While human security threats are present in interstate conflict, we mainly focus on intrastate conflict in this book. The reason for this is twofold. First, since the end of World War II intrastate conflict has been the dominant form of violent conflict. Second, because intrastate conflict is intricately connected to the governance and stability of the state, there will be both chronic and systemic threats that accompany a state's breakdown during conflict that will need to be addressed during any given peace process.

The long-term prospects for durable human security following a conflict are rooted in the nature of the **peace processes** that lead to the conflict's termination. Peace processes cover the wide range of activities intended to bring about a cessation of an ongoing violent conflict. These may include informal dialogue between parties, mediation by outside actors, formal negotiations, cease-fires, and, ultimately, peace treaties. Peace processes also include the participation of a wide range of actors, from those who directly participate in and perpetuate the violence, to the numerous nonviolent actors that make up civil society, and from foreign governments to international and regional organizations.

There are two ways that human security needs are addressed during peace processes. First is the attention given to human security problems independently of any other conflict resolution processes, including immediate humanitarian assistance and protection of vulnerable populations. Second are the approaches through which human security problems are addressed in any final agreement that terminates the conflict. Because peace processes tend to favor the interests of those that were most responsible for the violence, the needs of many of the most vulnerable populations are often ignored. Global activists and the United Nations have worked to address this gap by advocating for the rights and protection of noncombatant civilians during conflict. These efforts have resulted in some instances of greater participation by civil society actors in peace negotiations.

During conflict the question of responsibility for human security becomes strained. During these periods the state is often unable or unwilling to provide basic security for its citizens and may, in fact, be the one that poses the greatest threat, as discussed in chapter 3. In El Salvador, for example, the Truth Commission determined that during the state's twelve-year civil war, government forces were responsible for 95 percent of reported human rights violations. During conflict, tensions rise over who has the responsibility and authority to allocate humanitarian aid, protect vulnerable populations, and resolve the conflict itself. Some of these issues are exacerbated by the nature of today's conflicts. Most are communal in nature, meaning that the core contradiction between fighting parties are driven by issues linked to identity. Identity politics are understood as "political ideology, organization, and action that openly represents the interests of designated groups based on 'essential' characteristics such as ethnic origin or religion, and whose legitimacy lies in the support of important segments of such groups" (Eriksen 2001, 42). As discussed in chapter 3, when populations within a state see themselves as belonging to distinct identity-based subgroups, individuals may adopt a nativist perspective on security and rely on those subgroups for protection, which can create further cleavages in an already difficult ongoing conflict. In addition, international actors, even with supposedly good intentions, intervening in a conflict can unwittingly contribute to these divisions. For instance, a group that perceives humanitarian aid or other forms of assistance from international actors as being distributed unjustly or giving a rival group an advantage may lead to higher levels of mistrust toward the intervening actor. This mistrust could result in the aggrieved groups working to undermine the work of humanitarian actors. Such fracturing between groups makes the question of who has ultimate responsibility for security provision more difficult to resolve.

The need to independently address immediate human security concerns during conflict and in peace processes has become a key goal for many international humanitarian actors. How global institutions are designed and how different strategies are prioritized and pursued are important factors in how human security needs are addressed during conflict; however, the international system of states has not been particularly well suited to address these needs effectively. As *Human Security Now* argued, "The existing international security system is not designed to prevent and deal effectively with the new types of security threats. New multilateral strategies are required that focus on shared responsibility to protect people" (Commission on Human Security 2003, 23). As we will further explore in this chapter, there have been ongoing efforts by the international community to address these gaps. Yet, despite these attempts to bolster global institutions designed to respond to these crises, they remain weak and under constant challenge. These weaknesses are further amplified by recent backlashes to this global institutional framework. Therefore, when discussing peace processes, it is important to consider the ways in which these activities happen both within and outside official policy processes.

Furthermore, violent conflict often corresponds with the institutional breakdown of the state. Therefore, a peace process will work toward constituting a new ordering of those state institutions. How that state is constituted post-conflict has obvious ramifications for the likelihood of future conflict and consequently long-term human security. Perceptions of bias toward one group or another within newly formed political structures can contribute to a fragile peace. For instance, the state institutions that remain strongest during conflict are often those most closely linked to its security sector, which in many cases was a leading source of human insecurity. How the security sector is constituted after the end of armed conflict will be highly contested and have ramifications for post-conflict peace and justice. Therefore, there are a number of questions that should be considered when evaluating any given peace process. How will the new state reduce violence against its citizens? How will people's human rights be protected and what methods of redress will exist when those rights are violated? How will the post-conflict economy be constructed? Will inequalities, which may have been the source of the conflict, be adequately addressed? These questions don't have obvious answers and different actors will have different conclusions about the most appropriate outcomes.

This chapter, therefore, seeks to unravel the processes by which wars end and how different types of war termination efforts affect prospects for both durable and short-term human security, with a specific focus on the actors that work to address immediate human security needs and the creation of comprehensive peace accords. It will explore how multiple actors are involved in these processes and how they advocate (or fail to advocate) for human security approaches. Importantly, peace processes occur concurrently with violence and sometimes parties will simultaneously attempt to engage in both negotiation and violence. This duality between the simultaneous pursuit by some actors of war and peace often makes peace processes appear complicated, contradictory, and hypocritical. While it is easy to become cynical, recognizing the inherent messiness of these processes helps us develop a more realistic understanding of how they work. To demonstrate this complexity—and also to show how creative and purposeful engagement by activists during wartime can bring about peaceful transformations—this chapter will briefly examine the case of the Liberian civil war and the role of Mass Action for Peace.

ALL WARS MUST END?

Is it true that all wars must end? More importantly, what do those endings look like? Who are the so-called winners and losers? How does the type of ending impact the human security needs of the populations effected by war? In general, conflicts can end in four ways: (1) a **one-sided victory** in which one side is victorious over the other(s); (2) a formal **cease-fire** in which all sides agree to stop committing violence, but with no formal peace accord, although there might be some type of conflict regulation mechanisms put into place; (3) a formal **peace accord** in which all or most sides involved in the conflict agree to some form of post-conflict governance; or (4) the conflict has no clear resolution, meaning the fighting stops or continues at very low levels of activity without any process that oversaw that cessation (Kreutz 2010). A one-sided victory is most likely to occur in the first few years of an intrastate war. After ten years, however, it is very rare for one side to have a decisive victory (Brandt et al. 2008).

According to data from the Uppsala Conflict Data Program (UCDP) Conflict Termination dataset, only a small percentage of intrastate conflicts, in fact, end in a formal peace accord. Between 1990 and 2005, 18.4 percent of intrastate conflicts ended in a peace agreement and 19.7 percent ended in a cease-fire. Only 13.6 percent of conflicts during this period ended in one side being victorious. The vast plurality of conflicts, 48.3 percent, end with no clear resolution (Kreutz 2010). There is one important caveat when interpreting this data: the UCDP dataset looks at the termination of armed conflict, which is defined as violent events between two or more groups, of which one is a government, with just twenty-five or more battle deaths. It is not surprising, therefore, that many low casualty conflicts do not result in a formal peace process, as they never hit a threshold beyond which parties would be motivated to engage in complicated formal negotiations. That also means that the roots of many conflicts remain unresolved, despite there being a cessation to ongoing violence.

Unsurprisingly, the study of conflict termination has been largely concerned with the bargaining processes that occur between the various groups engaged in violence. These studies generally conceptualize these groups to be rational in that they have a relatively fixed set of preferences and political goals that they are pursuing through violent means. If the Clausewitzian dictum that "war is merely the continuation of policy by other means" is what we use to explain why wars begin, then it follows that peace processes are simply an additional "other means" for how those same armed actors resolve the disputes that initially led to war. Thus, these conflict termination models explain peace processes as negotiated bargains between a limited number of self-interested actors. The conflict terminates once they reach an outcome that is mutually acceptable among the actors at the negotiating table.

A common way to think about war termination is by presenting conflict as a linear progression that moves along an escalation/de-escalation continuum. This simplification helps us better understand many of the discrete events that happen throughout the process—and the various points at which warring parties might be compelled to seek a resolution. One common example is Lund's "Curve of Conflict," which maps the course of a conflict along two dimensions (Lund 1996). The first dimension is the intensity of the conflict, which ranges from Durable Peace to War, and the second dimension is the duration of the conflict, which is measured in stages. The stage and intensity of the conflict at a given point will determine which type of management techniques will or should be engaged. In the Lund model, prior to a conflict escalating to violence, various prevention techniques, such as routine and preventive diplomacy, would be employed with the intention to de-escalate the situation. Once violence breaks out, however, a new set of tools (i.e., crisis diplomacy, peacemaking, and peace enforcement) would be needed to manage the crisis, limit the violence, and bring parties toward resolution. Once the violent stage of the conflict has ended, tools focused on post-conflict peacebuilding and reconciliation would be employed. Similar models have been developed by Galtung (1996) as well as Ramsbotham, Woodhouse, and Miall (2016).

Escalation/de-escalation models, while useful in their basic framework, have several limitations that we should keep in mind, particularly when applying them to human security questions. First, rarely do conflicts follow such simple trajectories. Violence can be unpredictable, manifesting itself at multiple stages and at various levels of intensity. Therefore, it is not always clear what stage a conflict is in and consequently what would be the most effective conflict management approaches at any given time. Second, by placing conflict along a continuum it can create the impression that there is only a narrow selection of conflict management tools that can be used at any particular stage. As we will discuss throughout this chapter, a wide range of activities by a variety of actors constitute what we consider part of a peace process—particularly those that engage a human security approach—and these can occur during all stages of a conflict. A third issue is that these models are often elite focused and ignore the multiple "non-elite" actors that are engaged in peace processes at all stages of conflict. This begins with the term "conflict management," which implies the presence of at least one single actor who has both the authority and power to "manage" multiple violent actors. The assumption that such an actor exists is problematic, as the United Nations, the United States, Russia, and many other of the world's most powerful actors have repeatedly learned. In addition, the elite focus that has dominated security studies in the past under-examines the many nonviolent and grassroots actors that are engaged in peace activities, which make significant contributions to the nature of a peace process.

From a methodological standpoint limiting our explanations to a few key variables or actors is important when trying to explain complex phenomena. But what happens when our explanations for war initiation, escalation, and termination include only a small subset of the actors that experience armed conflict?

FROM CEASE-FIRES TO COMPREHENSIVE PEACE ACCORDS: INTEGRATING HUMAN SECURITY INTO CONFLICT TERMINATION

When neither side is able to achieve a military victory, violent parties must reach some mutual agreement between themselves on the conditions for conflict termination. Coming to such an agreement, however, can be challenging. Many conflicts can last decades with neither side ever able to gain a clear advantage. Parties with a history of conflict may find it difficult to commit to an agreement if they believe the other side might renege at some point in the future. Even if an agreement is reached, all sides might have a future incentive to restart the conflict if they believe violence could give them a better deal from what was previously negotiated.

Cease-fires, or agreements between fighting parties to stop using violence or otherwise mobilizing their forces against each other, are often seen as the first step toward reaching peace. Cease-fires usually do not involve much else beyond a non-use-of-force agreement. They can be used to provide the space for humanitarian actors to deliver aid or to start building trust between enemies with the hope that it leads to more formal peace negotiations. Belligerents, however, may also use the space provided by cease-fires to replenish their arms or to gain other advantages against the opposing side. When new windows of opportunity open up, parties may take advantage of their better strategic position and reinitiate hostilities. Thus, cease-fires are often violated and rarely bring lasting peace. These problems mean that peace negotiations will often focus on lessening the incentives for violent actors to go back on their commitments. It is for this reason that negotiations over **comprehensive peace accords**, agreements in which all the major parties in the conflict are involved in the negotiation process and go beyond basic issues of post-conflict governance, but also address the substantive issues that fueled the conflict (Joshi and Darby 2013), will focus on provisions that directly affect the fighting parties. Comprehensive peace accords are typically centered on agreements over policy and military reform, political reform and shared governance, and development issues.

The assumption that peace is best achieved by focusing on the interests of the armed actors has meant that human security concerns are often excluded from agreements or are only referenced in the most general terms. However, one of the core critiques of peace processes is that the overarching focus on the violent actors means that those who did not participate in the violence, but nevertheless suffered throughout the conflict, are ignored and continue to suffer deprivation long after the fighting has stopped. This raises the question of whether a peace process that overwhelmingly rewards the violent actors and does not address the victims can be seen as a just peace.

New research has demonstrated that we ignore the role of civil society and other nonviolent actors in conflict and peace processes at our own peril. This research suggests that when peace processes involve a greater segment of civil society—which consequently are also the actors most engaged with addressing human security concerns—they are more likely to be successful than those accords that narrowly focus on the interests of the armed actors (Paffenholz 2014, Wanis-St. John and Kew 2008). An examination of peace agreements shows that the more mechanisms are contained within an agreement, the more likely it is to succeed, and that a wider set of provisions within the agreement better integrates the complex interdependence between military, economic, and societal aspects of a post-conflict state (Badran 2014). Other research has shown that the inclusion of women contributes to the likelihood of an accord's success (Caprioli, Nielsen, and Hudson 2010, Nakaya 2003). There is a logic to these findings: when a deal is struck only between those that are capable of using violence, there are few incentives to stop them if they believe at some later date they can get a better deal by reinitiating hostilities; however, when more segments of society are brought into the peace process, more people have buy-in to the long-term success of the accord, meaning they will work to ensure a sustainable peace. This creates broader pressure on combatants to follow through on their commitments. While this does not guarantee that an armed actor will not try to take up arms at some future date, the interconnectedness of these more comprehensive peace accords makes that more difficult. Additionally, a comprehensive peace agreement is much more deeply rooted in the society's rule of law and becomes part of its constitutional legal framework. This creates mechanisms for future grievances to be more readily addressed through normal judicial processes.

One way to visualize the extent to which human security-focused provisions are included in comprehensive peace accords is by examining data from the University of Notre Dame's Peace Accord Matrix (PAM) (Joshi, Quinn, and Regan 2015). PAM is a dataset that consists of thirty-four peace accords negotiated between 1989 and 2012. As is evident in figure 6.1 most accords contain provisions for cease-fires, police and military reforms, economic development, and electoral reforms. Provisions that specifically address issues such as women's rights, children's rights, and cultural protections are far less likely to be included in an agreement. For instance, only seven of thirty-four accords in PAM had provisions specifically addressing women's rights. Those human security issues that are most likely to be included in agreements are those that address human rights in general and refugee/IDP issues. While evidence points to the importance of addressing broader human security issues within peace accords, they still often take a secondary position in official peace processes.

Nevertheless, there are a number of ongoing initiatives to promote more inclusive human security concerns within both the negotiation process and the final agreement. Security Council Resolution 1325 (2000), for instance, encourages more participation by women in peace processes (see chapter 10 for more discussion of Resolution 1325). There has also been increased pressure to include local civil society actors in the negotiation process. In the Colombian peace process, for example, victims were given the opportunity to testify before the negotiators, which was part of an effort by mediators to make victim rights a central component of the agreement. That said, the

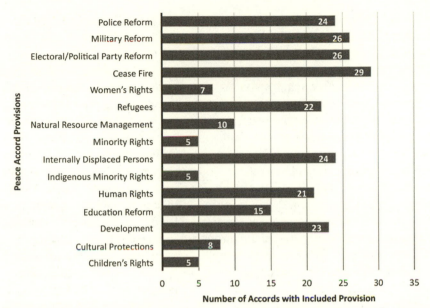

Figure 6.1. Frequency of Provision Types in Comprehensive Peace Accords. *Source*: Peace Accord Matrix (https://peaceaccords.nd.edu). See also Joshi, Quinn, and Regan (2015).

inclusion of human security issues in a peace accord does not necessarily guarantee that those issues will be addressed during implementation. Research on the inclusion of IDP provisions in peace accords, for instance, shows that many of the promises made toward those populations often go unfulfilled even as the peace holds (Andersen-Rodgers 2015).

Ultimately a peace accord serves as a marker between a period of violent conflict and a period of potential peace. As ongoing conflict represents the period in which human security threats are most severe, the simple act of stopping conflict may greatly reduce that threat. Still, it is not enough to simply stop the violence between competing forces. Political violence can easily transition to criminal violence if ex-combatants are unable to transition into a new role. In addition, populations that feel that a peace accord did not adequately address their grievances or lacks sufficient justice mechanisms for those who committed violent acts against them may choose to restart the conflict. Thus, the content of the peace accord matters, but, as we will examine here and in chapter 7, how provisions in an accord are actually implemented will make a significant difference in the level of human security that people will experience.

HUMAN SECURITY DURING CONFLICT: PROTECTION, ASSISTANCE, AND ADVOCACY

During conflict, human security threats are at their most extreme. During these times the three main activities human security actors engage in are protection, assistance, and advocacy. As discussed in chapter 5, protection involves the act of shielding noncombatants not just from physical harm but also guarding their basic human rights. In addition to basic protection activities, human security actors may engage in assistance activities, including the provision of immediate humanitarian aid to vulnerable populations. During conflict the responsibilities and capabilities of providing protection and assistance can become extremely complex as multiple actors seek to pursue their competing missions and interests (to get an idea of this complexity, consider the long list of security providers introduced in chapter 3, then consider that the long list there is just a small sample of the world's security providers). The third area that human security actors engage in is broad-based advocacy, as they attempt to create a normative discourse that pushes human security concerns into formal policymaking apparatuses. This section discusses this complex and interdependent web of actors and their efforts to provide protection and assistance to vulnerable populations, as well as advocate for their needs.

Ending violent conflicts is a complicated process and involves actors from many different sectors (i.e., the state, violent non-state actors, civil society), each with competing demands and visions of what a post-conflict society should look like. Different actors engage with a conflict in different ways—some actively participating in the violence, while others remain nonviolent throughout the conflict. Some may not directly commit violence but instead give support to violent actors. Because violence can have a polarizing effect on people, shaping perceptions between groups for generations, long-term mistrust of the other sides' intentions and motivations often emerges. As peace processes unfold, these histories will remain important as different groups evaluate how their grievances are being recognized and addressed through those mechanisms.

How each groups' interests are addressed or not addressed during a peace process has ramifications for long-lasting peace and the creation of durable human security. John Paul Lederach (1997) describes three levels of actors that are involved in peacebuilding processes. Level 1 actors—and the ones we are most likely to hear and read about in the news—are the military, political and religious elites. These are the groups that were most likely to be directing and engaging in violence. Therefore, they are the ones who are most likely to be involved in high-level negotiations to end the conflict and to be responsible for managing any cease-fire agreement. Lederach's important insight is that in order to build long-lasting peace, it is not just those who engage in the violence that need to be involved in peace processes. Level 2 actors, therefore, include respected members of different ethnic and religious groups, academics and intellectuals, and heads of higher-profile NGOs. Level 3 actors are made up of grassroots leadership that could include local leaders, leaders of indigenous NGOs, community developers, local health officials, and refugee camp leaders (Lederach 1997). While many will be excluded from the formal peace process, each of these entities brings its own agenda and influence to these processes, shaping the outcome in ways that may or may not contribute to improved human security. In addition to these domestic actors, intergovernmental organizations such as the United Nations, international NGOs, and other states will often become involved in these processes.

As we examine how different actors contribute or don't contribute to human security practices during conflict it is important to keep in mind that not all actors in a conflict behave in stereotypical ways or uniformly across conflicts. Each must make strategic decisions based on their specific needs, which are informed by their perceptions of the conflict and who is ultimately responsible for their security. Thus, someone being a military elite does not necessarily imply that they are not willing to engage in human security activities; they may, in fact, be a strong advocate for a cosmopolitan security perspective. Nor does it mean that a leader of a grassroots movement is engaging in activities that are always beneficial for peace. We should also keep in mind that few, if any, of these actors have the unilateral capability to bring about an end to the conflict or to protect human security. Instead, these processes rely on cooperation and compromise between many actors.

While many of the basic mechanisms that society has in place to protect individuals are highly strained during violent conflict, there also exists simultaneously a wide range of activities by a variety of actors meant to create the conditions for peace and to protect human security. These activities happen on two levels: the bottom up, which includes the engagement of domestic actors, including the conflict parties and local civil society; and the top down, which involves international engagement by other states, intergovernmental organizations such as the UN, and international nongovernmental organizations (INGOs) (see figure 6.2). Each of these actors will face different limitations and advantages when engaging with others. The nature of the system, though, gives distinct advantage to states as they have institutional advantages (i.e., membership in intergovernmental organizations, a diplomatic corps, legitimacy in the use of force, etc.) that most non-state actors lack (Andersen-Rodgers 2015). Next, we briefly discuss each of these actors. It should be recognized that the scope of this chapter does not allow us to engage all the ways in which these groups involve themselves with peace processes, and

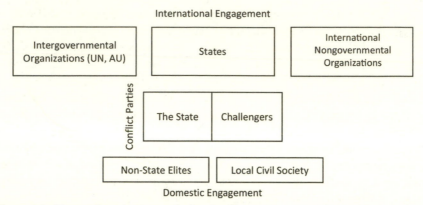

Figure 6.2. Human Security Actors during Conflict

some actors, such as elite economic interests, are not addressed. Instead, our focus is on the means by which they engage in human security practice.

Domestic Engagement

The fist area in which human security issues are engaged is on the domestic level. Domestic actors can act both as threats to and guarantors of human security. This section provides an overview of the actors involved in bottom-up activities related to peace processes.

Conflict Parties

The first set of actors to be considered are the conflict parties themselves, which typically consist of the state and the state's various challengers. According to Lederach's framework, these would be considered level 1 actors. During conflict, it is these actors that control the physical means to carry out widespread violence against civilian populations. States, in particular, have both the military capacity and the organizational capability to conduct war crimes, ethnic cleansing campaigns, crimes against humanity, and genocide. For example, it was the Bosnian Serb army that carried out the slaughter of 8,000 Muslim men and boys in Srebrenica. This level of atrocities is not limited to state actors, as violent non-state groups, such as the so-called Islamic State, have also carried out comparably atrocious attacks against civilian populations.

While armed actors, whether state or non-state combatants, are generally those who are most responsible for the breakdown of human security during conflict, they can also simultaneously serve as human security providers. The mass violation of a population's human security can create severe difficulties with both current and future governance, which conflict actors do care about, especially if they wish to assume control of the state. However, the provision of human security by these actors is typically uneven and limited narrowly toward those groups that they consider to be aligned with their interests. Populations that the armed actors do not consider essential in their ability to govern will be most threatened (Weinstein 2007).

Both the state and its challengers can be pressured to pursue human security policy, even during high levels of violent conflict. This pressure can result in limiting the types of force used and who they consider to be legitimate military targets. This pressure can come from multiple sources, including international actors and local civil society. Ultimately, post-conflict stability will require these actors to adopt, at least to some degree, a human security approach toward those populations to which they are linked. Thus, conflict actors must weigh the benefits of using violence to pursue their political goals against their long-term goals of effectively governing.

Local Civil Society Activism

While **civil society** is a very broad term, it loosely describes the sphere of voluntary action that is distinct from the state and economic spheres. Civil society can include religious institutions, humanitarian and charity organizations, advocacy networks, and other social groups, as discussed in chapter 3. Oftentimes, civil society advocates are the loudest voices advocating for the human security needs of a community during conflict. For instance, civil society activism can create community space for those affected by conflict. In the Democratic Republic of the Congo, domestic civil society actors— perhaps most well known among them Dr. Denis Mukwege and the staff of Panzi Hospital—worked together with transnational advocacy networks and were instrumental in providing care for and bringing attention to the needs of hundreds of thousands of survivors of conflict-related sexual violence (Crawford 2017).

Civil society contributes to what Mac Ginty refers to as everyday peace or "the practices and norms deployed by individuals and groups in deeply divided societies to avoid and minimize conflict . . . at both the inter- and intra-group levels" (Mac Ginty 2014, 553). In this way civil society may be able to provide space in which members from different communities can participate in normal interaction with each other. Of course, civil society does not always represent a unified voice and security providers can even work against each other. In Colombia, for example, different sectors of civil society staked diametrically opposed positions on the October 2016 plebiscite over the acceptance of the peace deal between the Colombian government and the

Revolutionary Armed Forces of Colombia (FARC). Those who opposed the terms of the peace treaty narrowly defeated those in support. After renegotiating the treaty, President Juan Manuel Santos did not present it for a vote the second time around.

Increasingly, local civil society actors are seen as important positive contributors to peace processes. A 2011 report by the United Nations Peacebuilding Support Office states that civil society has "a crucial role in peacebuilding through legitimizing processes and projects, mediating among state, society and international community, communicating local level perspectives and priorities to decision-makers and implementing concrete peacebuilding and development programmes" (United Nations Peacebuilding Support Office 2011, 3). That said, some have critiqued the extent to which civil societies concerns are addressed during these processes. A core critique is that the voices that donors and other elite actors listen to are those that most closely conform to already stated elite interests and that some local civil society organizations will, in fact, tailor their positions to attract international aid. Consequently, these critics argue, civil society serves as a means for amplifying elite views rather than acting as a counter-voice to it (Mac Ginty and Richmond 2013).

Civil society actors are aware of the potential physical threats facing them during conflict and often will engage in **strategic nonviolence**. According to Stephan and Chenoweth "nonviolent resistance is a civilian-based method used to wage conflict through social, psychological, economic, and political means without the threat or use of violence" (Stephan and Chenoweth 2008, 9). These strategies are used to bring attention to issues facing sectors of civil society. The use of nonviolent resistance, even during periods of violent conflict, can have important strategic advantages over violent methods. First, violently targeting nonviolent movements may have higher costs than targeting violent actors. Therefore, a dedication to nonviolent strategies may give those actors more freedom of movement than violent actors. Second, members of a regime, including civil servants, security forces, and the judiciary, are more likely to shift their allegiance toward nonviolent groups than violent groups. Third, the international community is more likely to denounce acts of violence against nonviolent groups than against violent groups (Stephan and Chenoweth 2008). That said, challenging violent actors remains risky, particularly in the midst of a conflict. A nonviolent movement that is accused of being aligned with one group over another may be enough to persuade the state to use violent tactics against it. In Syria, for example, President Assad continually equated the nonviolent protests against him as being aligned with violent forces as a way to justify to his supporters his violent response to their opposition.

The intensity and type of violence being perpetrated will also affect how civil society actors are able to act during conflict. Domestic human rights organizations may not be able to exist safely under intensely authoritarian regimes. In such situations, the most effective civil society actors may be those that come from long-standing institutions, such as churches, mosques, or other religious organizations. However, such organizations may be restricted on what or whom they are able or willing to advocate for. In addition, conflict itself can generate new civil society actors. Women, for example, may be able to move around combat zones more easily than men in some ways, as they are traditionally viewed as innocent civilians. This has allowed women to be some of the strongest advocates for peace during wartime. In Argentina, for example, a group of women whose children had been disappeared by the military regime during the Dirty War (1977–1983) began gathering in Buenos Aires' Plaza de Mayo in April 1977. Their status as grieving mothers and grandmothers made it difficult for the regime to target and intimidate them or frame their protest as a threat to the state, and the protest brought international attention to the human rights abuses being carried out by the Argentine government. Despite these important roles as advocates, women mostly remain outside the formal negotiating process; Security Council Resolution 1325 seeks to change this, but implementation has been slow.

It is also important to note those cases of what Semelin (2011) refers to as "civic action that is taken outside the framework of society" (2). Organizations that openly challenge the policies of one of the violent actors risk retribution—those who work to rescue potential victims of genocide being one such example. The White Helmets in Syria, ordinary individuals who work together to rescue civilians after airstrikes and bombings, have been persistently accused of "terrorist sympathies" or worse by proponents of the Assad regime. During such ongoing atrocities, any action that could be seen as potentially protecting a targeted group could also make the protector a potential target, stifling open civil society. In many cases, these choices to protect others are made by individuals without the backing of a broader organization. In these extreme circumstances the scope of what individuals can do is limited in the face of failing institutions and lack of external assistance and often requires a significant conflict-terminating event to stop ongoing mass atrocities. For instance, Jews continued to be murdered up until the days just prior to the Nazis' surrender to Allied forces and in Rwanda the genocide was not fully stopped until the Rwandan Patriotic Front's victory in July 1994 (Semelin 2011, 6).

While civil society can play a key role in promoting and providing human security, it is, therefore, important to recognize the limits of these capabilities. During violent conflict, civil society actors' resources are often stretched thin. Civil society is not constituted to respond to crises and once violence has started those resources can become increasingly scarce. In addition, civil society advocates must always determine the risks of challenging violent actors. While research on organized nonviolent resistance shows that it can be an effective tool, it is not always so, and any given individual activist must consider these very real risks, essentially creating a collective action problem for civil society activists. Civil society action in the Liberian civil war illustrates the strengths of and constraints on domestic security providers and advocates, as the next section discusses.

Liberia and Mass Action for Peace

The important contribution that civil society can make during conflict was highlighted by the actions of a group of women during the brutal civil war between the government of Liberia and Charles Taylor's National Patriotic Front of Liberia (NPLF) that began in 1989 and culminated in the 2003 Accra Peace Agreement. That conflict led to wide-scale displacement, the destruction of Liberia's economy, and devastating violence against the civilian population. Activism on the part of women's organizations throughout the conflict put pressure on the warring parties and the international mediators to come to end the conflict.

The effort, known as "Mass Action for Peace," may have appeared to the combatants as spontaneous but was a well-organized and strategic campaign that brought different Liberian women's groups from many different sectors of Liberian society together. Its key leader, Leymah Gbowee (who later received the Nobel Peace Prize for her efforts), organized women to gather in visible and public places dressed in white T-shirts bearing the organization's logo, white hair ties, and holding signs declaring the message, "The Women of Liberia Want Peace! Now!" (Gbowee 2011).

Later, the Mano River Women's Peace Network (MARWOPNET)—an organization made up of women from Liberia, Sierra Leone, and Guinea—formed in 2000 to promote peace within each of their countries and for the region as a whole. In 2001 it began a process to get leaders from these war-torn countries to begin talking with each other. After meeting with the respective leaders from each country, Presidents Charles Taylor of Liberia, Lansana Conte of Guinea, and Tejan Kabba of Sierra Leone, met at a three-day summit in Rabat, Morocco, in March 2002. This summit helped jump-start many of the discussions that would later lead to formal peace accords in Liberia, as well as Sierra Leone. During the negotiations MARWOPNET played an important role as an intermediary between the warring factions (Femmes Africa Solidarté 2005).

While this activism is widely credited with helping resolve the conflict in Liberia, these activists were not invited to be part of the formal negotiations. Instead, they held demonstrations outside and even blockaded negotiators into the room until combatants took their duty toward crafting a comprehensive peace accord seriously. Partly due to strong pressure from civil society, the Accra Peace Agreement went beyond the simple division of spoils between the armed belligerents and addressed many issues critical to human security. The Accra Peace Agreement ended Liberia's civil war and included provisions that dealt largely with the rehabilitation of children, women, the elderly, and disabled. The peace accord called for the post-conflict government to design programs specifically for these groups as well as for child combatants. One of the key questions with a peace accord is implementation and the institutions that will be responsible for it. The Accra Peace Agreement addresses implementation at the domestic level but also calls on various UN and regional agencies for assistance, including the UN Special Representative for Children in Armed Conflict, UNICEF, and the African Committee of Experts on the Rights and Welfare of the Child. Notably, the elections that followed the signing of the Accra Peace Agreement resulted in Africa's first elected female head of state, Ellen Johnson Sirleaf.

It is important not to overstate the importance of these networks in conflict termination. What the literature shows is that, yes, the broad participation of civil society and the addressing of civil society concerns within peace agreements improve their likelihood for success, but conflict actors still must be willing to cease their violent contestations of power. Charles Taylor had to step down from power in order for the conflict to come to an end, and it took a combination of domestic civil society action, sustained regional and international pressure, and acceptable peace agreement provisions to accomplish this.

International Engagement

There are multiple types of external actors that engage during civil wars including states (often pursuing their own national security interests), transnational advocacy networks, and international and regional organizations. These external engagements can impact the conflict both negatively and positively and have ramifications for how human security needs are met. It is at the international level that we observe the constant competition between the three different security approaches (national, global, and human) as different actors prioritize different forms of security.

States and Human Security during Peace Processes

A large part of international engagement into ongoing intrastate conflicts happens through different states' foreign policies supporting one side in pursuit of their own national security interests. States, particularly great powers, care greatly about the outcome of intrastate conflicts as a new government might have ramifications for the state's alliances and long-term security interests. This type of **proxy war** was front and center during the Cold War when the United States and the Soviet Union chose sides based on one's acceptance or rejection of Marxist ideologies. This type of support, however, continues outside the confines of the Cold War, as can be seen in Iran's support of the Houthis in Yemen and Russia's support of the Assad regime in Syria. This support does not necessarily reflect complete agreement with the goals of the group being supported but can sometimes be driven by a desire to weaken another state that supports an opposing side. This type of engagement can have long-term negative ramifications for human security since conflicts that experience external intervention in support of one side or another tend to last longer than conflicts without this type of intervention (Cunningham 2010). However, international engagement in the form of third-party guarantees in a peace agreement has also been shown to be a key variable for the successful resolution of civil wars (Walter 2002). Thus, states will often play an important role in the negotiation of final peace accords.

More rarely a state may intervene in a conflict solely to provide humanitarian assistance to a threatened population. While this typically would come through the auspices of the United Nations (as discussed next), in some instances intervention may happen unilaterally or through a regional organization, as happened in Kosovo in 1999. Justifications for such actions may happen for a myriad of reasons, including internalization of the general human security norm or the principles of R2P; internalization of strong norms specifically prohibiting the type of violence or weapons used (e.g., genocide or the use of chemical weapons); religious, ethnic, or other identification with the group targeted for violence; or domestic public pressure on the intervening state to take humanitarian action.

Some states have become vocal advocates for the human security approach and pressure other states to shape their policies in ways that improve human security. This has resulted in many states, particularly middle powers, formally banding together to work on mechanisms for strengthening the global human security architecture. For example, a number of states (including Austria, Brazil, Canada, France, Germany, Norway, the United Kingdom, and Uruguay, among others) have organized a Group of Friends of the Protection of Civilians, which has continued to put pressure on states to adhere to international humanitarian law and to condemn attacks on civilians and humanitarian workers.

The United Nations System as Human Security Actor

States face a number of constraints on how they can even implement a human security agenda if they so choose. The principle of sovereignty, as discussed in the previous chapter, means that unilateral interventions, even to enforce a widely accepted global norm, are suspect. It is for this reason that state advocates for human security have turned to the United Nations to advance this agenda. Thus, the United Nations has become a key actor in encouraging conflict parties to engage human security issues during peace processes. As discussed in previous chapters, the initial conceptualization of the United Nations was to maintain global security. Initially, the task of maintaining peace and security was considered something that should happen *between* states. Over time, however, the increased prevalence of intrastate wars expanded what the UN saw to be within its mandate to address peace and security issues. This has included a growing engagement with issues related to the protection of civilians during conflict and greater insistence that human security issues be addressed in peace accords overseen by a UN peacekeeping operation. We see this engagement on two levels. First is greater attention by the UN Security Council and the secretary-general to human security threats that intrastate conflicts generate. Second is the creation by the General Assembly of multiple UN agencies tasked with addressing systemic human security threats both in and out of conflict. Because the United Nations is made up of its Member States, its main task is engaging with governments and its institutional design is structured to facilitate that task. As discussed in chapter 5, however, principles of sovereignty limit what the United Nations can do within the territory of a state. These limits block the extent to which the UN as an international institution can successfully engage a human security approach.

The United Nations and Civilian Protection

The most pressing human security threat during conflict is direct or indirect violence against civilian populations. According to international humanitarian law, civilians are a protected class during conflict and intentionally targeting them constitutes a war crime. Yet, during the Cold War, the debate at the UN on civilian protection during intrastate conflict was limited to basic (and severely contested) questions on human rights and refugee issues (MacFarlane and Khong 2006). As chapter 2 discussed, a string of atrocities following the end of the Cold War, including the dissolution of Somalia, the genocide in Rwanda, and the massacre at Srebrenica, brought greater attention to the threats faced by civilians during conflict. Beginning in the mid-1990s, the United Nations began to adopt a series of resolutions, protocols, and guiding principles whose aim it was to protect civilians during armed conflict. This included efforts to develop a set of principles for states to follow regarding internally displaced populations and the creation of judicial instruments capable of trying and punishing individuals who commit war crimes. While

R2P, which was discussed in chapter 5, represented the normative framework for these efforts, the actual implementation of these norms has been applied unevenly.

The United Nations Security Council is the body specifically tasked with the "primary responsibility for the maintenance of international peace and security" (United Nations 1945, Article 24.1); therefore, the most direct way that the United Nations has engaged human security issues during ongoing conflicts has been through Security Council resolutions. Security Council resolutions can encompass a wide range of tools for addressing human security concerns during conflict. These tools include diplomatic engagement, such as offering good offices (i.e., using the prestige of the UN to help facilitate negotiations between groups in conflict), fact-finding missions, mediation, and civilian monitoring; the deployment of military force; the levying of sanctions; and the condemnation of one or more parties engaged in the conflict (Beardsley, Cunningham, and White 2017). However, because the Security Council is made up of individual nation-states, the security issues that it chooses to engage are limited to those that do not threaten one of the veto-wielding states' self-identified national security interests. This dynamic was particularly present during the Cold War, when the United States and the Soviet Union continually vetoed or threatened to veto Security Council resolutions that went against either of their interests, but it remains a challenge today (as the UN's paralysis in response to the atrocities in Syria suggests).

After the Cold War, there was renewed emphasis on creating a more effective UN system. Part of this derived from a new emphasis on resolving the record-high number of intrastate conflicts that were taking place at that time. These efforts largely came from the secretary-general's office beginning with the publication of *An Agenda for Peace* in 1992 but were also supported by a rare amount of Security Council consensus around greater international engagement in ongoing crises. This included the authorization of a number of new peacekeeping operations with increasingly involved mandates (discussed in more detail in chapter 7). The early optimism, however, was confronted with the harsh realities of intervention, with the UN being criticized for either acting only after mass atrocities had already happened, as was the case in Rwanda, or being impotent in the face of an ongoing atrocity, as was the case during the massacre at Srebrenica. Because the UN relies on Member States to supply military personnel to conduct its missions, it often makes rapid response to crises logistically impossible and imposes strict and extremely cautious rules of engagement once forces are on the ground.

To counter these issues, both the Security Council and the secretary-general's office began to codify the obligations that states had toward civilian populations during conflict. In September 1999, UN secretary-general

Kofi Annan issued on behalf of the UN Security Council a report on the protection of civilians (United Nations Security Council 1999). In that report, Annan gave a number of recommendations on how the UN and its Member States could better address civilian protection issues. These recommendations included encouraging states to ratify and implement international instruments designed to protect civilians and to punish war crimes, specifically supporting the creation of the International Criminal Court. Further, Annan urged states to follow new protocols regarding the rights and treatment of internally displaced populations as well as the treatment of humanitarians working in combat zones. This report was followed by a series of Security Council resolutions that further emphasized civilian protection during conflict.

Since the 1999 report, how civilian protection concerns are integrated into Security Council resolutions has become increasingly institutionalized. In 2007, Secretary-General Ban Ki-moon issued a new report on the protection of civilians that called for the creation of "a dedicated, expert-level working group to facilitate the systematic and sustained consideration and analysis of protection concerns" (United Nations Security Council 2007). The informal group of experts that was formed on this recommendation meets regularly to help craft language on civilian protection issues being addressed in Security Council resolutions. The recommendations are based on the evaluation of a conflict in six areas: (1) the conduct of hostilities and its impact on civilians; (2) violations and abuses of human rights; (3) humanitarian access; (4) protection issues related to displacement; (5) gender-based protection concerns, including sexual violence; and (6) protection concerns related to children. Additionally, the Commission on Human Rights and, since 2006, the Human Rights Council, as well as the High Commissioner for Human Rights (established in 1993), have been tasked by the Security Council with investigating and reporting on human rights violations all over the world with the purpose of better informing the Security Council on human rights violations when crafting resolutions. These efforts have resulted in more specific tasks related to civilian protection concerns within UN Security Council resolutions themselves.

Due to the voting rules of the Security Council, resolutions do not provide a consistent response to violations of humanitarian law. Many long-lasting conflicts are immune from Security Council resolutions due to the national security interests of one or more of the veto-wielding P5 members. For instance, a resolution was unable to pass regarding Kosovo in 1994 due to Russia's objection (which is what eventually led to the unauthorized NATO response). Israel's occupation of the Palestinian territories is essentially immune from Security Council interference due to the U.S. relationship with Israel. Any resolution on the conflict in Syria was largely watered down or rejected due to Russian support for the Assad regime. China, while often abstaining rather than vetoing, has continued to raise objections to resolutions that it sees as violating the principle of sovereignty and has, since 2007, often sided with Russia on vetoing resolutions that call for increased UN intervention. France, on the other hand, has pledged to not veto any resolution that directly responds to a humanitarian crisis.

To overcome the power politics of the Security Council, the UN General Assembly, which is made up of all Member States, has used its voting powers to create an expansive bureaucracy designed to help the UN respond to humanitarian crises around the world. Some of the earliest votes taken by the General Assembly concerned the rights of refugees, which eventually led to the Refugee Convention in 1951 and the creation of the UNHCR in 1950, which now provides support for displaced persons in conflicts around the world. As discussed in chapter 3, other UN agencies that have been tasked with providing assistance to people experiencing humanitarian crises include UNICEF and the World Food Programme. The end of the Cold War created an environment that led to a number of institutional changes within the UN to engage conflicts as they occur. These changes created a host of new agencies and reorganizations to already existing ones. While the Security Council is the body of the UN that is tasked with overseeing peace and security issues, numerous other agencies are engaged in tasks that facilitate various peace processes. These agencies have been given the institutional capacity to carry out the Security Council's resolutions when asked to, but are also able to engage in various activities even without an explicit mandate.

One major concern for UN agencies is determining when to become involved in a crisis situation and how to avoid multiple agencies overlapping with each other and NGOs also working in the area. The impetus for these changes started with General Assembly Resolution 46/182 in 1991, which called for strengthening the UN in its capacity to respond to complex humanitarian emergencies. While the resolution was primarily meant to respond to natural disasters, over time its framework has been used to provide mechanisms to mitigate humanitarian disasters caused by warfare. The resolution created two new tools for response: the Emergency Relief Coordinator, who serves as a focal point for the multiple agencies tasked with overseeing humanitarian emergencies; and the Interagency Standing Committee (ISAC), which includes all humanitarian partners from those working within the UN, to various relief funds, to the Red Cross Movement, to NGOs working in the field. ISAC works to ensure interagency and partner coordination during emergencies. In 1998, a number of additional reforms to improve this interagency coordination during conflict were enacted, including the creation of the United Nations Office for the Coordination of Humanitarian Affairs, tasked with overseeing these processes and to evaluate when humanitarian crises—both man-made and natural—are likely to emerge.

Has this attention to civilian protection made any difference? Certainly, the United Nations and its partners have been able to provide services that relieve immediate suffering. The UNHCR, in particular, has effectively provided both short- and long-term shelter for displaced populations. In addition, the UNHCR has helped states register displaced populations and develop mechanisms for resolving said displacement. The series of crises in the 2010s has been particularly brutal toward civilians and the abilities of the UN to effectively prevent these ongoing atrocities have been severely strained. At least in the foreseeable future, the UN (and regional organizations such as the African Union) will continue to face challenges as a human security actor due to lack of available resources and the constraints imposed on it by its Member States.

BOX 6.1. "THINK ABOUT IT . . ."—THE UNITED NATIONS AND CIVILIAN PROTECTION

Go to the United Nations' Peacekeeping website (http://www.un.org/en/peacekeeping/) and look through the list of ongoing United Nations peacekeeping missions. Find one that has a protection of civilians' mandate and read the resolutions establishing the mission. For example, the United Nations Multidimensional Integrated Stabilization Mission in Mali (MINUSMA) was established in April 2013 by Security Council Resolution 2100. In June 2014, Security Council Resolution 2164 extended and expanded the mandate. Both resolutions identify civilian protection as a key part of the UN mission.

Consider the following questions:

1. What does the language in the mandate authorizing the mission focus on?
2. Does the mandate provide mechanisms through which civilian protection can be achieved?

Use an online news search engine and research how the UN carried out its civilian protection mandate and answer the following questions:

1. If you were advising the UN Security Council on issues related to civilian protection, what recommendations would you give them?
2. How did the UN work to ensure civilian protection?
3. Can you find events in which civilians were targeted during the mission?
4. What challenges did the civilian protection effort face?

International Nongovernmental Organizations

The final type of actor engaged in human security practice during conflict are international nongovernmental organizations. These transnational organizations engage in activities which promote key norms for political behavior. NGOs at the international level have been a core voice in human security discourse in global politics and essential for filling the gap between the formal and informal policy processes. There are thousands of international NGOs throughout the world, which operate in a number of different ways and carry out various types of activities. As discussed in chapter 3, human rights organizations such as Human Rights Watch and Amnesty International, for example, work to document violations of international humanitarian law by conflict actors. Groups such as Médecins Sans Frontières and the International Committee of the Red Cross play a role in providing medical and other lifesaving services to civilians and injured combatants. In the face of inaction by European states, NGOs have been key actors in helping save the lives of refugees and migrants fleeing Libya by crossing the Mediterranean in overcrowded and dangerously inadequate vessels (Amnesty International 2017). Organizations such as Peace Brigades International put observers into conflict zones whose presence helps protect local human rights defenders. International NGOs play a key role in pressuring states and intergovernmental organizations to live up to obligations to protect the lives and rights of those affected by conflict.

A key role for international NGOs has been to help amplify local groups' voices be heard and recognized by more powerful local and global actors (Keck and Sikkink 1998). NGOs are frequently based in Western states and are led by individuals who have access to their government's foreign policy decision-makers and to high-level officials within the United Nations. This access can sometimes help bring attention, and in many cases protection, to groups working on human security–related issues in combat zones. This phenomenon, which Keck and Sikkink call the boomerang effect, helps open space for local civil society to better engage the political process. However, for this to be effective, the international NGO has to be aware of the local advocates and their activities on the ground and have actual influence with the governments or IGOs they are trying to pressure. Again, the context of these interactions will be an important factor in their overall success.

CONCLUSION

The resolution of conflict is complex. Human security demands that conflict resolution not only focus on the elimination of direct violence but also account for how any resolution process affects different populations. This raises a key question: is human security necessary to end a conflict and does an insistence on a human security approach in conflict resolution diminish the chances of ending the violence? Of course, the answer is not clear-cut and, as the previous discussion highlights, people from all groups in conflict will do what they can to best pursue their interests. Who is heard and how different groups' interests are integrated into a peace process will have impacts on the nature of the post-conflict peace.

This chapter has broadly examined a number of areas related to human security during conflict and the peace processes meant to bring those conflicts to an end. Since the end of the Cold War there has been heightened concern that warfare now disproportionally harms civilian populations. States are increasingly concerned that the internal instability caused by these conflicts threatens both their national security and the overall security of the global system. This has led many to advocate for policy approaches that emphasize a deeper engagement with human security. One of the primary ways that this is happening is through greater recognition within peace processes of the different types of actors that experience conflict. By broadening our scope beyond the conflict actors, we see a much more complex mosaic of interests, grievances, and needs. Activists on both the domestic and international levels have worked to highlight these issues and to promote an international legal framework that addresses the right of civilians during conflict. Of course, it cannot be ignored that many of those mechanisms are severely strained as the world faces increased threats to civilian protection manifest most visibly in the ongoing displacement crisis.

The next chapter examines these issues more closely as it looks at how human security concerns are addressed after conflict through peacebuilding and transitional justice.

Discussion Questions

1. Thinking about the many people and groups that are engaged in conflict, how might each be motivated or not motivated to address human security issues?
2. Scholars, policymakers, and practitioners are placing greater emphasis on the role of civil society in helping bring about long-term peace. How does civil society contribute to successful peace accords? Can you think of any ways in which the participation of civil society actors could undermine peace?
3. Does peace require human rights?
4. What are the main obstacles to civilian protection? Are there ways to realistically address these obstacles?

FURTHER READING AND WEB RESOURCES

Peace Accord Matrix. https://peaceaccords.nd.edu

Radhika Coomaraswamy. "Preventing Conflict, Transforming Justice, Securing the Peace: A Global Study on the Implementation of the Implementation of United Nations Security Council Resolution 1325." UN Women. 2015. Available at: http://wps.unwomen.org/en

Security Council Report. UN Documents on the Protection of Civilians. http://www.securitycouncilreport.org/un-documents/protection-of-civilians/

UCDP/PRIO Armed Conflict Dataset. https://www.prio.org/Data/Armed-Conflict/UCDP-PRIO/

Victoria Holt and Glyn Taylor. *Protecting Civilians in the Context of UN Peacekeeping Operations: Successes, Setbacks and Remaining Challenges*. New York: United Nations, 2009. Available at: http://reliefweb.int/sites/reliefweb.int/files/resources/B752FF2063E282B08525767100751B90-unocha_protecting_nov2009.pdf

For Deeper Discussion

Barbara F. Walter. *Committing to Peace: The Successful Settlement of Civil Wars*. Princeton, NJ: Princeton University Press, 2002.

John D. Brewer. *Peace Processes: A Sociological Approach*. London: Polity, 2010.

Leymah Gbowee. *Mighty Be Our Powers*. New York: Beast Books, 2011.

Margaret E. Keck and Kathryn Sikkink. *Activists beyond Borders: Advocacy Networks in International Politics*. Ithaca, NY: Cornell University Press, 1998.

United Nations Security Council. *Report of the Secretary-General on the Protection of Civilians in Armed Conflict*. S/2017/414. New York: United Nations, 2017.

REFERENCES

Amnesty International. *A Perfect Storm: The Failure of European Policies in the Central Mediterranean*. London: Amnesty International, 2017.

Andersen-Rodgers, David R. "Back Home Again: Assessing the Impact of Provisions for Internally Displaced Persons in Comprehensive Peace Accords." *Refugee Survey Quarterly* 34, no. 3 (2015): 24–45.

Andersen-Rodgers, David R. "No Table Necessary? Foreign Policy Crisis Management Techniques in Non-State Actor-Triggered Crises." *Conflict Management and Peace Science* 32, no. 2 (2015): 220–21.

Badran, Ramzi. "Intrastate Peace Agreements and the Durability of Peace." *Conflict Management and Peace Science* 31, no. 2 (2014): 193–217.

Beardsley, Kyle, David E. Cunningham, and Peter B. White. "Resolving Civil Wars before They Start: The UN Security Council and Conflict Prevention in Self-Determination Disputes." *British Journal of Political Science* (2017): 1–23.

Brandt, Patrick T., T. David Mason, Mehmet Gurses, Nicolai Petrovsky, and Dagmar Radin. "When and How the Fighting Stops: Explaining the Duration and Outcome of Civil Wars." *Defense and Peace Economics* 19, no. 6 (2008): 415–34.

Caprioli, Mary, Rebecca Nielsen, and Valerie M. Hudson. "Women and Post Conflict Settings." In *Peace and Conflict 2010*, by J. Joseph Hewitt, Jonathan Wilkenfeld and Ted Robert Gurr, 91–102. Boulder, CO: Paradigm, 2010.

Commission on Human Security. *Human Security Now*. New York: United Nations, 2003.

Crawford, Kerry F. *Wartime Sexual Violence: From Silence to Condemnation of a Weapon of War*. Washington, DC: Georgetown University Press, 2017.

Cunningham, David E. "Blocking Resolution: How External States Can Prolong Civil Wars." *Journal of Peace Research* 47, no. 2 (2010): 115–27.

Eriksen, Thomas Hylland. "Ethnic Identity, National Identity, and Intergroup Conflict: The Significance of Personal Experiences." In *Social Identity, Intergroup Conflict, and Conflict Resolution*, by Richard D. Ashmore, Lee Jussim and David Wilder, 42–68. Oxford: Oxford University Press, 2001.

Femmes Africa Solidarté. "Engendering the Peace Processes in West Africa: The Mano River Women's Peace Network." In *People Building Peace II: Successful Stories of Civil Society*, by Paul van Tongeren, Malin Brenk, Marte Hellema, and Juliette Verhoeven, 588–93. Boulder, CO: Lynne Rienner, 2005.

Galtung, Johan. *Peace by Peaceful Means: Peace and Conflict, Development and Civilization*. Oslo: PRIO, 1996.

Gbowee, Leymah. *Mighty Be Our Powers*. New York: Beast Books, 2011.

Joshi, Madhav, and John Darby. "Introducing the Peace Accords Matrix (PAM): A Database of Comprehensive Peace Agreements and Their Implementation, 1989–2007." *Peacebuilding* 1, no. 2 (2013): 256–74.

Joshi, Madhav, Jason Michael Quinn, and Patrick M. Regan. "Annualized Implementation Data on Intrastate Comprehensive Peace Accords, 1989–2012." *Journal of Peace Research* 52, no. 4 (2015): 551–62.

Keck, Margaret E., and Kathryn Sikkink. *Activists beyond Borders: Advocacy Networks in International Politics*. Ithaca, NY: Cornell University Press, 1998.

Kreutz, Joakim. "How and When Armed Conflicts End: Introducing the UCDP Conflict Termination Dataset." *Journal of Peace Research* 47, no. 2 (2010): 243–50.

Lederach, John Paul. *Building Peace: Sustainable Reconciliation in Divided Societies*. Washington, DC: United States Institute of Peace, 1997.

Lund, Michael. *Preventing Violent Conflicts*. Washington, DC: United States Institute of Peace, 1996.

Mac Ginty, Roger. "Everyday Peace: Bottom-Up and Local Agency in Conflict-Affected Societies." *Security Dialogues* 45, no. 6 (2014): 548–64.

Mac Ginty, Roger, and Oliver P. Richmond. "The Local Turn in Peace Building: A Critical Agenda for Peace." *Third World Quarterly* 34, no. 5 (2013): 763–83.

MacFarlane, S. Neil, and Yuen Foong Khong. *Human Security and the UN: A Critical History*. Bloomington: Indiana University Press, 2006.

Nakaya, Sumie. "Women and Gender Equality in Peace Processes: From Women at the Negotiating Table to Postwar Structural Reforms in Guatemala and Somalia." *Global Governance* 9, no. 4 (2003): 459–76.

Paffenholz, Thania. "Civil Society and Peace Negotiations: Beyond the Inclusion-Exclusion Dichotomy." *Negotiation Journal* 30, no. 1 (2014): 69–91.

Ramsbotham, Oliver, Tom Woodhouse, and Hugh Miall. *Contemporary Conflict Resolution*. 4th edition. London: Polity, 2016.

Semelin, Jacques. "Introduction: From Help to Rescue." In *Resisting Genocide: The Multiple Forms of Rescue*, by Jacques Semelin, Claire Andrieu and Sarah Gensburger, 1–14. New York: Columbia University Press, 2011.

Stephan, Maria J., and Erica Chenoweth. *Why Civil Resistance Works: The Strategic Logic of Nonviolent Conflict*. Vol. 33. 1 vol. International Security, 2008.

United Nations. *Charter of the United Nations*. New York, June 26, 1945.

United Nations Peacebuilding Support Office. *From Rhetoric to Practice: Operationalizing Ownership in Post-Conflict Peacebuilding*. Workshop Report, New York: United Nations, 2011.

United Nations Security Council. "Report of the Secretary-General on the Protection of Civilians in Armed Conflict." *S/2007/643*. New York, October 28, 2007.

United Nations Security Council. "Report of the Secretary-General to the Security Council on the Protection of Civilians in Armed Conflict." *S/1999/957*. New York, September 8, 1999.

Walter, Barbara F. *Committing to Peace: The Successful Settlement of Civil Wars*. Princeton, NJ: Princeton University Press, 2002.

Wanis-St. John, Anthony, and Darren Kew. "Civil Society and Peace Negotiations: Confronting Exclusion." *International Negotiations* 13 (2008): 11–36.

Weinstein, Jeremy M. *Inside Rebellion: The Politics of Insurgent Violence*. Cambridge: Cambridge University Press, 2007.

Chapter 7

Human Security and Peacebuilding

Learning Objectives

This chapter will enable readers to:

1. Understand the residual effects of conflict in post-conflict societies.
2. Define the difference between peacebuilding and state-building.
3. Understand the evolution of United Nations multidimensional peacekeeping operations.
4. Consider how different priorities in peacebuilding address human security issues differently.
5. Understand what is meant by the term "transitional justice" and the different mechanisms that have been used to try to achieve post-conflict justice.

The process of moving from war to a condition of sustained peace is called **peacebuilding** and involves a wide range of efforts, actions, and policies that fit within the human security approach. In 1992, *An Agenda for Peace* defined peacebuilding as "action to identify and support structures which will tend to strengthen and solidify peace to avoid relapse to conflict." Since then peacebuilding has evolved to be broadly understood as a range of activities aimed at rebuilding the political, economic, and social structures of post-conflict societies. These activities can include demobilization, disarmament, and reintegration (DDR) of combat troops; security sector reform; reforming political and judicial structures; establishing the rule of law; and the promotion of just socioeconomic development.

This chapter moves from the period of acute violent conflict and examines the processes that accompany post-conflict peacebuilding and justice. How post-conflict societies should be constituted has been an ongoing question of international politics. Because conflicts themselves are likely fought over this very question, the answer to this problem is never without contention and different actors will prioritize different security goals over others. Therefore, we start by examining the question of which threats to human security persist even after violent conflict has ended. This is followed by a discussion of two terms that are typically used to describe post-conflict activity—statebuilding and peacebuilding—and how human security approaches have been integrated into these activities. The chapter ends with an examination of the evolution of UN peace operations and efforts to create mechanisms better equipped to address justice for victims of atrocities.

In chapter 6, we examined how different types of actors address human security issues during ongoing conflicts. Because war creates threats to human security that are usually sudden and overtly violent, the human security approach in armed conflict is often directed toward immediate protection needs. In this chapter, we will continue to explore these issues, but we will shift our temporal frame to the post-conflict period. It is important to consider that (1) many of the activities aimed toward guaranteeing human security during conflict closely match the types of activities aimed toward guaranteeing human security after conflict (Zelizer and Oliphant 2013); and (2) post-conflict periods are rarely violence-free and, in fact, face a high likelihood of conflict recurrence (Quinn, Mason, and Gurses 2007). Another important contextual point to keep in mind is that civil wars can last for multiple decades (although most average between seven and twelve years), meaning that when peace is achieved, there are many who have known nothing but what it is to live in a state suffering from ongoing violence. Keeping in mind the human consequences of living through armed conflict, and how that experience shapes one's understanding of the world around them, is key to engaging a human security approach.

SECURITY THREATS AFTER CONFLICT

Human populations continue to face insecurities after violent conflict stops and stable state structures have been put in place. While some of those threats include direct violence from crime or not fully demobilized armed actors, many more derive from systematic, long-term threats associated with weak institutional performance that, if not addressed, can affect generations. For a population to be healthy they must have access to health services, which are often severely damaged during civil wars. Hazem Adam Ghobarah, Paul Huth, and Bruce Russett (2003), for example, demonstrate that civil wars have long-term negative consequences for public health long after the fighting has stopped. Using data from the World Health Organization, they show that the breakdown of health services due to conflict results in higher ongoing instances of infectious diseases, including tuberculosis and malaria. If these services are not reconstructed following the termination of conflict, civilian populations will continue to face long-term, systemic threats to their health.

Beyond the breakdown in health services, different sectors of society experience long-term consequences from conflict in different ways. Education systems and funding for education are often destroyed during civil wars (Lai and Thyne 2007), meaning children, especially girls, are less likely to attend or complete school, which damages their long-term economic prospects (Shemyakina 2011). For displaced populations, it can take years for solutions to their displacement to be resolved, if any resolution is possible (Smit 2012). In addition, combatants being integrated into post-conflict society will not only suffer from psychological distress but often lack the schooling and training necessary for skilled employment (Blattman and Annan 2010). This lack of opportunity may push some toward criminal endeavors. Conflict can also affect the types of economic activity that people are able to engage in and when the violence stops; it is not always the case that people can return to the employment they were previously trained in. For example, the use of landmines during conflict can render agricultural land unusable until the mines are cleared. If not adequately addressed during the post-conflict phase, these issues, and others, will have generational consequences. Post-conflict human security efforts, therefore, constitute essential activities designed specifically to prioritize and mitigate ongoing human misery that was suffered during the violence.

STATE-BUILDING, PEACEBUILDING, AND THE HUMAN SECURITY APPROACH: NEW WINE FOR OLD BOTTLES?

National and global security approaches have tended to prioritize state stability and economic recovery during post-conflict peacebuilding. As we've discussed in previous chapters, these approaches see conflict as best managed through the creation of a system of stable sovereign states. Overall, the argument goes, state stability decreases the types of breakdown that can trigger transboundary conflict, which for both security approaches is a core priority. Therefore, a narrow focus on **state-building**, which generally consists of reconstituting a core set of state institutions, a market economy, and basic rule-of-law provision, is central to these approaches (Richmond and Franks 2009). Definitions of peace are often framed within this narrow state-centric focus. For example, the annual Global Peace Index, published by the Institute for Economics & Peace, lists eight "pillars" of positive peace. These pillars include a well-functioning government, equitable distribution of resources, free flow of information, good relations with neighbors, high levels of human capital, acceptance of the rights of others, low levels of corruption, and a sound business environment. These pillars are heavily predicated on a very specific model of Westphalian sovereignty, which prioritizes the nation-state.

One driving argument for the emphasis on state-building is that post-conflict development requires a more stable environment for economic activity. Some research has shown that a combination of foreign aid and good governance by the post-conflict state leads to positive economic growth (Kang and Meernik 2005). However, uncertainty in the form of spoilers or even future elections, therefore, prevents the financial investment central to reconstituting the state (Flores and Nooruddin 2009). Thus, there is the ongoing question of what should be prioritized and when.

Peacebuilding, on the other hand, goes beyond the reconstitution of the state and attempts to create institutional frameworks and processes that address the roots of the conflict and establish processes for reconciliation with the intention of lessening the likelihood for conflict recurrence. Thus, peacebuilding focuses on questions of reconciliation and coexistence. This may include the establishment of truth commissions and the promotion of forgiveness between victims and perpetrators. As with state-building, peacebuilding in practice has been closely linked with the strengthening of state institutions.

By explicitly recognizing that long-term human insecurities persist after conflict has ended, the human security approach has challenged both the national security and global security approaches to look beyond what is seen as policies that are simply institutionally sufficient to stop ongoing violence and to shift toward questions related to how the newly constituted state actually serves its population. Because the outbreak of civil war is often connected to the underperformance of a country's government, the idea that post-conflict peacebuilding activities should seek to develop the mechanisms that address these pressing human needs has become a core global priority. Thus, there has been an ongoing shift to see post-conflict peacebuilding in the light of how governance structures function toward citizens, rather than simply whether those structures prevent future violent conflict.

What priority post-conflict peacebuilding should give to different types of human security issues, however, is an ongoing debate. It is important to distinguish between those policies that address a human security threat or problem but do not necessarily employ a human security *approach* and those that are designed to directly engage individuals' insecurities. While a strong state may be less likely to be violently challenged and, thus, presumably at a lesser risk for the recurrence of civil war, a post-conflict peace that only focuses on preventing violence (**negative peace**) and does not adequately provide social welfare, establish rights, and create post-conflict justice mechanisms (**positive peace**) can be a miserable environment to live in and, ultimately, undermine the prospects for durable human security.

Post-conflict activities have been given many different labels, and there is not always a clear distinction on which activities fall under which label and whether the use of a human security approach changes the fundamental nature of post-conflict policies. This has led some to ask whether human security is simply, as the parable goes, "new wine for old bottles" (Hanlon and Christie 2016). The breakdown of states puts tremendous strain on the international system and the states within it. This, in and of itself, may explain why both states and the global system as a whole have incentives to assist those states that are emerging from violent conflict. However, what form that assistance takes and which policies get prioritized over others will depend on the overall security perspectives of the actors crafting the policy. The motivation of states to address post-conflict stability issues in general does not mean that human security issues will also be addressed by default. Both the national and the global security approaches would prioritize activities that address what they see as the immediate threat to their own stability. This would mean that there would be a greater emphasis on state-building projects that emphasize stability, such as building up law enforcement and military institutions as well as a larger focus on political reform. While state-building may have a residual effect on overall human security, it is not clear that it would always be positive. In practice, this means that human insecurity would be addressed only to the extent that it assists in reconstituting the state.

The introduction of human security, therefore, has helped practitioners better evaluate these activities with humans as the referent. While state-building and peacebuilding may help reduce certain threats, their bias toward certain forms of institution building may insulate them from effectively addressing the residual human security needs of certain vulnerable populations after conflict. Therefore, we should ask ourselves whether the institutional focus of state-building and peacebuilding is sufficient to capture what Ryerson Christie refers to as the larger *ethos* of human security (Christie 2008). This is, in essence, the ongoing human security dilemma: whether the traditional approach to peace operations (typically conducted under the auspices of the UN), with its focus on building institutional capacity, is sufficient to address deeper-seated human security needs.

In analyzing peacebuilding and peacekeeping activities, therefore, it is important to recognize that these activities have justifications under both national and global security approaches. It is for this reason that discussions of peacebuilding are often focused on the role of intervenors. As was discussed in chapter 6, however, scholarship increasingly recognizes the critical role that local actors play in these processes. While there is a large body of research on why peacebuilding activities fail, scholars are now paying increasing attention to the factors that lead to successful post-conflict peacebuilding. As we have discussed in other chapters, there is an increased emphasis on the importance of local actors in these processes and the role that outside intervenors play in supporting these local initiatives.

BOX 7.1. "THINK ABOUT IT . . ."—EVERYDAY PEACE

When thinking about the concepts of peacebuilding and state-building we should try to understand them in relation to the types of community we ourselves would want to live in. Thus, it is sometimes useful to take mental stock of our own experiences and to consider how our own worldviews might influence the way we understand post-conflict peacebuilding.

Consider the following questions:

1. On a scale of 1–10 with 10 being "most peaceful," how would you describe the community that you live in? What contributes to that score?
2. What do you think contributes to peace and what contributes to violence in your own community? Would other people in your community agree with that assessment? Why or why not?
3. Examine table 7.1 and consider how each component is present in or absent from your community. Which activities would you give priority to? Why?
4. In what ways do you feel most vulnerable? What would have to happen for that vulnerability to lessen?
5. If you can, talk to others in your community about these questions. Are the answers the same or different? What surprised you most about their answers?

UNITED NATIONS PEACE OPERATIONS

The United Nations serves as the main global institution tasked with assisting post-conflict states through **peacekeeping** and peacebuilding activities. Regional organizations, such as the African Union, also play key roles in peacekeeping, but often in partnership with a United Nations mandate. Peacekeeping missions are authorized through UN Security Council Resolutions and are understood as the post-conflict "deployment of international personnel to help maintain peace and security" (Fortna 2008). Peacekeeping, however, was not a component of the UN as originally conceived, but has instead evolved as Member States saw a greater need for engagement in post-conflict peace. In its original conceptualization peacekeepers would begin a mission only once a cease-fire or peace accord had been signed and with the consent of the warring parties. The idea was that peacekeepers would serve as a neutral party observer between the previously warring factions. Nor has a human security component been a consistent component of peacekeeping mandates.

The first UN mission to deploy military forces with a purpose explicitly described as "peacekeeping" was the UN Emergency Force I (UNEF I) in 1956, which oversaw the withdrawal of British, French, and Israeli forces from the Sinai Peninsula and established a buffer zone between Israel and Egypt.[1] This original mission adhered to a strict global security framework and required consent from the sovereign authority of the territory. The **multidimensional peacekeeping** missions that have dominated post–Cold War peacekeeping look drastically different. Multidimensional peacekeeping missions seek to rebuild the state institutions that were destroyed during a civil conflict. The shift to these types of peacekeeping missions began in 1989 when the UN Transition Assistance Group (UNTAG) was sent to Namibia to aid in its decolonization from South Africa. The tasks for this operation were much wider than those of previous operations, and included a mandate to plan and supervise elections, oversee military disarmament and civilian policing, and assist in refugee return.[2] Since then, mandates for UN peace operations have more often reflected the multidimensional aspects of UNTAG than the simple monitoring mission of UNEF.

Today multidimensional peacekeeping has been institutionalized through a series of reorganizations and bureaucratic reforms. In 1992, the United Nations established the Department of Peacekeeping Operations to manage and report on ongoing peacekeeping missions. In 2000, the Brahimi Report provided the basis for many additional reforms, recommending that the UN develop permanent capacities to engage in comprehensive peacebuilding activities. This has resulted in a series of steps to better integrate all the different actors engaging in post-conflict peacebuilding. For instance, in 2005 the United Nations established the Peacebuilding Commission (PBC) in an attempt to better coordinate post-conflict peacebuilding activities among various UN agencies, donors, national governments, and international financial institutions. This shift toward multidimensional, comprehensive peace operations that integrates UN agencies, national governments, and various non-state actors has continued. In 2015 and 2017, both the General Assembly and the Security Council have approved joint resolutions that embrace a broader range of peacebuilding activities (United Nations General Assembly 2015, United Nations General Assembly 2017).

Throughout the 1990s, multidimensional peace operations were conducted in many locations, including El Salvador, Guatemala, Cambodia, East Timor, and Tajikistan. These types of operations were comprehensive and were designed to develop the institutions that would bring stability and presumably peace to the country. The series of UN operations in East Timor, for instance, included within their mandates multiple provisions meant to stabilize the newly independent state, including overseeing elections; managing the core administrative structures of the state and creating civil and social services; providing law enforcement and public security personnel; and assisting in maintaining the internal and external security of the country.[3] While many aspects of these missions have been considered successful, they have been criticized for giving too much of their attention to elite concerns and applying "cookie-cutter" models based on Western ideals of good governance and market economies, leaving many of the most vulnerable out of the decision-making processes.

Another important shift has been the timing in which a UN peace operation is called on to enter the field. *An Agenda for Peace* entertained the idea that the United Nations could take a more active role in preventing armed actors from carrying out violence with what was described as **peace enforcement**. A peace enforcement mission would differ from traditional peacekeeping and peacebuilding in that it would put a UN force onto the ground without full consent from all armed actors. While the idea of a rapid reaction force at the UN has been entertained since its founding, various institutional and political realities have prevented this from happening. As discussed in previous chapters, the Rwandan genocide and the Srebrenica massacre put pressure on the UN to better address atrocities before they happen. Consequently, the UN Security Council started to state explicitly that a peace operation should include protection of civilians within its mandate. The first to do so was Security Council Resolution 1270, which established the United Nations Mission in Sierra Leone (UNAMSIL) in 1999 to oversee the implementation of the recently signed Lomé Peace Agreement. The resolution invokes Chapter VII of the UN Charter to justify granting UN personnel the authority "to afford protection to civilians under imminent threat of physical violence" (United Nations Security Council 1999). Since then the protection of civilians has taken a more central role within UN mandates.

This growing call for civilian protection has meant that peacekeepers are more likely to stay in the field if a cease-fire or peace accord deteriorates. The UN Multidimensional Integrated Stabilization Mission in the Central African Republic (MINUSCA), for instance, lists the protection of civilians and the promotion and protection of human rights as its most immediate priority. Only after stating that priority does the mandate call for what would be considered more traditional peacekeeping and peacebuilding activities, such as security sector reform (SSR) and DDR. Thus, when the cease-fire that justified the mission began to unravel, UN forces remained in the country. Consequently, MINUSCA personnel have been the target of ongoing violence from militias and other actors. Additionally, the Central African Republic also shows the limitations of a deployment force to carry out its mandate successfully: even after the introduction of UN forces there have been multiple attacks on civilian populations and tens of thousands of new displacements. Similar dynamics exist in South Sudan.

Overall, scholarship on the effectiveness of United Nations peacekeeping has generally shown a positive effect. UN peacekeeping missions are associated with a higher likelihood that postwar peace will last (Fortna 2008) and an overall improvement in civilian protection when adequately deployed (Hultman, Kathman, and Shannon 2013). In addition, peacekeeping missions have also been shown to prevent armed conflict from spreading into neighboring states (Beardsley 2011). Additionally, United Nations peacekeeping operations have been able to undergo significant changes as the organization has "learned" how to carry out these activities. According to Howard, this learning has come from the UN's ability to gather information in the field to better understand the problems facing the post-conflict environment they are working in. This includes better coordination between agencies and partners on the ground and focusing on integrating itself into post-conflict settings in order to work with relevant parties and to develop policy from field operations rather than from UN headquarters (Howard 2008).

There have been a number of important ongoing critiques of UN peacebuilding activities. Paris argues that while the liberal market democracies that peace operations attempt to promote are not, in the long-term, a bad outcome, they are often implemented too quickly, leading to outcomes that ultimately undermine the peace (Paris 2004). Richmond and Franks contend that it is the liberal Westphalian models of peacekeeping overall that undermine their effectiveness (Richmond and Franks 2009). Autesserre (2014) highlights a number of practices that are inefficient, ineffective, or counterproductive. Practices such as deploying people who do not understand the language or local customs and placing intervenors in management positions over local staff can result in poor outcomes. Intervenors, no matter how well intentioned, will often favor thematic expertise rather than local custom and, due to the limited timeframes of their missions, may opt toward quicker, top-down, technical, and often quantifiable solutions. The overall inclination by peacekeepers to rely on their own expertise rather than working with local partners decreases the amount of local ownership that the population has toward any of these projects. For instance, who has the authority to make determinations of justice may differ from community to community. Thus, a justice system that is seen to have been imposed by an outside authority may be viewed as less legitimate to the local population than a justice system rooted in local traditions and customs—even if the two systems were to arrive at the exact same conclusions for any given case. These and other issues, such as using simplified explanations on the causes of the conflict, and collecting data on ongoing violence from other intervenors or local elites, can be counterproductive and even contribute to refueling violence.

Integrating Human Security into Post-Conflict Peace Operations

How extensive a UN mandate should be and how big an operation needs to be in order to meet that mandate has been an ongoing challenge for integrating human security practice into formal post-conflict peace operations. Chapter 4 of *Human Security Now* engages this challenge and highlights multiple clusters of what it considers to be human security activities that should happen during the post-conflict period (Commission on Human Security 2003, 60). These clusters include Public Safety; Humanitarian Relief; Rehabilitation and Restoration; Reconciliation and Coexistence; and Governance and Empowerment. Under each cluster is a set of practices that the report urges practitioners to engage in during post-conflict activities (see table 7.1). These approaches are not exclusive to each other and *Human Security Now* argues that, at least in theory, they should all be mutually pursued. The reality of limited resources, however, has meant that some activities have been prioritized over others.

Many of the practices *Human Security Now* recommends are identical to what earlier would have been considered state-building or peacebuilding practices. For example, under the Public Safety cluster, the first recommended practice is controlling armed elements, which includes enforcing cease-fires and disarming and demobilizing combatants. In addition, it recommends the building of national security institutions such as the police and military as well as the disarmament and dissolution of non-state armed actors. This fits in with the idea that it should be the state that has a monopoly on the means of violence. While these are accepted practices in state-building, they may not be necessary, and certainly are not sufficient, to guarantee human security. In fact, the state itself may be a key source for human insecurity; therefore, concentrating the means for violence in the state, without an appropriate check on its ability to apply that force, may lessen overall human security. The practice in the Public Safety cluster that is most closely tied to what would be considered human security is the protection of civilians. Nevertheless, even that adopts a state-centric approach, with the three main areas of focus consisting of establishing the rule of law and fighting criminal violence, clearing landmines, and collecting small arms. Each of these activities, however, assumes a benign state free from internal contention—a condition that is often not met in a post-conflict environment.

This question of whether human security is just simply new wine for old bottles is raised within other clusters as well. In the Reconciliation and Coexistence cluster, for example, most of the suggested practices in *Human*

Security Now fit within what would traditionally be considered peacebuilding practice. Suggested practices include such activities as setting up tribunals and truth commissions as well as establishing amnesties for lesser crimes. While the cluster also includes such activities as forgiveness promotion and reparation for victims, these ideas have long been a key component of peacebuilding practice.

Ultimately, we should ask how a focus on human security changes our perspectives on state-building and peacebuilding practice. For instance, it is not unreasonable to suggest that in order to establish durable human security, the use of violence should be limited to the state and that the state should use violence only in a way that conforms to universally accepted rights-based rule of law. The human security approach, therefore, helps identify the normative parameters by which institutional capacity building can take. This same question can be used when thinking about other areas of post-conflict peacebuilding by shifting our perspective from which outcomes lessen the prospects for violence to asking how different policy choices affect the short- and long-term human security of various groups.

Table 7.1 examines the main clusters and activities *Human Security Now* highlights as key to integrating human security into post-conflict peacebuilding. We present it as a helpful guide to critically think through the

Table 7.1. Timing and Responsibility of Core Peacebuilding Activities

Clusters and core activities identified in Human Security Now, *Chapter 4*	*When does it need to happen?*	*Primary responsibility lies with . . .*
Public Safety		
"Control Armed Elements • Enforce cease-fire • Disarm Combatants • Demobilize Combatants"	Immediately after agreement between combatants is reached.	International actors with cooperation from violent parties
"Protect Civilians • Establish law and order, fight criminal violence • Clear landmines • Collect small arms"	Early, but needs institutional structure in place. Internationals can provide, but not indefinitely.	International actors then transitioning to domestic government
"Build National Security Institutions • Police • Military • Integrate/dissolve non-state armed elements"	Early. Process is generally outlined in peace agreement.	Domestic government in cooperation with potential spoilers

(Continued)

Table 7.1. (Continued)

Clusters and core activities identified in Human Security Now, *Chapter 4*	When does it need to happen?	Primary responsibility lies with . . .
"Protect External Security • Combat illegal weapons and drug trade • Combat trafficking in people • Control borders"	Ongoing. Requires highly professionalized security institutions.	Domestic government with assistance from international actors and bordering states
Humanitarian Relief		
"Facilitate Return of Conflict Affected People • Internally displaced persons • Refugees"	Ongoing. Durable solution must lessen risk of future displacement and be agreed upon by displaced populations.	Domestic government with assistance from international actors (UNHCR)
"Assure Food Security • Meet nutrition standards • Launch food production"	Immediate and ongoing. Food aid to address acute hunger crisis. Long-term food production requires conditions for agriculture and markets.	Domestic government with assistance from international actors (WFP, FAO)
"Ensure Health Security • Provide access to basic health care • Prevent spread of infectious diseases • Provide trauma and mental health care"	Immediate and ongoing. Post-conflict populations have immediate medical needs. Long-term public health requires broad health infrastructure.	Domestic government with assistance from international actors (WHO)
"Establish Emergency Safety Net for People at Risk • Women (female-headed households); children (soldiers); elderly; indigenous people, missing people"	Immediate and long-term.	Domestic government with assistance from international actors
Rehabilitation and Reconstruction		
"Integrate Conflict-affected People • Internally displaced persons • Refugees • Armed combatants"	Long-term and requires both housing and employment solutions.	Domestic government with assistance from international actors
"Rehabilitate Infrastructure • Roads • Housing • Power • Transportation"	Long-term.	Domestic government with assistance from international actors
"Promote Social Protection • Employment • Food • Health • Education • Shelter"	Mostly long-term, but immediate if population is facing acute crisis.	Domestic government with assistance from international actors

Clusters and core activities identified in Human Security Now, Chapter 4	When does it need to happen?	Primary responsibility lies with . . .
"Dismantle War Economy • Fight criminal networks • Re-establish market economy • Provide micro-credit"	Immediate and ongoing. Requires progress in other areas (national security institutions, rehabilitate infrastructure, etc.).	Domestic government with assistance from international actors
Reconciliation and Coexistence		
"End Impunity • Set up tribunals • Involve traditional justice processes"	Early. Process is generally outlined in peace agreement.	Domestic government and/or international actors and/or local civil society
"Establish Truth • Set up truth commission • Promote forgiveness • Restore dignity of victims"	Early. Process is generally outlined in peace agreement.	Domestic government and/or international actors and/or local civil society
"Announce Amnesties • Immunity from prosecution for lesser crimes • Reparation for victims"	Early and ongoing. Process is generally outlined in peace agreement.	Domestic government and/or international actors and/or local civil society
"Promote Coexistence • Encourage community-based initiatives (long-term) • Rebuild social capital"	Ongoing.	Domestic government and local civil society
Governance and Empowerment		
"Establish Rule of Law Framework • Institute constitution, judicial system, legal reform • Adopt legislation • Promote human rights"	Early and ongoing. Process is generally outlined in peace agreement.	Domestic government with assistance from international actors
"Initiate Political Reform • Institutions • Democratic Processes"	Early and ongoing. Process is generally outlined in peace agreement.	Domestic government with assistance from international actors
"Strengthen Civil Society • Participation • Accountability • Capacity building"	Ongoing.	Local civil society with assistance from global civil society and legislation that assists these processes
"Promote Access to Information • Independent media • Transparency"	Ongoing.	Domestic government and local civil society

Adapted from Commission on Human Security 2003, 60.

questions raised in this chapter. While a full examination is too broad for the overall scope of this chapter, carefully working through each box helps conceptualize the core issues that this chapter addresses. The first column lists the main clusters and core activities identified in *Human Security Now* (Commission on Human Security 2003, 60). For each of the core activities within each cluster we examine two questions: when the core activity should take place and with whom the primary responsibility lies to implement the approach. We leave it to the reader to contemplate the overall impact that each of these activities would have on improving overall human security.

Working through the table, we can make several important observations regarding the integration of the human security approach into peacebuilding activities. First, international actors play an important role, but the ultimate success of their engagement will be based on local buy-in and the ability of the newly formed post-conflict government, in cooperation with international actors and local civil society, to implement these policies. Second, while most peacebuilding activities need to be started immediately after an agreed-upon peace, post-conflict structural conditions create obstacles. For instance, displaced populations will be unable to return if housing is unavailable or if the place they are returning to lacks basic security. Limited resources force governments and international actors to make choices on basic priorities. Should infrastructure spending prioritize those areas that support economic activity, such as paving a road to a factory, or should it prioritize a group that was victimized during the conflict, such as building housing so that a displaced population can return to its community? Finally, there is the question of how communities emerge from a period of long-term violence. In the next section, we will examine this in greater detail.

NO PEACE WITHOUT JUSTICE? TRANSITIONAL JUSTICE AND HUMAN SECURITY

Human security is grounded in the idea that both short-term and long-term security is best guaranteed when state institutions are designed to protect human rights and carry out the just application of the rule of law. Violent conflict breaks down the rule of law, leading to massive violations of people's rights and widespread atrocities. **Transitional justice**, therefore, is the process by which a state transitions from a period of conflict to a peaceful, democratic society with a focus on redress for victims. These processes are inherently entwined with the question of how atrocities carried out by regimes and other violent actors are punished and how victims receive justice. After civil wars victims and perpetrators must often live together in the same communities. If not remedied, long-standing resentment due to past injustices can form the narrative for future conflict.

Therefore, transitional justice is strongly linked to the question of reconciliation. **Reconciliation** is a process in which people work to overcome hatred and mistrust between groups to the extent that they can coexist with each other (Murithi 2009, Philpott 2012). How this actually occurs is complicated. According to Philpott, there are several important components of political reconciliation. First, reconciliation involves the state. The state has the capacity and the authority to carry out key acts of reconciliation, including trying and imprisoning war criminals, disbursing reparations to victims, and issuing formal apologies. While civil society and other non-state actors play important roles in the reconciliation process, the state is seen as key. Thus, for post-conflict reconciliation to succeed the state must adopt just institutions. Second, reconciliation includes punishment. Punishment may be reduced or creatively applied, but an important component of any justice process is that there is an appropriate response to wrongdoing. Third, reconciliation involves the personal participation of victims, perpetrators, and other members of the community. This participation is seen as a key first step to healing the wounds caused by violent conflict. Fourth, a reconciliation process must address what is known as "right relationship," that is, how the aggrieved parties reconcile enough between each other that they can live between each other in the day to day. Finally, reconciliation involves the idea that it returns to a previous condition. Of course, this is problematic in that pre-conflict states are usually built on unjust social structures. Thus, reconciliation is built on an ideal of justice and it leads us to wonder: if these ideals were unachievable in the past, how do they become achievable in the future?

Many cultures already have processes by which certain components of reconciliation take place. In post-genocide Rwanda, for example, a traditional form of justice called *gacaca* was used in some cases. This community-based form of justice requires the perpetrators to acknowledge their misdeeds, with the victims then being involved in determining how reparations should be made and how to best reintegrate the perpetrators back into the community. A similar process called *ubuntu* occurred in South Africa after apartheid, in which there was a strong push for victims to forgive. While these processes are aimed at helping communities find both the forgiveness and the common ground needed to move forward, some have argued that victims are often pressured to declare forgiveness and leave perpetrators with a false sense of absolution.

Accompanying these methods are more formal processes, such as **truth and reconciliation commissions (TRCs)**, the purpose of which is to correctly reveal the truth of what exactly happened during a conflict or system of injustice. To get to this truth, people are given immunity or reduced sentences to testify about their role in the conflict. When the commission finishes its work, it will typically produce a report detailing its findings. The use of such commissions is widespread, and TRCs have occurred in such places as Guatemala, South Africa, Chile, Argentina, and East Timor.

Another key concern in transitional justice processes is the question of reparations for victims. For those who have been displaced or have lost property, this includes creating the conditions for which they can return to their communities and be compensated for lost property. How to compensate victims who have lost loved ones or been permanently disabled due to the conflict may be even more problematic. Restitution also raises the question of who constitutes a victim. Does someone who was displaced due to deteriorating economic conditions caused by the conflict garner the same rights to compensation as someone who was displaced due to direct violence by one of the armed actors? What about those who chose to stay in their communities, often surviving through worse conditions than the displaced who were able to flee? Even when these definitional issues can be appropriately clarified, there remains the question of who has the responsibility to compensate. Post-conflict states are often strapped for resources and the pledges for compensation may never be fulfilled. International actors may be able to provide immediate aid, but such outside assistance could leave some feeling that those responsible were not appropriately held accountable.

One important criticism of truth and reconciliation processes is that, when used, perpetrators of war crimes can remain unpunished. Some will argue that this is an unfortunate consequence for achieving peace, whereas others will counter that this ignores the basic rights of victims. Post-conflict justice has always faced the challenge of determining what should be the proper balance between amnesty, reconciliation, and criminal prosecution against those who committed the worst acts. In order for justice to be properly administered, all parties should be in general agreement that the process is fair and impartial. Not only should victims have the right to receive justice for acts committed against them, but defendants should also have the right to defend themselves and have access to legal counsel during any proceedings. However, there are a number of obstacles to establishing fair and impartial justice mechanisms. In criminal law, if an action is not specifically recognized as a crime, it cannot be prosecuted. After conflict, there simply may not be specific enough domestic or international legal statutes which define the acts that were carried out by violent actors during conflict as criminal. This combination of weak judicial institutions and lack of political will has meant that victims of political violence have historically had very little legal recourse for seeking justice when state institutions are unable or choose not to act. These limitations have led many human rights and legal advocates to work to create more robust international law dedicated to prosecuting war crimes and crimes against humanity.

The idea that war crimes and crimes against humanity could be punishable under international law is not new. Following the end of World War I, the acts of violence carried out by Turkey against its Armenian population sparked the question of whether the 1907 Hague Convention extended to states that carried out unconscionable acts against their own citizens (Bassiouni 2011). As discussed in previous chapters, numerous treaties were ratified throughout the twentieth century to better codify what constitutes violations of international humanitarian law; however, this expansion was not necessarily accompanied by mechanisms through which those crimes could be easily prosecuted. If prosecutions were to happen, they were to happen via domestic judicial systems. In fact, one of the first actions taken by the UN General Assembly was to encourage Member States to arrest war criminals who had fled and to send them back to their respective countries in order to be tried.

A lack of an enforcement mechanism fostered a belief by combatants that war crimes would ultimately go unpunished, therefore removing any checks against their committing egregious acts. This problem of impunity has led to greater efforts to give international criminal jurisdiction to outside bodies. This shift toward international institutions is reflected in the reaction to the 1999 Lomé Peace Agreement, intended to bring the brutal civil war in Sierra Leone to a close. To convince guerrilla fighters to lay down their arms, the accord offered blanket amnesty to all rebel combatants. At the time, the argument for offering said amnesty was that it was the only condition under which rebel fighters would lay down their arms. Considering the brutality of the Sierra Leone Civil War (in 1999 Sierra Leone was ranked last in the world in average years of expected disability-free life at only 29.5 years), such an assumption may not appear unreasonable if it could guarantee that fighting would stop. This decision, however, came under intense scrutiny from human rights organizations, and in 2000 the United Nations Security Council voted, with the support of the Sierra Leone government, to create a court, the Special Court for Sierra Leone, that would have jurisdiction to try those accused of violating international humanitarian law. In the end, the court convicted members of the Civil Defense Forces (CDF), the Revolutionary United Front (RUF), and the Armed Forces Revolutionary Council (AFRC), as well as Charles Taylor, the former president of Liberia, for his support of the RUF. Similar international tribunals have been established in Rwanda, the former Yugoslavia, and Cambodia.

To try to help close this gap between international humanitarian law and domestic courts' inability to prosecute violators of said law, the **International Criminal Court (ICC)** was created as a permanent international body, based in The Hague, the Netherlands, with the authority to prosecute individuals (including heads of state) who are responsible for genocide, crimes against humanity, and war crimes. The ICC was established by the Rome Statute in

1998 and entered into force in July 2002. Currently, there are 124 state parties. By creating a permanent institution, the need to create ad hoc tribunals, as was done in the former Yugoslavia, Sierra Leone, and Cambodia, was eliminated. In addition, a permanent court would help more clearly codify what constituted prosecutable crimes. Importantly, the Rome Statute continues to give deference to the sovereign authority of a state's domestic courts, and takes cases only when a state's domestic judicial systems are unable or unwilling to do so, making it a court of last resort. Additionally, only crimes that have been committed on the territory of a state party or by an individual who is a citizen of a state party are subject to the ICC's jurisdiction. There are two exceptions to this: a state that is not party to the Rome Statute can accept the jurisdiction of the ICC or the alleged crimes can be referred to the ICC through a resolution of the UN Security Council.

While the ICC is a tremendous leap forward in international jurisprudence, it has faced a number of important criticisms. One criticism is its low rate of convictions. As of November 2017, there have only been four individuals found guilty. In addition, many other situations investigated by the court have not led to any indictment and were eventually dropped. A major obstacle for prosecutors is gathering the evidence sufficient to convict. It is not enough to know that atrocities happened, but conviction requires evidence against a specific individual giving an order or participating in an act. Another key criticism is the fact that there has yet to be a non-African case brought to trial.[4] This and the fact that the ICC has issued indictments for sitting heads of state in Sudan and Kenya have led some African countries to advocate for a collective withdrawal of the African Union from the body. This advocacy for withdrawal is not shared by all AU member states—Nigeria, Senegal, Burkina Faso, Cote d'Ivoire, and others have forcibly rejected such a move. In addition, after South Africa's president, Jacob Zuma, declared his intention to withdraw from the ICC, a South African court ruled that a withdrawal without parliament's approval was unconstitutional, thus revoking its announcement.

Another issue is the role of victims and how the ICC is perceived by victims. The ICC tries to involve victims at multiple stages in the proceedings, including allowing them, through their legal representatives, to question defense witnesses, challenge evidence, and serve as witnesses. In addition, if there is a conviction, victims can take part in the reparations proceedings (Turner 2017). The ICC has also established a Trust Fund for Victims, which is to support and implement programs designed to specifically address the harm caused by those convicted. Still, ICC proceedings are also notoriously slow and can take years to come to a close. Germain Katanga, for instance, spent almost seven years in detention before he was found guilty for crimes against humanity. Such lengthy trials deprive victims the closure they may be seeking. Some have complained that they must continue to survive in extremely depraved conditions, while those that contributed to those conditions exist in relative comfort while they await their trial. In fact, Bosco Ntaganda, the Congolese warlord, voluntarily turned himself in, determining, probably correctly, that a prison cell in The Hague would be more comfortable and safer than the forests of eastern Congo.

Does the existence of an international body with the authority to prosecute war crimes help lessen these crimes from occurring? If so, what impact does this have on human security? Research on this question is inconclusive, showing both positive and negative effects. Because the ICC is a court of last resort, the existence of such an outside body may incentivize states to improve their own judicial institutions in order to carry out said prosecutions on their own and avoid ICC interference. For instance, in June 2015 the Central African Republic passed a law creating the Special Criminal Court which would oversee, in cooperation with international judges and prosecutors, the prosecution of those who have committed war crimes. Despite the creation of the court, it has yet to hear a case. Simmons and Danner suggest that many countries with atrocious human rights records were willing to join the ICC as a signal to their domestic audiences that they were willing to play by the rules (Simmons and Danner 2010). Such capacity building by individual states could serve as a check on ongoing and future atrocities. However, little evidence exists that would suggest the ICC itself has a deterrent effect against future atrocities. In addition, Prorok (2017) finds that ICC involvement while a conflict is ongoing decreases the chance for peace and, in fact, prolongs conflict.

How to appropriately approach questions of transitional justice following conflict remains a difficult question to answer. The human security approach pushes us to think about how the newly constituted state addresses the question of mass atrocity committed during warfare. While it is possible to hold some individuals accountable for the most egregious atrocities, there will remain many others who participate in atrocities at some level but remain within their communities. How communities reconcile and move beyond these traumas remains an important part of the human security approach. Recognizing the deep hurts that conflict imposes on the populations that experience it, as well as the difficulty of adequately redressing these hurts, creates the conditions in which human security needs can be addressed.

REBUILDING SECURITY IN THE DEMOCRATIC REPUBLIC OF THE CONGO

To better highlight the many challenges the human security approach faces during peacebuilding and transitional justice, we will examine efforts to rebuild in the aftermath of protracted conflict in the Democratic Republic of the Congo. The dynamics of the conflict in DRC are complex. The DRC gained independence from Belgium on June 30, 1960, and almost immediately faced a political crisis, as early efforts to democratize devolved into ethnic competition. In 1964, a coup d'état brought Mobutu Sese Seko and his Popular Revolutionary Movement (MPR) to power. (In 1971, Mobutu changed the state's name from Congo to Zaire. It was changed to the Democratic Republic of the Congo in 1997 after Mobutu was overthrown.) While rhetorically Mobutu framed his one-party rule as the way to unify the country under the guise of nationalism, his method of rule had clear ethnic and regional biases and was more reflective of a mafia-style form of government than a functioning nation-state. Thus, when processes toward constitutional reform meant to pave the way for greater democratization began in April 1990, the underlying tensions brought about by Mobutu's rule exploded.

Multiple rebellions broke out across the territory and between ethnic groups. These conflicts were exacerbated by the aftermath of the Rwandan genocide in 1994, in which many Hutus who had participated in the genocide fled to refugee camps in eastern Zaire. In October 1996, an alliance between Uganda, Rwanda, and Burundi, as well as a group of Zairean dissidents, overthrew Mobutu under the pretense that they were protecting themselves from cross-border raids being carried out by Hutu extremists being sheltered in refugee camps in Zaire. The overthrow of Mobutu put Laurent-Désiré Kabila, a former guerrilla chief during the post-independence period, into power. Kabila quickly sought to consolidate his control over the territory. Meanwhile, other African powers, including Angola, Namibia, Zimbabwe, Uganda, and Rwanda, vied for influence, eventually leading to the second phase of the conflict, which began in 1998 and lasted through the Lusaka Ceasefire Agreement of July 1999 until the war's official end in July 2003 with the establishment of a transitional government. The consequences of this conflict have devastated the DRC, particularly in its eastern provinces, and violence and instability continued well past the war's formal end. Wartime casualties are difficult to measure, so estimates range from one million to more than five million deaths resulting from direct and indirect violence (Human Security Report Project 2011, International Rescue Committee 2007).[5]

The United Nations has played an ongoing role in the conflict. Beginning in 1996 the UN Security Council passed a series of resolutions calling on parties to cease hostilities and giving authorization for Member States to provide troops for a humanitarian force that would facilitate the return of humanitarian organizations into eastern Zaire (United Nations Security Council 1996). However, it wasn't until the Lusaka Ceasefire Agreement between the DRC and Angola, Namibia, Zimbabwe, Uganda, and Rwanda that a full UN peace operation was implemented. This mission, the United Nations Organization Mission in the Democratic Republic of the Congo

(MONUC), was established under Security Council Resolution 1279 and had fairly straightforward security goals: to oversee the cease-fire agreement and to provide information on security conditions throughout the country. Later the Security Council expanded MONUC's mission to supervise the country's democratic elections in 2006.

From the beginning MONUC faced a number of challenges—the first being the DRC's sheer size. DRC covers 905,000 square miles of territory, making it the second-largest state in Africa. In addition, the periods of conflict stalled economic development in the resource-rich state, and 77 percent of its population lives on less than $1.90 a day. A 2010 DRC government report on the prospects for achieving the Millennium Development Goals stated that the country had "no chance" of reaching the target for six goals by 2015 and only a "limited chance" of reaching the target for the remaining goals (Trefon 2011). Despite the cease-fire and the presence of a UN mission, civilians in DRC continued to experience massive violations of their human rights. The Rwandan army remained in DRC's eastern territory with the stated intention of defeating the Hutu militia, although multiple human rights organizations documented their involvement in human rights violations, including massacres of and sexual violence against civilians, by both Rwandan soldiers and the rebel groups the army was supporting. The amount of reported conflict-related sexual violence is staggering: while estimates of gender-based violence are also difficult to obtain, a 2011 study estimated that at one point 48 women per hour were raped (Peterman, Palermo, and Bredenkamp 2011). Responding to violence on such a large scale requires significant resources. Not only did MONUC lack the resources or the mandate to effectively address the ongoing violence, it had difficulty effectively working with the local populations it was trying to assist (Autesserre 2014). The ineffectiveness of these initial efforts by the United Nations to engage in peacebuilding, plus the UN's experience in other peacekeeping operations, led to a more extensive mandate when it authorized a reformed peace operation, United Nations Organization Stabilization Mission in the Democratic Republic of the Congo (MONUSCO), in May 2010.

This new mandate came after the March 23, 2009, agreement between the DRC government and one of the main rebel groups—the National Congress for the Defense of the People (CNDP)—and expanded the scope of the UN mission to protect civilians, humanitarian personnel, and human rights defenders facing imminent attack. In addition, it gave the mission the authorization to use "all necessary means" to carry out its mandate. MONUSCO also took more active measures to address the roots of the conflict, which stemmed from intercommunal rivalries being played out on a national stage. In 2012, for instance, MONUSCO participated with local and national leaders in dialogues between the Baruliro and Burundi communities. Despite the more extensive mandate, the peace operation still struggles to protect civilians. Civilian populations continue to be targeted and displaced: the Internal Displacement Monitoring Center estimates that more than two million people are currently internally displaced due to violence. When MONUSCO was unable to prevent the M23 guerrilla group from forcibly taking Goma in November 2012, the UNSC authorized a first-of-its-kind Force Intervention Brigade (FIB), which was then instrumental in defeating M23 and retaking the city (United Nations Security Council 2013).

Considering the extensive violations of human rights in DRC, justice has been hard to achieve. Multiple efforts have tried to bring about transitional justice, including a Truth and Reconciliation Commission that was completed in 2008 but lacked any substantial findings (Mould 2011). However, there has been some progress in empowering DRC's courts to investigate and try international crimes. The 2013 Law on the Organization, Functioning and Jurisdiction of the Courts gave civilian courts exclusive jurisdiction over international crimes, and in 2015 new laws were passed that put international crimes that would be covered under the Rome Statutes into the civilian Criminal Code (Thomson and Kihika 2017). In addition, international actors have been continually engaged in justice issues in DRC. Transnational human rights organizations, working with local civil society, have been important actors in documenting and drawing attention to crimes being committed and establishing mobile courts to help bring transitional justice mechanisms to more remote areas. In addition, the ICC has been actively engaged in DRC, eventually leading to the convictions of Thomas Lubanga Dyilo (for his involvement in enlisting and conscripting child soldiers) and Germain Katanga (for murder and attacking a civilian population).

DRC provides a sobering example of the difficulties that face peace operations. While the UN has been successful in helping consolidate post-conflict peace in a number of places, the brutality and the complexity of the conflict in DRC continue to frustrate both local and international peacemakers. UN peace operations have tried to provide the environment for peace to consolidate, but the complexity of the conflict, poor execution, and limited resources have stymied efforts to foster human security and overall stability.

CONCLUSION

This chapter has examined the peacebuilding processes that occur post-conflict. During this period, human security threats continue to persist as people try to regain normalcy and seek justice for atrocities perpetrated during armed conflict. Human security threats persist on two levels: First, the immediate and acute threats that arise from the actions of violent individuals and groups, whether they have an interest in attempting to reignite the conflict, new violent political actors seeking to take advantage of the uncertainty of the new environment, or criminal elements. Second, the long-lasting threats that result from the damage caused by the conflict. Without adequately addressing these long-lasting threats and focusing on society's long-term durable human security, any peace will have little positive impact on these vulnerable populations.

As the outset of this chapter discusses, initial international efforts to address post-conflict environments only dealt with human security issues as a side effect of more straightforward national and global security goals. Changes brought about by the end of the Cold War and by pressure from human rights advocates began to bring more focused attention to post-conflict peacebuilding approaches that focused on protecting civilian populations and addressing transitional justice concerns. While there have been failures in these attempts, these processes are fairly recent in terms of international practice, and there has been a steep learning curve. Today, we see greater attention to the role that civil society can play as well as local initiatives and more creative forms of justice. To the extent that peacebuilding efforts lay the foundation for sustainable peace, they contribute to durable human security, to which we now turn in the chapters in section III.

Discussion Questions

1. What are the advantages of the traditional state and global security approaches to peacebuilding? What is left out of these approaches?
2. How do the traditional and multidimensional approaches to peacekeeping differ? What are the advantages of and drawbacks to each approach?
3. What are the obstacles to effective long-term peace if those who were responsible for conducting atrocities are not held responsible for their crimes?
4. Why is it important to have local participation and support for peacebuilding efforts, including transitional justice processes? What are the implications of not having this participation and support?

NOTES

1. Two previous UN missions—the United Nations Truce Supervision Organization (UNTSO) of 1948 and the United Nations Military Observer Group in India and Pakistan (UNMOGIP) of 1949, both of which remain ongoing—are retrospectively considered peacekeeping operations.

2. The idea that UN missions should include a full spectrum of responses better designed to address the specific context of the conflict has led to greater use of the term "peace operations" to replace "peacekeeping" and "peacebuilding."

3. There were three successive peacekeeping missions in East Timor: United Nations Mission in East Timor (UNAMET) as a response to violence that followed its pro-independence vote in 1999, which was quickly proceeded by the United Nations Transitional Administration in East Timor (UNTAET), which oversaw the transition to independence from Indonesia, followed by the United Nations Mission of Support in East Timor (UNMISET), which oversaw the post-independence period up to 2005.

4. There have been preliminary examinations in Afghanistan, Colombia, UK nationals in Iraq, Palestine and Ukraine; and investigations in Georgia.

5. The International Rescue Committee estimates that 5.4 million people were killed, either directly or indirectly, due to the conflict. However, the Human Security Report Project at Simon Fraser University, using a different methodology, places that figure between one and two million.

FURTHER READING AND WEB RESOURCES

Global Peace Index, Vision of Humanity: http://visionofhumanity.org
International Criminal Court website: www.icc-cpi.int/Pages/Main.aspx
Milli Lake. "Ending Impunity for Sexual and Gender-Based Crimes: The International Criminal Court and Complementarity in the Democratic Republic of Congo." *African Conflict & Peacebuilding Review* 4, no. 1 (2014): 1–32.
United Nations General Assembly. *Report of the Panel on United Nations Peace Operations* (Brahimi Report). 2000. http://www.un.org/en/events/pastevents/brahimi_report.shtml
United Nations Peacekeeping website: www.un.org/en/peacekeeping/

For Deeper Discussion

Daniel Philpott. *Just and Unjust Peace: An Ethic of Political Reconciliation.* New York: Oxford University Press, 2012.
John Paul Lederach. *Building Peace: Sustainable Reconciliation in Divided Societies.* Washington, DC: United States Institute of Peace, 1997.
Oliver P. Richmond and Jason Franks. *Liberal Peace Transitions: Between Statebuilding and Peacebuilding.* Edinburgh: Edinburgh University Press, 2009.
Roland Paris. *At War's End: Building Peace after Civil Conflict.* Cambridge: Cambridge University Press, 2004.
Séverine Autesserre. *Peaceland: Conflict Resolution and the Everyday Politics of International Intervention.* New York: Columbia University Press, 2014.

REFERENCES

Autesserre, Séverine. *Peaceland: Conflict Resolution and the Everyday Politics of International Intervention.* New York: Columbia University Press, 2014.
Bassiouni, Cherif M. *Crimes against Humanity: Historical Evolution and Contemporary Application.* Cambridge: Cambridge University Press, 2011.

Beardsley, Kyle. "Peacekeeping and the Contagion of Armed Conflict." *The Journal of Politics* 73, no. 4 (2011): 1051–64.

Blattman, Christopher, and Jeannie Annan. "The Consequences of Child Soldiering." *The Review of Economics and Statistics* 92, no. 4 (2010): 882–98.

Boutros-Ghali, Boutros. *An Agenda for Peace: Preventive Diplomacy, Peacemaking and Peacekeeping*. New York: United Nations, 1992.

Christie, Ryerson. "The Human Security Dilemma." In *Environmental Change and Human Security: Recognizing and Acting on Hazard Impacts*, by P. H. Liotta, David A. Mouat, William G. Kepner, and Judith M. Lancaster, 253–69. Dordrecht: Springer, 2008.

Commission on Human Security. *Human Security Now*. New York: United Nations, 2003.

Flores, Thomas Edward, and Irfan Nooruddin. "Democracy under the Gun: Understanding Postconflict Economic Recovery." *Journal of Conflict Resolution* 53, no. 1 (2009): 3–29.

Fortna, Virginia Page. *Does Peacekeeping Work? Shaping Belligerents' Choices after Civil War*. Princeton, NJ: Princeton University Press, 2008.

Ghobarah, Hazem Adam, Paul Huth, and Bruce Russett. "Civil Wars Kill and Maim People—Long after the Shooting Stops." *American Political Science Review* 97, no. 2 (2003): 189–202.

Hanlon, Robert, and Kenneth Christie. *Freedom from Fear, Freedom from Want: An Introduction to Human Security*. Toronto: Toronto University Press, 2016.

Howard, Lisa Morjé. *UN Peacekeeping in Civil Wars*. Cambridge: Cambridge University Press, 2008.

Hultman, Lisa, Jacob Kathman, and Megan Shannon. "United Nations Peacekeeping and Civilian Protection in Civil War." *American Journal of Political Science* 57, no. 4 (2013): 875–91.

Human Security Report Project. *Human Security Report 2009/2010: The Causes of Peace and the Shrinking Costs of War*. Simon Fraser University, Oxford: Oxford University Press, 2011.

International Rescue Committee. *Mortality in the Democratic Republic of Congo: An ongoing Crisis*. New York: International Rescue Committee, 2007.

Kang, Seonjou, and James Meernik. "Civil War Destruction and the Prospects for Economic Growth." *Journal of Politics* 67, no. 1 (2005): 88–109.

Lai, Brian, and Clayton Thyne. "The Effect of Civil War on Education, 1980–97." *Journal of Peace Research* 44, no. 3 (2007): 277–92.

Mould, Verity. "State Failure and Civil Society Potential: Reconciliation in the Democratic Republic of Congo." *Journal of Conflict Transformation & Security* 1, no. 2 (2011): 73–82.

Murithi, Timothy. *The Ethics of Peacebuilding*. Edinburgh: Edinburgh University Press, 2009.

Paris, Roland. *At War's End: Building Peace after Civil Conflict*. Cambridge: Cambridge University Press, 2004.

Peterman, Amber, Tia Palermo, and Caryn Bredenkamp. "Estimates and Determinants of Sexual Violence against Women in the Democratic Republic of Congo." *American Journal of Public Health* 101, no. 6 (2011): 1060–67.

Philpott, Daniel. *Just and Unjust Peace: An Ethic of Political Reconciliation.* New York: Oxford University Press, 2012.

Prorok, Alyssa K. "The (In)compatibility of Peace and Justice? The International Criminal Court and Civil Conflict Termination." *International Organization* 71, no. 2 (2017): 212–43.

Quinn, Michael T., T. David Mason, and Mehmet Gurses. "Sustaining Peace: Determinants of Civil War Recurrence." *International Interactions* 33, no. 2 (2007): 167–93.

Richmond, Oliver P., and Jason Franks. *Liberal Peace Transitions: Between State-building and Peacebuilding.* Edinburgh: Edinburgh University Press, 2009.

Shemyakina, Olga. "The Effect of Armed Conflict on Accumulation of Schooling: Results from Tajikistan." *Journal of Development Economics* 95, no. 2 (2011): 186–200.

Simmons, Beth A., and Allison Danner. "Credible Commitments and the International Criminal Court." *International Organization* 64, no. 2 (2010): 225–56.

Smit, Anneke. *The Property Rights of Refugees and Internally Displaced Person: Beyond Restitution.* London: Routledge, 2012.

Thomson, Aileen, and Kasandre Sarah Kihika. *Victims Fighting Impunity: Transitional Justice in the African Great Lakes Region.* New York: International Center for Transitional Justice, 2017.

Trefon, Theodore. *Congo Masquerade: The Political Culture of Aid Inefficiency and Reform Failure.* London: Zed Books, 2011.

Turner, Jenia Iontcheva. "Defense Perspectives on Fairness and Efficiency at the International Criminal Court." In *Oxford Handbook on International Criminal Law,* by Kevin Jon Heller. Oxford: Oxford University Press, 2017.

United Nations General Assembly. "Follow-up to the Outcome of the Millennium Summit." *A/69/968-S/2015/490.* New York, June 30, 2015.

United Nations General Assembly. "Report of the Peacebuilding Commission." *A/17/768-S/2017/76.* New York, January 27, 2017.

United Nations Security Council. "Resolution 1080 (1996)." *S/RES/1080.* New York, November 15, 1996.

United Nations Security Council. "Resolution 1270 (1999)." *S/RES/1270.* New York, October 22, 1999.

United Nations Security Council. "Resolution 2098 (2013)." *S/RES/2098 (2013).* New York, March 28, 2013.

Zelizer, Craig, and Valerie Oliphant. "Introduction to Integrated Peacebuilding." In *Integrative Peacebuilding: Innovative Approaches to Transforming Conflict,* by Craig Zelizer, 3–30. Boulder, CO: Westview Press, 2013.

Section III

DURABLE HUMAN SECURITY

Chapter 8

The Cycle of Security: From Human Security in Armed Conflict to Durable Human Security

Learning Objectives

This chapter will enable readers to:

1. Identify human security concerns common to armed conflict and peacetime.
2. Connect the notions of freedom from fear and freedom from want with the issues discussed in sections II and III.

This short transitional chapter bridges the concepts presented in sections II and III to underscore the commonalities in human security and insecurity in armed conflict and in times of relative peace. The human security approach is often discussed in terms of "freedom from fear" and "freedom from want," with some states and organizations choosing to prioritize one or the other in keeping with national or organizational policy priorities. Ultimately, human insecurity in armed conflict and long-term insecurity are mutually reinforcing, just as freedom from fear and freedom from want are similarly reinforcing. When the conditions for human security exist in peacetime, the risk of violent conflict is diminished; when human security is taken into consideration in the transition from war to peace, peace is more sustainable. The reverse is also true. The cycle of security that connects human security in armed conflict to durable human security is the focus of this brief chapter. The first section of this chapter looks at human security in armed conflict and the notion of freedom from fear, while the second section examines durable human security and the notion of freedom from want. The third and final section offers an overview of the structure of section III.

HUMAN SECURITY IN ARMED CONFLICT AND
FREEDOM FROM FEAR

Threats related to human security in armed conflict are similar to threats that have traditionally been central to the state and global security approaches. Armed conflict, violence committed by non-state armed actors, transnational terrorism, the proliferation of weapons from small arms to nuclear arsenals, and mass displacement and migration all present threats to the physical safety of individuals and communities. These same threats affect the stability and security of states and—if sufficiently widespread—the global system. The narrow view of human security emphasizes the importance of freedom from fear. Preventing violence, resolving conflicts through peaceful means, rebuilding society and promoting reconciliation after the end of armed hostilities, protecting individuals from terrorist attacks, decreasing the availability of weapons of mass destruction and the flow of small arms to conflict zones, and protecting vulnerable populations from harm contribute to freedom from fear of direct violence or imminent physical harm.

Recall the 1994 Human Development Report's definition of human security as protection from both sudden and chronic threats, introduced in section I (United Nations Development Programme 1994, 3). Human security in armed conflict is concerned most immediately with sudden threats and, as the chapters in section II discuss, the breakdown of norms and institutions to such an extent that direct physical violence occurs. Establishing and protecting freedom from fear can resemble efforts to protect the state, which makes the narrow view of human security appear less daunting to scholars, practitioners, and policymakers than the wider view of human security. We cannot expect to achieve human security if the state is fragile, failing, or embroiled in armed conflict. In this respect, the human security and state security approaches are synchronous: when the state is secure it is better able to maintain institutions and promote or comply with norms that make the protection of individuals possible.

When positive societal norms and functional institutions that foster good governance are eroded and weakened, the protections from harm that individuals and communities enjoy in relative peacetime are also weakened or eliminated. For marginalized and vulnerable communities who do not enjoy the full protection of norms and institutions even in relative peacetime, insecurity is likely to worsen in armed conflict, especially if these individuals and communities are directly targeted for violence or perceived as threats to the state. Unlike efforts to protect state security, human security practice places individuals and communities at the center of all decisions and actions. In chapter 1 we discussed the internment of Japanese-Americans during World War II as a response to the Japanese attack on the U.S. naval base at Pearl Harbor and the fear among policymakers that individuals of Japanese descent may pose a security risk to the state. In cases like this one, human security and state security are in direct conflict and efforts to secure the state result in erosion of human rights, freedoms, and security. When the state perceives, anticipates, or experiences threats to its stability, it can respond in ways that degrade human security.

While the narrow view of human security is conceptually cleaner and more recognizable from the traditional security perspectives, it has still encountered resistance. The perception that human security is synonymous with the doctrine of Responsibility to Protect and military intervention in states' domestic affairs has led to some criticism of the human security approach as a way to impose Western values on non-Western states. As discussed in chapter 5, UN General Assembly Resolution 66/290, in response to critiques from state policymakers, practitioners, advocates, and scholars concerned with the erosion of the principle of non-intervention and the use of military means to respond to civil and human rights concerns, articulates the synchronous nature of human security and state security, noting that human security is distinct from responsibility to protect and does not advocate for the use of force (United Nations General Assembly 2012, 2). Human security in armed conflict and protection of freedom from fear must incorporate the perspectives, voices, and resources of human security actors at all levels, from local to global. It is important to note that bolstering human security in conflict zones does not need to involve military means, although exercising R2P through the UN Security Council may use military force as a last resort in situations involving grave and widespread threats to civilian populations.

The wider approach to human security, that which includes the well-being of individuals in armed conflict and in daily life outside of conflict zones, takes the cyclical nature of security into account. As the chapters in section III discuss, there are connections between the enjoyment of durable human security and the overall stability of states and the international system. Better protection of overall well-being, freedoms, rights, and opportunities through efforts at the local, state, and international levels may decrease the risk of armed conflict and the human insecurity that accompanies the breakdown of norms and institutions in conflict zones. We now turn briefly to this notion.

BOX 8.1. "THINK ABOUT IT . . ."—TRAFFICKING IN PERSONS

The United Nations Convention against Transnational Organized Crime and the Protocols Thereto defines trafficking in persons as

> the recruitment, transportation, transfer, harbouring or receipt of persons, by means of the threat or use of force or other forms of coercion, of

abduction, of fraud, of deception, of the abuse of power or of a position of vulnerability or of the giving or receiving of payments or benefits to achieve the consent of a person having control over another person, for the purpose of exploitation. Exploitation shall include, at a minimum, the exploitation of the prostitution of others or other forms of sexual exploitation, forced labour or services, slavery or practices similar to slavery, servitude or the removal of organs. (United Nations Office on Drugs and Crime 2004, 42)

Trafficking in persons is a violation of the human rights of victims and an extreme threat to their physical security and well-being.

People of all ages and genders can become vulnerable to trafficking. Economic insecurity may lead individuals to pursue educational and job opportunities abroad, responding to misleading advertisements or offers that place them in the hands of traffickers rather than with legitimate academic institutions or businesses. Mass migration and refugee flows often involve large numbers of unaccompanied children, women traveling with children, and other individuals desperately seeking safe passage out of situations of acute insecurity; these individuals are vulnerable to exploitation and trafficking. Other threats to durable human security or conflict-related insecurity may place individuals in a position of vulnerability through which they are more likely to fall victim to the many forms of trafficking in persons.

Trafficking in persons is a transnational criminal practice that exists in times of relative peace, in and around zones of armed conflict, and in wealthy and developing states alike. It is a human security threat and human rights violation that is tied to many of the forms of insecurity discussed in this book and to forms that we do not discuss here. Beyond its threat to the security of individuals, the UN Security Council Resolution 2331 (2016) also recognized that human trafficking can exacerbate armed conflict, contributing to the cycle of insecurity. Resolution 2331 is available through the UN website (http://www.un.org/en/ga/search/view_doc.asp?symbol=S/RES/2331(2016)).

The United Nations Office on Drugs and Crime (UNODC) maintains a Report on Trafficking in Persons and data on individual regions, victims, and traffickers (https://www.unodc.org/unodc/data-and-analysis/glotip.html). Review the latest report and consider the following questions.

1. How do patterns of trafficking in persons relate to threats to human security?

2. How might changes in security provision in armed conflict affect the practice of trafficking in persons?
3. What improvements in durable human security might decrease the prevalence of trafficking in persons?
4. What is your state doing to address the problem of trafficking in persons? Is your state's response focused on trafficking as a domestic (internal) problem or threat, foreign (external) problem or threat, or both? (Note: You may need to search beyond the UNODC for this information.)

FROM ARMED CONFLICT TO "PEACETIME": DURABLE HUMAN SECURITY AND FREEDOM FROM WANT

Durable human security relates to chronic or long-term threats to peace, security, and well-being. When a society has achieved durable human security individuals and communities live without fear of widespread violence or armed conflict and receive equal protection of, respect for, and provision of their rights and freedoms. Durable human security encompasses the dimensions of security and insecurity that are not necessarily rooted in active armed conflict but threaten the daily lives and livelihoods of individuals and communities—although the same violations of human rights and freedoms may exist and worsen in armed conflict. General Assembly Resolution 66/290 observes the cyclical nature of human security in times of armed conflict and times of relative peace: "Human security recognizes the interlinkages between peace, development and human rights, and equally considers civil, political, economic, social and cultural rights" (United Nations General Assembly 2012, 1). "Peacetime" is not always peaceful or secure for all people; this reality is at the heart of the wider view of human security. Durable human security is realized when individuals and communities enjoy freedom from fear *and* freedom from want; the concept of durable security draws from both freedoms for a broad view of human security.

Freedom from want was a crucial component of twentieth-century human rights discussions, including in U.S. president Franklin Roosevelt's "Four Freedoms" speech, the Universal Declaration of Human Rights, and the International Covenant on Economic, Social, and Cultural Rights (as discussed in chapters 1 and 4). As the 1994 Human Development Report notes, freedom from fear and freedom from want have both been integral aspects of human security efforts (even before the term "human security" gained traction), but over time state and international security practice came to favor efforts to protect freedom from fear over freedom from want (United Nations Development Programme 1994, 24). The narrow focus on freedom from fear has not been universal, of course; Japan has led efforts to secure freedom from want and improved well-being through economic development, joined by many Asian states that witnessed the effects of the 1997 Asian financial crisis and saw the importance of social safety nets (Hanlon and Christie 2016, 8–9).

Rights and protections like effective and accessible public health systems, access to adequate nutrition, access to stable employment and the ability to earn a livable wage, gender equality, access to quality education, racial and ethnic equality and freedom from discrimination on the basis of identity, and environment sustainability fall under the conceptual umbrella of freedom from want. These are the rights, freedoms, and protections that enable people to thrive, to participate actively as members of society, and to live their lives without fear of discrimination, repression, or harm. When these protections exist so too does durable human security. The idea of human security developed alongside a reemergence of interest in and discussion of human rights and human development within the international community, and especially at the UN, in the early 1990s. This was no coincidence; the establishment of human security depends in large part on the provision and fulfillment of human rights, recognition of the potential contributions of the individual to effective and sustainable economic development, and general recognition by the state and other international actors that the individual matters.

Human security requires good governance at all levels of society. When durable security exists, individuals, communities, and—by extension—states do not suffer the effects of widespread poverty, hunger, poor health, lack of access to education, gender-based violence and discrimination, racial, ethnic, or sectarian violence and discrimination, the effects of environmental degradation and destruction, or other day-to-day harms that inhibit well-being. Of course, insecurity can always exist within a society that generally enjoys high levels of human security; our point here is that these forms of insecurity will not be systematic or widespread, nor will they arise from entrenched norms or dysfunctional institutions. Good governance does not imply that the international community or an entity like the United Nations must intervene militarily whenever a threat to durable human security arises, thereby eliminating the last vestiges of state sovereignty, but rather that individuals, local communities, states, and the international community should collaborate to build the norms and institutions required to realize durable human security. In some cases, this may entail scaling up local capacity to improve gender equality or environmental protection (to name just two of the many examples). In other situations, this may involve transnational advocacy and international shaming in response to grave human rights violations. Further, it is important to recognize that human security cannot exist without state security, and state security is jeopardized by global instability; efforts to foster durable human security must balance these considerations with the overall goal of protecting individuals from long-term threats to their well-being.

The rights, opportunities, and freedoms that each individual and community prioritizes will vary across cultural contexts and experiences, which means there is no single universal prescription for achieving durable human security. Still, the ideal end state of durable human security is one in which individuals are self-sufficient and empowered to provide for themselves, their families, and their communities as they see fit (recall the diverging perspectives on security discussed in chapter 3); it is also one in which individuals are secure in their persons and free from the fear of violence. As the 1994 Human Development Report emphasizes, human security is not about "handouts" or paternalistic efforts to stifle individuals' ability to seize opportunities and reach goals on their own; instead, it is grounded in the recognition that insecurity generates dependence and an inability to thrive (United Nations Development Programme 1994, 24). When states are unable or unwilling to guarantee the various facets of durable human security, individuals, their communities, and, ultimately, the state will face insecurity and instability. It is this connection between durable human security and the more traditional security approaches that section III addresses.

Overview of Section III Chapters

The chapters that follow in section III explore some, but certainly not all, threats to durable human security. As noted in chapter 2, the broad view of human security, with its inclusion of threats to freedom from want and insecurity in situations of relative peace, is the subject of debate. By expanding the notion of security to issues that arise outside of armed conflict, scholars and practitioners risk rendering the concept of human security too unwieldy to study and apply in policy initiatives. We contend that this risk is outweighed by the utility of understanding chronic insecurity and its links to national and global instability. Widespread hunger may not trigger civil war on its own, but it can be a contributing factor to political instability (Lappé 1998). Gender inequality may not incite regional conflict, but research shows that states with high levels of gender inequality tend to resort to aggression first in conflict, use higher levels of violence in conflict than states with greater gender equality, and are more likely to experience civil war (Caprioli 2000, 2005, Caprioli and Boyer 2001, Hudson et al. 2012). Durable human security may lay the foundations for long-term peace and stability, which satisfies the central aim of the narrow view of human security rooted in freedom from fear. In addition to the moral imperative to concern ourselves with big problems like chronic hunger, the effects of climate change on future generations, pandemic disease, and gender inequality, there is analytical value in assessing the links between these problems and overall security.

The chapters in section II explore human security in armed conflict and, therefore, focus predominantly on freedom from fear and the narrow approach to human security. In contrast, each of the substantive chapters in section III draws out the links between the human security issue addressed—health security, gender inequality, environmental security, and food security—and national and global security. By highlighting the key connections between the human security approach and the more traditional security approaches, we aim to demonstrate both the potentially synchronous nature and the sources of conflict between the three security approaches as applied to issues that stand to be left out of discussions that adopt the narrow view of human security. The chapters in section III do not need to be read sequentially, although sections of chapter 12 build on some of the ideas presented in chapter 11. Since the issues highlighted in section III do not constitute the full scope of sources of insecurity that may be included in the broad view of human security, the aim of section III is not to provide an authoritative catalogue of every durable human security issue but rather to highlight several problems with the ultimate goal of enabling readers to think critically about other threats to well-being in today's world.

Discussion Questions

1. Consider your local community. Does your community enjoy freedom from fear and freedom from want? Are there any threats to these freedoms for the community as a whole or any subset of the community?
2. Why might states align their foreign policy priorities with either the idea of freedom from fear or freedom from want?
3. How does the wide view of human security—including both human security in conflict and durable human security—advance security provision? How does it challenge security provision?
4. Consider an acute conflict unfolding today. What obstacles to freedom from fear and freedom from want exist for the population affected by the conflict?

FURTHER READING AND WEB RESOURCES

Commission on Human Security. *Human Security Now.* New York: United Nations, 2003.

Robert J. Hanlon and Kenneth Christie. *Freedom from Fear, Freedom from Want: An Introduction to Human Security.* North York, Ontario: University of Toronto Press, 2016.

For Deeper Discussion

Mary Caprioli. "Primed for Violence: The Role of Gender Inequality in Predicting Internal Conflict." *International Studies Quarterly* 49 (2005): 161–78.

Roland Paris. "Human Security: Paradigm Shift or Hot Air?" *International Security* 26, no. 2 (2001): 87–102.

Shannon D. Beebe and Mary Kaldor. *The Ultimate Weapon Is No Weapon: Human Security and the New Rules of War and Peace.* New York: PublicAffairs, 2010.

REFERENCES

Caprioli, Mary. "Gendered Conflict." *Journal of Peace Research* 37, no. 1 (2000): 53–68.

Caprioli, Mary. "Primed for Violence: The Role of Gender Inequality in Predicting Internal Conflict." *International Studies Quarterly* 49 (2005): 161–78.

Caprioli, Mary, and Mark Boyer. "Gender, Violence, and International Crisis." *Journal of Conflict Resolution* 45, no. 4 (2001): 503–18.

Commission on Human Security. *Human Security Now.* New York: United Nations, 2003.

Hanlon, Robert J., and Kenneth Christie. *Freedom from Fear, Freedom from Want: An Introduction to Human Security.* North York, Ontario: University of Toronto Press, 2016.

Hudson, Valerie M., Bonnie Ballif-Spanvill, Mary Caprioli, and Chad F. Emmett. *Sex & World Peace.* New York: Columbia University Press, 2012.

Lappé, Francis Moore. *World Hunger: Twelve Myths.* New York: Grove Press, 1998.

United Nations Development Programme. *Human Development Report.* New York: Oxford University Press, 1994.

United Nations General Assembly. "Follow-up to Paragraph 143 on Human Security of the 2005 World Summit Outcome." *A/Res/66290.* New York, October 25, 2012.

United Nations General Assembly. "United Nations Millennium Declaration." *A/Res/55/2.* New York, September 18, 2000.

United Nations Office on Drugs and Crime. *United Nations Convention Against Transnational Organized Crime and the Protocols Thereto.* United Nations. Vienna, 2004.

Chapter 9

Health Security as Human Security

Learning Objectives

This chapter will enable readers to:

1. Discuss the impact of health threats on human security.
2. Discuss the impact of health threats on national and global security.
3. Identify the reciprocal influence of health on human security and human security on health.
4. Debate the extent to which health concerns constitute security threats.

Infectious disease outbreaks—like the H5N1 (avian flu), Ebola, cholera, and Zika scares—make it into the headlines of global news media and national and international policy agendas alike, triggering fear in a globalized world in which a public health crisis in one state threatens to affect the citizens and stability of another, or many others. When we think of human security as the absence of threats to an individuals' well-being and ability to thrive, it is clear that good health is necessary for the achievement of human security. The question then becomes: Which health issues constitute human security issues? Are acute health crises affecting large swaths of the global population the only relevant concerns or are noncommunicable, but debilitating, health issues viable human security concerns? In this chapter we explore health crises in relation to the human, state, and global security approaches. Of particular interest is the mutually reinforcing (and potentially mutually destructive) relationship between health and human security: health crises pose a potential threat to human security and human security offers a promising policy orientation toward global health issues. While the parameters according to which health issues are central to security have yet to be clearly

179

defined, what is clear is that health is an inextricable component of the complex web of issues that comprise human security.

HEALTH AS A HUMAN SECURITY ISSUE

The UNDP's 1994 Human Development Report includes threats to good health among the causes of individual insecurity, noting that daily concerns like health and employment were as important as protection from war to the architects of the UN system in their early discussions at the San Francisco Conference in 1945 (United Nations Development Programme 1994, 3). Twenty-one years after the San Francisco Conference, Article 12 of the International Covenant on Economic, Social and Cultural Rights (ICESCR) asserted the "right of everyone to the enjoyment of the highest attainable standard of physical and mental health," referencing infant mortality, environmental and industrial hygiene, the "prevention, treatment and control of epidemic, endemic, occupational and other diseases," and the provision of medical care to all. In recognition of the centrality of health to the pursuit of human security, the Human Development Report observes that primary health care is a component of human development, and one that states should support through foreign assistance (United Nations Development Programme 1994, 4). *Human Security Now* (2003) reiterates the need to provide basic health care at affordable costs (Commission on Human Security 2003, iv). **Health security** is concerned with the protection of individuals from sudden or chronic health threats and efforts to empower individuals to lead healthy lives. When we consider once again the definition of human security introduced by the Human Development Report (and discussed in the book's introduction), health security clearly relates to "safety from the constant threats of hunger, disease, crime and repression" and to "protection from sudden and hurtful disruptions in the pattern of our daily lives" (United Nations Development Programme 1994, 3). Good health is especially crucial to the empowerment—or freedom from want—aspect of human security.

Health concerns become durable or chronic human security issues when they arise from systemic inequality or deprivation created by societal norms surrounding individuals' health needs, the weakness or inefficiency of health care institutions, or from the structural instability imposed by active armed conflict or state collapse. A chronic disease like asthma in and of itself may impede an individual's ability to thrive: it can reduce attendance at school or work; it may limit options for locale due to environmental triggers like air pollution or allergens; it may affect the family budget if necessary prescription medications are expensive; and it may cause severe symptoms or death without timely professional medical attention. Such a disease certainly constitutes an individual hardship. Yet we would consider a chronic disease (including asthma) to be a human *security* threat if it is the result of a widespread problem arising from a lack of institutional protections or from harmful societal norms; examples of such problems include extreme air pollution, substandard housing conditions for marginalized or impoverished groups, or lack of access to quality medical care and affordable medications for certain groups or society as a whole. The scale of the problem and the nature of contributing factors (societal norms or state institutions) turn an individual issue into a human security issue, especially if the problem arises from the state's failure to protect the population (or some segment of it) from harm.

Some health security concerns arise more quickly, as the disease outbreaks referenced at the start of this chapter suggest. An **epidemic** (an unusually high incidence of disease in a community or the spread of disease to a new locality) or **pandemic** (the spread of disease across borders or on a global scale) constitutes a sudden threat to human security due to the potential for widespread effects on individuals and institutions alike. An infectious disease outbreak that spreads quickly through a population or carries devastating effects on a large scale is a sudden health threat. In addition to threatening many individuals' health in a short period of time, it carries the potential to overwhelm health care institutions, cut economic productivity, and create social and political unrest. Such an outbreak is also potentially exacerbated by structural issues like lack of access to medical services, insufficient institutional capacity to treat certain health problems, or unequal distribution of expertise and resources. Social, cultural, or religious norms that impede individuals' access to medical care can magnify the impact of chronic and sudden health concerns alike; refusing international health experts' requests for access to the sick and delaying medical care for a female family member due to inequality within the household are two such examples. Norms and traditions surrounding care of the sick and deceased may also lead to the spread of infectious diseases through unsafe handling of bodies, as was the case during the 2014 Ebola outbreak when transmission occurred through contact with bodily fluids containing the virus during funeral rites.

As with all aspects of human security, the provision of health care, the protection of individuals from sudden or chronic health threats, and the extent to which individuals are empowered to lead healthy lives will vary with respect to factors such as state stability and resources, shifting international political relationships, and attributes related to the individual (including nationality, ethnicity, religion, sex, gender, age, marital status, and socioeconomic standing). While there is some overlap across states and regions, different types of health challenges confront the Global South and Global North, with infectious diseases constituting serious threats to health in the South and **"lifestyle" diseases** (chronic health conditions arising from a societal shift toward a sedentary lifestyle) in the North. Related to this variation in health concerns is the problem of inequality in the distribution of resources and capabilities to prevent, diagnose, and treat health problems, but this problem is not as clearly divided between the North and South, as high levels of inequality and discrepancies in access to quality medical care persist across the globe (Yukping and Thomas 2010, 448). When infectious diseases or lifestyle diseases become pervasive, they threaten the economic and political stability of the state, and potentially the region or the globe, as well as the well-being of the individual. Health security, then, is relevant not only to international actors concerned with human security but to those who adopt a state or global security approach as well.

Health Crises as Threats to State and Global Stability

Health concerns become state security concerns, from the traditional state security approach, when they begin to affect economic and political stability (two primary indicators of the state's well-being from a state security perspective). When they are widespread throughout the population, both chronic and acute health threats create the potential for economic loss due to decreased productivity in the workforce, loss of tourism income, and the state's reallocation of resources to mitigating the problem. When determining the effect of a health threat on state stability and security, we should consider two key factors: the scale of the problem (how widespread it is, in terms of the population affected) and the immediacy of the threat (how quickly the threat originates and spreads). Scale and immediacy may be, but are not always, related. Cardiovascular disease was the leading cause of death among men and women in the United States between 1999 and 2014, making this a widespread problem but not an immediate threat to the state (Centers for Disease Control and Prevention 2015). Cardiovascular disease, then, would not qualify as a threat to state security unless it challenged the political and economic stability of the state. The 2001 anthrax outbreak in the United States, in contrast, affected a small number of people but quickly became a state security concern. Four letters containing anthrax spores were mailed to U.S. senators and news agencies in September and October 2001; a total of 22 people contracted anthrax, a total of 43 people tested positive for exposure, 10,000 people were deemed at risk for exposure, and of the 22 people who contracted the disease, 5 died (Centers for Disease Control and Prevention 2016). Anthrax had not been diagnosed in the United States since 1976, and the intentional release of the spores within threatening letters so soon after the 9/11 attacks suggested a larger threat to the state. The U.S. government explicitly recognized the anthrax outbreak as a national security threat, and we can consider the threat's immediacy and the potential for a large-scale outbreak as key factors, as well as the broader political environment in which the U.S. government and public were on alert for terrorist threats.

A health crisis can become a matter of political stability not only because of the direct impact of the disease on economic productivity and the health of the population but also because of the way in which a state handles—or fails to address—the situation. When a state downplays the effect of disease, fails to build and maintain an effective health care infrastructure, is unable or unwilling to prevent the spread of infectious disease, or otherwise falls short in providing for the basic health needs of the population, there is potential for unrest and the government risks losing its legitimacy. When viewed through the lens of state security, health problems are prioritized on the basis of their impact on the state and its political and economic stability; this means that disproportionately more resources will be devoted to the potential threat of **bioterrorism** (see box 9.1) than to pervasive health problems like Alzheimer's disease and cardiovascular disease. Still, health is one area in which states come together regularly to cooperate in response to regional and global concerns, in addition to threats that directly affect the state's national interests. Collaborative efforts may take the form of initiatives focused on the eradication of one specific disease (like malaria or polio) or multilateral institutions dedicated to global or regional public health (e.g., the Pan American Health Organization or the World Health Organization) (Meslin and Garba 2016, Rugemalila et al. 2007).

Health security, like other sudden and chronic human security threats, can quickly transition from a state security concern to a global security issue. Infectious disease outbreaks are difficult, if not impossible, to contain in our globalized world. Disease-causing bacteria and viruses can travel across state borders in people, animals, and objects, and a total shutdown of state borders is not only politically fraught but also practically infeasible. Even chronic diseases impose an increasing burden on a growing number of states as pollution in major cities compromises the clean air necessary for good health and modern technology reinforces a sedentary lifestyle. The global security approach, like the state security approach, considers health issues to be security threats when they jeopardize the economic and political stability of the system. As in the state security approach, we should consider the scale and immediacy of health threats to determine whether they affect global security. An acute health threat, like the 2014 Ebola outbreak, the 2015–2016 Zika virus epidemic, or the ongoing burden of malaria, poses a challenge to global stability when it is unprecedented in scope or nature (and therefore unpredictable in its scale and effects), when states lack the capacity to contain and eliminate the outbreak, when a large portion of the global population is affected, or when cross-border political or economic relations are jeopardized as a result of the outbreak.

BOX 9.1. "THINK ABOUT IT . . ."—BIOTERRORISM

Bioterrorism involves the "deliberate release of viruses, bacteria, or other germs (agents) used to cause illness or death in people, animals, or plants" (Centers for Disease Control and Prevention n.d.). Examples of bioterrorism agents include anthrax, cholera, ricin toxin, and small-pox. Bioterrorism agents may be found in nature or they may be diseases that were eradicated long ago and exist only in laboratories. It is the act of deliberate exposure within a population to cause harm and incite panic that turns diseases into weapons. It is important to note that turning disease agents into weapons capable of inflicting harm on a large scale has proven difficult to date, and incidents of bioterrorism have created relatively few casualties (when compared with incidence of naturally occurring disease in a population or other forms of terrorism). Still, because bioterrorism agents are difficult for intelligence agencies and security screeners to detect, the threat of their use by nefarious actors remains a security concern for states and populations confronting twenty-first-century terrorism.

Consider the following questions:

1. Given the parameters we have discussed for health security issues and the deliberate and political nature of a terrorist attack, does bioterrorism most closely resemble a human security, state security, or global security threat?
2. How might the response to a bioterrorism attack differ with each approach?
3. How might good health security, or human security in general, limit the effectiveness of a bioterrorism attack?
4. If you directed a state's health policy agency, like the Centers for Disease Control and Prevention (CDC) in the United States, what recommendations would you make to ensure the highest level of preparedness for an act of bioterrorism?

RESPONSIBILITY FOR HEALTH SECURITY

From the perspective of a state or an international organization, determining whether, when, where, and how to respond to health concerns as security issues can be difficult. States may decide individually to include global health issues among their foreign policy priorities. For example, Cuba's medical internationalism melds foreign policy and community health care. The state's initiatives at home and abroad—which reach back to a deployment of medical professionals to Algeria and Guinea-Bissau in the 1960s—seek to provide community-based health care services, empower marginalized individuals and communities, and build up institutional capacity with the end goal of eliminating structural violence (Huish and Kirk 2007, 78–79, Huish and Spiegel 2008, 45). Cuba's international medical policy efforts are thus in line with both the egalitarian aims of the state's Revolution and the central goals of human security. Japan, in its foreign policy efforts to promote global health, has explored this multifaceted issue area and contributed to the immense progress made in the global battle against HIV/AIDS, tuberculosis, and malaria (Llano and Shibuya 2011, Takemi 2016, 21). Japan's human security approach centers on the principle of freedom from want and the aspects of human security most closely related to what we call durable human security, making global health a central initiative for the state. A state that has adopted a human security approach will likely include health concerns among important security issues.

Yet even in the face of a devastating health crisis that presents clear challenges not only to human security but to national, regional, or global stability as well, international coordination can be difficult. At the international level, states can formally discuss and coordinate their efforts through the World Health Organization, which was established in 1948 to direct and coordinate international health policy efforts to promote physical, mental, and social well-being. The WHO functions under the auspices of the UN and supports states by promoting evidence-based health policy options, providing technical advice on health issues, disseminating health research, setting norms and standards, and assessing health trends and crises (World Health Organization 2016). The World Health Assembly, the WHO's decision-making body, consists of all WHO member states and provides a forum for discussion and coordination, much like the UN's General Assembly. It receives and considers reports and instructions from the WHO Executive Board, an elected body of thirty-four health experts. States look to the WHO for advice and assessments on health security concerns. Having a technically focused international organization can alleviate some of the challenges surrounding global collaboration in response to health threats, but it cannot guarantee that states or other human security actors respond quickly or comprehensively.

The Ebola outbreak in West Africa, which began in March 2014, made headlines in the global media but the international community's response was not immediate, leaving NGOs like Médecins Sans Frontières to do much of the initial work required to train local hospital staff to treat patients and control the spread of the virus (Médecins Sans Frontières 2014). In July 2014 the WHO convened a ministerial-level meeting to bring state representatives together to determine collectively the best way to stem transmission and treat the affected populations (World Health Organization Regional Office for Africa 2014). Two months later, UN secretary-general Ban Ki-moon spoke to the UN Security Council and described Ebola as a security concern requiring "a level of international action unprecedented for an emergency" in the form of the UN Mission for Ebola Emergency Response (UNMEER) (United Nations Security Council 2014). Once the international community recognized the Ebola outbreak as a security concern and a threat not only to human security but to national and regional stability as well, the issue received priority status from international organizations and foreign states (Fidler 2004, Katz and Singer 2007). Not all health concerns will register as national or international security priorities (Ban 2003, Katz and Singer 2007), so the question of responsibility for health security is central to the discussion here.

Just as we must limit the scope of issues included under the banner of health security, we must also observe that many health concerns are not security threats to the state, region, or international community. If we accept that major health concerns (those that are life-altering or life-threatening) are human security concerns when they arise from or are exacerbated by normative or institutional factors within society, like lack of access to medical care, then we must explore the concept of responsibility for the provision of health security. Recall the table illustrating justifications for protection in a world in which human security norms are present (chapter 1, table 1.2). When states provide protection against and treatment of health security threats affecting the individual, they may do so in the interest of state preservation, because addressing health concerns is the appropriate thing to do because it is politically expedient to address health concerns, or some combination of these motivations. When international actors cooperate to address health threats affecting individuals, they may similarly do so because it is the appropriate thing to do or because it would be too politically costly not to act. Thus, we can see potential for both normative and rational political motivations driving responsibility to prevent and respond to health crises.

We cannot consider *all* health concerns to be human, national, regional, or global security threats because casting the net of "health security" too broadly risks diverting resources and attention away from health crises that are more imminently threatening (Katz and Singer 2007). Examples of imminent health threats to the state include the 1918 influenza pandemic, the 1947 New York City smallpox outbreak, the global HIV/AIDS epidemic, and the 2014 Ebola outbreak; these health crises threatened to overwhelm resources, harm large swaths of the population, upset economic stability, and contribute to political unrest. In such cases health security becomes not only a human security issue but a state—and perhaps even regional or global—security issue. If we apply the logic of conditional sovereignty (as discussed in chapter 5 with respect to R2P) to health security, we can formulate a process through which responsibility to address health concerns transfers from state to global entities. As chronic or acute health threats arise, it is first the responsibility of the state to assess the nature of the health issue and mobilize resources to address it. Failing successful action, whether because the state lacks adequate capacity to handle the threat or because the threat is transnational in scope, the international community has a responsibility to assist the state in its efforts to mitigate the crisis. Collaboration on health issues brings together NGOs, UN or regional agencies, the WHO and other global and regional health policy organizations, and other state agencies as necessary to exchange expertise to improve global understanding of the problem and the best solution.

When Human Security Actors Create Insecurity: Cholera in Haiti

We cannot neglect the role that state and non-state actors potentially play in creating, not just mitigating, threats to health security. Chronic health problems and infectious disease outbreaks can result from environmental factors (like the spread of mosquitos that transmit malaria or Zika to new regions), shifting lifestyle trends (e.g., the sedentary workday in developed states), the evolution of viruses and bacteria over time (and especially the increased drug resistance related to the widespread overuse of antibiotics), and other natural and man-made conditions. Major health crises can also be caused by human action, and, very unfortunately, sometimes these crises occur in conjunction with other human security threats and as a direct result of efforts to respond to those threats.

The cholera outbreak in Haiti that began in October 2010 is one such instance, as the infection-causing bacteria were traced to the base used by UN peacekeepers deployed to assist in the aftermath of the devastating 2010 earthquake. Latrine sewage containing human waste from a contingent of peacekeepers recently deployed from Nepal, a state in the midst of a cholera outbreak at the time, leaked into the Meille River and reintroduced cholera-causing bacteria into the water (Katz 2016a, 2016b, Gladstone 2016b). The six-year epidemic carries an official death toll of 9,200 victims, but a Doctors without Borders study emphasizes that incomplete data collection and lack of access to health clinics suggest the death toll is much higher than the official account (Gladstone 2016a). The deadly unintended consequences of the UN Humanitarian Stabilization Mission in Haiti (MINUSTAH) and the organization's official denial of the link between its peacekeepers and the outbreak (until August 2016) have called into question the legitimacy of the multilateral mission in Haiti: if those who came to restore human security introduced a health crisis and did little to address the problem, then the mission's costs may outweigh the benefits. Families of cholera victims in Haiti have pressed the UN for restitution, but the organization has denied fault, refused payment, and claimed diplomatic immunity when asked to appear in court; at the time of writing, the families' lawsuit asking for financial redress for those affected by cholera was pending a decision in the Second Circuit Court of Appeals in New York (Katz 2016a). The UN launched a cholera eradication effort in Haiti, but fund-raising efforts fell short, leading to delays in the delivery of vaccines to vulnerable populations and in the reconstruction of Haiti's water and sanitation systems to prevent further spread of the bacteria (Archibold and Sengupta 2014). For years after the initial introduction of cholera on the island, the infection continued to threaten the health security of the Haitian population—with heightened concern about the disease spreading in the aftermath of hurricanes and flooding—and contributed to concerns about the UN's legitimacy as an international organization.

The cholera epidemic in Haiti is a tragic example of how well-intended human security efforts can inadvertently create new, albeit unintended, human security threats. The far-reaching effects of the cholera outbreak in Haiti also illustrate the ways in which health crises present challenges to state and global security and stability. When human security actors create health crises they face moral and political imperatives to rectify the situation, whether unilaterally or through collaboration with states and non-state actors.

CONCLUSION: GOOD HEALTH AND HUMAN SECURITY

Health is a human security issue when it arises from norms, institutions, or acute crises and threatens or constrains individuals' well-being and ability to thrive. Although chronic diseases (e.g., diabetes or rheumatoid arthritis) and sudden health problems (like a heart attack or stroke) threaten an individual's overall well-being or even their survival, the inclusion of health within the range of security issues requires us to consider the scale and impact of the threat. Because assigning an issue a "security" label requires human security actors—including states and international organizations—to prioritize that issue, we must take care not to broaden the scope of human security so extensively that we dilute its meaning. Health is always a human concern, but we include health problems as human security issues when they arise from harmful societal norms or a lack of institutional protections, or when they threaten society and its institutions on a large scale. Health security issues can quickly become state and global security threats, especially when infectious diseases become epidemics or pandemics. The potential for rapid transmission of an infectious disease in our globalized world means that even states and international organizations that prioritize a traditional approach to security find reasons to protect against health threats. Health threats not only cross geopolitical borders, but health security easily traverses the already permeable borders between the three approaches to security.

In September 2015 UN secretary-general Ban Ki-moon unequivocally asserted that "human security depends on health security" (UN News Centre 2015). There is a reciprocal relationship between health and human security: good health is at the root of an individual's ability to thrive, so progress in one begets progress in the other. Health is closely related to other aspects of durable human security, including food security, gender equality, environmental stability, poverty, and protection of human rights. If an individual's basic health needs are not met, the individual cannot realize opportunities to thrive, to pursue a fulfilling livelihood, and to contribute to the political, social, and economic advancement of society. By the same token, when other aspects of durable human security are in place (and certainly also in times of acute armed conflict) it is difficult to ensure that the individual can lead a healthy life. Efforts to provide for human security in general pave the way for health security in particular. Health security and overall human security, then, are reciprocal influences, and policy decisions must account for the interrelated nature of health and human security more broadly.

Two key predicaments confronting states, international organizations, and other human security actors are (1) when and how to respond to health security threats should they occur and (2) where the primary responsibility for the response to health threats lies. The notion of conditional sovereignty, or sovereignty as the state's responsibility to protect its citizens from threats, tells us that the state bears the primary and enduring obligation to address the health needs of its people. When the state lacks the capacity to respond to a health crisis the international community also bears a responsibility to assist the state in finding a way to address the threat. The international response to the Ebola outbreak, discussed previously, demonstrates this sense of communal responsibility (however imperfect) to assist states or regions facing a health crisis: international assistance came after NGOs and states in the affected region called for help, and delivery of financial aid and coordination between donor states and the governments of Guinea, Liberia, Sierra Leone, Nigeria, and Senegal were welcome efforts. Still, the questions of when and how to respond and who bears primary responsibility for the response are pervasive in human security matters, and political debate can stall assistance. In addition, while the *need* to respond to a global pandemic or a regional epidemic is fairly clear (even though the questions of who, when, and how to persist), other health-related concerns do not register as human security threats to all human security actors and state or international policymakers. One such dilemma is whether or not health care is a human right that states should provide for their citizens. There is global variation in the extent to which states have the political will, historical precedent, and capacity to guarantee adequate and affordable access to health care. If we accept the premise that good health is central to human security, and we further accept that societal norms and institutions—including the capacity of and access to the health care system—either foster or degrade health security, then the question of responsibility for the provision of health care is relevant to human security policy.

Health security issues and required responses can be exceptionally clear in some cases and exceedingly murky with respect to others, as is the case with other issues related to durable human security. Lingering questions remain surrounding the threshold with which we assess health concerns as human *security* concerns and the responsibility to act once a human security threat arises and is considered a priority, and the global community will likely resolve these questions only on a case-by-case basis for the foreseeable future.

Discussion Questions

1. Is there a clear threshold beyond which a chronic disease becomes a human security threat?
2. Under what circumstances might a state have strategic (self-interested) incentives to incorporate health security into its foreign policy initiatives?
3. Does universal health care contribute to or detract from overall health security within a population? Is health care a human right?
4. Is the difference between health as a human security issue or a state or global security issue meaningful? Is the difference more or less clear regarding health concerns than other human security concerns?
5. How might the response to an epidemic differ from the response to a pandemic within each of the three approaches to security (human, national, and global)?
6. Undernutrition and malnutrition are health concerns that stem from food insecurity. How do the overlapping security concerns affect human security actors' ability to respond to these threats?

FURTHER READING AND WEB RESOURCES

Centers for Disease Control and Prevention—Cholera in Haiti: http://www.cdc.gov/haiticholera/

Centers for Disease Control and Prevention—Ebola Updates: https://www.cdc.gov/vhf/ebola/outbreaks/2014-west-africa/previous-updates.html

Centers for Disease Control and Prevention-Global health partnerships: http://www.cdc.gov/globalhealth/partnerships.htm

Katsuya Okada. "Japan's New Global Health Policy: 2011–2015." *The Lancet* 376 (2010): 938–40.

Maryam Zarnegar Deloffre. "Human Security in the Age of Ebola: Towards People-centered Global Governance." *E-International Relations* (2014). http://www.e-ir.info/2014/10/25/human-security-in-the-age-of-ebola-towards-people-centered-global-governance/

Pan American Health Organization: http://www.paho.org/hq/

World Health Organization: http://who.int/en

World Health Organization—Chronic Disease: http://www.who.int/nutrition/topics/2_background/en/

World Health Organization—Malaria: http://www.who.int/mediacentre/factsheets/fs094/en/

For Deeper Discussion

David P. Fidler. "Germs, Norms and Power: Global Health's Political Revolution." *Law, Social Justice & Global Development Journal* 2004, no. 1 (2004). http://elj.warwick.ac.uk/global/04-1/fidler.html

Haruko Sugiyama, Ayaka Yamaguchi, and Hiromi Murakami. *Japan's Global Health Policy: Developing a Comprehensive Approach in a Period of Economic Stress.* New York: Rowman & Littlefield, 2013.

Lawrence D. Brown. "The Political Face of Public Health." *Public Health Reviews* 32 (2010): 155–73.

Zaryab Iqbal. "Health and Human Security: The Public Health Impact of Violent Conflict." *International Studies Quarterly* 50, no. 3 (2006): 631–49.

REFERENCES

Archibold, Randal C., and Somini Sengupta. "U.N. Struggles to Stem Haiti Cholera Epidemic." *New York Times*, April 19, 2014.

Ban, Jonathan. "Health as a Global Security Challenge." *Seton Hall Journal of Diplomacy and International Relations* 4 (2003): 19–28.

Centers for Disease Control and Prevention. *A History of Anthrax.* 2016. http://www.cdc.gov/anthrax/resources/history/ (accessed September 23, 2016).

Centers for Disease Control and Prevention. *Bioterrorism Overview.* https://emergency.cdc.gov/bioterrorism/overview.asp (accessed September 22, 2016).

Centers for Disease Control and Prevention. "Underlying Cause of Death, 1999–2014." *CDC WONDER Online Database.* 2015. https://wonder.cdc.gov/ucd-icd10.html (accessed December 18, 2017).

Commission on Human Security. *Human Security Now.* New York: United Nations, 2003.

Fidler, David P. "Germs, Norms and Power: Global Health's Political Revolution." *Law, Social Justice & Global Development* 1 (2004). https://www2.warwick.ac.uk/fac/soc/law/elj/lgd/2004_1/fidler/

Gladstone, Rick. "Cholera Deaths in Haiti Could Far Exceed Official Count." *New York Times*, March 18, 2016a.

Gladstone, Rick. "Lawmakers Urge John Kerry to Press U.N. for Haiti Cholera Response." *New York Times*, June 29, 2016b.

Huish, Robert, and Jerry Spiegel. "Integrating Health and Human Security into Foreign Policy: Cuba's Surprising Success." *International Journal of Cuban Studies* 1, no. 1 (2008): 42–53.

Huish, Robert, and John M. Kirk. "Cuban Medical Internationalism and the Development of the Latin American School of Medicine." *Latin American Perspectives* 34, no. 6 (2007): 77–92.

Katz, Jonathan M. "The Killer Hiding in the CDC Map." *Slate*, April 24, 2016a.

Katz, Jonathan M. "U.N. Admits Role in Cholera Epidemic in Haiti." *New York Times*, August 17, 2016b.

Katz, Rebecca, and Daniel A. Singer. "Health and Security in Foreign Policy." *Bulletin of the World Health Organization* 85, no. 3 (March 2007).

Llano, Rayden, and Kenji Shibuya. *Japan's Evolving Role in Global Health*. Seattle, WA: National Bureau of Asian Research, 2011.

Médecins Sans Frontières. *Ebola: International Response Slow and Uneven*. December 2, 2014. http://www.doctorswithoutborders.org/article/ebola-international-response-slow-and-uneven (accessed September 2, 2016).

Meslin, Eric M., and Ibrahim Garba. "International Collaboration for Global Public Health." In *Public Health Ethics: Cases Spanning the Globe*, by Drue H. Barrett, Leonard H. Ortmann, Angus Dawson, Carla Saenz, Andreas Reis, and Gail Bolan, 241–84. Springer International Publishing, 2016. https://link.springer.com/content/pdf/10.1007%2F978-3-319-23847-0.pdf

Rugemalila, Joas B., Olumide A. T. Ogundahunsi, Timothy T. Stedman, and Wen L. Kilama. "Multilateral Initiative on Malaria: Justification, Evolution, Achievements, Challenges, Opportunities, and Future Plans." *American Journal of Tropical Medicine and Hygiene* 77, no. 6, Supplement (2007): 296–302.

Takemi, Keizo. "Japan's Global Health Strategy: Connecting Development and Security." *Asia-Pacific Review* 23, no. 1 (2016): 21–31.

UN News Centre. "'Human Security Depends on Health Security,' Ban Says, Calling on Nations to Be Proactive." September 26, 2015.

United Nations Development Programme. *Human Development Report 1994: New Dimensions of Human Security*. New York: Oxford University Press, 1994.

United Nations Security Council. *With Spread of Ebola Outpacing Response, Security Council Adopts Resolution 2177 (2014) Urging Immediate Action, End to Isolation of Affected States*. September 18, 2014. http://www.un.org/press/en/2014/sc11566.doc.htm (accessed September 2, 2016).

World Health Organization. *About WHO*. 2016. http://www.who.int/about/what-we-do/en/ (accessed October 11, 2016).

World Health Organization Regional Office for Africa. *Special Ministerial Meeting on Ebola Virus Disease in West Africa Accra, Ghana, 2–3 July 2014*. July 2014. http://www.afro.who.int/en/clusters-a-programmes/dpc/epidemic-a-pandemic-alert-and-response/epr-highlights/4187-special-ministerial-meeting-ebola-accra-2-3-july-2014.html (accessed September 2, 2016).

Yuk-ping, Catherine Lo, and Nicholas Thomas. "How Is Health a Security Issue? Politics, Responses and Issues." *Health Policy and Planning* 25 (2010): 447–53.

Chapter 10

Gender Inequality and Security

Learning Objectives

This chapter will enable readers to:

1. Identify indicators of gender inequality.
2. Discuss the impact of gender inequality on human security.
3. Discuss the impact of gender inequality on national and global security.
4. Compare efforts to improve gender equality.

Gender inequality is a problem that plagues every society to some extent—and in some places harm is much more egregious than in others. Chapter 4 discussed the universality of human rights—the concept that all people are entitled to the same basic rights simply because they are human. In reality, discrimination on the basis of gender is pervasive and it creates a wide range of injustices and abuses that lead to insecurity and the unequal fulfillment of rights. This chapter explores gender inequality and its connection to human, national, and global security. In this chapter we will examine global efforts to improve gender equality and introduce efforts related to two states in particular: Afghanistan and Sweden. These examples illustrate a variation in gender inequality as well as the ways in which various non-state and governmental actors can influence gender equality–focused initiatives.

GENDER AND GENDER INEQUALITY

In informal discussion people often conflate the terms "sex" and "gender," using them interchangeably and sometimes inappropriately in context.

193

Strictly speaking, **sex** refers to the biological differences in human reproductive systems—a person is born with male genitalia, female genitalia, or with a combination of the two. **Gender** refers to the personal sense of a person as male, female, both, or neither, as well as the societal expectations for a person's behavior, appearance, and expression on the basis of their sex. For example, if a person is born female, that person is socialized to act, speak, dress, and live within the boundaries of what society considers feminine at the time. A person who is born male is similarly expected to embody and express masculine traits and behaviors. The severity of societal expectations varies across time and culture; some communities, states, or cultures condemn the subversion of gender expectations more harshly than others. Societal expectations for how people should behave, live, and love on the basis of gender are **gender norms**. Just like all other norms, gender norms are subject to change over time. For example, during the mass mobilization of World War II, women in the United States took over jobs in factories, traditionally masculine jobs they had previously been discouraged or outright barred from taking, because so many working-age men were away at war. What is considered feminine at one point in time may fall out of fashion in another era as society's needs or values change. Accordingly, gender roles, behaviors, and expectations vary across *cultures*. The two states discussed in the vignettes in this chapter—Afghanistan and Sweden—are neither the most gender-unequal nor the most gender-equal states in the world, but men's and women's experiences, expectations for behavior, roles, and opportunities are in sharp contrast.

Sex and gender are intricately tied together (Goldstein 2001, 2), and it is difficult to separate the concepts and their real-world implications completely. What is important to underscore, however, is that gender is a socially constructed concept: gender norms and expectations for appropriate behavior, appearance, and lifestyle are based on a consensus within society about what it means to be male, female, masculine, feminine, man, woman, or somewhere along the spectrum between those identities. We say "spectrum," because although it is common to discuss sex and gender as two binary (either X or Y) concepts, it is more realistic to acknowledge that many people are born female but identify as male, or are born male but identify as female, or both, or neither. **Gender identity** is the gender with which a person associates on the inside (one's sense of self as male, female, or somewhere between or completely unrelated to the two) and is not necessarily identical to one's sex. **Gender expression** is the outward reflection of one's gender and is also not necessarily tied to one's sex; gender expression encompasses dress, mannerisms, speech, hairstyle, and other visible or audible traits a person may adopt on the outside to reflect a sense of gender identity. Sex and gender are not truly binary concepts.[1]

Gender inequality arises when one group is privileged over others on the basis of sex and gender. Across the globe, gender inequality almost universally means that men and boys receive a larger share of resources and enjoy more freedoms, rights, and opportunities than women and girls. Such inequality is most often the result of **patriarchy**, or "rule by fathers," which privileges masculinity (and men and boys) over all other identities and people. In a patriarchal, gender unequal society women, girls, and LGBTQ persons are discriminated against on the basis of their gender identity, gender expression, or sexuality. Gender norms create or reinforce inequality in many contexts.

Discrimination and violence on the basis of sex and gender can be subtle, structural, overt, or all of these at the same time. So how do we know gender inequality exists and how can we compare the situations in different areas of the world? One way to measure gender inequality is the UNDP's **Gender Inequality Index (GII)**. Recognizing gender inequality as a "major barrier to human development," UNDP introduced the GII in the Human Development Report 2010 (United Nations Development Programme 2010, 90). The GII measures the position of women relative to men in a given state on the basis of female reproductive health, empowerment, and economic status. No state has achieved gender parity, or complete equality between men and women, but the GII gives us a sense of how much a particular state needs to do to improve the status of women. Specifically, it provides a measurement of the loss of potential human development (recall that UNDP was the first agency to discuss human development directly) stemming from disparities between male and female economic status, empowerment, and health. To provide several examples, in 2014 Slovenia ranked 1st (closest to gender parity), Sweden ranked 6th, China ranked 40th, the United States ranked 55th, Saudi Arabia ranked 56th, Chile ranked 65th, and Afghanistan ranked 152nd (United Nations Development Programme 2015).

Another helpful measure of gender inequality is the World Economic Forum's **Global Gender Gap Index (GGGI)**, which focuses on the economic disparities between males and females. The GGGI 2015 measures economic participation and opportunity, educational attainment, political empowerment, and health and survival in 140 states' economies. The GGGI 2015 ranked Iceland closest to parity, placing Sweden 4th, Slovenia 9th, United States 28th, Chile 73rd, China 91st, and Saudi Arabia 134th (World Economic Forum 2015). Afghanistan was not ranked. As is clear from our examples, the types of indicators used to measure gender equality determine how a particular state fares in the rankings, so it is always best to use multiple measures when feasible in order to form as complete a picture as possible.

Both the GII and the GGGI compare males and females; this binary approach is common within policy circles, although recognition of the impact of gender norms on LGBTQ persons has started to emerge in recent years.

Progress toward gender equality is not just a women's issue, and "gender" should never be considered synonymous with "women." Gender inequality, discrimination, and violence affect men and boys—especially those who do not fit the heterosexual masculine social ideal—and LGBTQ persons as well as women and girls. Indeed, our viewpoint here is that gender inequality in all of its many forms negatively affects human security for all and—by extension—detracts from state and global security. Much of the focus on gender inequality in foreign and domestic policy has focused on improving conditions for women and girls. As such, many of the examples in this chapter focus on gender inequality's effects on women and girls in particular, with the acknowledgment that the picture is far more complex than such examples describe.

GENDER (IN)EQUALITY AND HUMAN (IN)SECURITY

Gender inequality is a significant barrier to the realization of human security because it creates legal, social, economic, and political constraints on individuals and inhibits their ability to thrive—and in many places on the likelihood that a person will survive to old age or even past early childhood. The entrenched view that some people have less intrinsic worth than others because of their sex or gender leads to differential treatment within the home, schools, workplaces, political institutions, and daily social encounters. Girls may drop out of school or attend infrequently if schools do not have facilities to allow them to manage menstruation privately (Hudson et al. 2012, 27). A family may not send a girl child to school if school fees are high, her labor is needed at home, she is married early, there is little anticipated return on the investment of education because a woman's prospects for employment are few, travel to school is dangerous, or the school itself is threatened by groups opposed to girls' education. In states with lower levels of gender equality women may face obstacles to obtaining a divorce, even from an abusive spouse, or family laws may prohibit a woman from maintaining custody of her children in the event of a divorce (Hudson et al. 2012, 31). Even the prosecution of violent crimes can be unequal and subjective when gender inequality exists, placing a higher burden of proof on female survivors, especially in the event of a sexual offense like rape (Westmarland and Gangoli 2011). When gender norms privilege males and marginalize or discriminate against females, it can be difficult for women and girls to pursue an education, obtain and keep paid employment, decide if and when to have children, seek out adequate health care, participate in political processes, and have a stake in household financial decisions.

Extreme dangers like natural disasters and war are made worse by gender inequality. In societies with higher levels of gender equality, women are more likely to survive natural disasters; as levels of inequality increase, however, women suffer violence, exploitation, and death at higher rates than men. Some reasons relate directly to the onset of disaster, as in the following examples: if girls are not taught how to swim or not allowed to swim, they are more likely to die in the event of a flood, typhoon, or tsunami; or if social norms require women and girls to wear heavy or restrictive clothing, it is more difficult for them to flee dangers such as rising flood waters, fires, man-made violence, or other threats. Others are less directly tied to the onset of a disaster than to the breakdown of stability that follows; women and girls in societies with lower levels of gender inequality are more vulnerable to trafficking, sexual violence and exploitation, and domestic violence in times of instability (United Nations Development Programme 2010). In armed conflict as in natural disasters, women and girls are also more likely to carry the burden of caring for young and elderly family members, which constrains their ability to flee or evacuate. Daily activities such as fetching water or cooking fuel can place women and girls in harm's way, especially when they have to travel long distances through active conflict zones.

Devaluing people on the basis of gender makes them more likely to suffer physical violence, poverty and deprivation, and psychological harm. Because of discriminatory gender norms that favor males over females, there are an estimated 163 million "missing" girls and women in the world; they have been lost to sex-selective abortion, female infanticide, childhood mortality, maternal mortality, suicide, and violence in many forms (Hudson et al. 2012, 28). Gender inequality creates both imminent physical and chronic threats to human security, which makes it an issue that shapes the prospects for durable human security. Initiatives that work to improve gender equality also enhance durable or long-term human security; when foreign or domestic policy initiatives attempt to change entrenched norms or understandings about the relative worth of people of different genders, they expand opportunities for all individuals. Girls' education is often cited as one of the highest-yield investments in developing states (Coleman 2004, Herz and Sperling 2004, Sperling, Winthrop, and Kwauk 2016); when state governments, foreign aid, or foreign investments fund girls' education, the payoffs for families and society far outweigh the short-term costs. Education is a powerful equalizer that creates opportunities for individuals to thrive, one of the hallmarks of durable human security. When girls and women have better access to education—and when a state has higher levels of gender equality in general—birth rates and child mortality rates fall, childhood nutrition improves, communities become more stable, public health improves, the economy strengthens, and governance institutions become more democratic (Coleman 2004). In short, increased gender equality can lead to improved durable human security.

Gender inequality becomes a human security issue when it arises from societal norms that diminish the value of individuals on the basis of gender and thereby threaten the security of those individuals for the reasons discussed previously. Gender inequality may be entrenched in a state's institutions because of the existence of strong gender norms that devalue individuals on the basis of gender, and when societal norms and state institutions perpetuate threats to well-being, the situation is one of human insecurity. Efforts to promote positive social norms that value individuals of all genders and to reform institutions like family law, political processes, employment protections, and educational systems (to name only a few) can dramatically improve the human security situation.

THE LINKAGES BETWEEN GENDER AND STATE AND GLOBAL SECURITY

Gender equality improves the prospects for state and global security as well as human security, so in addition to the normative rationale for treating people of all genders equally—such a stance holds that all human beings are entitled to the same rights, freedoms, and opportunities, regardless of gender—there are clear strategic or instrumental reasons for doing so. States with high levels of domestic gender equality are more stable and less inclined toward aggressive foreign policy behaviors that endanger the delicate balance of global security; states with political, social, and economic gender equality are less likely to resort to military action to settle their international disputes (Caprioli 2000, 65). Furthermore, states with higher levels of gender equality employ lower levels of violence during international crisis situations (Caprioli and Boyer 2001, 515). Gender inequality is not only a predictor of state behavior on the international level; however, states with high levels of gender inequality are also more likely to experience intrastate or civil conflict (Caprioli 2005).

Issues of gender inequality are often overlooked as central to state and global security, as "gender" translates (to many) as "women's issues" or social issues (Caprioli 2005, Hudson et al. 2012). If we start to untangle the complex web of gender relations and norms, we can begin to see the consequences of discrimination and violence, not just for individuals but for society as a whole and the state and its foreign relations by extension. Hudson and den Boer caution that exaggerated gender inequality, characterized by excessively high **male:female sex ratios** (the number of males per 100 females in a population) resulting from son preference, sex-selective abortion, and discrimination against and abuse of girls and women, has led in some states (their study focuses explicitly on China and India) to a "surplus" of men. This surplus—men who are unable to marry and live within the traditional family unit—contributes to instability within the state, which in turn affects the way in which the state makes governance and foreign policy decisions (Hudson and den Boer 2002, 6). Even if a state does not have such a surplus of restive men, gender-based violence, and inequality are still concerns relevant to security studies and policy. In their research, Hudson, Ballif-Spanvill, Caprioli, and Emmett argue that all of the international relations can be traced back to gender relations: the global financial crisis beginning in 2008 could have taken a different turn if there had been more women sitting in the boardrooms of key actors; the HIV/AIDS epidemic relates back to sexual violence and exploitation, disproportionately affecting girls and women; and overpopulation and the accompanying social and economic strains could be alleviated through women's empowerment and improved reproductive freedom (Hudson et al. 2012, 1–3). If state and international policies, civil society efforts, and economic investments do more to address gender inequality, they will also begin to address some of the world's most pressing problems.

Sweden's Feminist Foreign Policy: Gender at the Center of International Affairs

Sweden has written gender equality into its domestic and foreign policies, demonstrating that states can (and do) make gender a pillar of statecraft. At the center of its stance on gender equality is the principle of fairness, the notion "that everyone, regardless of gender, has the right to work and support themselves, to balance career and family life, and to live without the fear of abuse of violence" (Swedish Institute 2016). This principle is in line with the central tenets of human security and the concept of durable human security. Ranked 6th in the 2014 GII and 4th in the 2015 GGGI, Sweden has consistently received praise for its gender equality measures at home and abroad and has been at the top of the GII since the World Economic Forum began assessing states in 2006. Sweden's government has made **feminist foreign policy**—an approach to foreign affairs that emphasizes women's participation, rights, and empowerment and gender equality—a cornerstone of its international initiatives and security measures. In her 2016 Statement of Government Policy, Minister for Foreign Affairs Margot Wallström contended that the "situation in the world calls for a feminist foreign policy that aims to strengthen women's representation and access to resources" (Wallström 2016). Having previously served as the UN Secretary-General's Special Representative on Sexual Violence in Armed Conflict (2010–2012), Wallström was acutely aware of the very real impact of gender-based violence and discrimination, and, upon her appointment as foreign minister in 2014, the Swedish government adopted a feminist foreign policy approach. Factoring gender into foreign policy is still a novel approach, and one that led to a diplomatic skirmish with Saudi Arabia in 2015 (Nordberg 2015, Taylor 2015), but it places at the heart of international politics the notion that states and the international community as a whole are more secure when the entire population has full and equal access to rights and opportunities to thrive.

GLOBAL EFFORTS TO IMPROVE GENDER EQUALITY

The link between gender equality and more peaceful international politics is suggested not just in the academic literature but also in international policy. Decades-long advocacy efforts by women's rights groups, human rights organizations, the UN and other multilateral organizations, and states supportive of gender equality initiatives have resulted in several international agreements that hold states accountable in the face of gender-based discrimination, violence, and inequality in representation. In its earliest days the UN declared that all people are equal and entitled to the same rights, regardless of sex (United Nations 1945) and established the Commission on the Status of Women (CSW), tasked with informing and creating policies to promote gender equality, under the Economic and Social Council (ECOSOC). The **Convention on the Elimination of All Forms of Discrimination against Women** was signed on December 18, 1979, and came into effect on September 3, 1981, during the UN Decade for Women (1976–1985). The binding agreement defines gender-based discrimination and establishes steps that **states parties** (states that have signed and ratified the Convention) should take to end discrimination against women, including changes to the state's legal system, establishment of public institutions to prevent discrimination, and measures to prevent discriminatory actions. Several states have not signed the treaty (including Iran, Somalia, Sudan, Tonga, and the Holy See—the Vatican), and some have signed but not ratified it (including the United States and Palau). Of the 189 states parties, about 50 states have ratified CEDAW with reservations to specific articles, which limit a state's full compliance with the Convention in keeping with preexisting national laws or cultural or religious constraints. CEDAW's adoption provided a legal foundation upon which gender equality advocates could work toward more extensive and inclusive protections.

The 1990s saw tremendous transnational advocacy around human rights in general and women's human rights and gender equality in particular. The end of the Cold War created more space for discussions of non-traditional security issues (as we have discussed in previous chapters), including human security, the rights and security of women and children, and gender issues (Hudson 2010, 69–72). In addition to a shifting global political landscape, the genocidal wars in the former Yugoslavia and Rwanda featured sexual and gender-based violence on a massive scale, creating greater global public awareness of the extreme brutality that can result from destructive gender norms. In 1995, during the Fourth World Conference on Women in Beijing and on the heels of global press coverage of gender-based violence in war, women's human rights advocates secured another international agreement. The **Beijing Platform for Action** established women's rights as human rights, made commitments to protecting women's human rights, and called for a global shift in thinking about gender equality as a broader issue of concern for all people rather just than one half of the population. Shortly thereafter, the Millennium Development Goals made gender equality and women's empowerment explicit objectives to be met by 2015. MDG Number 3 (MDG 3), "promote gender equality and empower women," and MDG Number 5 (MDG 5), "reduce by three quarters the maternal mortality ratio," dealt explicitly with both structural and imminent physical threats to the well-being of women and girls in the pursuit of an end to poverty, hunger, disease, and human insecurity. The Sustainable Development Goals, adopted in 2015 with a target date of 2030, similarly address gender-based discrimination and inequality—specifically, in SDG 5, "Achieve gender equality and empower all women and girls," noting that despite the progress made under the MDGs, women and girls still suffer violence and discrimination. Because gender norms are so deeply entrenched in culture and society, and because these norms typically privilege one group of people over all others, gender equality is an elusive objective.

At the start of the new millennium, and thanks to sustained transnational advocacy, gender became an item on the UN Security Council's agenda, as well. The Security Council adopted **Resolution 1325** in October 2000. Chapter 6 introduced Resolution 1325 in the context of comprehensive peace accords, and it is important to revisit it as an achievement in the push for women's involvement in international decision-making processes. The resolution was the first in what would become the Security Council's **Women, Peace, and Security (WPS)** agenda, which is a set of Security Council resolutions that call, in part, for greater participation of women in conflict resolution and peacebuilding processes. Recognizing that war disproportionately affects women and girls (for reasons including those we discussed as threats to durable human security previously) and that female voices have historically been absent from peace processes, WPS aims to improve female participation in decision-making, enhance the protection of women and girls in armed conflict, and prevent the outbreak of armed conflict. The logic behind Resolution 1325 and WPS in general is that by making negotiations and peace processes more representative of society, peace agreements and conflict resolution will be more effective in the long run. In other words, there is a link between the human security of women and girls and the long-term stability of states.

Hudson et al. assert that the security of women serves as the basis for national and global stability—without eliminating gender inequality and gender-based violence and discrimination we cannot expect to end armed conflict or achieve national or global security. More to the point, they articulate that gender equality initiatives and efforts to improve women's security do not stand to detract from men's security and opportunities; the ability of *all* individuals to thrive is key to stability and security (Hudson et al. 2012, 200). Progress toward these goals can be made through partnerships and collaboration between a wide array of domestic and international actors. The initiatives and goals discussed here are clearly global in scope and objectives, but of course not all progress toward gender equality happens on the international level, and the next section offers a glimpse into two different approaches to gender equality in foreign and domestic policy.

BOX 10.1. "THINK ABOUT IT . . ."—SUSTAINABLE DEVELOPMENT GOAL 5

SDG 5 aims to achieve gender equality and empower women and girls across the globe. In addition to ending gender-based discrimination and violence, SDG 5's targets include specific customs, practices, and entrenched norms.

Three of the targets are as follows:

- "Eliminate all harmful practices, such as child, early and forced marriage and female genital mutilation."
- "Recognize and value unpaid care and domestic work through the provision of public services, infrastructure and social protection policies and the promotion of shared responsibility within the household and the family as nationally appropriate."
- "Ensure women's full and effective participation and equal opportunities for leadership at all levels of decision-making in political, economic, and public life."

For each of the targets, consider the following:

1. How does the listed custom, practice, or norm inhibit gender equality?

2. To what extent is the custom, practice, or norm an issue in your state or community?
3. What are potential sources of opposition and obstacles to change?
4. How might local, national, regional, or global actors make a difference?

(Targets excerpted from United Nations. 2015. "Goal 5: Achieve gender equality and empower all women and girls." http://www.un.org/sustainabledevelop ment/gender-equality/)

Gender Equality in Afghanistan: Opportunities and Obstacles

Gender inequality in Afghanistan has been a frequent topic in Western policy circles and popular discourse for more than a decade (Hirschkind and Mahmood 2002). The oppression of women under the Taliban regime became a prominent foreign policy issue in the build-up to armed intervention in Afghanistan in response to the September 11, 2001, attacks on New York City and Washington, DC; systemic violations of women's human rights were cited as grounds for humanitarian intervention (Kandiyoti 2008, 155). Calls for recognition of the hardships women and girls faced under the Taliban emphasized the grim reality facing those who happened to be born female: under Taliban rule women could not seek employment; girls' schools were closed; universities could not educate women; women and girls had extremely limited freedom of movement; physical violence and corporal punishment were common responses to transgressions of Taliban rules; and— perhaps the most common imagery used in Western discussions—women and girls were required to wear the *burqa* (Hirschkind and Mahmood 2002, 340). Years later, progress toward gender equality in the post-conflict reconstruction phase has been slower than advocates hoped it would be, as evidenced by the poor GII ranking discussed at the outset of this chapter (the state ranked 152nd in the UNDP's 2014 gender inequality assessment). The issue of gender inequality in Afghanistan brings up important questions: When a population experiences widespread gender inequality and gender-based violence and discrimination, who is responsible for bringing about positive change? Further, which local, national, regional, or global actors are best positioned to foment successful long-term change?

The difficulty of addressing gender inequality in Afghanistan, in conjunction with the multilateral armed intervention to depose the Taliban regime, stems from the fact that such efforts often focused on Islamic norms and law as inherently oppressive, emphasized the importance of achieving

Western visions of women's rights and empowerment for Afghan women, and overlooked the disproportionate impact of armed conflict on women. When approaches to gender equality fail to maintain an analytical view of current conditions and how those conditions came to be, and neglect the voices of affected individuals, initiatives premised on noble objectives fall short in their application. As one study of U.S. popular and political condemnation of women's oppression in Afghanistan observes, "A number of commentators, in discussions that preceded the war, regularly failed to connect the predicament of women in Afghanistan with the massive military and economic support that the US provided, as part of its Cold War strategy, to the most extreme of Afghan religious militant groups" (Hirschkind and Mahmood 2002, 341); in other words, the effort to stand with the women and girls of Afghanistan accounted for only some of the root causes of their insecurity. The Western feminist campaign to secure Afghan women's rights also established an artificial juxtaposition of subordinate/oppressed veiled and liberated/empowered uncovered women and girls, applying a broad brush that equated voluntary observance of religious and cultural norms of modesty with the extreme political dictates of a governing regime, thus inadvertently stripping away female agency and choice where it may have been present (Hirschkind and Mahmood 2002, 352) and leading to divisions among transnational women's rights advocates over the best approach to demonstrating solidarity with Afghan women (Kandiyoti 2008, 155). These two observations point to a potential pitfall of gender equality initiatives (or those related to many other human security issues): to create successful and lasting change, local, national, regional, and global actors must appreciate the context in which they work, seek out support and input from beneficiaries (those whose lives are affected by the intervention or initiative), and ultimately ensure that they appreciate the *humanity* and agency of the subjects of policies and discussions.

In fact, collaboration between the Government of the Islamic Republic of Afghanistan, Afghan civil society groups, transnational women's rights groups, and foreign government agencies has led the state to make an extraordinary number of commitments to improving the security of women and girls and expanding their opportunities to thrive. The state's revised constitution now specifies legal rights and protections for women and girls. In 2003 Afghanistan officially ratified the Convention on the Elimination of Discrimination against Women (it signed the convention in 1980). Afghanistan's history, governance structure, and relationship between the government and local civil society and international donors create both opportunities for and obstacles to lasting change; the influence of local governing bodies throughout much of the state means that centralized change at the level of the central government may not always diffuse effectively (Kandiyoti 2008, 175–77). As a result, the numerous positive legal changes (improvements on paper) do not necessarily affect the daily lives, security, and opportunities of women and girls in Afghanistan (Barr 2013).

CONCLUSION: GENDER EQUALITY AT HOME AND ABROAD

No state can boast complete gender equality. Whether a state ranks first or last in the gender equality indexes we introduced in this chapter, there are always avenues to reduce gender-based disparities in the provision of basic needs and opportunities and ensure freedom from violence and discrimination on the basis of sex, gender, or sexuality. The two vignettes in this chapter—gender equality in Afghanistan and feminist foreign policy in Sweden—illustrate differing approaches and obstacles to empowering women and girls and reducing gender-based violence and discrimination. As with any of the human security issues we discuss in this book—both in armed conflict and in "peacetime"—there is no "one size fits all" solution to gender inequality that will work in every region, state, and locality. Instead, when devising policies and programs to empower women, LGBTQ persons, and other marginalized groups, civil society, states, and international organizations must consider the context-specific obstacles and influences that affect the prospects for gender equality.

As we discussed previously, gender equality influences national and global peace and stability; the more a state ensures equal protection and opportunity for all people, regardless of gender, the less likely it is to engage in aggressive foreign policy behaviors and the more likely it is to experience social and political stability within its borders. The relationship between gender equality and peace goes the other way, as well: the experience of armed conflict, state violence, intervention, and insurgency also affects the prospects for gender equality. Political repression, sectarian violence, displacement, and war can create conditions under which progress toward gender equality rolls back. For example, among Syrian refugees living in Jordan, Iraq, and Lebanon, the rate of child marriage has increased for girls (from 12 percent in prewar Syria 2011 to 25 percent in 2013) amid families' concerns related to limited resources, lack of opportunities for education and employment, and threats of sexual violence and harassment (Save the Children 2014). Gender inequality and gender-based violence and discrimination are serious impediments to an individual's ability to thrive, and foreign, domestic, and security policy must take them into account (Hudson et al. 2012). What is abundantly clear, in both academic research and the practice of international politics, is that gender inequality creates real barriers to the achievement of durable human security.

Discussion Questions

1. How do the different measures of gender inequality vary? Is this variation problematic? Why or why not?
2. To what extent should gender concerns factor in to a state's foreign policy framework?
3. To what extent should gender concerns factor in to a state's domestic policy framework?
4. What are the advantages of pursuing gender equality initiatives derived from grassroots domestic actors, organizations, or movements? What are the disadvantages?
5. What are the advantages of pursuing gender equality initiatives derived from international actors, organizations, or movements? What are the disadvantages?

NOTE

1. We note here that sexuality—the romantic or sexual preference for persons of a particular sex—is a concept that is distinct from both sex and gender. A person's sex and gender do not necessarily determine that person's sexuality; a female may identify as female and prefer other females, a male may identify as male and prefer females, a female may identify as male and prefer males, and so on.

FURTHER READING AND WEB RESOURCES

The Malala Fund: https://www.malala.org/girls-education

United Nations Development Programme. *Human Development Report—the Real Wealth of Nations: Pathways to Human Development.* 2010. http://hdr.undp.org/en/content/human-development-report-2010

United Nations Development Programme. Gender Inequality Index: http://hdr.undp.org/en/content/gender-inequality-index-gii

United Nations Millennium Development Goals and beyond 2015. Goal 3: Promote Gender Equality and Empower Women: http://www.un.org/millenniumgoals/gender.shtml

United Nations Office of the High Commissioner on Human Rights. Committee on the Elimination of Discrimination against Women: http://www.ohchr.org/en/hrbodies/cedaw/pages/cedawindex.aspx

United Nations Sustainable Development Goals. Goal 5: Achieve Gender Equality and Empower All Women and Girls: http://www.un.org/sustainabledevelopment/gender-equality/

UN Women. Fourth World Conference on Women, Beijing Platform for Action. 1995. http://www.un.org/womenwatch/daw/beijing/platform/

The WomanStats Project: http://www.womanstats.org

World Economic Forum. Global Gender Gap Report 2014: http://reports.weforum.org/global-gender-gap-report-2014/

Additional Sources for Research on Gender Equality in Afghanistan

Equality for Peace and Democracy. *Afghanistan Gender Equality Report Card: Evaluating the Government of Afghanistan's Commitments to Women and Gender Equality*. 2015. Accessed August 4, 2016. http://www.epd-afg.org/wp-content/uploads/2014/03/GERC-English.pdf

UNICEF. "Afghanistan—Basic Education and Gender Equality." Accessed August 4, 2016. http://www.unicef.org/afghanistan/education.html

United Nations. "Consideration of Reports Submitted by States Parties under Article 18 of the Convention on the Elimination of All Forms of Discrimination against Women—Afghanistan." CEDAW/C/AFG/1–2. 2011.

United Nations Development Programme. "Gender Equality Project (GEP II)." Accessed August 4, 2016. http://www.af.undp.org/content/afghanistan/en/home/operations/projects/womens_empowerment/gepii.html

Ziba Mir-Hosseini. "Beyond 'Islam' vs. 'Feminism.'" *IDS Bulletin* 42, no. 1 (2011). Accessed August 4, 2016. http://www.zibamirhosseini.com/documents/mir-hosseini-article-beyond-islam-vs-feminism--2011.pdf

Additional Sources for Research on Gender Equality Policy in Sweden

Government Offices of Sweden. *Swedish Foreign Service action plan for feminist foreign policy 2015–2018 including focus areas for 2016*. 2015. Accessed August 4, 2016. http://www.government.se/information-material/2015/12/swedish-foreign-service-action-plan-for-feminist-foreign-policy-20152018-including-focus-areas-for-2016/

Reid Standish. "How Sweden Is Pursuing Its 'Feminist Foreign Policy' in the Age of Erdogan, Putin, and Trump." *Foreign Policy*, July 29, 2016.

United Nations. "Consideration of Reports Submitted by States Parties under Article 18 of the Convention on the Elimination of All Forms of Discrimination against Women—Sweden." CEDAW/C/SWE/7. 2006.

For Deeper Discussion

Laura J. Shepherd, ed. *Gender Matters in Global Politics: A Feminist Introduction to International Relations*. New York: Routledge, 2010.

Michele L. Swers. *The Difference Women Make: The Policy Impact of Women in Congress*. Chicago: University of Chicago Press, 2002.

Natalie Florea Hudson. *Gender, Human Security and the United Nations: Security Language as a Political Framework for Women*. New York: Routledge, 2010.

REFERENCES

Barr, Heather. "Afghanistan: Failing Commitments to Protect Women's Rights." Human Rights Watch, July 11, 2013.

Caprioli, Mary. "Gendered Conflict." *Journal of Peace Research* 37, no. 1 (2000): 53–68.

Caprioli, Mary. "Primed for Violence: The Role of Gender Inequality in Predicting Internal Conflict." *International Studies Quarterly* 49 (2005): 161–78.

Caprioli, Mary, and Mark Boyer. "Gender, Violence, and International Crisis." *Journal of Conflict Resolution* 45, no. 4 (2001): 503–18.

Coleman, Isobel. "The Payoff from Women's Rights." *Foreign Affairs* 83, no. 3 (2004): 80–95.

Goldstein, Joshua. *War and Gender: How Gender Shapes the War System and Vice Versa*. New York: Cambridge University Press, 2001.

Herz, Barbara, and Gene B. Sperling. *What Works in Girls' Education: Evidence and Policies from the Developing World*. New York: Council on Foreign Relations, 2004.

Hirschkind, Charles, and Saba Mahmood. "Feminism, the Taliban, and Politics of Counter-Insurgency." *Anthropological Quarterly* 75, no. 2 (2002): 339–54.

Hudson, Natalie Florea. *Gender, Human Security and the United Nations: Security Language as a Political Framework for Women*. New York: Routledge, 2010.

Hudson, Valerie M., and Andrea den Boer. "A Surplus of Men, a Deficit of Peace." *International Security* 26, no. 4 (2002): 5–38.

Hudson, Valerie M., Bonnie Ballif-Spanvill, Mary Caprioli, and Chad F. Emmett. *Sex & World Peace*. New York: Columbia University Press, 2012.

Kandiyoti, Deniz. "The Politics of Gender and Reconstruction in Afghanistan: Old Dilemmas or New Challenges?" In *Gendered Peace: Women's Struggles for Post-War Justice and Reconciliation*, by Donna Pankhurst, 155–85. New York: Routledge, 2008.

Nordberg, Jenny. "Who's Afraid of a Feminist Foreign Policy?" *The New Yorker*, April 15, 2015.

Save the Children. *Too Young to Wed: The Growing Problem of Child Marriage among Syrian Girls in Jordan*. London: Save the Children, 2014.

Sperling, Gene B., Rebecca Winthrop, and Christina Kwauk. *What Works in Girls' Education: Evidence for the World's Best Investment*. Washington, DC: The Brookings Institution, 2016.

Swedish Institute. *Gender Equality in Sweden*. June 21, 2016. https://sweden.se/society/gender-equality-in-sweden/ (accessed August 4, 2016).

Taylor, Adam. "How Saudi Arabia Turned Sweden's Human Rights Criticisms into an Attack on Islam." *The Washington Post*, March 24, 2015.

United Nations. "Charter of the United Nations." October 24, 1945.

United Nations Development Programme. *Gender and Disasters*. New York: United Nations Development Programme, 2010.

United Nations Development Programme. *Gender Inequality Index (GII)*. 2015.

United Nations Development Programme. "Human Development Report—The Real Wealth of Nations: Pathways to Human Development." 2010.

Wallström, Margot. "Statement of Government Policy in the Parliamentary Debate on Foreign Affairs 2016." *Government Offices of Sweden*. February 24, 2016. http://www.government.se/speeches/2016/02/statement-of-government-policy-in-the-parliamentary-debate-on-foreign-affairs-2016/ (accessed August 4, 2016).

Westmarland, Nicole, and Geetanjali Gangoli, eds. *International Approaches to Rape*. Portland, OR: The Policy Press, 2011.

World Economic Forum. "The Global Gender Gap Index 2015." 2015. http://widgets.weforum.org/gender-gap-2015/

Chapter 11

Climate Change and Environmental Security

Learning Objectives

This chapter will enable readers to:

1. Differentiate between climate change and global warming.
2. Identify the effects of global warming and climate change.
3. Discuss the connections between climate change and human security.
4. Discuss the connections between climate change and states and global security.
5. Identify the difficulties related to global cooperation to address climate change.

In Paris in December 2015, the international community agreed on a set of goals to try to slow or reverse the course of climate change and prevent its most catastrophic effects. As a problem that is truly global in scope, climate change affects each of the three types of security—human, national, and global—but prior international agreements have failed to generate cooperation among states. At the time of writing, the fate and effectiveness of the Paris Agreement remain uncertain. There is broad scientific consensus that climate change is man-made and poses a serious threat to the stability of ecosystems and human communities. A 2015 global public opinion poll conducted by Pew Research shows that majorities in the forty states polled view climate change as a serious threat. The poll also indicates that individuals in Latin America and sub-Saharan Africa are more concerned about climate change than those in other regions, and that individuals in the United States and China—the world's largest emitters of greenhouse gases—are less concerned. Regardless, more than three-quarters of respondents surveyed indicated that they view policy changes as essential in the fight against climate change. When there is variation in perceptions of the seriousness of a problem like climate change, and particularly when the top contributors to that problem fail to view it as urgent, identifying the problem as a security threat in any sense and finding a comprehensive multilateral solution to the problem will be difficult.

This chapter examines climate change and the role of environmental instability in shaping human, national, and global security. The chapter begins with a brief discussion of the scientific evidence for climate change. Following the exploration of the science of climate change, the chapter delves into the security implications within each approach addressed by the book—human, state, and global security. The security section also looks at the existential threat faced by the Marshall Islands as global warming leads to sea level rise and flooding of the island nation. The next section examines international efforts to regulate greenhouse gas emissions and set goals to prevent the worst effects of climate change. The chapter closes with a look at bottom-up efforts to address climate change and conclusions in the context of current international affairs.

GLOBAL WARMING AND CLIMATE CHANGE

In 1824 Jean Baptiste Joseph Fourier, a French physicist, first proposed the **greenhouse effect**, wherein gases (including water vapor and carbon dioxide [CO_2]) help to warm the earth by trapping radiation in the atmosphere. He likened the planet's atmosphere to a glass cover over a box in sunlight: the sun's rays warm the box and the air under the glass cover, which is in contact with the sun-warmed box, remains warm as the glass keeps the air (and heat radiation) from escaping (American Institute of Physics 2016). As early as 1824, then, scientists had an awareness of the link between gases in the atmosphere and the temperature of the earth. In 1896 Svante Arrhenius, a Swedish chemist, observed that industrialization enhances the greenhouse effect of Earth's atmosphere through the burning of coal. Throughout the twentieth century, engineers and scientists continued to document the effects of increased CO_2 in the atmosphere and the overall warming of the earth, but international political recognition remained muted until the last quarter of the century (BBC News 2013).

Wallace Broecker, a scientist in the United States, published a short piece in *Science*, in 1975, titled "Climatic Change: Are We on the Brink of a Pronounced Global Warming?" (Broecker 1975). He predicted a period of "rapid warming" in the twenty-first century with "global temperatures warmer than any in the last 1000 years" (Broecker 1975, 460–61). Indeed, NASA data on global surface temperatures and Arctic sea ice extent indicate that 2016 broke records, with average temperatures during the first six months of the year 1.3 degrees Celsius warmer than late nineteenth-century temperatures (NASA 2016). **Global warming** is a term that refers to overall increases in the average temperatures of the earth's oceans and atmosphere. Global warming is caused by high concentrations of CO_2 and other greenhouse gases in the atmosphere, which trap heat and warm the earth through the greenhouse effect. The term **climate change** is used to describe sustained changes in global or regional climate patterns that stem from overall warming. Climate change can be seen in the increased prevalence of extreme weather like strong hurricanes or blizzards, increased frequency of droughts or polar vortexes, or changing levels of precipitation. While the terms "global warming" and "climate change" are often used interchangeably, they refer to two distinct phenomena. Of course, they're closely related: global warming causes climate change.

The Earth has experienced warming and cooling trends (or climatic changes) throughout its history, but there is scientific consensus that the current warming trend, in which average temperatures are increasing at a rate unseen in the past 1,300 years, is due to human activity—particularly the high levels of carbon dioxide and other greenhouse gas emissions present in the atmosphere since the Industrial Revolution (IPCC 2007, 5, NASA 2017). The earth has experienced warming and cooling trends over time in the past, but the pace and degree of the current shift are unlike the naturally occurring cycles evident in Earth's history. In 1981, atmospheric physicists at NASA published an article in *Science* observing a 0.2-degree Celsius rise in global temperatures from the 1960s to 1980 and warning that global warming linked to atmospheric carbon dioxide could lead to drought-prone regions, melting sea ice, and climate shifts in the twenty-first century (Hansen et al. 1981). Global climate change may be a subject of urgent consideration—and sometimes intense political debate—now, but climate scientists have pointed to the warming trend and its grave implications for decades.

The difficult question from a security perspective becomes: what do states and other security actors *do* about global warming and climate change? States, for their part, are often inclined toward the nationalist or state security perspective where concessions and efforts to mitigate the effects of climate change are concerned, and this orientation to a truly global security problem makes cooperative solutions elusive. Climate change offers us a case study through which we can see how the various approaches to security may align in theory but conflict in practice. When viewed in terms of short- and long-term threats to individuals and communities, the vicious cycle of insecurity, and the potential for chronic human insecurity to breed national and global instability, climate change constitutes a clear security concern according to each of the three approaches—in theory. In practice, especially as international **regimes** seeking to mitigate the effects of climate change lack sufficient support from key carbon-emitting states, political decision-makers have placed efforts to bolster human security against climate-related threats at odds with efforts to strengthen and protect national security and the domestic economy. Before we turn to the difficulty of cooperating to address the effects of climate change, we should first examine the rationale for considering global climate change a security concern.

THE SECURITY IMPLICATIONS OF CLIMATE CHANGE

The effects of climate change interact with other dimensions of human security, as well as national and global security, to create the potential for a range of short- and long-term security issues. For this reason, any discussion of climate change is also a discussion of food security, migration, and armed conflict, as well as a host of other acute and chronic security threats within each of the three approaches. Global warming and climate change are already contributing to sea level rise (due to melting sea ice), shifting weather patterns, extreme weather events, displacement, famine, and public health concerns like the spread of mosquito-borne illness to historically cooler regions. Still, it is difficult at this time to anticipate the exact effects of climate change. The degree of insecurity created by climate change will vary according to a region or state's geography, the strength of institutions and ability to mitigate climate-related threats, and future innovation and technological advances (Salehyan 2008). Despite the fact that there is a high level of consensus among climate scientists that the warming trend throughout the past century is linked to human activity (NASA 2017), the fact that the effects are not uniformly visible in the near term has opened climate change up to political debate within some states, especially within the United States. If states are unable or unwilling to adapt to the shifts brought about by climate change, states, their populations, and the broader global community will face security threats in the years to come.

We classify the environmental effects of climate change as threats to durable human security. The Intergovernmental Panel on Climate Change (IPCC) has warned that the long-term effects of climatic shifts will affect individual security and well-being through changes to affected economies, loss of traditional culture and knowledge, resource scarcity, and mass migration (Adger et al. 2014). When combined with flaws in state institutions and insufficient state capacity to shelter people from or compensate for climate-related challenges, these effects on individuals' lives and livelihoods become human security problems. In addition to its classification as a durable human security concern, climate change is likely to lead to acute security threats—including armed conflict—if the chronic security issues go unaddressed or if short-term changes or extreme weather events are significant enough to trigger upheaval (Barnett and Adger 2007, Hendrix and Glaser 2007, Meier, Bond, and Bond 2007). For instance, sustained drought (due to shifting weather patterns) and famine (due to state unwillingness or lack of capacity to provide sufficient food security) may lead to unrest, displacement, armed conflict, and state instability (Adger et al. 2014, Jones, Mattiacci, and Braumoeller 2017, Notaras 2011). Climate change in and of itself may not lead directly to armed conflict, but a combination of resource scarcity or rapid mass displacement due to extreme weather events with political, social, and economic institutions that contribute to chronic insecurity may lay the groundwork for acute insecurity, unrest, and armed conflict (Evans 2010, Jones, Mattiacci and Braumoeller 2017). The effects of climate change serve to exacerbate existing durable and acute security threats, worsening human security and—if left unchecked—state and global security. In considering climate change as a security concern at the individual, state, and global levels, we account for both chronic and acute threats and the interconnectedness of the three approaches to insecurity.

Climate Change and Human Security

The connection between human security and climate change is already visible, especially in island nations and low-lying areas of larger states, drought-prone regions, and the Arctic. Extreme weather events like strong hurricanes and floods devastate communities and displace families, insufficient rainfall or drought reduces the access to and availability of food and safe drinking water in affected regions, desertification triggers migration and resource competition, sea level rise forces people in coastal communities to abandon their homes, and melting ice in the Arctic forces indigenous communities to adapt their livelihoods and cultural traditions or move away as the landscape changes. The effects of climate change are most immediately and harshly felt by individuals and communities who rely on natural resources to sustain their livelihoods and who have little support from the state (whether because of a lack of willingness or a lack of capacity) to compensate for chronic or abrupt scarcity or displacement (Salehyan 2008). It follows, then, that individuals and communities within underdeveloped states in geographically vulnerable positions—such as hot, arid climates and low-lying coastal regions—will suffer the earliest and most intense security threats linked to climate change.

Climate change constitutes a durable human security threat, using the threshold we have discussed throughout the book, when its effects create or exacerbate other chronic security issues. For instance, climate change is linked to food insecurity when persistent drought leads to insufficient agricultural yields, which in turn lead to rising food prices and lack of availability of and access to nutritious foods. In early 2017, the UN issued a warning that famine in Somalia would likely occur unless international humanitarian organizations took quick action. Poor rainfall in the previous two seasons led to insufficient water supply for crops and livestock, leading to food shortages and financial instability for individuals and families; the Famine Early Warning Systems Network of the Food and Agriculture Organization estimated in February 2017 that 6.2 million people (out of a population of roughly 10.5 million people) in Somalia were in need of humanitarian assistance. Just six years prior, in 2011, famine devastated Somalia and cost more than a quarter million lives (UN News Centre 2017). Famine in Somalia provides an example of the interaction between various forms of human insecurity: drought, political instability, armed conflict, and poverty all contribute to the context in which famine becomes widespread and threatens a large portion of the population. While poor rainfall is not the only factor contributing to famine in Somalia, drought serves to exacerbate and combine with the political and socioeconomic factors to create human insecurity. Similarly, floods, tropical storms, tsunamis, and other natural disasters can severely damage agriculture and alter the price and availability of certain foods, contributing to food insecurity and economic instability around the world (Food and Agriculture Organization of the United Nations 2015). When the state lacks the capacity or willingness to safeguard its population from the worst effects of climate change, situations of human insecurity result.

Individuals living in coastal communities are at risk of displacement and unemployment if their homes gradually become unlivable due to rising tides, forcing individuals or entire communities to move inland and jeopardizing livelihoods, financial stability, and cultural traditions. The populations of the Marshall Islands, Tuvalu, and other island nations face the threat of displacement from rising sea levels, as do communities in low-lying coastal regions in larger states. Retreating waters also trigger migration and instability. Melting glaciers and shrinking lakes deplete the necessary freshwater reserves that are essential to the survival of communities, driving migration to urban centers or regions with more reliable access to water. Communities in the Andean plain have been forced to migrate to the Amazon Basin as a result of dwindling freshwater reserves, and the rapid depletion of Lake Chad has displaced millions in Cameroon, Chad, Niger, and Nigeria and exacerbated the security threat posed by the insurgent group Boko Haram (Benko 2017). Displaced individuals are at greater risk of chronic insecurity as they work to start over in a new community, often with considerably fewer financial, social, and material resources than they once possessed.

Climate change can also pose acute, short-term but severe human security threats. These threats come in the form of natural disasters affecting states and their populations without regard for the level of development or institutional capacity. Natural disasters present human security threats when the state lacks the capacity to remove people from harm's way to safer areas and respond with effective reconstruction and assistance after the threat has passed; this problem is not limited to developing or impoverished states, as wealthy states can still find themselves underprepared to handle the human security challenges posed by natural disasters. Further, the same state may respond differently to separate events on the basis of a number of factors, including the political or cultural centrality of the location and communities affected, lessons learned from past disaster responses, and human and financial resources available for emergency management. For example, the U.S. Federal Emergency Management Agency (FEMA) responded differently to Hurricane Sandy in 2012 than it did to Hurricane Katrina in 2005. After the inadequate response to Katrina, a devastating category 5 storm that made landfall in the Gulf Coast states from Florida to Texas and affected an estimated half million people and 90,000 square miles, the U.S. Congress passed the aptly named Post-Katrina Emergency Management Reform Act of 2006 (U.S. Government Accountability Office 2008). The deadly and costly efforts of insufficient coordination among federal agencies and between federal, state, and local agencies during and after Katrina led to the 2006 FEMA law and changes within the agency. When Hurricane Sandy, a category 3 storm, made landfall in the northeastern United States, FEMA had already deployed emergency response teams to the region. Prior to the 2006 law and agency reforms, FEMA worked under the view that emergency responders could begin working only once an area was already devastated; the 2006 law clarified FEMA's role and allowed for a preemptive emergency response, which was visible during and after Sandy's course (Starks 2012). Adequate responses to human insecurity created by natural disasters require significant resources and coordination of emergency management agencies and processes; as extreme weather events become more common, states and humanitarian relief agencies will have to bear the cost of these efforts in order to prevent or mitigate significant human suffering.

Climate Change and Its State and Global Security Linkages

As we have discussed in previous chapters, states do not immediately recognize all human security threats as state-level or national security concerns. There is a significant (and somewhat unpredictable) threshold before a climate-related issue moves from the area of human security to that of state security; for this reason, there may be more concern among individuals and

communities before the state is driven *by national or political interests* to recognize climate change as a security threat. The push for action to reverse the
course of climate change is bottom-up in some—but certainly not all—states.

Much of the rhetoric on climate change focuses on protecting resources
for future generations (e.g., the children and grandchildren of today's adults),
but national security policymaking usually operates on the basis of clear and
present threat, so there is a critical gap between the implications for human
security and the willingness of states to act. Evidence of this gap lies in the
difficulty of securing international cooperation on binding greenhouse gas
emission reduction agreements. If the state operates on a rational basis, making cost-benefit calculations prior to each action or policy decision, then a
state that is not immediately affected by climate change will hesitate to act in
response to the future threat if the costs of changing its behavior are high and
immediate and the benefits of that change are diffuse and in the future. Still,
even within the United States—a top carbon-emitting state and one with a
political faction that downplays the risks related to climate change—security
professionals have begun to advocate for political recognition of the linkages
between climate change and national security threats. Central to this advocacy is the notion that the deprivation, disruptions, and physical insecurity
created by extreme weather events, sea level rise, and desertification are
threat multipliers, or phenomena that make existing security threats worse
(Powers 2015, Revkin 2017). In addition, states and international institutions
like the International Monetary Fund and World Bank have made the argument that investments in clean energy, carbon pricing, and climate change
adaptation make good economic sense for states (The World Bank 2013).
Zambia, for instance, has been affected by climate change through droughts,
floods, and a resulting increase in poverty. Recognizing the economic impact
of climate change, the state has committed a significant share of its national
budget to climate change adaptation programs, removal of unnecessary fossil
fuel subsidies, and support for clean energy sources like solar and hydroelec-
tric power (The World Bank 2013, Zambian Development Agency 2017).
States facing the prospect of losing large portions or the entirety of their territory to sea level rise or unstable food supplies caused by desertification and
drought will view the effects of climate change as both a human security and
a national security threat, as Zambia's national budget suggests.

Climate change is, by definition, a global security concern. The melting
ice in the Arctic directly affects the territorial integrity of eight states—Canada, Denmark, Finland, Iceland, Norway, Russia, Sweden, and the United
States—and threatens to create a "tipping point" for global climate change
(Harvey 2016). The atmosphere does not contain borders, so the greenhouse
gas emissions released by one state do not stay within that state; all states
share the costs of high concentrations of greenhouse gas emissions, even

if they did not contribute equally to the problem. As the effects of climate change displace populations, more states will have to grapple with the decision to take in or keep out climate refugees. If inhospitable climates, drought, flooding, resource conflicts, and food insecurity create massive migration flows, the states these populations leave, those they travel through, and those in which they seek to settle will face the prospect of destabilization (Benko 2017). Climate-related threats do not observe borders and can destabilize entire regions if states do not have sufficient resources and institutional capacity to mitigate the effects of extreme weather events, droughts, sea level rise, famine, and resource conflicts. Of all of the durable and acute security threats discussed in this book, climate change is the one most directly linked to truly global instability and insecurity.

Because no single state can mitigate or solve climate change acting alone, this particular security concern constitutes a **collective action problem**. In a collective action problem, all actors (states in this particular case) have an interest in creating a solution to a problem that affects everyone. Nevertheless, solutions often come at some cost and this makes it difficult to convince individual actors to work toward any given solution. Since states will feel the effects of climate change differently, with states in the Global South likely to face the harshest effects earlier than wealthier states in the Global North, states will possess varying degrees of motivation or urgency to contribute to climate change mitigation and adaptation efforts.

The Marshall Islands: Rising Seas and International Advocacy

The states that are already experiencing the effects of climate change within their own borders are among the most vocal advocates of the need to recognize climate change as a global security threat. As these states naturally view climate change as a clear and immediate threat, the calculation of costs and benefits favors immediate and decisive action. One state is the Marshall Islands, a sovereign nation made up of twenty-nine atolls and five islands situated in the Pacific Ocean between Australia and Hawaii. In 2008 and 2013 the capital city of Majuro flooded, engulfed by high tides and surging waves. In April 2016, severe drought due to insufficient rainfall led President Hilda Heine to request emergency assistance from the U.S. government, with whom the Marshall Islands has had a Compact of Free Association since 1986. This compact of free association has facilitated migration from the Marshall Islands to the United States, leaving the former with a shrinking population as the island nation itself shrinks.

Flooding and the related salinization of freshwater on the islands and atolls, drought, prospects for economic and educational opportunities within the United States and elsewhere, and the after-effects of U.S. nuclear missile tests have contributed to a steady out-migration of the Marshallese population (Milman 2016, Milman and Ryan 2016). As the small island nation stands to lose its population and territory as the seas rise, it was active in building a coalition to support "vulnerable nations on the frontline of climate change" in advance of the United Nations Climate Change Conference, the 21st session of the Conference of Parties, or **COP 21**, in Paris in December 2015 (Komai 2015). The Coalition of High Ambition Nations pushed for a warming limit of 1.5 degrees Celsius above preindustrial average global temperatures. For states like the Marshall Islands, warming above 1.5 degrees poses an existential threat.

At present, the world is at 1 degree Celsius above preindustrial levels, and scientists are beginning to grapple with the exact ramifications of average global surface temperature increases of 1.5 and 2 degrees. The IPCC's Fifth Assessment Report, released in phases between September 2013 and November 2014, projects that global warming is likely to exceed the 1.5-degree mark by the end of the twenty-first century, and temperatures are likely to exceed the 2-degree mark in some scenarios. For island states like the Marshall Islands, drought-prone regions, and many developing states, 2 degrees above preindustrial temperatures would likely cause mass displacement due to sea level rise and dangerous heat, widespread food insecurity, frequent extreme weather events, irreversible coral reef die-off, and loss of territory (Silberg 2016), whereas staying below the 1.5-degree increase would reduce the likelihood of these catastrophic changes. The Coalition of High Ambition Nations is not a formal negotiating group, but it has continued to advocate for climate change mitigation in the months after COP 21. The coalition is also broader than just the states that are immediately affected by climate change; it includes more than 100 wealthy and developing states concerned by the alarming warming trend and its global effects. The Paris Agreement calls on states to limit warming to below 2 degrees Celsius and to pursue efforts to limit warming to 1.5 degrees above preindustrial levels; this agreement fell short of the Coalition's goals, leaving the most vulnerable states' futures in question. In the next section, we will take a look at how the international community has attempted to regulate the factors leading to climate change through multilateral agreements and the difficulty of achieving effective cooperation.

BOX 11.1. "THINK ABOUT IT . . ."—CLIMATE REFUGEES

Rising sea levels will leave coastal areas uninhabitable in the coming years and, as a result, populations will move inland when they can or seek to migrate to larger states when they cannot. The discussion of climate change–related migration often focuses on island nations, as they are the first to face significant—and existential—territorial threats from sea level rise.

Less commonly discussed are the regions within larger states, including the United States, that currently face human security threats from sea level rise. Isle de Jean Charles, an island in the Louisiana bayou, has long been home to members of the Biloxi-Chitimacha-Choctaw tribe. The waters of the Gulf of Mexico have steadily encroached on Isle de Jean Charles, which has lost more than 90 percent of its land to rising waters since 1955 (Davenport and Robertson 2016, Houten 2016).

In January 2016, the U.S. Department of Housing and Urban Development directed $1 billion in grants to thirteen U.S. states to support climate change adaptation. Isle de Jean Charles received $48 million to move the entire community, a population of about sixty people, inland (Beller and Depp 2016, Davenport and Robertson 2016, Houten 2016).

The residents of Isle de Jean Charles are **climate refugees**, individuals and communities forced by the effects of climate change to relocate from their homes. Like refugees fleeing man-made violence and destruction, climate refugees face the challenges of loss of livelihood, physical insecurity, and loss of cultural and ancestral traditions as they seek safety and stability in a new place.

Read the stories of Isle de Jean Charles in *National Geographic*, *Smithsonian Magazine*, and the *New York Times* and consider the human security impact of climate change on this community.

Beller and Depp 2017 (*Smithsonian Magazine*) is available online here: http://www.smithsonianmag.com/science-nature/residents-louisiana-island-americas-first-climate-refugees-180959585/

Davenport and Robertson 2016 (*New York Times*) is available online here: http://www.nytimes.com/2016/05/03/us/resettling-the-first-american-climate-refugees.html

Van Houten 2016 (*National Geographic*) is available online here: http://news.nationalgeographic.com/2016/05/160525-isle-de-jean-charles-louisiana-sinking-climate-change-refugees/

1. How do climate refugees differ from other displaced persons?
2. What are the most pressing security issues facing climate refugees?

3. What is the state's role in providing protection for climate refugees? Does the international community have a role to play?
4. What other aspects of human security do you see in the story of the residents of Isle de Jean Charles?

GLOBAL COOPERATION AND NATIONAL INTEREST: EFFORTS AND OBSTACLES

If we apply the concept of responsibility for security provision to the problem of global climate change, it is apparent that international agreements made by states would offer the most efficient path toward necessary policy changes. When states agree to limit their greenhouse gas emissions and encourage the development of clean energy sources and new technologies to reduce human contributions to climate change—and implement these agreements—that represents an important step toward providing security for the regions and populations that are most vulnerable to the effects of climate change.

Yet, coordination to slow or reverse the course of climate change is difficult. The international community is made up of nearly 200 states, all with different—sometimes competing—interests and varying levels of risk associated with climate change. Since a large share of greenhouse gas emissions come from the private sector, efforts to curb them require states to regulate economic activity; some governments are more willing to do this than others. International efforts to address climate change have sought to mitigate the collective action problem that makes states' cooperation in this area so challenging. The collective action problem in this particular case is created by (1) the shared or diffuse environmental effects of any one state's behavior, (2) the immediate economic and political costs of changing such behavior, and (3) the shared and chronologically distant benefits of taking action to combat climate change. Since some states—particularly those least negatively affected by climate change in the near future—have short-term economic or political interests in *not* cooperating, international efforts have to make cooperation as politically feasible, efficient, and cheap as possible. Alternatively, or in addition, such efforts must make reneging or not joining the effort too costly.

Effective agreements to address climate change require a cosmopolitan approach to security, one that requires states to contribute to a solution and perhaps—though not always—compromise short-term state economic gains for a future global (shared) benefit. Agreement is possible, as the international community has shown several times. Nevertheless, the substance and effectiveness of global agreements focused on climate change remain in question as the world continues to warm.

INTERNATIONAL AGREEMENTS: TOP-DOWN SOLUTIONS

When states come together to draft, sign, and ratify agreements to address shared problems, they take a top-down approach to problem-solving. The agreement reached will ideally change state-level policies and shape international-level coordination among states. Here we focus on four such agreements, three directly related to climate change and one that predates the climate change regime. Table 11.1 highlights key agreements on climate change.

A precursor to the international agreements on climate change is the **Montreal Protocol**, a treaty adopted by forty-six states in August 1987. The Montreal Protocol focuses specifically on protection of the ozone layer, and as such it lies outside of the climate change regime. As an early international effort to address a global public good (the ozone layer), the Montreal Protocol gives us an idea of what a successful environmental policy change looks like. The **ozone layer** is a portion of the earth's stratosphere that acts as a "sunscreen" for the planet and its inhabitants, absorbing the sun's ultraviolet radiation. Its depletion leaves humans especially vulnerable to skin cancer. The multilateral Montreal Protocol aims to reduce the production and use of ozone-depleting substances, including chlorofluorocarbons (CFCs), hydrochlorofluorocarbons (HCFCs), and hydrofluorocarbons (HFCs), noting that depletion of the ozone layer would pose dangers to human and environmental health. The Montreal Protocol entered into force in August 1989 and was eventually ratified by 197 parties (all UN Member States, the European Union, Niue, the Cook Islands, and the Holy See). It was the first UN treaty to achieve universal ratification, or ratification by all states. The narrowly focused agreement has contributed to national-level policies that have effectively improved the integrity of the ozone layer by reducing or slowing the increase of concentrations of ozone-depleting substances. Since the Montreal Protocol has enjoyed success in regulating states' contributions to a global problem (ozone layer depletion), it stands to reason that agreements regulating

Table 11.1. Timetable of Key International Agreements Forming the Climate Regime

1992	United Nations Framework Convention on Climate Change adopted (entered into force in 1994)
1997	Kyoto Protocol signed (entered into force in 2005)
2015	Paris Agreement signed (entered into force in 2016)

greenhouse gases and seeking to reverse the course of climate change could work as well, given the right framing and adequate global support.

Collaboration focused on climate change as a complex set of problems is most directly traced back to the **United Nations Framework Convention on Climate Change (UNFCCC).** The UNFCCC was adopted at the United Nations Conference on Environment and Development (or the Earth Summit) in June 1992 and entered into force on March 21, 1994. The UNFCCC, like the Montreal Protocol, has been ratified by 197 parties (all UN Member States, the European Union, the Cook Islands, Niue, and Palestine). A first step toward facilitating cooperation among states to address the factors contributing to climate change, the UNFCCC's central focus is the "stabilization of greenhouse gas concentrations in the atmosphere at a level that would prevent dangerous anthropogenic interference with the climate system" (United Nations 1992, 9). As a framework convention, the UNFCCC does not place legally binding restrictions on greenhouse gas emissions or provide enforcement mechanisms. Instead, the UNFCCC functions as a framework or starting place for more specific, legally binding agreements. Efforts to reach such agreements began to take shape shortly after the UNFCCC entered into force, as states and organizations realized the need for explicit guidelines, regulations, incentives, and enforcement mechanisms.

The **Kyoto Protocol** followed the UNFCCC and committed states through legally binding emissions reduction targets. The Kyoto Protocol was signed on December 11, 1997, in Kyoto, Japan. It entered into force on February 16, 2005, and has been ratified by 192 parties (of note: the United States signed but did not ratify the Protocol and Canada withdrew in 2012). Building on and implementing the UNFCCC, the Kyoto Protocol tasks states, primarily developed states, with reducing their greenhouse gas emissions. State Parties to the Protocol share a "common but differentiated" responsibility to reduce their emissions; the notion of differentiated responsibility comes from the observation, central to the Kyoto Protocol, that developed states bear the primary burden for greenhouse gas emissions reduction; it was industrialization within these states (powered by fossil fuel consumption) that contributed most to the current concentrations of greenhouse gases in the atmosphere. The downside of holding only developed states accountable to the Protocol's goals is that these states face an economic disincentive to comply, as they fear competition from states whose industries are not regulated by the Protocol's emissions limits. Indeed, the United States did not ratify, Canada withdrew during the first commitment period (which ran from 2008 to 2012), and Russia, Japan, and New Zealand are not participating in the second commitment period (2013 through 2020). As a result, the Kyoto Protocol applies to a modest portion of the world's emissions (an estimated 14 percent) and has been the subject of criticism for its inability to generate substantial policy change, curb emissions, or promote alternative approaches that may be more effective (European Council 2016, Prins and Rayner 2007).

The **Paris Agreement** is the most recent and most comprehensive follow-up to the UNFCCC and the Kyoto Protocol. As we discussed in the previous section, the Paris Agreement resulted from negotiations before and during COP 21 in November and December 2015. The global agreement, which entered into force on November 4, 2016, has 195 signatories, and 144 of those have ratified the agreement at the time of writing this book.[1] Like the Kyoto Protocol, the Paris Agreement builds on the UNFCCC and places legally binding restrictions on signatories, although each state party determines its own national commitments to the effort. Recall that the Paris Agreement aims to limit global warming below 2 degrees Celsius above preindustrial levels, and to pursue efforts to stay below an increase of 1.5 degrees Celsius. The half-degree difference is significant, especially for island nations, coastal regions, drought-prone regions, coral reefs, and states whose populations are dependent on agriculture and other natural resources. Unlike the Kyoto Protocol, the Paris Agreement requires all states to set **nationally determined contributions (NDCs)**, or national goals aimed at reducing greenhouse gas emissions, pursuing clean and renewable energy sources, and mitigating the effects of climate change. The agreement requires a global stocktaking every five years in an effort to ensure transparent monitoring and reporting of progress toward NDCs. Extending the shared obligations to developing states—especially those with large economies like Brazil, China, India, and Mexico—addressed some of the criticism the Kyoto Protocol faced. The United States never ratified the Kyoto Protocol in large part because of policymakers' concern that economic competitors would not be held to the same environmental standards and would therefore have an edge over the developed states bound by the Kyoto Protocol's regulations. By holding all states accountable for reducing greenhouse gas emissions and limiting global warming in an effort to reduce the likelihood of catastrophic climate change, the Paris Agreement unites parties in a collective effort to address a global problem. The hard-fought agreement, however, continues to face challenges as states begin the work of implementing policy changes at home in an era of uncertain global cooperation.

SECURITY PROVISION FROM BELOW? NEW PROSPECTS IN AN UNCERTAIN TIME

A trend of nationalist sentiment has swept through traditional **donor states** in Europe and the United States. Donor states contribute a large share of the financial resources necessary to sustain international agencies and

coordination efforts, and an inward turn among these states presents an obstacle to global efforts to solve a number of human security problems. If donor
states adopt isolationist or nationalist stances, issues like mass displacement
and the Syrian refugee crisis, cases of famine and global hunger in general,
and action to slow climate change are substantially more difficult to address.
As the United States reverses course on environmental protection and climate
change policies under a new presidential administration and increasingly
polarized legislature, the future of the multilateral climate regime could lie
in a number of different directions. As with any international coordination
effort, the withdrawal (whether the withdrawal is a formal legal or de facto
one) of one major player risks the destabilization of the entire effort. Without
the United States working to meet its Paris Agreement commitments, China
and the European Union may be poised to assume leadership of the regime
or attempt to pick up the slack left by the United States. Alternatively, the
withdrawal of one top emitter may lead other states to default on their commitments if they come to view the regime as untenable or as an obstacle to
their own state interests.

Human security problems can be resolved through persistent, well-
coordinated, bottom-up approaches. While the prospect of tackling climate
change without the buy-in of key states is daunting, a critical mass of cities,
industries, and advocacy networks may find ways to close gaps left by states.
One such path involves coordinated leadership through cities. Oslo, Norway,
has aggressively pursued sustainable urban development and aims to restrict
privately owned vehicles from the city center by 2019, divest fossil fuels
from pensions, and encourage the use of zero-emissions electric bicycles and
vehicles (France-Presse 2015). Cities are projected to be home to two-thirds
of the world's population by 2050, so efforts like Oslo's have the potential
to wield significant pressure on world leaders and influence the course of
climate change (Cho 2016). Global coordination efforts are not limited to
interstate coordination efforts, as Cities Climate Leadership Group (C40), a
network of the world's largest cities devoted to addressing climate change,
demonstrates. Founded in London in 2005, C40 is an initiative of eighty
megacities, which include "600 million people and one quarter of the global
economy" (C40 Cities n.d.), and a networking platform through which cities
can exchange ideas and expertise. C40 is one network within several united
in the cause to bring cities to the forefront of the fight against climate change;
the broader coalition also includes ICLEI–Local Governments for Sustainability, United Cities and Local Governments, and UN Habitat. The coalition
oversees the Compact of Mayors, which was founded in September 2014 by
former UN secretary-general Ban Ki-moon and former New York City mayor
Michael Bloomberg. The Compact of Mayors similarly provides a platform
for city leaders to take collective action to tackle climate change, including

through public outreach and commitments to international agreements like the Paris Agreement, investments, support for research, and sustainable urban development (Compact of Mayors n.d.). In June 2016 the Compact of Mayors merged with the Global Covenant of Mayors to form the Global Covenant of Mayors for Climate and Energy, now comprising 644 cities and nearly 7 percent of the global population (Compact of Mayors n.d.).

Whether or not such bottom-up efforts can succeed without state cooperation remains unclear, but it is notable that popular pressure for action has increased as many of the world's regions have begun to feel the effects of climate change. While the way forward on climate change is uncertain, if states are unable to coordinate top-down security provision, then increased awareness of insecurity among communities and cities may trigger a different approach to international coordination led from below.

Discussion Questions

1. Why might states' national interests positively or negatively influence their willingness to participate in global efforts to slow the effects of climate change? Which states are least likely to participate? Which states are most likely to participate?
2. What are the implications of climate change–related migration for national and global security?
3. Why is it difficult for states to cooperate to curb greenhouse gas emissions and pursue efforts to mitigate and adapt to climate change?
4. Does global coordination among cities offer advantages over the more traditional, state-led approach? What are the potential disadvantages of this type of global bottom-up approach?

NOTE

1. The United States announced its plans to withdraw from the agreement in June 2017. The formal process for withdrawal does not permit signatories to begin the exit process until three years after the agreement entered into force.

FURTHER READING AND WEB RESOURCES

1987 Montreal Protocol: http://ozone.unep.org/en/treaties-and-decisions/montreal-protocol-substances-deplete-ozone-layer
1992 Rio Earth Summit: http://www.un.org/geninfo/bp/enviro.html
1992 United Nations Framework Convention on Climate Change: http://unfccc.int/essential_background/convention/items/6036.php
1997 Kyoto Protocol: http://unfccc.int/kyoto_protocol/background/items/2879.php

2015 Paris Agreement: http://unfccc.int/paris_agreement/items/9485.php
Arctic Council: http://www.arctic-council.org/index.php/en/
Benko, Jessica. "How a Warming Planet Drives Human Migration." *New York Times.* April 19, 2017. https://www.nytimes.com/2017/04/19/magazine/how-a-warming-planet-drives-human-migration.html?_r=0 (accessed April 27, 2017)
Intergovernmental Panel on Climate Change (IPCC): https://www.ipcc.ch/
IPCC Fifth Assessment Report: https://www.ipcc.ch/report/ar5/
NASA on Sea Ice: https://www.nasa.gov/content/goddard/nasa-study-shows-global-sea-ice-diminishing-despite-antarctic-gains
National Snow and Ice Data Center on Sea Ice Levels 2016: http://nsidc.org/arctic seaicenews/
Republic of the Marshall Islands Intended Nationally Determined Contribution: http://www4.unfccc.int/ndcregistry/PublishedDocuments/Marshall%20Islands%20First/150721%20RMI%20INDC%20JULY%202015%20FINAL%20SUBMITTED.pdf
Yale Environment 360 on 1.5 degrees: https://e360.yale.edu/features/what_would_a_global_warming_increase_15_degree_be_like
Yale Program on Climate Change Communication: http://climatecommunication.yale.edu

For Deeper Discussion

Indigenous Communities in the Arctic: http://www.e-ir.info/2014/04/10/arctic-indigenous-peoples-climate-change-impacts-and-adaptation/
James Hansen TED Talk on Climate Change: https://www.ted.com/talks/james_hansen_why_i_must_speak_out_about_climate_change/up-next
James Hansen on the Paris Agreement: https://www.theguardian.com/environment/2015/dec/12/james-hansen-climate-change-paris-talks-fraud
Nature on 1.5 degrees: http://www.nature.com/nclimate/journal/v6/n7/full/nclimate3000.html
Nature on Warming in Southwest Asia: http://www.nature.com/nclimate/journal/v6/n2/full/nclimate2833.html

REFERENCES

Adger, W. Neil, et al. "Human Security." In *Climate Change 2014: Impacts, Adaptation, and Vulnerability. Part A: Global and Sectoral Aspects. Contribution of Working Group II to the Fifth Assessment Report of the Intergovernmental Panel on Climate Change*, by Christopher B. Field et al., 755–91. Cambridge: Cambridge University Press, 2014.
American Institute of Physics. *The Discovery of Global Warming.* February 2016. http://history.aip.org/history/climate/simple.htm#L_M085 (accessed May 10, 2017).
Barnett, Jon, and W. Neil Adger. "Climate Change, Human Security and Violent Conflict." *Political Geography* 26, no. 6 (2007): 639–55.

BBC News. "A Brief History of Climate Change." September 20, 2013. http://www.bbc.com/news/science-environment-15874560 (accessed May 10, 2017).

Beller, Thomas, and Ben Depp. "America's First 'Climate Refugees.'" *Smithsonian Magazine*, June 29, 2016.

Benko, Jessica. "How a Warming Planet Drives Human Migration." *New York Times*. April 19, 2017. https://www.nytimes.com/2017/04/19/magazine/how-a-warming-planet-drives-human-migration.html?_r=0 (accessed April 27, 2017).

Broecker, Wallace S. "Climatic Change: Are We on the Brink of a Pronounced Global Warming?" *Science* 189, no. 4201 (August 1975): 460–63.

C40 Cities. *About C40*. http://www.c40.org/about (accessed May 8, 2017).

Cho, Renee. *Cities: the Vanguard Against Climate Change*. Earth Institute, Columbia University. November 10, 2016. http://blogs.ei.columbia.edu/2016/11/10/cities-the-vanguard-against-climate-change/ (accessed May 8, 2017).

Compact of Mayors. *About*. https://www.compactofmayors.org/history/ (accessed May 8, 2017).

Davenport, Coral, and Campbell Robertson. "Resettling the First American 'Climate Refugees.'" *New York Times*, May 2, 2016.

European Council. "International Agreements on Climate Action." *European Council*. June 14, 2016. http://www.consilium.europa.eu/en/policies/climate-change/international-agreements-climate-action/ (accessed April 27, 2017).

Evans, Alex. "Resource Scarcity, Climate Change, and the Risk of Violent Conflict." *World Development Report 2011* (Word Bank), 2010.

Food and Agriculture Organization of the United Nations. "The Impact of Disasters on Agriculture and Food Security." November 2015. http://www.fao.org/3/a-i5128e.pdf (accessed April 14, 2017).

France-Presse, Agence. "Oslo Moves to Ban Cars from City Centre within Four Years." *The Guardian*, October 19, 2015.

Hansen, J., et al. "Climate Impact of Increasing Atmospheric Carbon Dioxide." *Science* 213 (1981): 957–66.

Harvey, Fiona. "Arctic Ice Melt Could Trigger Uncontrollable Climate Change at Global Level." *The Guardian*. November 25, 2016. https://www.theguardian.com/environment/2016/nov/25/arctic-ice-melt-trigger-uncontrollable-climate-change-global-level (accessed May 5, 2017).

Hendrix, Cullen S., and Sarah M. Glaser. "Trends and Triggers: Climate, Climate Change and Civil Conflict in Sub-Saharan Africa." *Political Geography* 26, no. 6 (2007): 695–715.

IPCC. "Summary for Policymakers." In *Climate Change 2007: The Physical Science Basis. Contribution of Working Group I to the Fourth Assessment Report of the Intergovernmental Panel on Climate Change*, by S. Solomon et al. Cambridge: Cambridge University Press, 2007.

Jones, Benjamin T., Eleonora Mattiacci, and Bear F. Braumoeller. "Food Scarcity and State Vulnerability: Unpacking the Link between Climate Variability and Violent Unrest." *Journal of Peace Research* (2017): 335–50.

Komai, Makereta. *Marshall Islands & St. Lucia Spearhead Work of Coalition of High Ambition Nations*. December 5, 2015. http://www.sprep.org/climate-change/

marshall-islands-a-st-lucia-spearhead-work-of-coalition-of-high-ambition-nations (accessed April 28, 2017).

Meier, Patrick, Doug Bond, and Joe Bond. "Environmental Influences on Pastoral Conflict in the Horn of Africa." *Political Geography* 26, no. 6 (2007): 716–35.

Milman, Oliver. "Obama Declares Disaster as Marshall Islands Suffers Worst-Ever Drought." April 28, 2016. https://www.theguardian.com/world/2016/apr/28/obama-marshall-islands-drought (accessed April 28, 2017).

Milman, Oliver, and Mae Ryan. "Lives in the Balance: Climate Change and the Marshall Islands." September 15, 2016. https://www.theguardian.com/environment/2016/sep/15/marshall-islands-climate-change-springdale-arkansas (accessed April 28, 2017).

NASA. *2016 Climate Trends Continue to Break Records.* July 19, 2016. https://www.nasa.gov/feature/goddard/2016/climate-trends-continue-to-break-records (accessed May 10, 2017).

NASA. "Scientific Consensus: Earth's Climate Is Warming." *Global Climate Change: Vital Signs of the Planet.* May 5, 2017. https://climate.nasa.gov/scientific-consensus/ (accessed May 7, 2017).

Notaras, Mark. *Food Insecurity and the Conflict Trap.* United Nations University. August 31, 2011. https://ourworld.unu.edu/en/food-insecurity-and-the-conflict-trap) (accessed March 30, 2017).

Powers, Jon. *Climate Change Is the "Mother of All Risks" to National Security.* November 6, 2015. http://time.com/4101903/climate-change-national-security/ (accessed April 28, 2017).

Prins, Gwyn, and Steve Rayner. "Time to Ditch Kyoto." *Nature* 449 (October 2007): 973–75.

Revkin, Andrew. *Trump's Defense Secretary Cites Climate Change as National Security Challenge.* March 14, 2017. https://www.propublica.org/article/trumps-defense-secretary-cites-climate-change-national-security-challenge (accessed April 28, 2017).

Salehyan, Idean. "From Climate Change to Conflict? No Consensus Yet." *Journal of Peace Research* 45, no. 3 (2008): 315–26.

Silberg, Bob. "Why a Half-Degree Temperature Rise Is a Big Deal." *NASA.* June 29, 2016. https://climate.nasa.gov/news/2458/why-a-half-degree-temperature-rise-is-a-big-deal/ (accessed April 29, 2017).

Starks, Tim. "Katrina's Lessons Seen in Response to Sandy." *Congressional Quarterly.* December 9, 2012. http://public.cq.com/docs/weeklyreport/weeklyreport-000004197197.html (accessed May 7, 2017).

The World Bank. *World Bank, IMF Leaders Make Economic Case for Climate Action.* October 9, 2013. http://www.worldbank.org/en/news/feature/2013/10/08/world-bank-imf-leaders-make-economic-case-for-climate-action (accessed May 5, 2017).

U.S. Government Accountability Office. "Actions Taken to Implement the Post-Katrina Emergency Management Reform Act of 2006." *U.S. Government Accountability Office.* November 21, 2008. http://www.gao.gov/products/GAO-09-59R (accessed May 7, 2017).

UN News Centre. *Urgent Scale-Up in Funding Needed to Stave Off Famine in Somalia, UN Warns.* February 2, 2017. http://www.un.org/apps/news/story. asp?NewsID=56094#.WPEChFLMyi4 (accessed April 14, 2017).

United Nations. "United Nations Framework Convention on Climate Change." 1992. http://unfccc.int/files/essential_background/convention/background/application/ pdf/convention_text_with_annexes_english_for_posting.pdf (accessed May 10, 2017).

van Houten, Carolyn. "The First Official Climate Refugees in the U.S. Race against Time." *National Geographic*, May 25, 2016.

Wike, Richard. "What the World Thinks about Climate Change in 7 Charts." *Pew Research Center Fact Tank.* April 18, 2016. http://www.pewresearch.org/ fact-tank/2016/04/18/what-the-world-thinks-about-climate-change-in-7-charts/ (accessed May 7, 2017).

Zambian Development Agency. *2017 Budget Aims to Restore Economic Growth.* 2017. http://www.zda.org.zm/?q=content/2017-budget-aims-restore-economic-growth (accessed May 5, 2017).

Chapter 12

Food Security

Learning Objectives

This chapter will enable readers to:

1. Discuss the sources and types of food insecurity.
2. Recognize the effects of chronic hunger, famine, and food price instability on human security.
3. Recognize the potential linkages between food security and national and global security.
4. Compare situations of food insecurity in the current global context.

Food is essential to life. Without food, or with insufficient quantities of nutritious food, an individual loses the ability to work, learn, participate in social and political life, fend off disease, or flee natural disasters or man-made violence. When you think of hunger, do you think of a security threat? Do you think, instead, of a moral failing that so many people go without food in our world of plenty? It is indeed morally reprehensible that one in nine people in the world experiences chronic hunger and that almost half of all deaths in children under five years old are caused by hunger, but it is also a concern that is central to human security, and a problem that can contribute to national and global instability.

In this last chapter in the section on durable human security, we explore one of the most fundamental dimensions of human security: food security. In this chapter, we discuss the roots and effects of hunger, malnutrition, and undernutrition, and dysfunctional distribution of resources. The discussion revisits human security concepts introduced in previous chapters in an effort to underscore the interdependent nature of human security issues in general, the chronic and acute

nature of food insecurity in particular, and the need for international cooperation to address the causes and effects of food insecurity. The chapter vignettes
explore variation in state strength and hunger by examining famine in South
Sudan and food deserts in the United States; both situations demonstrate that
food insecurity is not a problem isolated within fragile or impoverished states.

HUNGER AS A HUMAN SECURITY THREAT

In its articulation of human security as a new concept in 1994, the United
Nations Development Programme included hunger among the threats facing
individuals and communities across the globe: "Human security is relevant to
people everywhere, in rich nations and in poor. The threats to their security
may differ—hunger and disease in poor nations and drugs and crime in rich
nations—but these threats are real and growing" (United Nations Development Programme 1994, 15). Hunger presents a threat to durable human
security, a chronic or acute problem that disrupts the daily lives and impedes
the opportunities of individuals and whole communities when states lack the
capacity or political will to address it.

In 1996, 185 states and the European Community met at the headquarters
of the Food and Agriculture Organization in Rome to commit to the elimination of hunger and malnutrition (World Food Summit 1996). This global
discussion yielded the World Food Summit Plan of Action and, therein, the
following definition of food security: "Food security exists when all people,
at all times, have physical and economic access to sufficient, safe and nutritious food to meet their dietary needs and food preferences for an active and
healthy life" (World Food Summit 1996). When individuals and communities
can afford food that meets their cultural, nutritional, and lifestyle needs, and
the supply of that food is steady, we can reasonably assume that the situation
is one of relative food security.

Food preferences are included in the World Food Summit's definition
of food security not to suggest that individuals experience food insecurity
when they lack access to their favorite foods, like ice cream or a good steak.
Instead, the use of the term "food preferences" points to entrenched and
sometimes strict cultural or religious norms and dietary guidelines, like keeping kosher or eating halal. It also recognizes that individuals may adhere
to nutritional guidelines linked to health conditions or allergies (like celiac
disease or peanut allergy) or personal morality (as in the case of a vegetarian
or vegan who opposes the consumption of animals or animal by-products for
moral reasons). In each of these cases, it would be inappropriate and even
unethical to ask an individual to accept food that does not meet their preferences, and the lack of availability of acceptable food makes it difficult for that
individual to meet their nutritional requirements.

Definitions and Dimensions of Food Security

Food security depends on the fulfillment of four dimensions, including food access, availability, use, and stability (Food and Agriculture Organization 2006, 1). **Food access**, or entitlement, refers to an individual's ability to purchase or otherwise acquire a sufficient amount of nutritious food to sustain their daily activities (Food and Agriculture Organization 2006, Sen 1981). If the price of food suddenly spikes or the individual loses their paid employment, access to food becomes more difficult. **Food availability** refers to the supply of food in the region (Food and Agriculture Organization 2006, 1). If an individual lives in a food desert (see the section on causes of food insecurity), if their state is the target of comprehensive sanctions, or if drought has reduced crop yields, food availability will decrease. **Food use** or utilization refers to overall "nutritional well-being" achieved through the combination of a nutritious diet, "clean water, sanitation, and health care" (Food and Agriculture Organization 2006, 1). **Food stability** combines the factors of access and availability; it refers to an individual's access to food at all times, without sudden or cyclical disruptions such as those that result from economic recession, climate change, natural disasters, armed conflict, or famine (Food and Agriculture Organization 2006, 1).

Hunger, undernutrition, and malnutrition are related, but distinct, challenges to food security. **Chronic hunger**, also referred to as undernourishment, is the long-term "inability to acquire enough food, defined as a level of food intake insufficient to meet dietary energy requirements" (Food and Agriculture Organization 2015, 53). **Undernutrition** may result from "undernourishment, and/or poor absorption and/or poor biological use of nutrients consumed as a result of repeated infectious disease" and manifests as being underweight, too short, dangerously thin, or deficient in essential vitamins and minerals (Food and Agriculture Organization 2015, 53). **Malnutrition** is the result of taking in too few, too many, or the wrong nutrients such that the body does not receive the necessary balance of essential nutrients to maintain daily activities (Food and Agriculture Organization 2015, 53). Individuals and communities may experience periods of food insecurity without clearing the thresholds for hunger as a long-term condition, undernutrition, or malnutrition. In such cases, unemployment, poverty, food price increases, displacement, or other factors may create a situation of **episodic food insecurity**, in which an individual, family, or community's access to food is limited or unpredictable, but not long-term or chronic (Coleman-Jensen et al. 2016, United States Department of Agriculture 2016).

These conditions do not exist in a vacuum, of course. Drought, flooding, and displacement due to climate change can disrupt the supply or availability of and individuals' access to healthy foods in a region, especially when states lack the capacity to absorb shocks to the food supply (Parry et al. 2007).

Armed conflict can limit or wipe out agricultural production and displace large portions of a population, laying the dangerous groundwork for **famine**, as in South Sudan (see the section on causes of food insecurity). A famine is a situation of extreme, usually deadly, food insecurity resulting from severe lack of access to and availability of food. Indeed, parties to conflict may intentionally wield starvation as a weapon, withholding food and humanitarian relief from besieged civilians to force negotiations or surrender, as witnessed in the Syrian civil war (United Nations Security Council 2016). Oppressive regimes may similarly use hunger and poverty as tools to try to crush political opposition and maintain control over the population (Lappé 1998, 122–46). Economic instability, global food price increases, and poverty limit an individual's access to nutritious foods, a problem that affects low-income households in the United States (see the section on causes of food security in this chapter). Gender inequality can jeopardize a woman or young girl's nutrition if she is served last in a household that barely has enough to eat. Undernutrition or malnutrition rob individuals of the energy needed to engage in daily activities (like paid employment or schoolwork), thereby depriving them of opportunities and further decreasing their ability to maintain access to food (Sen 1999, 162).

If human security exists when individuals and communities are safe from chronic and acute threats to their well-being, freedoms, and physical security, then mitigating and preventing chronic hunger and episodic food insecurity must be central to any effort to promote overall human security. There is enough food in the world to feed everyone; the global quantity of food is not a direct cause of food insecurity (Clapp 2014, Lappé 1998, 8–14). Food-related threats become a human security issue when their root causes lie in flawed societal or political institutions and norms or in the complete breakdown of institutions, norms, and other protections in situations of acute insecurity. When food insecurity threatens a large portion of the population (as in famine or widespread chronic hunger), targets one community on the basis of identity (as in strategic starvation or famine), aligns with socioeconomic disparity (as in food deserts and insufficient social support), or results from climate change–related problems like drought or flooding, then the state's institutions, norms, capacity to protect, or some combination of these are at work and hunger becomes a human security issue.

The Link between Food Security and State and Global Security

When does food insecurity shift from a human security problem to a state or global security problem? As we have discussed throughout the book, the three approaches to security are synchronous; security and insecurity at all levels can operate as mutually reinforcing or mutually destructive. In chapter 11 on climate change and environmental security, we highlighted the complex linkages between environmental security and state instability, referencing the growing body of research on the interaction between resource scarcity or abrupt climate disruptions, insufficient state capacity to ease the effects of human security threats, and unrest or armed conflict (Evans 2010, Jones, Mattiacci, and Braumoeller 2017, Notaras 2011). Food security plays a similar role, and environmental stability and food security often go hand in hand.

The armed conflict in Syria is one example of the role food insecurity can play in exacerbating broader insecurity within a state or region. Insufficient rainfall in Syria in the years prior to the civil war led to low agricultural yields, displaced agricultural producers, migration from rural to urban areas, increased employment, and widespread discontentment with the Assad regime (Schwartzstein 2016). The chain of events, unfolding as part of the broader Arab Spring resistance movement, contributed to the outbreak of civil war in March 2011. Deteriorating national security further reduces human security, as has been the case with respect to food insecurity, among other forms of acute insecurity, in Syria's civil war: decreased food production, economic instability, currency depreciation, reduced government-funded social supports, and siege warfare created conditions in which food access and availability have been severely threatened, if not entirely eliminated (Schwartzstein 2016, World Food Programme n.d.).

Rising food prices also served as a contributing factor in Egypt's January 25 revolution in 2011, and food scarcity fueled protests and uprisings in Venezuela in 2017. As Francis Moore Lappé argues, the myth that a population can be "too hungry to revolt" is just that—a myth; recent history offers many accounts in which individuals and communities mobilized against the state in response to food insecurity, poverty, and insufficient government efforts to protect the population from harm (Lappé 1998, 122–28).

Even beyond the context of armed conflict and unrest, a malnourished or undernourished population is one that creates hefty economic costs realized in terms of poor school performance among children and adolescents and decreased productivity among working adults (Fan 2014). Indeed, in many places the potential for a vicious cycle exists in which weak institutions, high food prices, economic instability, conflict, and food insecurity contribute to one another and threaten individual lives and state stability (Hendrix and Brinkman 2013). If crises and situations of instability go unchecked, state insecurity can create ripple effects for regional and global security.

FOOD INSECURITY: CAUSES AND EXAMPLES

Food insecurity can threaten individuals and communities in wealthy states, poor states, conflict zones, and states without active armed conflict. Recall the dimensions of food security: availability, access, utilization, and stability.

To enjoy food security an individual must have reliable, regular access to nutritious and appropriate foods at a reasonably predictable and affordable price. Food scarcity, which affects not only availability but also access and stability, is usually not the result of insufficient quantities of food in a region; rather, it is often an issue of access limited by government policies, armed actors' strategies, entrenched social inequalities, or some combination of these factors. Amartya Sen observes that famines do not occur in wealthy developed countries, not because there is an absence of poverty but because there are social safety nets in place to prevent widespread starvation and provide for basic necessities (Sen 1981, 7). Robert Paarlberg cites the Irish Potato Famine (1876–1878), the Holodomor famine in Ukraine during the wider Soviet famine (1932–1933), and famine in China's Great Leap Forward (1959–1961) as examples of widespread, deadly, and *man-made* situations of acute hunger in non-democratic states (Paarlberg 2010, 3). Paarlberg notes that democratic governance is related to better food security because individuals in non-democracies "lack the opportunity to take organized political action" and "serious food policy errors are often made" (Paarlberg 2010, 3). Famines do not happen by accident; they result from failed policies or the imposition of deliberate harm.

The effects of environmental degradation and climate change compound the effects of government policies: drought, desertification, flooding, deforestation, and changing weather patterns are already disrupting the stability of food sources around the world and, as chapter 11 suggests, these problems will only worsen with time if states maintain the status quo with respect to the environment (Food and Agriculture Organization 2016, Lappé 1998, 41–57). When states lack the capacity or political will to compensate for agricultural instability and other climate-related effects on food sources, food security is jeopardized.

It is also important to note here that food insecurity is not a direct result of overpopulation; the challenge of matching food production with global population growth is more complicated than the economist Thomas Robert Malthus originally postulated in 1798. Malthus made the argument that food production cannot keep pace with world population growth in *An Essay on the Principle of Population*; the central premise of his argument holds that since food production requires "fixed assets such as land that can only be expanded slowly," but the human population grows exponentially with each generation (Paarlberg 2010, 8), widespread hunger and suffering are inevitable. Technological innovation has contradicted Malthus' argument and overall world food production has, to date, kept pace with population growth. Still, the links between overpopulation, the earth's capacity to feed billions more humans, and food insecurity require continued study and should remain the focus of careful policymaking. To continue to ensure that food production can support the nutritional needs of all people, state and global policies must address the social and economic inequalities related to poverty, high fertility rates, and distribution of resources (Lappé 1998, 40, Sen 1999, 205–206), and alter demand for resource-intensive foods like livestock (Smith 2014). State- and global-level policymakers and opinion shapers have considerable work to do when it comes to protecting global food security in the long term.

For hunger to pose a human *security* threat, it must be the result of short-comings in the state's institutions, norms, or ability to protect the population. As with other threats to human security, food insecurity, even when widespread, will not threaten *everyone* in an affected region or state. Sen's observation on famines is illustrative here:

> While famines involve fairly widespread acute starvation, there is no reason to think that it will affect all groups in the famine affected nation. Indeed, it is by no means clear that there has ever occurred a famine in which all groups in a country have suffered from starvation, since different groups typically do have very different commanding powers over food, and an over-all shortage brings out the contrasting powers in stark clarity. (Sen 1981, 43)

The causes of food insecurity are all rooted, at least to some degree, in politics and other forms of insecurity. The question is not whether there is enough food in the world to feed everyone, but instead whether or not individuals are blocked in some way from accessing necessary nutrients. As a result, food insecurity will threaten some individuals and communities more than others. To explore the causes of food insecurity and the broad range of contexts in which hunger threatens well-being, we turn briefly to two examples: food insecurity in the United States and famine in South Sudan.

BOX 12.1. "THINK ABOUT IT . . ."—STAPLE FOODS IN DEMAND

In January 2013, British newspaper *The Guardian* published an article provocatively titled "Can Vegans Stomach the Unpalatable Truth about Quinoa?" (Blythman 2013). In it, the author cited the steep increase in the price of quinoa from 2006 onward, noting that the sudden demand for the Andean staple grain among health-conscious eaters in the Global North placed it out of reach for the Peruvians and Bolivians who have long cultivated and relied on it.

Three years later, in May 2016, *The Economist* ran another story on the effects of quinoa demand. This piece noted that quinoa consumption in Peru fell more gradually than the grain's price rose, and that the average household spent only 0.5 percent of its budget on quinoa, contradicting the earlier claim that sudden price shocks caused by skyrocketing demand threatened the food security of lower-income households in the areas where quinoa is grown. The article in *The Economist* highlighted the link between higher quinoa prices and higher incomes for quinoa growers (*The Economist* 2016). A study by several economists confirms this reassurance, finding that the increased price of quinoa has improved the economic well-being of quinoa-producing households and, to a lesser but still notable extent, the general welfare of the surrounding population where quinoa is grown (Bellemare, Fajardo-Gonzalez, and Gitter 2016, 25).

Still, the overall effects of increased demand for a traditional staple food are complex. Concerns range from environmental degradation (LeVaux 2013) and the threat of falling prices (*The Economist* 2016), resulting from scaled-up production of quinoa in the Andes and new regions, to broader societal outcomes—including wages for agricultural workers, nutritional changes, and resource distribution, among other factors—linked to shifting quinoa prices (Bellemare, Fajardo-Gonzalez and Gitter 2016).

Consider the following questions related to changing dietary fads and North–South relations:

1. How does demand for a food or product in the Global North affect the livelihoods and well-being of communities in the Global South? Are there other notable examples of fad foods or products or is the case of quinoa exceptional?
2. Should states have an obligation to shield their agricultural producers from price shocks? What would be the effects of such an effort?
3. Noting that European producers have started to cultivate quinoa, which could increase supply and decrease the global price of the grain, should states or international organizations regulate, limit, or encourage efforts to cultivate traditional crops outside of their region of origin?
4. Take a look through your cabinets or pantry. Where does your food come from? Has it crossed borders and/or oceans, traveled across your own state, or is it locally grown? What do you take into consideration when purchasing your food and what does this suggest about your own degree of food security as an individual?

Food Insecurity in the United States

A report by the U.S. Department of Agriculture (USDA) Economic Research Service estimates that 12.7 percent of American households (15.8 million households comprising 42.2 million people) "were food insecure at some time during the year" in 2015 (Coleman-Jensen et al. 2016, 6). These households did not necessarily experience food insecurity throughout the entire year, and food insecurity in the United States is frequently temporary or episodic rather than chronic. Of the households that experienced food insecurity, 6.3 million "were food insecure to the extent that eating patterns of one or more household members were disrupted and their food intake reduced, at least some time during the year, because they could not afford enough food" (Coleman-Jensen et al. 2016, 6). Although the number of food insecure households in the United States decreased from a high of 17.85 million households in 2011 at the height of the economic recession (Coleman-Jensen et al. 2016, 7), 15.8 million food insecure households is a staggering figure for a society known for its wealth, prosperity, and dietary excesses. When we consider that the USDA Economic Research Service's survey omits homeless families and individuals, likely reducing the reported figures below the actual scale of food insecurity (Coleman-Jensen et al. 2016, 11), the numbers offer additional cause for concern.

As the USDA Economic Research Service's Food Access Research Atlas illustrates, food access varies across and within regions of the United States, with significant numbers of low-income individuals without access to supermarkets concentrated around cities (United States Department of Agriculture Economic Research Service 2017a). **Food deserts**, areas with a high population of low-income households and lack of access to available, affordable, and nutritious food sources within a set distance (usually ½ to 1 mile in urban areas and 10–20 miles in rural regions), contribute to food insecurity, affecting both the access and the availability dimensions of food security. Food access in the United States can be measured using proximity to supermarkets, farmers' markets, or other healthy food sources, as well as family income, average neighborhood income, family vehicle access, and accessibility of public transportation (United States Department of Agriculture Economic Research Service 2017b). These factors can tell us about the inequality of food security in the United States, but they are also part of the bigger picture of inequality and human insecurity in a diverse nation.

Family income, availability of supermarkets, vehicle possession, and availability of public transportation are linked to other forms of social and economic inequality: food security in the United States is more common for "households with incomes near or below the Federal poverty line, households with children headed by single women or single men, women and men living alone, and Black- and Hispanic-headed households" (Coleman-Jensen et al. 2016, vi). Income inequality continues to rise in the United States and, as it does, it leaves more individuals and households to survive at or below the federal poverty line, placing them at risk for food insecurity, among other hardships (Posey 2016, United States Census Bureau 2015). Income inequality, for its part, is compounded by flaws in U.S. social norms, especially racial inequality and gender inequality (Kochhar 2014, Patten 2016), which place individuals and communities at greater risk of insecurity because of institutionalized factors that limit their opportunities and threaten their personal safety. Although famine is rare in a state with social safety nets, like the United States, food insecurity is exacerbated when these social support resources are unavailable, underfunded, or unattainable. Low-income individuals and families in the United States may be eligible for support through the Supplemental Nutrition Assistance Program (SNAP), an aid initiative run by the Department of Agriculture's Food and Nutrition Service, if they meet the program's requirements. SNAP remains a subject of political debate within the United States, and it has come into more intense focus when policymakers have sought to reduce government spending through the budgetary process. Food security, then, relates to questions of societal cohesion, public views of the state's role in providing for the well-being and economic stability of its population, and the prioritization of domestic aid initiatives in times of economic hardship and prosperity.

Famine in South Sudan

In February 2017 the UN declared a famine in South Sudan and warned that 100,000 people faced starvation, with an additional one to five million in urgent need of food assistance (BBC News 2017, Beaubien 2017, Oxfam International 2017). The declaration of famine seldom comes lightly; the UN had not declared one since 2011. The Famine Early Warning Systems Network (FEWS NET) classified all regions of South Sudan in the "stressed" through "famine" levels of food insecurity for the period June to September 2017, citing the impact of conflict-related displacement and active armed conflict on agricultural production, aid delivery, and economic stability (Famine Early Warning Systems Network 2017). The severe food insecurity in South Sudan demonstrates the link between armed conflict—an acute human security threat—and food security—a durable human security issue. While we classify food security as a durable human security concern, it is important to recognize the cyclical links between durable and acute human security threats.

South Sudan became an independent state on July 9, 2011. Since its independence, the government has faced protracted conflict with armed groups across much of the state, having separated from Sudan after the Second Sudanese Civil War and struggled to rebuild infrastructure, develop economically, and improve human security following more than two decades of fighting. In December 2013, political struggles between President Kiir and Riek Machar, his former deputy, led to a civil war within the new state. The South Sudanese Civil War has created high levels food insecurity by decreasing agricultural productivity, limiting humanitarian organizations' access to vulnerable populations, disrupting trade throughout the state, and affecting individuals' ability to find paid employment to maintain household economic stability (and, thus, food security).

Armed conflict in general is a major driver of food insecurity because it creates physical insecurity that hampers food production (by threatening farmers and other food producers), destroys or renders inaccessible land that would have otherwise been used for agriculture, and displaces communities. Active hostilities also jeopardize aid delivery by shutting down routes to vulnerable populations. The presence of UN peacekeepers (through the UN Mission in South Sudan, or UNMISS) and humanitarian agencies likely prevented more severe food insecurity at the onset of famine, but humanitarian agencies are unable to operate in armed conflict zones when the security of their staff members is threatened. Such has been the case in South Sudan. U.S.-based news outlet National Public Radio reported that in February 2017, when the UN declared a famine in two of the state's regions, a U.S. humanitarian organization called Samaritan's Purse evacuated its staff amid active fighting; shortly thereafter, its remaining contingent of South Sudanese staff members were abducted (Beaubien 2017). Hostile conditions make aid delivery difficult, if not impossible, and increase the severity of food insecurity.

As the examples of food insecurity in the United States and South Sudan demonstrate, this particular human security threat can arise in peacetime as well as in armed conflict. Food insecurity is not limited to the Global South; it can strike any community when the political context and institutions create a situation of limited access to sufficient quantities of nutritious food. Who, then, bears the responsibility of providing for food security when it is threatened? We now turn to this question.

PROTECTION AGAINST HUNGER

The responsibility to protect individuals and communities from chronic hunger or acute food insecurity is shared, like many durable human security initiatives, among local actors, states, and the international community. States have varying degrees of social safety nets and food assistance programs, depending on the type of government, capacity for investment in social program, and domestic and international political priorities. State-level initiatives can go a long way toward causing chronic hunger and food insecurity, but also toward ameliorating these threats if policymakers are willing to prioritize them (Bailey 2014). Since widespread, chronic food insecurity is itself an indicator of underdevelopment, states may not have the resources needed to fix the root causes of hunger.

Three agencies within the United Nations system are tasked with responding to hunger and food insecurity: the **Food and Agriculture Organization**, the **World Food Program (WFP)**, and the **International Fund for Agricultural Development (IFAD)**. The FAO was created in October 1945. Its primary functions are to serve as a discussion forum through which states can develop policy responses to hunger and to disseminate technical information to improve food security in developing states. The WFP was founded in 1961 as the UN's food assistance agency. While the FAO helps states work through policy options and negotiations to address food insecurity, the WFP provides humanitarian assistance directly to regions in need. The WFP's mission is to offer immediate aid and expertise with the long-term objective of a food secure world. IFAD, a financial institution focused on assisting the rural poor in developing states, formed in 1977. Its central objectives are to improve well-being and food security and reduce poverty in developing states through loans and grants to increase access to agricultural technology and related skills. The FAO, WFP, and IFAD are all headquartered in Rome, Italy. As Jennifer Clapp and Marc Cohen observe, the UN's food agencies "have more balanced North–South representation on their governing bodies and are significant players in norm setting, data collection, technical assistance, and emergency aid" (Clapp and Cohen 2009, 6). In addition to the UN agencies, the Bretton Woods institutions (the World Bank and International Monetary Fund), Group of 7, and Organisation for Economic Co-operation and Development have traditionally provided funding in accordance with the policy priorities and interests of donor states in the Global North, and this includes food assistance and loans or grants (Clapp and Cohen 2009, 6). States in the Global North no longer hold a monopoly on food assistance outside of the UN framework; however, China has emerged as an influential donor state since the start of its "Go Global" foreign policy strategy in 2005 (Zhang 2016).

Realization of global goals focused on eradicating hunger, as articulated by Millennium Development Goal 1 (eradicate extreme poverty and hunger) and Sustainable Development Goal 2 (end hunger, achieve food security and improved nutrition, and promote sustainable agriculture), requires the participation of security actors throughout the international community. It also requires deliberate, well-coordinated policies that empower communities in need, as well as accurate measurements of the scope of food insecurity. The 2015 Millennium Development Goals Report (the MDGs concluded in 2015) calculates that the "proportion of under-nourished people in the developing regions has fallen by almost half since 1990, from 23.3 per cent in 1900–1992 to 12.9 per cent in 2014–2016" (United Nations 2015, 4) in spite of challenges posed by food price insta-bility, economic recession, armed conflict, political instability, and climate change–related threats (United Nations 2015, 20). This represents progress toward achieving overall food security. Still, hundreds of millions of people around the world continue to suffer from extreme food insecurity, which is why the SDGs were designed to "pick up where the MDGs left off" (United Nations 2015, 23). SDG 2 is more comprehensive in nature than MDG 1, with targets focused on ending hunger for all people, ending malnutrition, doubling agricultural productivity, improving sustainability and resilience in agriculture, and easing trade restrictions, among other targets, to be reached by 2030 (United Nations n.d.).

One problem with the increased level of detail in SDG 2, according to Michelle Jurkovich, is that the international community does not yet have a fully reliable way to measure progress toward ending food insecurity. A big reason why there is no international consensus on an appropriate way to measure food security outcomes is that there is some ambiguity about what, exactly, "hunger" is (Jurkovich 2016). Recall the start of this chapter—specifically, the discussion about malnutrition, chronic hunger, and undernu-trition. Should security providers focus on one type of food insecurity over the others, all three, or only on extreme food insecurity like that which we see in famines? What about food price instability and its effects on episodic food insecurity among the poor and working classes in developed states? In order to protect individuals and communities from food insecurity, or any form of insecurity, decision-makers and security providers must understand the nature and scope of the threat.

Protection against hunger, then, requires continued collaboration not only among local, state-level, and global actors but also among those who study food security and those who implement programs to provide for it. An important message to take away from this chapter is that although hunger is a problem in states that have fewer resources, it is not a human security threat that is limited to any particular region of the world. To understand the complex nature of food insecurity and work toward a solution to it, we must be willing to look at its diverse causes. Food insecurity has the potential to be globally devastating in scope; it also has the potential to be a security problem of the past if the world harnesses the right mix of technology, aid, and adjusted habits.

Discussion Questions

1. Is there a fundamental difference between chronic hunger and famine? Should the policy responses differ?
2. How might local civil society actors assist with improvements in food security? What can state-level actors do? How can international organizations best serve the goal of eliminating hunger?
3. Do populations in wealthy, developed states have an obligation to change their dietary habits to maximize the efficiency of food production? Why or why not?
4. If given the task, how would you measure progress toward achieving complete global food security?

FURTHER READING AND WEB RESOURCES

Famine Early Warning Systems Network (FEWS NET): https://www.fews.net
Food and Agriculture Organization, *The State of Food and Agriculture 2016*: http://www.fao.org/publications/sofa/2016/en/
Oxfam International, "Famine in South Sudan": https://www.oxfam.org/en/emergencies/famine-south-sudan
United Nations Millennium Development Goals: http://www.un.org/millenniumgoals/
United Nations Sustainable Development Goals: http://www.undp.org/content/undp/en/home/sustainable-development-goals.html
United States Department of Agriculture Economic Research Service, "Food Access Research Atlas": https://www.ers.usda.gov/data/fooddesert/
United States Department of Agriculture Food and Nutrition Service, "Supplemental Nutrition Assistance Program": https://www.fns.usda.gov/snap/supplemental-nutrition-assistance-program-snap

For Deeper Discussion

Alex de Waal. *Famine That Kills*. Oxford: Oxford University Press, 2005.
Roger Thurow and Scott Kilman. *Enough: Why the World's Poorest Starve in an Age of Plenty*. New York: PublicAffairs, 2010.

REFERENCES

Adger, W. Neil, et al. "Human Security." In *Climate Change 2014: Impacts, Adaptation, and Vulnerability. Part A: Global and Sectoral Aspects. Contribution of Working Group II to the Fifth Assessment Report of the Intergovernmental Panel on Climate Change*, by Christopher B. Field et al., 755–91. Cambridge: Cambridge University Press, 2014.
Bailey, Robert. "Food and Human Security." In *Routledge Handbook of Human Security*, by Mary Martin and Taylor Owen, 188–96. New York: Routledge, 2014.

BBC News. "Why Are There Still Famines?" March 15, 2017. http://www.bbc.com/news/world-africa-39039255 (accessed July 5, 2017).

Beaubien, Jason. "Why the Famine in South Sudan Keeps Getting Worse." *NPR*, March 14, 2017.

Bellemare, Marc F., Johanna Fajardo-Gonzalez, and Seth R. Gitter. "Foods and Fads: The Welfare Impacts of Rising Quinoa Prices in Peru." *Working Paper No. 2016–06*. Towson University Department of Economics Working Paper Series, March 2016.

Blythman, Joanna. "Can Vegans Stomach the Unpalatable Truth about Quinoa?" *The Guardian*, January 16, 2013.

Clapp, Jennifer. "World Hunger and the Global Economy: Strong Linkages, Weak Action." *Journal of International Affairs* 67, no. 2 (January 2014): 1–17.

Clapp, Jennifer, and Marc J. Cohen. *The Global Food Crisis: Governance Challenges and Opportunities*. Waterloo, Ontario: Wilfrid Laurier University Press, 2009.

Coleman-Jensen, Alisha, Matthew Rabbitt, Christian Gregory, and Anita Singh. *Household Food Security in the United States in 2015*. United States Department of Agriculture, 2016.

Evans, Alex. "Resource Scarcity, Climate Change, and the Risk of Violent Conflict." *World Development Report 2011* (Word Bank), 2010.

Famine Early Warning Systems Network. *Conflict Displaces Well over 100,000 in April as Extreme Levels of Food Insecurity Persist*. April 2017. http://www.fews.net/east-africa/south-sudan (accessed May 25, 2017).

Fan, Shenggen. *Ending World Hunger and Undernutrition by 2025*. June 2, 2014. http://www.ifpri.org/blog/ending-world-hunger-and-undernutrition-2025 (accessed June 2, 2017).

Food and Agriculture Organization. "Policy Brief: Food Security." June 2006. http://www.fao.org/forestry/13128-0e6f36f27e0091055bec28ebe830f46b3.pdf (accessed May 26, 2017).

Food and Agriculture Organization. *The State of Food and Agriculture: Climate Change, Agriculture and Food Security*. Rome, 2016.

Food and Agriculture Organization. "The State of Food Insecurity in the World." Rome, 2015.

Hendrix, Cullen S., and Henk-Jan Brinkman. "Food Insecurity and Conflict Dynamics: Causal Linkages and Complex Feedbacks." *Stability: International Journal of Security & Development* 2, no. 2 (2013): 1–18.

Jones, Benjamin T., Eleonora Mattiacci, and Bear F. Braumoeller. "Food Scarcity and State Vulnerability: Unpacking the Link between Climate Variability and Violent Unrest." *Journal of Peace Research* (2017): 335–50.

Jurkovich, Michelle. "Venezuela Has Solved Its Hunger Problem? Don't Believe the U.N.'s Numbers." *Monkey Cage–The Washington Post*, September 21, 2016.

Kochhar, Rakesh. *Wealth Inequality Has Widened along Racial, Ethnic Lines since End of Great Recession*. September 12, 2014. http://www.pewresearch.org/fact-tank/2014/12/12/racial-wealth-gaps-great-recession/ (accessed June 2, 2017).

Lappé, Francis Moore. *World Hunger: Twelve Myths*. New York: Grove Press, 1998.

LeVaux, Ari. "It's OK to Eat Quinoa." *Slate*, January 25, 2013.

Notaras, Mark. *Food Insecurity and the Conflict Trap*. United Nations University. August 31, 2011. https://ourworld.unu.edu/en/food-insecurity-and-the-conflict-trap (accessed March 30, 2017).

Oxfam International. *Famine in South Sudan*. May 4, 2017. https://www.oxfam.org/en/emergencies/famine-south-sudan (accessed May 25, 2017).

Paarlberg, Robert. *Food Politics: What Everyone Needs to Know*. Oxford: Oxford University Press, 2010.

Parry, M. L., O. F. Canziani, J. P. Palutikof, P. J. van der Linden, and C. E. Hanson. *Climate Change 2007: Working Group II: Impacts, Adaptation and Vulnerability*. Intergovernmental Panel on Climate Change, Cambridge: Cambridge University Press, 2007.

Patten, Eileen. *Racial, Gender Wage Gaps Persist in U.S. despite Some Progress*. July 1, 2016. http://www.pewresearch.org/fact-tank/2016/07/01/racial-gender-wage-gaps-persist-in-u-s-despite-some-progress/ (accessed June 2, 2017).

Posey, Kirby G. *Household Income: 2015*. United States Census Bureau, U.S. Department of Commerce, 2016.

Schwartzstein, Peter. "Inside the Syrian Dust Bowl." *Foreign Policy*, September 5, 2016.

Sen, Amartya. *Development as Freedom*. New York: Anchor Books, 1999.

Sen, Amartya. *Poverty and Famines: An Essay on Entitlement and Deprivation*. Oxford: Oxford University Press, 1981.

Smith, Pete. "Malthus Is Still Wrong: We Can Feed a World of 9–10 Billion, But Only by Reducing Food Demand." *Proceedings of the Nutrition Society* 74 (2014): 187–90.

The Economist. "Against the Grain." May 21, 2016.

United Nations Development Programme. *Human Development Report*. New York: Oxford University Press, 1994.

United Nations Security Council. *Starvation by Siege Now "Systematic" in Syria, Assistant Secretary-General Tells Security Council, amid Warnings That Tactic Could Be War Crime*. January 15, 2016. https://www.un.org/press/en/2016/sc12203.doc.htm (accessed May 26, 2017).

United Nations. *Sustainable Development Goal 2*. https://sustainabledevelopment.un.org/sdg2 (accessed June 2, 2017).

United Nations. *The Millennium Development Goals Report*. New York: United Nations, 2015.

United States Census Bureau. "Real Household Income at Selected Percentiles: 1967–2014." *United States Census Bureau Library*. September 16, 2015. https://www.census.gov/library/visualizations/2015/demo/real-household-income-at-selected-percentiles—1967-to-2014.html (accessed June 2, 2017).

United States Department of Agriculture. *Frequency of Food Insecurity*. October 4, 2016. https://www.ers.usda.gov/topics/food-nutrition-assistance/food-security-in-the-us/frequency-of-food-insecurity/ (accessed May 26, 2017).

United States Department of Agriculture Economic Research Service. *Documentation*. May 22, 2017b. https://www.ers.usda.gov/data-products/food-access-research-atlas/documentation/ (accessed May 24, 2017).

United States Department of Agriculture Economic Research Service. *Food Access Research Atlas*. May 18, 2017a. https://www.ers.usda.gov/data-products/food-access-research-atlas/ (accessed May 24, 2017).

World Food Programme. *10 Facts about Hunger.* September 30, 2015. https://www. wfp.org/stories/10-facts-about-hunger (accessed May 26, 2017).

World Food Programme. *Syrian Arab Republic.* http://www1.wfp.org/countries/ syrian-arab-republic (accessed May 31, 2017).

World Food Summit. "Rome Declaration on World Food Security." November 13, 1996. http://www.fao.org/docrep/003/w3613e/w3613e00.htm (accessed May 26, 2017).

Zhang, Junyi. *Chinese Foreign Assistance, Explained.* July 19, 2016. https://www. brookings.edu/blog/order-from-chaos/2016/07/19/chinese-foreign-assistance-explained/ (accessed June 2, 2017).

Section IV

APPLYING HUMAN SECURITY

Chapter 13

Is Human Security Possible in the Twenty-First Century?

Learning Objectives

This chapter will enable readers to:

1. Recognize the political and institutional requirements of human security.
2. Become familiar with the status of human security efforts within the United Nations system.
3. Think critically about the feasibility of the human security approach in the current era.

When policymakers, practitioners, and scholars talk about security, what do they mean? Whose security matters and how do we know what security looks like? Who or what is responsible for ensuring security? The human security approach demands a shift in thinking about these questions. In short, it requires scholars, policymakers, and security providers to embrace the individual as the subject of security theory, policy, and practice.

How useful is this approach in the twenty-first century? The broad view of human security accepts the importance of "protection from sudden and hurtful disruptions in the pattern of our daily lives" and "safety from the constant threats of hunger, disease, crime and repression," or what we refer to as human security in acute conflict and durable human security. Our focus throughout the book has been on the question of responsibility for security provision and in each of the prior chapters we have discussed the need to consider security challenges using the human, state, and global security approaches to ensure comprehensive policy responses, assistance efforts, and academic research.

Human security, we contend, does not replace the state or global security approaches; instead, human security offers a third approach to security provision that re-centers analysis, policy, and practice at the level of the individual, while also laying the groundwork for the kind of sustainable peace and stability that has the potential to improve state and global security. To the extent that the human security approach fills in gaps left in analysis and implementation of security policy, we suggest that this third approach is not only useful but also essential to meet the security challenges of the twenty-first century.

To round out the discussion of human security and its interaction with traditional security approaches, the chapter's first section synthesizes the requirements for establishing effective human security discussed throughout the book. The book's first chapter recalled the UNDP's 1994 Human Development Report and its first articulation of the term "human security"; in an effort to conclude our analysis of the emerging human security norm, the second section of this chapter briefly assesses the current status of the human security approach at the United Nations. The third section explores the need for multiple security approaches and perspectives when dealing with one of many complex threats facing security providers, individuals, states, and the global community in the twenty-first century—transnational terrorism; this section sets the stage for the thought exercise provided in chapter 14. The final section closes with enduring questions related to human security's feasibility in a rapidly shifting global political landscape.

REQUIREMENTS OF HUMAN SECURITY

If we accept the notion that human security exists when individuals and their communities are free from chronic, long-term threats to their well-being and acute, sudden threats to their physical safety, then security provision requires protection against the effects of weapons and armed conflict as well as protection against systematic adversity and human rights violations. Human security is cyclical: positive advances in protection and empowerment in post-conflict reconstruction spill over into peacetime, strengthening institutions and bolstering positive norms; erosion of human security in peacetime contributes to the conditions that create armed conflict. Acknowledging the cycle of security, we turn to a question: what needs to happen to achieve overall human security, both in conflict and post-conflict settings and in the long term? In this section, we revisit the factors that contribute to high levels of human security.

In section I, we explored the historical and political conditions that led to the emergence of the human security approach, with a particular focus on the UN. Three changes in the international community laid the groundwork for a new approach to security provision: the changing nature of war and the shift toward intrastate conflicts; the UN's increased influence after the end of the Cold War and its rigid bipolar international political structure; and a reaffirmation of the importance of human rights. To observe that a new approach to human security emerged in the 1990s is not to imply that states and other security providers—or the researchers who study them—have prioritized this approach above traditional state security or even global security; as we discussed in chapter 1, states will often operate with their national interests at top of mind and pursue policies or actions that promote human security as a result of mixed motivations (see table 1.3). Because human security and state security are often synchronous, however, it is possible for states to pursue their security while also accounting for the human security of their citizens and foreign populations.

Achieving human security requires stability, good governance, and effective collaboration among security providers. These requirements place human security in line with the state and global security approaches in some respects, and in conflict with them in others. As chapter 3 details, for security providers to promote the norms and values central to human security—including the protections and freedoms included in the notions of freedom from fear and freedom from want—states and the international system must be stable. Stability is a key foundation for the institutions and norms required to pursue human security. This basic structural precursor places the human security approach neatly in line with the state and global security approaches when the state's norms and institutions align with the core tenets of human security. Nevertheless, strong and stable states can—and do—still tolerate or perpetrate human rights violations, systematic discrimination and inequality, and other forms of insecurity that affect individuals and their communities without necessarily upsetting the state's ability to govern. In these cases, human security and state security are directly at odds, and strengthening the state will not improve human security without significant changes in the state's governing institutions and norms.

Protection of freedom from fear and the insecurity that accompanies acute conflict requires a stable state and an absence of widespread violence. As the chapters in section II explore, the breakdown in governance that both leads to and stems from intrastate conflict creates high levels of human insecurity. Armed conflict, mass displacement, widespread human rights violations, and protracted post-conflict instability degrade not only human security but also state security—and regional or global stability if the conflict involves numerous or highly influential international actors. Because a breakdown in the state's capacity and willingness to provide a safe, secure, and equitable environment leads to acute insecurity, efforts to rebuild and restore justice after armed conflict must work to address the roots of conflict through inclusive processes that aim to promote sustainable peace for all (not just to bring active hostilities to an end).

Durable human security is realized when societal norms and governance institutions prioritize the protection of human rights, human development, and individual well-being and opportunities to thrive. In contrast, flawed norms and institutions lead to a lack of durable human security characterized by systematic threats to well-being. The chapters in section III discuss the linkages between durable human security issues such as food security, environmental protection, gender equality, and health security and overall state and global security and stability: by laying the foundation for empowered, self-sufficient, healthy, and engaged citizens, human security practice has the potential to support overall state and global stability. The key prerequisite for this synchronous, positive interaction is that the state must view its own security as tied to the well-being of its people; the historical record and contemporary crises tell us that this is far from a foregone conclusion.

As we noted at the outset of this chapter, the human security approach requires a shift in thinking about who is at the center of security and what security looks like; while some states, NGOs, the UN, and other security providers are working to promote a human security norm, we do not yet live in a world characterized by human security for all. How do we work toward improving human security for all? In one word: collaboration. Chapter 3 enumerates a list of security providers and each of the chapters in sections II and III similarly conveys the importance of a range of state and non-state actors working to promote human security. When security providers communicate, share resources and expertise, and—most crucially—ensure the inclusion of local stakeholders, efforts to protect the safety and well-being of individuals and their communities are more successful. When efforts to provide security are out of sync with the security perspectives (nativist, nationalist, or cosmopolitan) of the populations of intervening or donor states and the populations of states receiving assistance or targeted for intervention, they are less likely to succeed in creating positive change. As the next section discusses, human security cannot be seen as a one-dimensional solution that simply evokes states' responsibility to intervene in situations of armed violence in other states. Instead, human security is a lens through which practitioners, policymakers, and scholars can work to apply diverse insights and experiences to the most pressing and complex problems arising in the twenty-first century.

THE STATUS OF HUMAN SECURITY: THE VIEW FROM THE UN

Where does human security stand nearly two decades into the twenty-first century? As chapter 2 discusses, the concept of human security came about amid renewed international optimism and hope for collaboration among states and non-state actors to promote human rights and development. After September 2001, shifting foreign policy priorities of the United States (a veto-wielding permanent Security Council member, key UN donor, and influential state) and its allies threatened to sideline the human security approach in favor of more traditional security efforts to respond to the threat of transnational terrorism. The UN-authorized intervention in Libya (addressed in chapter 5) provided another blow to human security as critics viewed the operation's transition from civilian protection to use of force to topple a norm-violating regime, stoking concerns that R2P serves simply as a guise for intervention in states' domestic affairs. In a world marked by challenges to global collaboration, emerging threats to security at all levels, persistent inequality within and between states, and disparate views on the responsibility for security provision, the human security approach is not as readily compelling now as it must have seemed in 1994. Still, if we look at the work undertaken by the UN and its Member States, as well as global civil society, it is clear that the sun has not set on human security.

UN General Assembly Resolution 66/290 (referenced in chapters 3 and 5), primarily in its emphasis on the differences between human security as a general approach and the doctrine of Responsibility to Protect, signals an attempt by UN agencies to respond to the challenges facing human security providers in a world still characterized by traditional approaches to security. Rather than serving as an extension of powerful states' political interests, human security is, to the UN General Assembly, "an approach to assist Member States in identifying and addressing widespread and cross-cutting challenges to the survival, livelihood and dignity of their people" (United Nations General Assembly 2012, 1). The key to consensus on human security is the idea of cross-cutting threats: the notion that states cannot respond effectively to novel, transnational challenges to their own security and that of their populations without accounting for the factors that improve individual well-being and physical security.

Efforts to institutionalize the human security approach throughout relevant UN agencies continue. In 2014, twenty years after the UNDP's articulation of the term "human security" in its annual Human Development Report, the UN Human Security Unit released a strategic plan to advance human security initiatives at the UN with new clarity. Building on the 2005 World Summit Outcome document and General Assembly Resolution 66/290, the strategic plan articulates the twin goals of mainstreaming human security in UN activities and extending "global awareness of human security and the usage of the human security approach" (United Nations Human Security Unit 2014, 13). A year later, the HSU released its Framework for Cooperation to ensure UN system-wide application of human security principles. The Framework notes that the human security approach is "people-centred, comprehensive, context-specific and prevention-oriented" (United Nations Human Security

Unit 2015, 2) and that its application is "both timely and essential in supporting the United Nations system to further integrate and enhance its efforts to improve people's aspirations for greater peace, development and a life lived in dignity" (United Nations Human Security Unit 2015, 12). In essence, better understanding of the human security approach, its purpose, and the benefits of its application in security policy and practice is vital. We agree. Human security as a third approach to security studies and practice can indeed conflict with traditional security priorities, but it also complements and strengthens efforts to improve state and global stability.

Progress toward the Sustainable Development Goals and the response to global challenges like mass displacement and climate change will likely be the bellwethers of the success of the human security approach in the twenty-first century. In the wake of the 2008 global financial crisis and in the midst of persistent threats from transnational terrorist actors and resurgent nativist and nationalist tendencies throughout the globe, the cosmopolitan perspective on security is a tough sell in many influential constituencies concerned by the effects of globalization and increased interdependence on their communities. When the populations of donor states fail to see the value in promoting global human security and instead pursue policies and actions motivated by local or national interest (self-interest, as discussed in chapter 1), the UN-centered human security approach is weakened. The United Kingdom's Brexit vote and the U.S. presidential and congressional elections of 2016 point to a rejection of cosmopolitanism by slim majorities of voters in both states. Whether these decisions signal a broader trend remains to be determined.

Furthermore, it is imperative that discussions of human security include historically underrepresented voices and perspectives, especially those from the Global South and global civil society. Human security practiced from the bottom up, beginning with local security provision and influencing governance at higher levels, ensures that efforts to enhance safety and well-being are in line with the realities and perspectives of the population in need of assistance. General Assembly Resolution 66/290 signals awareness of the need to take Global South states' concerns into account, and the drafting process for the Sustainable Development Goals showed similar promise of inclusion, but UN agencies must take care to ensure that human security efforts empower, rather than subdue or silence, security beneficiaries.

For the UN to institutionalize the human security approach and ensure its meaningful implementation by Member States, it must continue to highlight the value and strategic benefits of people-centered security policies and initiatives. We focus on the UN here because of its position at the center of human security discourse from the mid-1990s onward and its function as an institution that fosters collaboration among states and between states and non-state actors. The same imperatives apply to other security providers seeking to promote and implement human security. With this in mind, we turn to an issue that is rarely addressed using the human security approach: transnational terrorism.

HUMAN SECURITY AND THE THREAT OF TERRORISM

Andrew Kydd and Barbara Walter contend that terrorism is a way for non-state actors, generally the weaker party in any conflict with a state, to signal commitment to the issue at hand. Terrorist actors use violence as a way to persuade rivals and sympathizers (whether foreign or domestic state governments or populations) of their willingness and ability to create harm and impose costs in pursuit of a goal (Kydd and Walter 2006, 50). The use of random violence spreads fear and has the potential to generate instability, especially in fragile or post-conflict states where governance institutions have insufficient capacity to provide security. Individual civilians, people uninvolved in any decision-making capacity related to the conflict of interest between terrorists and their state targets, bear the brunt of the costly message terrorists send through violent acts. Terrorism, then, constitutes a human security issue because of its role in violating the principle of freedom from fear of violence and creating physical harm to individuals.

The threat of transnational terrorism in the twenty-first century—as created by groups like al Qaeda or the so-called Islamic State (also known as Daesh, ISIS, or ISIL)—is a cross-cutting challenge that has the potential to affect human security as well as state security and global stability. We focus here and in chapter 14 on **transnational terrorism**, operations of a terrorist group that involve activities or presence in more than one state, because the response to this form of terrorism requires some degree of international coordination to address a complex threat. For instance, terrorist organizations do not legally hold territory, so how should a state respond to a terrorist attack without violating the sovereignty of the state in which the terrorist group operates? The answer to this question will vary based on the relationship between the two states, the involvement of the UN and other collective security organizations, and the nature and magnitude of the threat. Any form of terrorism presents a threat to both human and state security, but transnational terrorism adds layers of complexity to the challenge and response.

When we consider the policy responses to terrorist attacks or the general threat of terrorism, it is clear that the focus is less on the protection of human security than on preservation of state security. Attacks may be met with policy concessions (when the state targeted by terrorists engages in some form of compromise with the group), defensive efforts by the state to thwart future attacks (e.g., increasing airport security or screening visitors to popular tourist sites), offensive use of force by the state to punish the group or prevent future attacks (e.g., using drone strikes to target terror cells or engaging in a military operation to take back territory held by the group), or some combination thereof. When we think about ways to combat violent extremism, however, we tend not to consider long-term efforts to strengthen human security, opting instead for short-term responses to prevent or respond to immediate threats and long-term efforts to improve the state's capacity. A key focus of the UN Counter-Terrorism Implementation Task Force is state capacity: the UN's Global Counter-Terrorism Strategy emphasizes the need to safeguard civil aviation and ports, strengthen efforts to combat money laundering (a source of funding for terrorist activities), and secure nuclear and chemical materials to prevent access by nefarious actors (United Nations Counter-Terrorism Implementation Task Force n.d.). States that do have sufficient capacity to anticipate and respond to terrorist threats may also engage in actions that undermine human security and violate human rights, including the use of torture, detention without due process, repression of civil society groups and journalists, and use of military force (which often creates civilian casualties) (Office of the United Nations High Commissioner for Human Rights 2008).

Precisely because the potential responses to the threat of terrorism conflict with the human security approach, this issue provides a useful lens on the approach's opportunities and challenges. The state security–focused response to the threat of terrorism—whether that threat arises from domestic extremist ideologies or transnational actors—places the state's ability to govern, guard its borders, and secure its assets at the highest priority level. The human security approach stands to offer a comprehensive response to terrorism, albeit over the long term, and can be used effectively in conjunction with the state security approach (Christie 2010, 174–76). State and international responses to terrorism would look different if the focus of these responses were the human security of the target state's population (those who experience an attack or face the threat of one) as well as the population from which the terrorist group seeks to recruit new members and garner support. Such an approach might involve empowering local actors as well as states to create the foundation for durable human security and invalidating the terrorist organization's message. Transnational terrorism presents a challenge to each of the security approaches, but this particular challenge also highlights not only the conflicts between but also the synchronous nature of the three approaches we have addressed throughout the book. Chapter 14 will ask readers to contemplate the application of human security to this particular issue.

HUMAN SECURITY IN A CHANGING WORLD: THEORY AND ACTION

We now return to the question of whether human security is possible in the twenty-first century, with its complex threats, interconnectedness, and rapid changes. We conclude that, yes, human security is possible. It is not only possible but also essential to utilize the insights from this approach to craft comprehensive local, state, and international policies and implement programs to assist and empower individuals and communities. Human security is not only a normative approach—although caring for our fellow humans is a moral endeavor; it also carries strategic benefits, allowing states to adopt domestic and foreign policies that better provide a basis for long-term peace. As we have sought to demonstrate in each of the preceding chapters, high levels of human security improve state and global stability.

There are, of course, enduring challenges that policymakers, practitioners, and scholars should not ignore. Effective human security efforts require dialogue to bridge the gaps between academics, states, NGOs, IGOs, and civil society. To navigate conflicting perspectives on who ought to provide security and for whom security ought to be provided, open and inclusive dialogue about security challenges and the ideal way forward is essential. Furthermore, such discussions must include diverse perspectives, especially from those for whom security is provided and those who have been underrepresented in international forums, including states and civil society from the Global South. The human security approach requires security providers to talk *with*, not talk *to*, the populations they aim to empower and assist. Finally, security providers must be content to embrace long-term solutions, even if they do not yield immediate results. Although the signs of success in some areas of human security provision are quickly visible (e.g., establishing a safe zone for civilians in acute conflict or getting children back to school after the end of armed conflict), fostering human security is inherently a lengthy and complex process with generational, not necessarily rapid, results.

As a third approach to security policy and practice, human security offers a comprehensive view of contemporary threats, responsibility to address insecurity, and beneficiaries of efforts to provide security. The complexity of the human security approach presents challenges, but in a world defined more by gray areas than stark contrasts and clear ways forward, we maintain that it is essential to consider and work to protect the security and well-being of individuals and their communities.

Discussion Questions

1. Consider the factors that contribute to human security. What do you see as the most essential factors?
2. What political, institutional, structural, or logistical barriers prevent the full participation of Global South states and advocates in discussions of human security?
3. How likely is human security to be a priority among state security policymakers in the twenty-first century? If you were a security policymaker, would you prioritize human security?

4. Have evolving efforts to define and pursue human security at the UN yielded significant advances? Where have the efforts succeeded? Where have they fallen short?
5. How useful is the distinction between human, national, and global security?

FURTHER READING AND WEB RESOURCES

Andrew H. Kydd and Barbara F. Walter. "The Strategies of Terrorism." *International Security* 31, no. 1 (2006): 49–80.

United Nations Counter-Terrorism Implementation Task Force. "UN Global Counter-Terrorism Strategy." n.d. https://www.un.org/counterterrorism/ctitf/en/un-global-counter-terrorism-strategy (accessed July 14, 2017).

United Nations Human Security Unit. *Framework for Cooperation for the System-Wide Application of Human Security*. New York, September 2015.

United Nations Trust Fund for Human Security. "Human Security Approach." n.d. http://www.un.org/humansecurity/human-security-unit/human-security-approach (accessed July 13, 2017).

For Deeper Discussion

James Lebovic. *Deterring International Terrorism and Rogue States: US National Security Policy after 9/11*. New York: Routledge, 2007.

Ryerson Christie. "Critical Voices and Human Security: To Endure, to Engage or to Critique?" *Security Dialogue* 41, no. 2 (2010): 169–90.

REFERENCES

Christie, Ryerson. "Critical Voices and Human Security: To Endure, to Engage or to Critique?" *Security Dialogue* 41, no. 2 (2010): 169–90.

Kydd, Andrew H., and Barbara F. Walter. "The Strategies of Terrorism." *International Security* 31, no. 1 (2006): 49–80.

Office of the United Nations High Commissioner for Human Rights. *Human Rights, Terrorism, and Counter-terrorism*. Geneva: United Nations, 2008.

United Nations Counter-Terrorism Implementation Task Force. *UN Global Counter-Terrorism Strategy*. https://www.un.org/counterterrorism/ctitf/en/un-global-counter-terrorism-strategy#poa3 (accessed July 14, 2017).

United Nations Development Programme. *Human Development Report*. New York: Oxford University Press, 1994.

United Nations General Assembly. "2005 World Summit Outcome." *A/Res/60/1*. New York, October 24, 2005.

United Nations General Assembly. "Follow-Up to Paragraph 143 on Human Security of the 2005 World Summit Outcome." *A/Res/66/290*. New York, October 25, 2012.

United Nations General Assembly. "Open Working Group of the General Assembly on Sustainable Development Goals." *A/67/L.48/Rev.1*. New York, January 15, 2013.

United Nations Human Security Unit. *Framework for Cooperation for the System-Wide Application of Human Security*. New York, September 2015.

United Nations Human Security Unit. *Strategic Plan 2014–2017*. New York: United Nations, 2014.

Chapter 14

Human Security: From Theory to Action

Learning Objectives

This chapter will enable readers to:

1. Apply the concepts presented in the book to a current security problem.
2. Think critically about policy solutions using the various approaches to security.
3. Identify obstacles to effective security policymaking.
4. Recognize areas of conflict and reinforcement across the different approaches to security.

The subtitle of this book, "Theory and Action," implies that human security is an idea that should be put into practice. As professors of international relations and security studies our initial interest in these fields was not motivated by a sacrosanct devotion to the protection of the state. Instead, and like many of the hundreds of students that we have taught, we were drawn to the discipline because we wanted to discover ways to make the world a better place in which to live. We hope that this book helps you, whether the student, the instructor, or the security practitioner, develop frameworks that can lead to purposeful and positive action.

The purpose of this final section is to help you think about how we would apply the human security approach even in cases in which national and global security approaches have tended to dominate. First, we want to reiterate that when we discuss the human security approach we are discussing an approach to policymaking that sees the individual as the referent of security and which focuses on addressing what we have identified as human security threats. That is, threats to individuals that are the result of systemic flaws or breakdowns in the norms and institutions tasked with security provision. We have divided this book into two areas of human security practice: first, insecurity during acute conflict; and second, problems that undermine durable human security. It is clear, though, that the two areas are heavily intertwined with each other—or cyclical—as the lack of durable human security contributes to acute conflict and the presence of acute conflict undermines durable human security.

The "action" part of the book's subtitle happens on two levels: the extent to which human security informs the decision-making apparatuses of states, intergovernmental organizations, and local and international nongovernmental organizations and the institutionalization of human security practice and prioritization within each of these actors' organizational structures. A key question of this book has been how the integration of human security into the policy processes changes the scope and direction of those policies. One way to think through this question is to examine a policy process that has lacked a consistent human security approach and think through what would be different if such an approach were to be applied in practice.

In the previous chapter, we challenged the reader to think about how a human security approach might be engaged when responding to transnational terrorism. Transnational terrorism, which deliberately targets civilian populations, poses a dire threat to human security, but the policy approaches that have most often been pursued to address that threat have been largely national and global security–centric, with a heavy reliance on military force. That it has been almost two decades since the September 11 terrorist attacks with little to show in terms of positive outcomes from these policies begs for a reevaluation of how the world responds to violent extremism.

Violent extremism, of which transnational terrorism is a manifestation, poses a serious threat to communities, states, and the global system as a whole. Therefore, it comes as no surprise that security providers on all levels have sought to respond to threats posed by violent extremist groups. National security responses to violent extremism have focused on efforts to debilitate extremist groups abroad, often through military force, including the targeting of members, or potential members, of those groups inside their own countries. What has become readily clear is that these policies have often resulted in indiscriminate targeting of people and communities unaffiliated with extremist groups to begin with. These policies can lead to a backlash as individuals who would have otherwise been indifferent or even supportive of the intervening state develop grievances stemming from what they see as unjust acts. Violent extremist groups recognize and often recruit new members from these newly aggrieved communities. Global security also sees the rise of violent extremism as a threat, particularly when it preys on weak institutions, slows economic development, and contributes to mass displacement. Recall that global security responses tend to favor policies that contribute to overall stability of the international system. This approach deploys top-down solutions meant to strengthen cooperation between states and seeks to support both state and global institutions tasked with combatting transnational terrorism. While either of these two approaches may lead to greater security for at least some individuals, their prioritization of the state or system leaves others vulnerable. Would a human security approach to transnational terrorism fare any better?

In this chapter, we do not presume to provide a human security–based policy prescription for transnational terrorism—that in itself would require an additional volume. Instead, we provide a basic outline for how one can begin to engage these questions within the context of a classroom simulation, group discussion, or independent thought exercise. Simulations have been shown to give participants the opportunity to discover new ideas about the environment they are exploring (Boyne 2012, Newmann and Twigg 2000, Shellman and Turan 2006). Simulations should challenge your assumptions about how the world works and improve understanding of interdependent decision-making. The following provides guidelines for designing an in-class or group simulation around, or independent contemplation of, human security. Building on chapter 13, we use the case of transnational terrorism as an example to highlight the ways in which the three security approaches can both counteract and complement each other. Most importantly, the exercise should help us think about the interdependent nature of any policymaking process. A well-designed simulation helps participants think about how different key actors utilize different types of security approaches. We have purposefully left the details of the exercise vague in order to accommodate the interests of diverse groups of participants and the independent reader.

THINKING ABOUT HUMAN SECURITY PRACTICE THROUGH A SIMULATED WORLD

During a simulation participants are asked to develop responses to revealed crises. Typically, in a turn-based simulation environment, choices by one actor would have implications for others; thus each turn would result in a corresponding reaction by affected groups—which would then inform the next round of decision-making. There are multiple variations that one can take, including creating an environment in which only some participants are dedicated to the human security approach. What is key is that the simulation has a pedagogical purpose and should be designed to create an experience that generates deeper insight into how the ideas presented in this book would be applied in a real-world scenario. Thus, a simulation that leads to a "failed" outcome may be just as, if not more, valuable than one that results in a "success." What constitutes failure or success should also be a point for consideration, regardless of whether the exercise involves a large or small group.

As this book has made clear, human security requires the engagement of a broad range of actors at the state, supranational, and subnational levels. The inclusion of multiple actors into a policy process broadens the scope of the policies that are likely to be considered. Additionally, every enacted policy elicits a reaction by those whom the policy effects. In real-world policymaking not having a clear understanding of all the stakeholders who might be affected by a decision can be detrimental to a policy's chances for success. For instance, a stakeholder that is left out, either deliberately or through oversight, may try to complicate or block successful implementation of a policy. Therefore, consideration of which actors or roles to include in a simulation is crucial. Of course, the parameters of the simulated environment (e.g., number of participants or time to conduct the simulation) will constrain which actors may or may not be included, but looking beyond the obvious actors may produce insights that may otherwise be missed.

Another key consideration in simulation design is whether the roles participants are assigned lean toward the specific or the general. In a simulation in which roles are specific, participants would be representing states, organizations, or people that exist in the real world. In a general simulation, participants would play the roles of generic states, organizations, or people that represent approximations of real-world entities. Thus, a specific simulation could fall along the lines of France experiencing a terrorist attack by the so-called Islamic State, whereas a general simulation would fall along the lines of State A experiencing a terrorist attack by a terrorist organization based in State B. Both approaches have their advantages and disadvantages. A specific simulation works well for participants who are part of, are likely to be part of, or have been studying a specific institution, state, or decision-making structure. Knowledge of that structure, as well as any cultural nuances associated with that role, helps them better evaluate the possibilities of applying a human security approach to the scenario. Specific simulations work best if the participants are able to carry out extensive research on their roles prior to beginning the simulation. On the other hand, a general simulation can give more freedom regarding the overall design and can help avoid biases based on preconceived notions of the assigned role, assuming, of course, that the roles are well enough designed and communicated to the participants to avoid caricatures or stereotypes. Of course, either approach requires careful planning by the designer as well as seriousness by the participants. Box 14.1 gives some examples of the roles that might be included for a simulation that examines transnational terrorism. A note for those who may be working through the exercise independently: you may work through each of the actors in box 14.1 and consider what their respective viewpoints and options would be, allowing you to gain a deeper understanding of the complexity of the problem and potential responses.

BOX 14.1. POSSIBLE ROLES FOR SIMULATION ON TRANSNATIONAL TERRORISM

The terrorist actor—One problem when engaging in a simulation that includes groups that are violent extremists is that it is tempting to portray them with broad strokes or ascribe to them more power and influence than they may actually have. Therefore, it might be useful for the instructor or other group leader to take on this role and to have a predetermined set of actions that happen at various stages of the simulation to which other roles must respond.

The target state (the state that was attacked)—Depending on the size of the simulation, this can include multiple actors and agencies within the state. The capabilities of that state should be clear, particularly if the use of military force is an included option in the simulation.

The state or states where the transnational terrorist actor is based—Again, depending on the size of the simulation, this can include multiple actors and agencies within the state. Also, since transnational terrorist groups tend to exist mainly in states with weak institutions, the capabilities of this state should be made clear.

The United Nations or other international or regional organization—The United Nations has been an important voice for articulating the human security norm and related concepts. A simulation could include roles for the secretary-general and his staff within the Secretariat or others from specialized agencies, such as UNHCR. Couching the entire simulation within the framework of a General Assembly or Security Council debate can help form the parameters of the simulation.

Non-state actors—The role of various non-state actors brings important normative voices into the simulation. These non-state actors could include victims of the terrorist group; civil society actors in the state that was attacked; civil society actors in the state where the transnational terrorist group is based; and international nongovernmental organizations, including human rights advocates and humanitarian actors.

Once specific roles are determined a simulation can be designed around two basic guiding frameworks. The first approach is to have participants mimic as closely as possible the anticipated real-world behavior of the role that they are playing. The purpose of this approach is to help the participant better understand the decision-making processes of someone she may not have otherwise been familiar with at the start of the simulation or to gain experience playing a role that the participant will likely take on in real life. A second approach to simulation design is to constrain the decision-making process according to certain prescribed parameters that allow the participant to consider how a different approach to the problem might result in a different outcome. In designing a simulation that incorporates human security it may work best to design it using the second approach since many of the assigned roles do not currently incorporate human security into their policymaking. Thus, to create the simulation environment we must first consider the different actors that would have a stake in the policies being pursued and consider: (1) the ways that those actors have confronted a similar situation in the past, and (2) what a human security response for any given actor would actually look like.

THE THREE BOXES: PROBLEM, POLICY, AND OUTCOME

A good simulation should derive insight into the problem being simulated. Therefore, it is important to be neither too complex nor too simple. A simulation that is too complex runs the risk of overwhelming and confusing participants. An overly simple simulation runs the risk of leading the participants toward a predetermined outcome that may come across as contrived.

Therefore, we recommend that the simulation be structured around what we call the three boxes (see figure 14.1). Each box represents a specific stage of the simulated environment. Box 1 is the problem phase. Box 2 is the policy phase. Box 3 is the desired outcome phase. In the problem phase (box 1) each role conceptualizes what the exact problem is that the actors are trying to solve. It is likely that different actors will conceptualize the problem very differently and prioritize different dimensions of the problem. For example, in a simulation focusing on transnational terrorism, how might a civil society actor in the state where a transnational terrorist cell is based view the problem of terrorism differently from foreign policy decision-makers in a state that has been targeted by that terrorist organization? After conceptualizing the problem, each role should clearly identify what their desired outcome would be

Box 1 Perception of the Problem	Box 2 Policy Options	Box 3 Ideal Outcome

Figure 14.1. The Three Boxes

(box 3). Comparing boxes 1 and 3 for each role against each other will show many instances of convergence. Many roles will share similar conceptualizations of the problem as well as a similar desired outcome. Of course, many will not. If, for instance, you choose to have participants take on the role of the terrorist organization it is likely that they will disagree with many others on both the problem and the ideal outcome.

It is in box 2 where much of the actual simulation takes place. The policy phase represents the concrete actions of each of the roles within the simulation. This phase should expose the participant to two aspects of the decision-making process: (1) the importance of nuts and bolts in policymaking, and (2) the interdependence of each decision. Thus, throughout the simulation participants should be able to articulate the details of their choices and each role should be given the chance to respond to the actions of others; thus the simulation should consist of multiple stages. How many total stages occur will depend on the amount of time scheduled to conduct the simulation or discussion and the expected complexity of each policy choice.

The box 2 phase allows the simulation designer to manipulate the environment in such a way that it gives participants the chance to think critically about how different approaches create different outcomes. In the following section we will discuss how one might integrate the human security approach into a simulation with a transnational terrorism scenario.

APPLYING A HUMAN SECURITY APPROACH

A human security approach to the problem of transnational terrorism may not seem obvious to many of the actors engaged in the policy process. Research has shown that states responding to crises triggered by non-state actors are more prone to violent crisis management techniques than states responding to crises triggered by other states (Andersen-Rodgers 2015). The use of force as a response, though, runs the risk of striking more than just the intended target and potentially producing what Kilcullen (2009) describes as an "accidental guerrilla," in which local political struggles are drawn into international conflict. However, as this book has argued, constructing policies within a human security framework can wield outcomes that address problems in such a way that a broader range of people's interests are considered. What, then, would a human security approach look like when responding to transnational terrorism? First, policies would prioritize the security of individuals. Although security providers may adopt the human security approach for a number of reasons (recall the discussion in chapter 1), human security accommodates the cosmopolitan perspective on security and may involve a range of actors who consider the security of others alongside their own immediate interests.

s derived from a human security approach would be grounded
n of people's human rights. Third, although the concept and
ped through discussions at the UN, human security would
tions over external imposition, as the former offer more hope
for long-term stability. Fourth, the human security approach would consider
how proposed policies contribute to durable human security.

An additional consideration for any scenario that involves transnational
terrorism is the question of whether the use of force would fit into a human
security approach. The decision to use force has broad implications for
people's security. Contemplation of who is targeted, the means by which they
are targeted, and when they are targeted all potentially threaten the human
security of people on the ground who have no connection to the terrorist
cell. Think, for instance, about a drone strike on a suspected training camp.
How certain are you that the tents or structures and people being observed
via satellite are who you think they are? What if, instead, they are a wedding
party, as was the case when on December 12, 2013, a U.S. drone mistakenly
fired on a wedding in Yemen, killing 12 people and injuring 24 more (Draper
2014)? When force is used is also an important consideration. Human security is grounded in human rights and two core human rights are that one has
the right to be presumed innocent until proven guilty and the right to a public
trial. National security responses to transnational terrorism have often labeled
suspected groups as combatants without certainty of their status as such, giving states justification to expand who qualifies as a target. Therefore, when
designing the simulation, it is important to build in clear instructions about
any of the participants' capacities for force and realistic consequences of that
use.

Ultimately, developing a simulated environment can help draw distinctions between the multiple approaches to security. In the previous chapter
we argued that human security requires good governance and collaboration
between security providers. This idea is not necessarily contradictory to
national and global security approaches. What should become clear, however,
is how the normative requirements of the human security approach constrain
certain policy choices but also open up new avenues for responding to threats.
How, then, is this applied to a simulation on transnational terrorism?

To start, we could consider the issues associated with living in a community in which members of a violent extremist group are present. Because
of the proximity to the violent extremist group, local actors are faced with a
number of security challenges. Openly defying violent extremists can result
in one becoming a target of that group; thus local actors will often be reluctant
to openly challenge these groups. This may appear to an outside observer
as collusion. Such an interpretation might loosen the constraints that a state
might have when formulating a policy response involving the use of force,

which, in turn, may mean a greater number of people will be killed. However, applying the human security approach broadens our understanding of who is a security provider and also takes into account the strategic choices that many civilians must take in order to stay alive. A human rights organization that applies normative pressure on states or local civil society organizations that provide aid and humanitarian assistance to effected communities are also security providers within a human security framework. Amplifying these voices within the simulation may lead to new insights into policymaking and the consequences of different actions.

Another potential area of consideration is each actor's determination of whether they should act unilaterally or in collaboration with others. Unilateralism, particularly for a powerful actor, may seem appealing, but it also means that this actor alone is liable for the consequences of their response. This question also applies to local actors who must consider the pros and cons of collaborating with other actors, particularly foreign powers or intergovernmental organizations such as the UN. Applying the human security approach shifts this question to the role of greater collaboration between various stakeholders.

There are, of course, many additional directions such a simulation can take, and we encourage you to think about these processes and how they would be applied within a real-world policy environment. By going through such exercises, both the difficulties and the practicalities of security practice will become clearer and, hopefully, assist in future policy planning.

CONCLUSION

This chapter provides the building blocks for creating an interactive learning experience and the foundation for a group discussion on the practicalities of applying the human security approach to real-world policymaking. As we have argued throughout this book, human security is a practice that security providers can choose to engage. While there is a diverse range of actors who apply the human security approach in their decision-making, they are often met with skepticism or are undermined in their efforts when issues traditionally associated with state-centric security concerns arise. Ultimately, we hope that this book can engage deeper and more critical thinking about the practice of human security.

Discussion Questions

1. In what ways does the desire to apply the human security approach become constrained when key actors choose not to engage such an approach?

2. A key variable in international relations is power. How does power play into the simulation or thought exercise set up here? How do weaker roles gain leverage over more powerful roles? In what ways is power constrained based on the strategies of weaker roles?

3. Some roles in the simulation are by definition motivated by the human security norm (i.e., a human rights NGO), whereas others are not. When those roles that do not typically engage a human security approach do so, how does it change the outcome of the simulation?

4. How does the use of force undermine the ability of human security actors to pursue their goals? Is the use of force anathema to human security practice? Why or why not?

REFERENCES

Andersen-Rodgers, David R. "No Table Necessary? Foreign Policy Crisis Management Techniques in Non-State Actor-Triggered Crises." *Conflict Management and Peace Science* 32, no. 2 (2015): 220–21.

Boyne, Shawn Marie. "Crisis in the Classroom: Using Simulations to Enhance Decision-Making Skills." *Journal of Legal Education* 62, no. 2 (2012): 311–22.

Draper, Lucy. *The Wedding That Became a Funeral: U.S. Still Silent One Year on from Deadly Yemen Drone Strike*. December 12, 2014. http://www.newsweek.com/wedding-became-funeral-us-still-silent-one-year-deadly-yemen-drone-strike-291403 (accessed July 14, 2017).

Kilcullen, David. *The Accidental Guerrilla: Fighting Small Wars in the midst of a Big One*. Oxford: Oxford University Press, 2009.

Newmann, William W., and Judyth L. Twigg. "Active Engagement of the Intro IR Student: A Simulation Approach." *PS: Political Science and Politics* 33, no. 4 (2000): 835–42.

Shellman, Stephen M., and Kürsan Turan. "Do Simulations Enhance Student Learning? An Empirical Evaluation of an IR Simulation." *Journal of Political Science Education* 2 (2006): 19–32.

Glossary

Acute conflict—conflict that has a substantial probability of violence.

Anarchic—a system that has no overarching authority capable of punishing rule violators.

Battle deaths—deaths that occur due to combat in two-sided conflict with at least one of those sides being a state.

Beijing Platform for Action—adopted in September 1995; established women's rights as human rights, made commitments to protecting women's human rights, and called for a global shift in thinking about gender equality as a broader issue of concern for all people rather just than one-half of the population.

Bioterrorism—the deliberate use of viruses, bacteria, or other disease agents to cause harm to people, animals, or plants for a political or strategic purpose.

Cease-fire—an agreement between fighting parties to stop using violence or otherwise mobilizing their forces against each other. These agreements are often seen as the first step toward reaching peace.

Chronic hunger—also referred to as undernourishment, is caused by long-term lack of access to the availability of sufficient quantities of nutritious food.

Civil and political rights—human rights that allow individuals to participate fully in society—including and especially in political processes—without fear of discrimination or harm. Civil and political rights were conceived to protect individuals from state repression, discrimination, and overreach and rights such as freedom of assembly, speech, and religion as well as security of person and property.

Civil society—the sphere of voluntary action that is distinct from the state and economic spheres. Civil society can include religious institutions, humanitarian and charity organizations, advocacy networks, and other domestic and international actors.

Civilian protection—the idea that civilians should be shielded from harm during armed conflict.

Climate change—describes sustained changes in global or regional climate patterns that stem from the overall warming of the earth.

Climate refugees—individuals and communities forced by the effects of climate change to relocate from their homes.

Collective action problem—a situation in which actors have an interest in creating a solution to a problem that affects everyone, but since solutions come at some cost it is difficult to convince individual actors to contribute to any given solution.

Collective security organizations—international organizations tasked with the provision of security for their member states, regions, or the global system. These organizations, made up of states, seek to cooperate to protect all of their members and allies from harm.

Collective security system—an international structure in which predatory behavior by one state elicits a collective response by all international actors.

Comprehensive peace accords—agreements in which all the major parties in the conflict are involved in the negotiation process and in which the substantive issues fueling the conflict are addressed.

Convention on the Elimination of All Forms of Discrimination against Women (CEDAW)—signed on December 18, 1979, and came into effect on September 3, 1981, during the UN Decade for Women (1976–1985); the binding agreement defines gender-based discrimination and establishes steps that states parties should take to end discrimination against women, including changes to the state's legal system, establishment of public institutions to prevent discrimination, and measures to prevent discriminatory actions.

COP 21—the 21st Conference of Parties, held in Paris in December 2015. The Paris Agreement on climate change resulted from this international conference.

Cosmopolitan perspective on security—views security as best provided through global cooperation and acceptance of norms and governance institutions. The cosmopolitan perspective leads individuals to see their security as closely aligned with the security of others around the world, regardless of differences in identity, nationality, and experiences.

Cultural relativism—an approach that views an individual's or society's morals, values, norms, and beliefs as rooted in their culture, history, and experiences.

Divine right of kings—a governing principle that held that rulers were not subject to human authority but to divine—or absolute—authority.

Donor states—wealthy states that contribute a large share of the financial resources necessary to sustain international agencies and coordination efforts.

Durable human security—durable human security includes the dimensions of security that are not necessarily related to armed conflict—though they may certainly exist in wartime—but threaten the daily lives and livelihoods of individuals and communities. Durable human security incorporates the concepts of freedom from want and freedom from fear, as both are essential for the realization of long-term, sustainable human security.

Economic, social, and cultural rights—human rights to the services and resources that allow individuals to thrive. Such rights include the right to food, housing, and education.

Epidemic—an unusually high incidence of disease in a community or the spread of disease to a new locality.

Episodic food insecurity—a situation in which an individual, family, or community's access to food is limited or unpredictable.

Famine—a situation of extreme, usually deadly, food insecurity resulting from severe lack of access to and availability of food.

Feminist foreign policy—an approach to foreign affairs that emphasizes women's participation, rights, and empowerment and gender equality.

First-generation rights—the earliest human rights discussed by philosophers and political actors. These rights establish the basis for a more participatory and less discriminatory society in which individuals do not need to fear state-perpetrated interference or harm.

First Geneva Convention (1864)—pertains to the welfare of wounded combatants and establishes a right to medical care and protection for International Committee of the Red Cross members working in war zones.

Food access—also referred to as entitlement (Sen 1981), is determined by an individual's ability to purchase or otherwise acquire a sufficient amount of nutritious food to sustain daily activities.

Food and Agriculture Organization (FAO)—founded in 1945 to serve as a discussion forum through which states can develop policy responses to hunger and to disseminate technical information to improve food security in developing states.

Food availability—the supply of food in the region

Food deserts—areas with a high population of low-income households and lack of access to available, affordable, and nutritious food sources within a set distance (usually ½ to 1 mile in urban areas and 10–20 miles in rural regions), contribute to food insecurity, affecting both the access and availability dimensions of food security.

Food stability—refers to an individual's access to food at all times, without sudden or cyclical disruptions such as those that result from economic recession, climate change, natural disasters, armed conflict, or famine.

Food use—also referred to as food utilization, refers to overall nutrition achieved through the combination of a healthy diet, access to quality health care, clean water, and sanitation.

Fourth Geneva Convention (1949)—outlines the rights of and protections for civilians in armed conflict.

Gender—the personal sense of a person as male, female, both, or neither, as well as the societal expectations for a person's behavior, appearance, and expression on the basis of their sex.

Gender expression—the outward reflection of one's gender and is also not necessarily tied to one's sex; gender expression encompasses dress, mannerisms, speech, hairstyle, and other visible or audible traits a person may adopt on the outside to reflect a sense of gender identity.

Gender identity—the gender with which a person associates on the inside (one's sense of self as male, female, or somewhere between or completely unrelated to the two); not necessarily identical to one's sex, though it may be.

Gender inequality—when one group is privileged over others on the basis of sex and gender.

Gender Inequality Index (GII)—measures the position of women relative to men in a given state on the basis of female reproductive health, empowerment, and economic status.

Gender norms—societal expectations for how people should behave, live, and love on the basis of gender.

Geneva Conventions—international treaties that outlined rights and protections related to combatants, prisoners of war, and civilians caught up in armed conflict.

Global Gender Gap Index (GGGI)—measures economic participation and opportunity, educational attainment, political empowerment, and health and survival in 140 states' economies.

Global security—an approach to security that focuses on the protection of the stability of the system of states.

Global warming—refers to overall increases in the average temperatures of the earth's oceans and atmosphere. Global warming is caused by high concentrations of carbon dioxide and other greenhouse gases in the atmosphere, which trap heat and warm the earth through the greenhouse effect.

Globalized—a description of our interconnected world. The globalized world in which we live allows people from all over the globe to exchange goods, services, and ideas; it also allows security threats to cross borders quickly and easily.

Greenhouse effect—a process wherein gases (including water vapor and carbon dioxide) help to warm the earth by trapping radiation in the atmosphere.

Hague Convention of 1899—the multilateral treaty that proposed a framework for conflict prevention through mediation, protocols for declarations of war, and rules for humane treatment of prisoners.

Hague Convention of 1907—outlawed the use of poison gas and aerial bombing.

Health security—or the protection of individuals from sudden or chronic health threats and efforts to empower individuals to lead healthy lives.

Human development—an approach that focuses on advancing the well-being of people instead of or in addition to increasing the economic wealth of a state; the focus of human development is on expanding the capability and opportunities of people.

Human Development Index (HDI)—a measure of growth that attempts to account for human capabilities and opportunities instead of simply measuring gross domestic product (GDP).

Human rights—the rights to which all human beings are entitled, regardless of their nationality, sex, ethnicity, race, religion, language, state or territory of residence, or any other factor or status. Human rights are universal (meaning all humans everywhere are entitled to them) and inalienable (meaning no one can deprive another human of that person's rights except through the due process of law).

Human security—exists when individuals and communities are safe from both chronic, long-term threats and from more sudden and overtly violent threats.

Human security approach—an effort or policy that seeks to ensure the protection of individuals and communities from harm.

Human security norm—a consensus, among a significant group of states and international organizations, that individuals and communities are entitled to protection from harm and that outside actors (including foreign states or organizations) may help to provide this protection as necessary.

Humanitarian assistance—provision of aid and support without the use of force, in response to natural disasters, famine, or public health crises in another state.

Humanitarian intervention—the use of force within another state to protect people from harm, when another government's policies and instability cause destruction and insecurity.

Humanitarian organizations—organizations that seek to protect individuals from harm, regardless of political affiliation, ethnic or racial identity, or any other characteristic. These organizations are unaffiliated with state governments (we often call them non-state actors) and provide aid in response to natural disasters, war and armed conflict, and public health crises.

Indirect violence—harm caused to civilians due to the indirect consequences of war such as decreased access to food, clean water, or health care.

Intergovernmental organizations (IGOs)—organizations formed by and comprosed of member states; these international-level actors help states to cooperate and coordinate efforts to address specific sets of issues.

Internally displaced persons (IDPs)—people who are displaced from their homes due to conflict or natural disasters, but remain inside their country and do not cross an international border.

International Bill of Human Rights—consists of the Universal Declaration of Human Rights; the International Covenant on Economic, Social and Cultural Rights; and the International Covenant on Civil and Political Rights.

The International Covenant on Economic, Social and Cultural Rights (ICESCR) (1966)—multilateral treaty that obligates parties to protect economic, social, and cultural rights.

International Covenant on Civil and Political Rights (ICCPR) (1966)—multilateral treaty that obligates parties to protect civil and political rights.

International Criminal Court (ICC)—a legal institution created as a permanent international body, based in The Hague, the Netherlands, with the authority to prosecute individuals, including heads of state, who are responsible for genocide, crimes against humanity, and war crimes.

International Fund for Agricultural Development (IFAD)—founded in 1977, a financial institution focused on assisting the rural poor in developing states. Its central objectives are to improve well-being and food security and reduce poverty in developing states through loans and grants to increase access to agricultural technology and related skills.

International human rights law—a body of international agreements, conventions, and treaties that outline the basic rights and freedoms to which individuals are entitled.

International humanitarian law—the rules of warfare that place limitations on the use of force by states and the conduct of combatants acting on behalf of states.

International order—the political, economic, and normative arrangements in the international system.

Intrastate wars—civil wars or wars that are fought within states instead of between two or more states.

Jus ad bellum—limits the causes for which war is justifiable, such as self-defense or civilians persecuted by their government.

Jus in bello—expectations for moral behavior in warfare, such as special protections for injured or surrendering combatants.

Jus post bellum—expectation that the parties to armed conflict will rebuild and restore a just order after hostilities end.

Just War Theory—a framework for when, how, and for what reasons governments may engage in warfare.

Just wars—wars fought with good intentions for one's own state or on behalf of others.

Kyoto Protocol—an international agreement within the UN climate change framework. The Kyoto Protocol was signed on December 11, 1997, in Kyoto, Japan, and it entered into force on February 16, 2005. It was ratified by 192 parties and committed signatories to emissions reduction targets.

"Lifestyle" diseases—chronic health conditions arising from a societal shift toward a sedentary lifestyle.

Male:female sex ratios—the number of males per 100 females in a population.

Malnutrition—a condition that results from taking in too few, too many, or the wrong nutrients such that the body does not receive the necessary balance of essential nutrients to maintain daily activities.

Millennium Development Goals (MDGs)—adopted in September 2000; global objectives for eradicating poverty and promoting equality, rights, and opportunity.

Montreal Protocol—a treaty adopted by forty-six states in August 1987. The Montreal Protocol focuses specifically on the protection of the ozone layer.

Multidimensional peacekeeping—an intervention that seeks to rebuild the state institutions that were destroyed during a conflict. The tasks for this type of operation are much wider than those of traditional peacekeeping operations.

Nationalist perspective on security—closely aligned with the traditional or state security and global security approaches. According to this perspective, the individual believes security is best provided by the state for the citizens of the state. The state is the primary provider of security and the individual expects to receive protection from the state, as established by the notion of the social contract.

National security—an approach to security that prioritizes the safety and stability of the political entity of the state and its territorial integrity; a state that is secure is able to defend its borders, protect its population from outside threats, and continue its political and economic functions.

Nationally determined contributions (NDCs)—national goals aimed at reducing greenhouse gas emissions, pursuing clean and renewable energy sources, and mitigating the effects of climate change. NDCs are linked to the Paris Agreement.

Nativist perspective on security—according to this perspective, security is best provided by a group or groups below the level of the state, including sectarian, ethnic, religious, racial, or other identity groups.

Natural law—refers to a foundational, unchanging morality that guides all human behavior at all times in all places.

Natural rights—rights to which all rational human beings are entitled. The concept of natural rights formed the philosophical and legal foundation for the concept of human rights.

Negative peace—a situation characterized by the absence of violence.

Negative rights—a term used to indicate that a certain right requires someone to abstain from a specific action; the enjoyment of such rights requires the government or other entities or people from affecting an individual's choices, freedoms, or beliefs, or actions.

Nongovernmental organizations (NGOs)—organizations that focus on a particular issue or set of issues and operate independently of states and IGOs.

Norm—a commonly accepted belief or idea that provides standards for behavior.

One-sided victory—a war termination in which one side militarily defeated the other.

One-sided violence—violence perpetrated against noncombatants without fear of reciprocation.

Ozone layer—a portion of the earth's stratosphere that acts as a "sunscreen" for the planet and its inhabitants, absorbing the sun's ultraviolet radiation. Its depletion leaves humans especially vulnerable to skin cancer.

Pandemic—the spread of disease across borders or on a global scale.

Paris Agreement—the most recent and most comprehensive follow-up to the UNFCCC and the Kyoto Protocol. Resulting from COP 21 negotiations, the Paris Agreement has 195 signatories and it entered into force on November 4, 2016. The agreement invites states to abide by nationally determined contributions (NDCs) to lower greenhouse gas emissions and tackle climate change.

Patriarchy—"Rule by fathers"; a system of entrenched norms and inequality that privileges masculinity (and men and boys) over all other identities and people.

Peacebuilding—the creation of institutional frameworks and processes that address the roots of a conflict and establish processes for reconciliation with the intention of lessening the likelihood for conflict recurrence.

Peacekeeping—an intervention that is typically authorized by the United Nations and involves the deployment of international military, police, and civilian personnel tasked with maintaining peace and security after a ceasefire or peace agreement.

Peace accord—an agreement between all or most conflict parties that outlines post-conflict governance.

Peace enforcement—a UN operation put into place without full consent of the warring parties with the intention of enforcing a peace.

Peace processes—the range of activities intended to bring about a cessation of violent conflict. These include informal meetings between parties, formal negotiations, cease-fires, and formal peace treaties.

Permanent five members (P5)—the permanent five members of the UN Security Council (China, France, Russia, the United Kingdom, and the United States) that have power to veto any resolution.

Positive peace—a situation that adequately provides social welfare, establishes rights, and facilitates justice.

Positive rights—a term used to indicate that the provision of a certain right requires someone (usually the government, but possibly also an agency, institution, or fellow human) to *do something* or take action to provide that right if necessary.

Principle of non-intervention—a strict interpretation of sovereignty implies that states are not to intervene in other states' affairs, including the use of force to stop states from violating their citizens' human rights.

Proxy war—armed conflict in which foreign states become involved in pursuit of their own national interests related to the outcome of the conflict.

Reconciliation—a process in which people work to overcome hatred and mistrust between groups to the extent that they can coexist with each other.

Refugees—people who are displaced from their homes and cross an international border. Refugees are granted legal rights under the 1951 Convention relating to the Status of Refugees.

Regimes—sets of international norms, rules, and expectations that facilitate cooperation among states.

Regional blocs—formal multilateral institutions that reduce barriers to economic and political cooperation; examples include the European Union (EU), Association of Southeast Asian Nations (ASEAN), the African Union (AU), the Cooperation Council for the Arab States of the Gulf (or the Gulf Cooperation Council, GCC), and the Organization of American States (OAS).

Responsibility to Protect (R2P)—the doctrine that holds that states are obligated to protect civilians from what are known as the four crimes: genocide, war crimes, ethnic cleansing, and crimes against humanity.

Second-generation rights—rights that establish not only certain individual liberties but also work toward a more egalitarian society in which individuals' basic needs (food, shelter, education, and employment) are met.

Second Geneva Convention (1906)—applies to sailors in armed forces and expands the protections of the First Geneva Convention to war at sea.

Security provision—the general practice of preventing or mitigating harm, or providing assistance and resources in response to situations of insecurity at the individual, state, or international level.

Self-determination—the notion that citizens of a territory have the right to choose for themselves what type of political system they are to live under and that the government is tasked with the protection of their rights.

Self-help system—view of the international system driven by the idea that states are on their own when it comes to guaranteeing their security.

Self-interest—protection for oneself in its most basic form.

Sex—the biological differences in human reproductive systems that lead to the identification of a person as male, female, both, or neither.

Social contract—the agreement between individuals and a government that the latter will provide for the common security in exchange for the allegiance of its people.

Sovereign equality—the principle that all states are legally equal to each other.

Sovereignty—the idea that a state has legal jurisdiction over its territory and that other states are not to interfere in each other's internal affairs.

Sovereignty as responsibility—the notion that having the status of sovereignty means that a state has certain obligations to protect the human rights of its citizens.

Sustainable Development Goals (SDGs)—adopted in 2015 with a target date of 2030; expand on and continue the work of the MDGs with a specific focus on sustainability.

State—a centralized political entity that holds territory, has a stable population, and is recognized as legitimate by its population and the other states in the world.

State-building—a practice that generally consists of reconstituting a core set of state institutions, a market economy, and basic rule-of-law provisions following a conflict.

States parties—states that have signed and ratified an international agreement.

Strategic nonviolence—nonviolent resistance used to draw attention to and put pressure on an oppressive regime.

Structural violence—the loss of life due to indirect factors such as poorly functioning health care systems, agriculture, water supplies, inequality, and other indirect physical, resource-related, or institutional threats.

Terrorism—the use of violence by non-state actors toward nonmilitary targets and noncombatant populations; the ultimate goal is to send a message to the state in which the terrorist organization is based, the population of that state, or to foreign states and populations.

Third-generation rights—rights pertaining to specific groups of people.

Third Geneva Convention (1949)—establishes protections for prisoners of war.

Threat multipliers—phenomena, situations, or actors that make existing security threats more dangerous.

Transitional justice—the process by which a state transitions from a period of conflict to a peaceful, democratic society with a focus on redress for victims.

Transnational advocacy networks—a grouping of individuals and organizations connected through their pursuit of a common goal.

Transnational terrorism—operations of a terrorist group that involve activities or presence in more than one state.

Truth and reconciliation commission (TRC)—a formal process with the purpose of correctly revealing the truth of what happened during a conflict or system of injustice.

Undernutrition—a condition resulting from lack of access to or availability of sufficient nutrients or the body's inability to use nutrients consumed as a result of disease.

United Nations Framework Convention on Climate Change (UNFCCC)—an international convention adopted at the Earth Summit in Rio de Janeiro in June 1992. It entered into force on March 21, 1994. The UNFCCC has been ratified by 197 parties. It seeks to facilitate cooperation among states to address the factors contributing to climate change.

United Nations Security Council Resolution 1325—adopted October 31, 2000; situated women, girls, and the gendered effects of war within the scope of peace and security, and therefore on the Security Council's agenda.

Universal Declaration of Human Rights (1948)—international agreement that documents much of what we understand about human rights today; forms the basis of current definitions of human rights and fundamental freedoms.

Women, Peace, and Security (WPS)—policy agenda comprising a set of Security Council resolutions that call, in part, for greater participation of women in conflict resolution and peacebuilding processes.

World Food Program (WFP)—founded in 1961 to provide humanitarian assistance directly to regions in need. The WFP's mission is to offer immediate aid and expertise with the long-term objective of a food secure world.

References

Adger, W. Neil, et al. "Human Security." In *Climate Change 2014: Impacts, Adaptation, and Vulnerability. Part A: Global and Sectoral Aspects. Contribution of Working Group II to the Fifth Assessment Report of the Intergovernmental Panel on Climate Change*, by Christopher B. Field et al., 755–91. Cambridge: Cambridge University Press, 2014.

Adler, Emanuel, and Vincent Pouliot. "International practices." *International Theory* 3, no. 1 (2011): 1–36.

Alderman, Liz. "Greek Villagers Rescued Migrants. Now They Are the Ones Suffering." *New York Times*, August 17, 2016.

American Institute of Physics. *The Discovery of Global Warming*. February 2016. http://history.aip.org/history/climate/simple.htm#L_M085 (accessed May 10, 2017).

Amnesty International. *A Perfect Storm: The Failure of European Policies in the Central Mediterranean*. London: Amnesty International, 2017.

Andersen-Rodgers, David R. "Back Home Again: Assessing the Impact of Provisions for Internally Displaced Persons in Comprehensive Peace Accords." *Refugee Survey Quarterly* 34, no. 3 (2015): 24–45.

Andersen-Rodgers, David R. "No Table Necessary? Foreign Policy Crisis Management Techniques in Non-State Actor-Triggered Crises." *Conflict Management and Peace Science* 32, no. 2 (2015): 220–21.

Archibold, Randal C., and Somini Sengupta. "U.N. Struggles to Stem Haiti Cholera Epidemic." *New York Times*, April 19, 2014.

Autesserre, Séverine. *Peaceland: Conflict Resolution and the Everyday Politics of International Intervention*. Cambridge: Cambridge University Press, 2014.

Badran, Ramzi. "Intrastate Peace Agreements and the Durability of Peace." *Conflict Management and Peace Science* 31, no. 2 (2014): 193–217.

Bailey, Robert. "Food and Human Security." In *Routledge Handbook of Human Security*, by Mary Martin and Taylor Owen, 188–96. New York: Routledge, 2014.

Ban, Jonathan. "Health as a Global Security Challenge." *Seton Hall Journal of Diplomacy and International Relations* 4 (2003): 19–28.

Barnett, Jon, and W. Neil Adger. "Climate Change, Human Security and Violent Conflict." *Political Geography* 26, no. 6 (2007): 639–55.

Barnett, Michael, and Martha Finnemore. *Rules for the World: International Organizations in Global Politics*. Ithaca, NY: Cornell University Press, 2004.

Barr, Heather. "Afghanistan: Failing Commitments to Protect Women's Rights." Human Rights Watch, July 11, 2013.

Bassiouni, Cherif M. *Crimes against Humanity. Historical Evolution and Contemporary Application*. Cambridge: Cambridge University Press, 2011.

BBC News. "A Brief History of Climate Change." September 20, 2013. http://www.bbc.com/news/science-environment-15874560 (accessed May 10, 2017).

BBC News. "Why Are There Still Famines?" March 15, 2017. http://www.bbc.com/news/world-africa-39039255 (accessed July 5, 2017).

Beardsley, Kyle. "Peacekeeping and the Contagion of Armed Conflict." *The Journal of Politics* 73, no. 4 (2011): 1051–64.

Beardsley, Kyle, David E. Cunningham, and Peter B. White. "Resolving Civil Wars before They Start: The UN Security Council and Conflict Prevention in Self-Determination Disputes." *British Journal of Political Science* (2017): 1–23.

Beaubien, Jason. "Why the Famine in South Sudan Keeps Getting Worse." *NPR*, March 14, 2017.

Bellamy, Alex J. *Global Politics and the Responsibility to Protect: From Words to Deeds*. London: Routledge, 2011.

Bellemare, Marc F., Johanna Fajardo-Gonzalez, and Seth R. Gitter. "Foods and Fads: The Welfare Impacts of Rising Quinoa Prices in Peru." *Working Paper No. 2016–06*. Towson University Department of Economics Working Paper Series, March 2016.

Beller, Thomas, and Ben Depp. "America's First 'Climate Refugees.'" *Smithsonian Magazine*, June 29, 2016.

Benko, Jessica. "How a Warming Planet Drives Human Migration." *New York Times Magazine*. April 19, 2017. https://www.nytimes.com/2017/04/19/magazine/how-a-warming-planet-drives-human-migration.html?_r=0 (accessed April 27, 2017).

Blattman, Christopher, and Jeannie Annan. "The Consequences of Child Soldiering." *The Review of Economics and Statistics* 92, no. 4 (2010): 882–98.

Blythman, Joanna. "Can Vegans Stomach the Unpalatable Truth about Quinoa?" *The Guardian*, January 16, 2013.

Boutros-Ghali, Boutros. *An Agenda for Peace: Preventive Diplomacy, Peacemaking and Peacekeeping*. New York: United Nations, 1992.

Boyne, Shawn Marie. "Crisis in the Classroom: Using Simulations to Enhance Decision-Making Skills." *Journal of Legal Education* 62, no. 2 (2012): 311–22.

Brandt, Patrick T., T. David Mason, Mehmet Gurses, Nicolai Petrovsky, and Dagmar Radin. "When and How the Fighting Stops: Explaining the Duration and Outcome of Civil Wars." *Defense and Peace Economics* 19, no. 6 (2008): 415–34.

Broecker, Wallace S. "Climatic Change: Are We on the Brink of a Pronounced Global Warming?" *Science* 189, no. 4201 (August 1975): 460–63.

C40 Cities. *About C40.* http://www.c40.org/about (accessed May 8, 2017).

Caprioli, Mary. "Gendered Conflict." *Journal of Peace Research* 37, no. 1 (2000): 53–68.

Caprioli, Mary. "Primed for Violence: The Role of Gender Inequality in Predicting Internal Conflict." *International Studies Quarterly* 49 (2005): 161–78.

Caprioli, Mary, and Mark Boyer. "Gender, Violence, and International Crisis." *Journal of Conflict Resolution* 45, no. 4 (2001): 503–18.

Caprioli, Mary, Rebecca Nielsen, and Valerie M. Hudson. "Women and Post Conflict Settings." In *Peace and Conflict 2010*, by J. Joseph Hewitt, Jonathan Wilkenfeld and Ted Robert Gurr, 91–102. Boulder, CO: Paradigm, 2010.

Carpenter, R. Charli. "Governing the Global Agenda: Gate-keeping and Issue Adoption in Transnational Advocacy Networks." In *Who Governs the Globe?*, by Deborah Avant, Martha Finnemore and Susan Sell. Cambridge University Press, 2010.

Carpenter, R. Charli. "Setting the Advocacy Agenda: Theorizing Issue Emergence and Nonemergence in Transnational Advocacy Networks." *International Studies Quarterly* 51, no. 1 (2007): 99–120.

Carpenter, R. Charli. "Vetting the Advocacy Agenda: Networks, Centrality and the Paradox of Weapons Norms." *International Organization* 65, no. 1 (2011): 69–102.

Carpenter, Charli. "'Women and Children First': Gender, Norms, and Humanitarian Evacuation in the Balkans 1991–1995." *International Organization* 57, no. 4 (2003): 661–94.

Cederman, Lars-Erik, Nils B. Weidmann, and Kristian Skrede Gleditsch. "Horizontal Inequalities and Ethnonationalist Civil War: A Global Comparison." *American Political Science Review* 105, no. 3 (2011): 478–95.

Centers for Disease Control and Prevention. *A History of Anthrax.* 2016. http://www.cdc.gov/anthrax/resources/history/ (accessed September 23, 2016).

Centers for Disease Control and Prevention. *Bioterrorism Overview.* https://emergency.cdc.gov/bioterrorism/overview.asp (accessed September 22, 2016).

Centers for Disease Control and Prevention. "Underlying Cause of Death, 1999–2014." *CDC WONDER Online Database.* 2015. https://wonder.cdc.gov/ucd-icd10.html (accessed December 18, 2017).

Cho, Renee. *Cities: the Vanguard against Climate Change.* Earth Institute, Columbia University. November 10, 2016. http://blogs.ei.columbia.edu/2016/11/10/cities-the-vanguard-against-climate-change/ (accessed May 8, 2017).

Christie, Ryerson. "Critical Voices and Human Security: To Endure, to Engage or to Critique?" *Security Dialogue* 41, no. 2 (2010): 169–90.

Christie, Ryerson. "The Human Security Dilemma." In *Environmental Change and Human Security: Recognizing and Acting on Hazard Impacts*, by P. H. Liotta, David A. Mouat, William G. Kepner, and Judith M. Lancaster, 253–69. Dordrecht: Springer, 2008.

Clapp, Jennifer. "World Hunger and the Global Economy: Strong Linkages, Weak Action." *Journal of International Affairs* 67, no. 2 (January 2014): 1–17.

Clapp, Jennifer, and Marc J. Cohen. *The Global Food Crisis: Governance Challenges and Opportunities.* Waterloo, Ontario: Wilfrid Laurier University Press, 2009.

Cohen, Roberta. "From Sovereignty to R2P." In *The Routledge Handbook of the Responsibility to Protect*, by W. Andy Knight and Frazer Egerton, 7–21. New York: Routledge, 2012.

Coleman-Jensen, Alisha, Matthew Rabbitt, Christian Gregory, and Anita Singh. *Household Food Security in the United States in 2015*. United States Department of Agriculture, 2016.

Coleman, Isobel. "The Payoff from Women's Rights." *Foreign Affairs* 83, no. 3 (2004): 80–95.

Commission on Human Security. *Human Security Now*. New York: United Nations, 2003.

Compact of Mayors. *About*. https://www.compactofmayors.org/history/ (accessed May 8, 2017).

Cranston, Maurice. "Are There Any Human Rights?" *Daedalus* 112, no. 4 (1983): 1–17.

Cranston, Maurice. "Human Rights: Real and Supposed." In *Political Theory and the Rights of Man*, by D. D. Raphael, 43–51. Bloomington: Indiana University Press, 1967.

Cranston, Maurice. *What Are Human Rights?* New York: Basic Books, 1962.

Crawford, Kerry F. *Wartime Sexual Violence: From Silence to Condemnation of a Weapon of War*. Washington, DC: Georgetown University Press, 2017.

Cunningham, David E. "Blocking Resolution: How External States Can Prolong Civil Wars." *Journal of Peace Research* 47, no. 2 (2010): 115–27.

Davenport, Coral, and Campbell Robertson. "Resettling the First American 'Climate Refugees.'" *New York Times*, May 2, 2016.

Davidson, Joe. "Uncle Sam Didn't Welcome Gay Employees." *The Washington Post*, March 2, 2012.

"Declaration of Independence." *United States National Archives*. 1776. http://www.archives.gov/exhibits/charters/declaration_transcript.html (accessed July 3, 2017).

Doyle, Michael W. "The Politics of Global Humanitarianism: The Responsibility to Protect before and after Libya." *International Politics* 53, no. 1 (2016): 14–31.

Draper, Lucy. *The Wedding That Became a Funeral: U.S. Still Silent One Year on from Deadly Yemen Drone Strike*. December 12, 2014. http://www.newsweek.com/wedding-became-funeral-us-still-silent-one-year-deadly-yemen-drone-strike-291403 (accessed July 14, 2017).

Edwards, Adrian. *Global Forced Displacement Hits Record High*. June 20, 2016. http://www.unhcr.org/en-us/news/latest/2016/6/5763b65a4/global-forced-displacement-hits-record-high.html (accessed June 23, 2017).

Eriksen, Thomas Hylland. "Ethnic Identity, National Identity, and Intergroup Conflict: The Significance of Personal Experiences." In *Social Identity, Intergroup Conflict, and Conflict Resolution*, by Richard D. Ashmore, Lee Jussim and David Wilder, 42–68. Oxford: Oxford University Press, 2001.

European Council. "International Agreements on Climate Action." *European Council*. June 14, 2016. http://www.consilium.europa.eu/en/policies/climate-change/international-agreements-climate-action/ (accessed April 27, 2017).

Evans, Alex. "Resource Scarcity, Climate Change, and the Risk of Violent Conflict." *World Development Report 2011* (Word Bank), 2010.

Evans, Gareth. "The Evolution of the Responsibility to Protect: From Concept and Principle to Actionable Norm." In *Theorising the Responsibility to Protect*, by Ramesh Thakur and William Maley, 16–37. Cambridge: Cambridge University Press, 2015.

Famine Early Warning Systems Network. *Conflict Displaces Well over 100,000 in April as Extreme Levels of Food Insecurity Persist*. April 2017. http://www.fews. net/east-africa/south-sudan (accessed May 25, 2017).

Fan, Shenggen. *Ending World Hunger and Undernutrition by 2025*. June 2, 2014. http://www.ifpri.org/blog/ending-world-hunger-and-undernutrition-2025 (accessed June 2, 2017).

Femmes Africa Solidarté. "Engendering the Peace Processes in West Africa: The Mano River Women's Peace Network." In *People Building Peace II: Successful Stories of Civil Society*, by Paul van Tongeren, Malin Brenk, Marte Hellema, and Juliette Verhoeven, 588–93. Boulder, CO: Lynne Rienner, 2005.

Fidler, David P. "Germs, Norms and Power: Global Health's Political Revolution." *Law, Social Justice & Global Development* 1 (2004). https://warwick.ac.uk/fac/ soc/law/elj/lgd/2004_1/fidler/

Finnemore, Martha. *The Purpose of Intervention: Changing Beliefs about the Use of Force*. Ithaca, NY: Cornell University Press, 2004.

Finnemore, Martha, and Kathryn Sikkink. "International Norm Dynamics and Political Change." *International Organization* 52, no. 4 (1998): 887–917.

Flores, Thomas Edward, and Irfan Nooruddin. "Democracy under the Gun: Understanding Postconflict Economic Recovery." *Journal of Conflict Resolution* 53, no. 1 (2009): 3–29.

Food and Agriculture Organization. "Policy Brief: Food Security." June 2006. http:// www.fao.org/forestry/13128-0e6f36f27e0091055bec28ebe830f46b3.pdf (accessed May 26, 2017).

Food and Agriculture Organization. *The State of Food and Agriculture: Climate Change, Agriculture and Food Security*. Rome, 2016.

Food and Agriculture Organization. "The State of Food Insecurity in the World." Rome, 2015.

Food and Agriculture Organization. "The Impact of Disasters on Agriculture and Food Security." November 2015. http://www.fao.org/3/a-i5128e.pdf (accessed April 14, 2017).

Fortna, Virginia Page. *Does Peacekeeping Work? Shaping Belligerents' Choices after Civil War*. Princeton, NJ: Princeton University Press, 2008.

France-Presse, Agence. "Oslo Moves to Ban Cars from City Centre within Four Years." *The Guardian*, October 19, 2015.

Gaglias, Alexis. "The Hidden Heroes of Greece's Refugee Crisis." *The Huffington Post*, June 2, 2016.

Galtung, Johan. *Peace by Peaceful Means: Peace and Conflict, Development and Civilization*. Oslo: PRIO, 1996.

Gbowee, Leymah. *Mighty Be Our Powers*. New York: Beast Books, 2011.

Ghobarah, Hazem Adam, Paul Huth, and Bruce Russett. "Civil Wars Kill and Maim People—Long after the Shooting Stops." *American Political Science Review* 97, no. 2 (2003): 189–202.

Gifkins, Jess. "R2P in the UN Security Council: Darfur, Libya and Beyond." *Cooperation and Conflict* 51, no. 2 (2016): 148–65.

Gladstone, Rick. "Cholera Deaths in Haiti Could Far Exceed Official Count." *New York Times*, March 18, 2016a.

Gladstone, Rick. "Lawmakers Urge John Kerry to Press U.N. for Haiti Cholera Response." *New York Times*, June 29, 2016b.

Global Centre for the Responsibility to Protect. "R2P References in United Nations Human Rights Council Resolutions." October 3, 2016. http://www.globalr2p.org/resources/977 (accessed February 24, 2017).

Goldstein, Joshua. *War and Gender: How Gender Shapes the War System and Vice Versa*. New York: Cambridge University Press, 2001.

Grayson, Kyle. "Securitization and the Boomerang Debate: A Rejoinder to Liotta and Smith-Windsor." *Security Dialogue* 34, no. 3 (2003): 337–43.

Hanlon, Robert J., and Kenneth Christie. *Freedom from Fear, Freedom from Want: An Introduction to Human Security*. North York, Ontario: University of Toronto Press, 2016.

Hansen, J., et al. "Climate Impact of Increasing Atmospheric Carbon Dioxide." *Science* 213 (1981): 957–66.

Harvey, Fiona. "Arctic Ice Melt Could Trigger Uncontrollable Climate Change at Global Level." *The Guardian*. November 25, 2016. https://www.theguardian.com/environment/2016/nov/25/arctic-ice-melt-trigger-uncontrollable-climate-change-global-level (accessed May 5, 2017).

Hehir, Aidan. "Assessing the Influence of the Responsibility to Protect on the UN Security Council during Arab Spring." *Cooperation and Conflict* 51, no. 2 (2016): 166–83.

Hehir, Aidan. *The Responsibility to Protect: Rhetoric, Reality and the Future of Humanitarian Intervention*. New York: Palgrave Macmillan, 2012.

Henderson, Stacey. "The Arms Trade Treaty: Responsibility to Protect in Action?" *Global Responsibility to Protect* 9, no. 2 (2017): 147–72.

Hendrix, Cullen S., and Henk-Jan Brinkman. "Food Insecurity and Conflict Dynamics: Causal Linkages and Complex Feedbacks." *Stability: International Journal of Security & Development* 2, no. 2 (2013): 1–18.

Hendrix, Cullen S., and Sarah M. Glaser. "Trends and Triggers: Climate, Climate Change and Civil Conflict in Sub-Saharan Africa." *Political Geography* 26, no. 6 (2007): 695–715.

Herz, Barbara, and Gene B. Sperling. *What Works in Girls' Education: Evidence and Policies from the Developing World*. New York: Council on Foreign Relations, 2004.

High-Level Panel of Eminent Persons on the Post-2015 Development Agenda. *A New Global Partnership: Eradicate Poverty and Transform Economies through Sustainable Development*. United Nations, 2013.

High-Level Panel on the Post-2015 Development Agenda. *About*. http://www.post2015hlp.org/about/ (accessed June 21, 2017).

Hirschkind, Charles, and Saba Mahmood. "Feminism, the Taliban, and Politics of Counter-Insurgency." *Anthropological Quarterly* 75, no. 2 (2002): 339–54.

Hoffmann, Stanley. *Duties beyond Borders: On the Limits and Possibilities of Ethical International Politics*. Syracuse, NY: Syracuse University Press, 1981.

Houten, Carolyn Van. "The First Official Climate Refugees in the U.S. Race against Time." *National Geographic*, May 25, 2016.

Howard, Lisa Morjé. *UN Peacekeeping in Civil Wars*. Cambridge: Cambridge University Press, 2008.

Hudson, Natalie Florea. *Gender, Human Security and the United Nations: Security Language as a Political Framework for Women*. New York: Routledge, 2010.

Hudson, Valerie M., and Andrea den Boer. "A Surplus of Men, a Deficit of Peace." *International Security* 26, no. 4 (2002): 5–38.

Hudson, Valerie M., Bonnie Ballif-Spanvill, Mary Caprioli, and Chad F. Emmett. *Sex & World Peace*. New York: Columbia University Press, 2012.

Huish, Robert, and Jerry Spiegel. "Integrating Health and Human Security into Foreign Policy: Cuba's Surprising Success." *International Journal of Cuban Studies* 1, no. 1 (2008): 42–53.

Huish, Robert, and John M. Kirk. "Cuban Medical Internationalism and the Development of the Latin American School of Medicine." *Latin American Perspectives* 34, no. 6 (2007): 77–92.

Hultman, Lisa, Jacob Kathman, and Megan Shannon. "United Nations Peacekeeping and Civilian Protection in Civil War." *American Journal of Political Science* 57, no. 4 (2013): 875–91.

Human Security Report Project. *Human Security Report 2009/2010: The Causes of Peace and the Shrinking Costs of War*. Simon Fraser University, Oxford: Oxford University Press, 2011.

IPCC. "Summary for Policymakers." In *Climate Change 2007: The Physical Science Basis. Contribution of Working Group I to the Fourth Assessment Report of the Intergovernmental Panel on Climate Change*, by S. Solomon et al. Cambridge: Cambridge University Press, 2007.

Jones, Benjamin T., Eleonora Mattiacci, and Bear F. Braumoeller. "Food Scarcity and State Vulnerability: Unpacking the Link between Climate Variability and Violent Unrest." *Journal of Peace Research* (2017): 335–50.

Joshi, Madhav, and John Darby. "Introducing the Peace Accords Matrix (PAM): A Database of Comprehensive Peace Agreements and Their Implementation, 1989–2007." *Peacebuilding* 1, no. 2 (2013): 256–74.

Joshi, Madhav, Jason Michael Quinn, and Patrick M. Regan. "Annualized Implementation Data on Intrastate Comprehensive Peace Accords, 1989–2012." *Journal of Peace Research* 52, no. 4 (2015): 551–62.

Jurkovich, Michelle. "Venezuela Has Solved Its Hunger Problem? Don't Believe the U.N.'s Numbers." *The Monkey Cage–The Washington Post*, September 21, 2016.

Kaldor, Mary. *Human Security: Reflections on Globalization and Intervention*. Cambridge: Polity, 2007.

Kandiyoti, Deniz. "The Politics of Gender and Reconstruction in Afghanistan: Old Dilemmas or New Challenges?" In *Gendered Peace: Women's Struggles for Post-War Justice and Reconciliation*, by Donna Pankhurst, 155–85. New York: Routledge, 2008.

Kang, Seonjou, and James Meernik. "Civil War Destruction and the Prospects for Economic Growth." *Journal of Politics* 67, no. 1 (2005): 88–109.

Katz, Jonathan M. "The Killer Hiding in the CDC Map." *Slate*, April 24, 2016a.

Katz, Jonathan M. "U.N. Admits Role in Cholera Epidemic in Haiti." *New York Times*, August 17, 2016b.

Katz, Rebecca, and Daniel A. Singer. "Health and Security in Foreign Policy." *Bulletin of the World Health Organization* 85, no. 3 (March 2007).

Keck, Margaret E., and Kathryn Sikkink. *Activists beyond Borders*. Ithaca, NY: Cornell University Press, 1998.

Kilcullen, David. *The Accidental Guerrilla: Fighting Small Wars in the midst of a Big One*. Oxford: Oxford University Press, 2009.

Kochhar, Rakesh. *Wealth Inequality Has Widened along Racial, Ethnic Lines since End of Great Recession*. September 12, 2014. http://www.pewresearch.org/fact-tank/2014/12/12/racial-wealth-gaps-great-recession/ (accessed June 2, 2017).

Komai, Makereta. *Marshall Islands & St. Lucia Spearhead Work of Coalition of High Ambition Nations*. December 5, 2015. http://www.sprep.org/climate-change/marshall-islands-a-st-lucia-spearhead-work-of-coalition-of-high-ambition-nations (accessed April 28, 2017).

Kreutz, Joakim. "How and When Armed Conflicts End: Introducing the UCDP Conflict Termination Dataset." *Journal of Peace Research* 47, no. 2 (2010): 243–50.

Kydd, Andrew H., and Barbara F. Walter. "The Strategies of Terrorism." *International Security* 31, no. 1 (2006): 49–80.

Lacina, Bethany, and Nils Petter Gleditsch. "Monitoring Trends in Global Combat: A New Dataset of Battle Deaths." *European Journal of Population* 21 (2005): 145–66.

Lai, Brian, and Clayton Thyne. "The Effect of Civil War on education, 1980–97." *Journal of Peace Research* 44, no. 3 (2007): 277–92.

Lappé, Francis Moore. *World Hunger: Twelve Myths*. New York: Grove Press, 1998.

Lederach, John Paul. *Building Peace: Sustainable Reconciliation in Divided Societies*. Washington, DC: United States Institute of Peace, 1997.

Liotta, P. H. "Boomerang Effect: The Convergence of National and Human Security." *Security Dialogue* 33, no. 4 (2002): 473–88.

Llano, Rayden, and Kenji Shibuya. *Japan's Evolving Role in Global Health*. Seattle, WA: National Bureau of Asian Research, 2011.

LeVaux, Ari. "It's OK to Eat Quinoa." *Slate*, January 25, 2013.

Lund, Michael. *Preventing Violent Conflicts*. Washington, DC: United States Institute of Peace, 1996.

Mac Ginty, Roger. "Everyday Peace: Bottom-Up and Local Agency in Conflict-Affected Societies." *Security Dialogues* 45, no. 6 (2014): 548–64.

Mac Ginty, Roger, and Oliver P. Richmond. "The Local Turn in Peace Building: A Critical Agenda for Peace." *Third World Quarterly* 34, no. 5 (2013): 763–83.

MacFarlane, S. Neil, and Yuen Foong Khong. *Human Security and the UN: A Critical History*. Bloomington: Indiana University Press, 2006.

Mallavarapu, Siddharth. "Colonialism and the Responsibility to Protect." In *Theorising the Responsibility to Protect*, by Ramesh Thakur and William Maley, 305–22. Cambridge: Cambridge University Press, 2015.

MDG Gap Task Force. *Millennium Development Goal 8: Taking Stock of the Global Partnership for Development*. New York: United Nations, 2015.

Médecins Sans Frontières. *Ebola: International Response Slow and Uneven*. December 2, 2014. http://www.doctorswithoutborders.org/article/ebola-international-response-slow-and-uneven (accessed September 2, 2016).

Médecins Sans Frontiéres. *G7 Fails to Provide Humane Response to Global Displacement Crisis*. May 27, 2017. http://www.doctorswithoutborders.org/article/g7-fails-provide-humane-response-global-displacement-crisis (accessed July 14, 2017).

Meier, Patrick, Doug Bond, and Joe Bond. "Environmental Influences on Pastoral Conflict in the Horn of Africa." *Political Geography* 26, no. 6 (2007): 716–35.

Meslin, Eric M., and Ibrahim Garba. "International Collaboration for Global Public Health." In *Public Health Ethics: Cases Spanning the Globe*, by Drue H. Barrett, Leonard H. Ortmann, Angus Dawson, Carla Saenz, Andreas Reis, and Gail Bolan, 241–84. Springer International Publishing, 2016. https://link.springer.com/content/pdf/10.1007%2F978-3-319-23847-0.pdf

Milman, Oliver. "Obama Declares Disaster as Marshall Islands Suffers Worst-Ever Drought." April 28, 2016. https://www.theguardian.com/world/2016/apr/28/obama-marshall-islands-drought (accessed April 28, 2017).

Milman, Oliver, and Mae Ryan. "Lives in the Balance: Climate Change and the Marshall Islands." September 15, 2016. https://www.theguardian.com/environment/2016/sep/15/marshall-islands-climate-change-springdale-arkansas (accessed April 28, 2017).

Mould, Verity. "State Failure and Civil Society Potential: Reconciliation in the Democratic Republic of Congo." *Journal of Conflict Transformation & Security* 1, no. 2 (2011): 73–82.

Murithi, Timothy. *The Ethics of Peacebuilding*. Edinburgh: Edinburgh University Press, 2009.

Nakaya, Sumie. "Women and Gender Equality in Peace Processes: From Women at the Negotiating Table to Postwar Structural Reforms in Guatemala and Somalia." *Global Governance* 9, no. 4 (2003): 459–76.

NASA. *2016 Climate Trends Continue to Break Records*. July 19, 2016. https://www.nasa.gov/feature/goddard/2016/climate-trends-continue-to-break-records (accessed May 10, 2017).

NASA. "Scientific consensus: Earth's Climate Is Warming." *Global Climate Change: Vital Signs of the Planet*. May 5, 2017. https://climate.nasa.gov/scientific-consensus/ (accessed May 7, 2017).

Newmann, William W., and Judyth L. Twigg. "Active Engagement of the Intro IR Student: A Simulation Approach." *PS: Political Science and Politics* 33, no. 4 (2000): 835–42.

Nianias, Helen. "Refugees in Lesbos: Are There Too Many NGOs on the Island?" *The Guardian*, January 5, 2016.

Nordberg, Jenny. "Who's Afraid of a Feminist Foreign Policy?" *The New Yorker*, April 15, 2015.

Notaras, Mark. *Food Insecurity and the Conflict Trap*. United Nations University. August 31, 2011. https://ourworld.unu.edu/en/food-insecurity-and-the-conflict-trap (accessed March 30, 2017).

Office of the United Nations High Commissioner for Human Rights. *Human Rights, Terrorism, and Counter-terrorism*. Geneva: United Nations, 2008.

Oxfam International. *Famine in South Sudan.* May 4, 2017. https://www.oxfam.org/en/emergencies/famine-south-sudan (accessed May 25, 2017).

Paarlberg, Robert. *Food Politics: What Everyone Needs to Know.* Oxford: Oxford University Press, 2010.

Paffenholz, Thania. "Civil Society and Peace Negotiations: Beyond the Inclusion-Exclusion Dichotomy." *Negotiation Journal* 30, no. 1 (2014): 69–91.

Paris, Roland. *At War's End: Building Peace after Civil Conflict.* Cambridge: Cambridge University Press, 2004.

Paris, Roland. "Human Security: Paradigm Shift or Hot Air?" *International Security* 26, no. 2 (2001): 87–102.

Parry, M. L., O. F. Canziani, J. P. Palutikof, P. J. van der Linden, and C. E. Hanson. *Climate Change 2007: Working Group II: Impacts, Adaptation and Vulnerability.* Intergovernmental Panel on Climate Change, Cambridge: Cambridge University Press, 2007.

Patten, Eileen. *Racial, Gender Wage Gaps Persist in U.S. despite Some Progress.* July 1, 2016. http://www.pewresearch.org/fact-tank/2016/07/01/racial-gender-wage-gaps-persist-in-u-s-despite-some-progress/ (accessed June 2, 2017).

Peterman, Amber, Tia Palermo, and Caryn Bredenkamp. "Estimates and Determinants of Sexual Violence against Women in the Democratic Republic of Congo." *American Journal of Public Health* 101, no. 6 (2011): 1060–67.

Pettersson, Thérése, and Peter Wallensteen. "Armed Conflicts, 1946–2014." *Journal of Peace Research* 52, no. 4 (2015): 536–50.

Philpott, Daniel. *Just and Unjust Peace: An Ethic of Political Reconciliation.* New York: Oxford University Press, 2012.

Pinker, Steven. *The Better Angels of Our Nature: Why Violence Has Declined.* New York: Penguin Books, 2011.

Posey, Kirby G. *Household Income: 2015.* United States Census Bureau, U.S. Department of Commerce, 2016.

Powers, Jon. *Climate Change Is the "Mother of All Risks" to National Security.* November 6, 2015. http://time.com/4101903/climate-change-national-security/ (accessed April 28, 2017).

Prins, Gwyn, and Steve Rayner. "Time to Ditch Kyoto." *Nature* 449 (October 2007): 973–75.

Prorok, Alyssa K. "The (In)compatibility of Peace and Justice? The International Criminal Court and Civil Conflict Termination." *International Organization* 71, no. 2 (2017): 212–43.

Quinn, Michael T., T. David Mason, and Mehmet Gurses. "Sustaining Peace: Determinants of Civil War Recurrence." *International Interactions* 33, no. 2 (2007): 167–93.

Ramsbotham, Oliver, Tom Woodhouse, and Hugh Miall. *Contemporary Conflict Resolution.* 4th edition. London: Polity, 2016.

Reveron, Derek S., and Kathleen A. Mahoney-Norris. *Human Security in a Borderless World.* Boulder, CO: Westview Press, 2011.

Revkin, Andrew. *Trump's Defense Secretary Cites Climate Change as National Security Challenge.* March 14, 2017. https://www.propublica.org/article/trumps-defense-secretary-cites-climate-change-national-security-challenge (accessed April 28, 2017).

Richmond, Oliver P., and Jason Franks. *Liberal Peace Transitions: Between State-building and Peacebuilding*. Edinburgh: Edinburgh University Press, 2009.

Rome Statute of the International Criminal Court. *A/CONF.183/9*. Rome, July 17, 1998.

Royal Embassy of Saudi Arabia Information Office. "Statement by Saudi Ambassador Al-Jubeir on Military Operations in Yemen." *PR Newswire*. March 25, 2015. http://www.prnewswire.com/news-releases/statement-by-saudi-ambassador-al-jubeir-on-military-operations-in-yemen-300056316.html (accessed July 1, 2017).

Rugemalila, Joas B., Olumide A. T. Ogundahunsi, Timothy T. Stedman, and Wen L. Kilama. "Multilateral Initiative on Malaria: Justification, Evolution, Achievements, Challenges, Opportunities, and Future Plans." *American Journal of Tropical Medicine and Hygiene* 77, no. 6, Supplement (2007): 296–302.

Sagan, Scott D., and Kenneth N. Waltz. *The Spread of Nuclear Weapons: A Debate Renewed*. 2nd. New York: W. W. Norton, 2002.

Sandbu, Martin. "Critics Question Success of UN's Millennium Development Goals." *Financial Times*, September 15, 2015.

Salehyan, Idean. "From Climate Change to Conflict? No Consensus Yet." *Journal of Peace Research* 45, no. 3 (2008): 315–26.

Save the Children. *Too Young to Wed: The Growing Problem of Child Marriage among Syrian Girls in Jordan*. London: Save the Children, 2014.

Schwartzstein, Peter. "Inside the Syrian Dust Bowl." *Foreign Policy*, September 5, 2016.

Secretary-General, United Nations. *An Agenda for Peace: Preventive Diplomacy, Peacemaking and Peace-Keeping*. A/47/277-S/24111, 1992.

Semelin, Jacques. "Introduction: From Help to Rescue." In *Resisting Genocide: The Multiple Forms of Rescue*, by Jacques Semelin, Claire Andrieu and Sarah Gensburger, 1–14. New York: Columbia University Press, 2011.

Sen, Amartya. *Development as Freedom*. New York: Anchor Books, 1999.

Sen, Amartya. *Poverty and Famines: An Essay on Entitlement and Deprivation*. Oxford: Oxford University Press, 1981.

Sharp, Gene. "Nonviolent Action in Acute Interethnic Conflicts." In *The Handbook of Interethnic Coexistence*, by Eugene Weiner, 371–81. New York: Continuum Publishing, 1998.

Shellman, Stephen M., and Kürsan Turan. "Do Simulations Enhance Student Learning? An Empirical Evaluation of an IR Simulation." *Journal of Political Science Education* 2 (2006): 19–32.

Shemyakina, Olga. "The Effect of Armed Conflict on Accumulation of Schooling: Results from Tajikistan." *Journal of Development Economics* 95, no. 2 (2011): 186–200.

Silberg, Bob. "Why a Half-Degree Temperature Rise Is a Big Deal." *NASA*. June 29, 2016. https://climate.nasa.gov/news/2458/why-a-half-degree-temperature-rise-is-a-big-deal/ (accessed April 29, 2017).

Simmons, Beth A., and Allison Danner. "Credible Commitments and the International Criminal Court." *International Organization* 64, no. 2 (2010): 225–56.

Smit, Anneke. *The Property Rights of Refugees and Internally Displaced Person: Beyond Restitution*. London: Routledge, 2012.

Smith, Pete. "Malthus Is Still Wrong: We Can Feed a World of 9–10 Billion, But Only by Reducing Food Demand." *Proceedings of the Nutrition Society* 74 (2014): 187–90.

Sperling, Gene B., Rebecca Winthrop, and Christina Kwauk. *What Works in Girls' Education: Evidence for the World's Best Investment*. Washington, DC: The Brookings Institution, 2016.

Starks, Tim. "Katrina's Lessons Seen in Response to Sandy." *Congressional Quarterly*. December 9, 2012. http://public.cq.com/docs/weeklyreport/weeklyre-port-000004197197.html (accessed May 7, 2017).

Stephan, Maria J., and Erica Chenoweth. *Why Civil Resistance Works: The Strategic Logic of Nonviolent Conflict*. Vol. 33. 1 vol. International Security, 2008.

Swedish Institute. *Gender Equality in Sweden*. June 21, 2016. https://sweden.se/society/gender-equality-in-sweden/ (accessed August 4, 2016).

Takemi, Keizo. "Japan's Global Health Strategy: Connecting Development and Security." *Asia-Pacific Review* 23, no. 1 (2016): 21–31.

Taylor, Adam. "How Saudi Arabia Turned Sweden's Human Rights Criticisms into an Attack on Islam." *The Washington Post*, March 24, 2015.

The Economist. "Against the Grain." May 21, 2016.

The World Bank. *World Bank, IMF Leaders Make Economic Case for Climate Action*. October 9, 2013. http://www.worldbank.org/en/news/feature/2013/10/08/world-bank-imf-leaders-make-economic-case-for-climate-action (accessed May 5, 2017).

Thomson, Aileen, and Kasandre Sarah Kihika. *Victims Fighting Impunity: Transitional Justice in the African Great Lakes Region*. New York: International Center for Transitional Justice, 2017.

Tran, Mark. "Mark Malloch-Brown: Developing the MDGs Was a Bit like Nuclear Fusion." *The Guardian*, November 16, 2012.

Trefon, Theodore. *Congo Masquerade: The Political Culture of Aid Inefficiency and Reform Failure*. London: Zed Books, 2011.

Turner, Jenia Iontcheva. "Defense Perspectives on Fairness and Efficiency at the International Criminal Court." In *Oxford Handbook on International Criminal Law*, by Kevin Jon Heller. Oxford: Oxford University Press, 2017.

UNICEF. *Female Genital Mutilation/Cutting: A Global Concern*. New York: UNICEF, 2016.

UN News Centre. "'Human Security Depends on Health Security,' Ban Says, Calling on Nations to Be Proactive." September 26, 2015.

UN News Centre. *Urgent Scale-Up in Funding Needed to Stave Off Famine in Somalia, UN Warns*. February 2, 2017. http://www.un.org/apps/news/story.asp?NewsID=56094#.WPEChFLMyi4 (accessed April 14, 2017).

United Nations. "Beijing Declaration and Platform for Action." *Fourth World Conference on Women*. September 15, 1995. http://www.un.org/womenwatch/daw/beijing/platform/ (accessed December 3, 2015).

United Nations. *Charter of the United Nations*. New York, June 26, 1945.

United Nations. *Sustainable Development Goals*. https://sustainabledevelopment.un.org/sdgs (accessed July 5, 2017).

United Nations. *Sustainable Development Goal 2*. https://sustainabledevelopment.un.org/sdg2 (accessed June 2, 2017).

United Nations. *The Millennium Development Goals Report*. New York: United Nations, 2015.

United Nations. "United Nations Framework Convention on Climate Change." 1992. http://unfccc.int/files/essential_background/convention/background/application/pdf/convention_text_with_annexes_english_for_posting.pdf (accessed May 10, 2017).

United Nations. *We Can End Poverty: Millennium Development Goals and beyond 2015*. http://www.un.org/millenniumgoals/ (accessed June 21, 2017).

United Nations Counter-Terrorism Implementation Task Force. *UN Global Counter-Terrorism Strategy*. https://www.un.org/counterterrorism/ctitf/en/un-global-counter-terrorism-strategy#poa3 (accessed July 14, 2017).

United Nations Development Programme. *Background on the Goals*. http://www.undp.org/content/undp/en/home/sustainable-development-goals/background.html (accessed June 21, 2017).

United Nations Development Programme. *Gender and Disasters*. New York: United Nations Development Programme, 2010.

United Nations Development Programme. *Gender Inequality Index (GII)*. 2015.

United Nations Development Programme. "Human Development Report—The Real Wealth of Nations: Pathways to Human Development." 2010.

United Nations Development Programme. *Human Development Report 1994: New Dimensions of Human Security*. New York: Oxford University Press, 1994.

United Nations General Assembly. "2005 World Summit Outcome." *A/Res/60/1*. New York, October 24, 2005.

United Nations General Assembly. "Follow-Up to Paragraph 143 on Human Security of the 2005 World Summit Outcome." *A/Res/66/290*. New York, October 25, 2012.

United Nations General Assembly. "Follow-Up to the Outcome of the Millennium Summit." *A/69/968-S/2015/490*. New York, June 30, 2015.

United Nations General Assembly. "Implementing the Responsibility to Protect: Report of the Secretary General." *A/63/677*. New York, January 12, 2009.

United Nations General Assembly. "Open Working Group of the General Assembly on Sustainable Development Goals." *A/67/L.48/Rev.1*. New York, January 15, 2013.

United Nations General Assembly. "Report of the Panel on United Nations Peace Operations." *A/55/305-S/2000/809*. New York, August 21, 2000a.

United Nations General Assembly. "Report of the Peacebuilding Commission." *A/17/768-S/2017/76*. New York, January 27, 2017.

United Nations General Assembly. "The Future We Want." *A/Res/66/288*. New York, September 11, 2012.

United Nations General Assembly. "Transforming Our World: the 2030 Agenda for Sustainable Development." *A/Res/70/1*. New York, October 21, 2015.

United Nations General Assembly. "United Nations Millennium Declaration." *A/55/L.2*. New York, September 8, 2000b.

United Nations High Commissioner for Refugees. "Lesvos Island-Greece Fact-sheet." *UNHCR*. November 12, 2015. http://www.unhcr.org/en-us/protection/operations/5645ddbc6/greece-factsheet-lesvos-island.html (accessed June 23, 2017).

United Nations High Commissioner for Refugees. *With 1 Human in Every 113 Affected, Forced Displacement Hits Record High*. June 20, 2016. http://www. unhcr.org/afr/news/press/2016/6/5763ace54/1-human-113-affected-forced-displacement-hits-record-high.html (accessed July 4, 2017).

United Nations Human Security Unit. *Framework for Cooperation for the System-Wide Application of Human Security*. New York, September 2015.

United Nations Human Security Unit. *Strategic Plan 2014–2017*. New York: United Nations, 2014.

United Nations Office on Drugs and Crime. *United Nations Convention Against Transnational Organized Crime and the Protocols Thereto*. United Nations. Vienna, 2004.

United Nations Peacebuilding Support Office. *From Rhetoric to Practice: Operationalizing Ownership in Post-Conflict Peacebuilding*. Workshop Report, New York: United Nations, 2011.

United Nations Security Council. "Letter Dated 24 May 1994 from the Secretary-General to the President of the Security Council." *S/1994/674*. New York, May 27, 1994.

United Nations Security Council. "Report of the Secretary-General to the Security Council on the Protection of Civilians in Armed Conflict." *S/1999/957*. New York, September 8, 1999.

United Nations Security Council. "Report of the Secretary-General on the Protection of Civilians in Armed Conflict." *S/2007/643*. New York, October 28, 2007.

United Nations Security Council. "Resolution 1080 (1996)." *S/RES/1080*. New York, November 15, 1996.

United Nations Security Council. "Resolution 1270 (1999)." *S/RES/1270*. New York, October 22, 1999.

United Nations Security Council. "Resolution 1970 (2011)." *S/RES/1970*. New York, February 26, 2011.

United Nations Security Council. "Resolution 1973 (2011)." *S/RES/1973*. New York, March 17, 2011.

United Nations Security Council. "Resolution 2098 (2013)." *S/RES/2098 (2013)*. New York, March 28, 2013.

United Nations Security Council. *Starvation by Siege Now "Systematic" in Syria, Assistant Secretary-General Tells Security Council, amid Warnings That Tactic Could Be War Crime*. January 15, 2016. https://www.un.org/press/en/2016/sc12203.doc.htm (accessed May 26, 2017).

United Nations Security Council. *With Spread of Ebola Outpacing Response, Security Council Adopts Resolution 2177 (2014) Urging Immediate Action, End to Isolation of Affected States*. September 18, 2014. http://www.un.org/press/en/2014/sc11566.doc.htm (accessed September 2, 2016).

United States Census Bureau. "Real Household Income at Selected Percentiles: 1967–2014." *United States Census Bureau Library*. September 16, 2015. https://www.census.gov/library/visualizations/2015/demo/real-household-income-at-selected-percentiles—1967-to-2014.html (accessed June 2, 2017).

United States Government Accountability Office. "Actions Taken to Implement the Post-Katrina Emergency Management Reform Act of 2006." *U.S. Government Accountability Office*. November 21, 2008. http://www.gao.gov/products/GAO-09-59R (accessed May 7, 2017).

United States Senate. *Employment of Homosexuals and Other Sex Perverts in Government*. Interim Report, Washington, DC: United States Government Printing Office, 1950.

Wallström, Margot. "Statement of Government Policy in the Parliamentary Debate on Foreign Affairs 2016." *Government Offices of Sweden*. February 24, 2016. http://www.government.se/speeches/2016/02/statement-of-government-policy-in-the-parliamentary-debate-on-foreign-affairs-2016/ (accessed August 4, 2016).

Walter, Barbara F. *Committing to Peace: The Successful Settlement of Civil Wars*. Princeton, NJ: Princeton University Press, 2002.

Wanis-St. John, Anthony, and Darren Kew. "Civil Society and Peace Negotiations: Confronting Exclusion." *International Negotiations* 13 (2008): 11–36.

Weinstein, Jeremy M. *Inside Rebellion: The Politics of Insurgent Violence*. Cambridge: Cambridge University Press, 2007.

Weisman, Steven R. "Irate over 'Stingy' Remark, U.S. Adds $20 Million to Disaster Aid." *New York Times*, December 29, 2004.

Westmarland, Nicole, and Geetanjali Gangoli, eds. *International Approaches to Rape*. Portland, OR: The Policy Press, 2011.

Wike, Richard. "What the World Thinks about Climate Change in 7 Charts." *Pew Research Center Fact Tank*. April 18, 2016. http://www.pewresearch.org/fact-tank/2016/04/18/what-the-world-thinks-about-climate-change-in-7-charts/ (accessed May 7, 2017).

Wilkenfeld, Jonathan. *Myth and Reality in International Politics: Meeting Global Challenges through Collective Action*. New York: Routledge, 2015.

World Economic Forum. "The Global Gender Gap Index 2015." 2015. http://widgets.weforum.org/gender-gap-2015/

World Health Organization. *About WHO*. 2016. http://www.who.int/about/what-we-do/en/ (accessed October 11, 2016).

World Health Organization. "Media Centre." *Female Genital Mutilation*. February 2016. http://www.who.int/mediacentre/factsheets/fs241/en/ (accessed June 30, 2016).

World Health Organization Regional Office for Africa. *Special Ministerial Meeting on Ebola Virus Disease in West Africa Accra, Ghana, 2–3 July 2014*. July 2014. http://www.afro.who.int/en/clusters-a-programmes/dpc/epidemic-a-pandemic-alert-and-response/epr-highlights/4187-special-ministerial-meeting-ebola-accra-2-3-july-2014.html (accessed September 2, 2016).

Yuk-ping, Catherine Lo, and Nicholas Thomas. "How Is Health a Security Issue? Politics, Responses and Issues." *Health Policy and Planning* 25 (2010): 447–53.

Zambian Development Agency. *2017 Budget Aims to Restore Economic Growth*. 2017. http://www.zda.org.zm/?q=content/2017-budget-aims-restore-economic-growth (accessed May 5, 2017).

Zampano, Giada, Liam Moloney, and Jovi Juan. "Migrant Crisis: A History of Displacement." *The Wall Street Journal*, September 22, 2015.

Zelizer, Craig, and Valerie Oliphant. "Introduction to Integrated Peacebuilding." In *Integrative Peacebuilding: Innovative Approaches to Transforming Conflict*, by Craig Zelizer, 3–30. Boulder, CO: Westview Press, 2013.

Index

Note: Page references for figures are italicized.

About the Authors

David Andersen-Rodgers is associate professor of political science and coordinator of the peace and conflict resolution minor at California State University, Sacramento. He has worked in Washington, D.C., as a researcher and Scoville fellow at the Federation of American Scientists. He received his PhD in government and politics from the University of Maryland (2004). He holds a BA in peace and world security studies from Hampshire College (1995). His teaching and research has focused on a wide range of issues pertaining to peace and conflict, including small arms and light weapons proliferation, foreign policy decision-making and non-state-actor-triggered crises, and internally displaced persons during peace processes. His most recent scholarship has been published in *Conflict Management and Peace Science*, *Refugee Survey Quarterly*, and the *Journal of Global Initiatives*.

Kerry F. Crawford is assistant professor of political science at James Madison University. She received a PhD in political science from George Washington University (2014) and a BA in political science from St. Mary's College of Maryland (2007). She was the International Studies Association's 2015–2016 James N. Rosenau Postdoctoral Fellow. Her teaching and research interests include international affairs; conflict-related sexual violence; human security; international ethics and norms; United Nations peacekeeping operations; and women, peace, and security. Dr. Crawford's first book, *Wartime Sexual Violence: From Silence to Condemnation of a Weapon of War* (2017), examines the impact of advocates' framing of sexual violence as a weapon of war on international efforts to mitigate conflict-related sexual violence. Her previous research has been published in print in *Journal of Global Security Studies, Gender and Development, Armed Forces & Society,* and *Air and Space Power Journal,* and online through openDemocracy, the Monkey Cage (*Washington Post*), and the United States Institute of Peace.